T0329926

Economy Studies

Economy Studies

A Guide to Rethinking Economics Education

Sam de Muijnck and Joris Tieleman

Amsterdam University Press

Cover and interior design: Matterhorn Amsterdam

ISBN   978 94 6372 604 7
e-ISBN   978 90 4855 280 1 (pdf)
DOI   10.5117/9789463726047
NUR   781 / 840

Table of Contents

Additional online resources

www.economystudies.com

Part IV: Background Materials
Introduction to the Background Materials
Background Material 1: Economic Approaches
Background Material 2: Interdisciplinary Economics
Background Material 3: Rethinking the History of Economic Thought & Methods
Background Material 4: Coordination & Allocation Mechanisms
Background Material 5: Research Methods & Philosophy of Science
Background Material 6: Teaching Materials

Short Versions of the Book
Economy Studies for Students
Economy Studies for Program Directors and Deans
Economy Studies for Secondary Education
Economy Studies for Business Schools
Economy Studies for Public Administration & Law Programs
Economy Studies for Economics 101
Economy Studies for Microeconomics
Economy Studies for Macroeconomics
Economy Studies for Econometrics
Economy Studies for Labour Economics
Economy Studies for Public Economics
Economy Studies for Environmental Economics
Economy Studies for Development Economics
Economy Studies for Industrial Organisation
Economy Studies for Finance
Economy Studies for Monetary Economics
Economy Studies for International Economics
Economy Studies for Game Theory
Economy Studies for Behavioural Economics

Summary

1 Rethinking Economics Education

Humanity is wealthier, more connected and more technologically advanced than ever. Access to healthcare is rapidly expanding and poverty levels keep dropping in most parts of the world. At the same time, societies around the globe are facing a multitude of challenges. To name a few: climate change, biodiversity loss and resource depletion, growing inequalities and power concentrations, economic instability and soaring levels of private and public debt, ageing and migration, social polarisation and rising authoritarian nationalist populism. And, back on the table since 2020: pandemics.

Tackling such challenges requires a deep comprehension of the economy, which the current system of economics education does not sufficiently provide. Economists need a real-world understanding of how various industries work, how they are intertwined with each other, how economic power works, what roles states play and how these are embedded in our society at large. It also requires open minds which can look at issues from a variety of perspectives. A single theoretical framework cannot provide the answers to every question. A range of approaches which prioritise different methodologies, assumptions, units of analysis and outcomes, is necessary for gaining a good understanding of the economy and its issues. Economists need to be able to think critically, select the tools which are most relevant for the context and problem at hand, and understand the limitations and uncertainties of the conclusions that they draw from them. Finally, it requires an awareness and an explicit discussion of the moral dilemmas and normative trade-offs involved in economic decisions. In short, economists have a lot on their plate.

Economists also have a lot of influence, for good and for bad. Firstly, as key policy experts and advisors, economists largely run many of the most powerful public-sector organisations in the world: central banks, ministries of finance, social and economic affairs, the IMF and the World Bank. In the private sector, economists co-direct the behaviour of banks and other large companies. Secondly, the economic *ideas* that float around most prominently in our society exert an influence far beyond the formal advisory reports of professional economists, guiding decision-making of citizens everywhere. Economic thinking influences even those who do not become economists, as economists have a central role in the public debate and many citizens are taught basic economics in secondary or tertiary education.

The growing societal importance of economists and economic ideas has sparked a lively debate around the content and structure of economics education. A worldwide movement of students and academics calls for more pluralist, real-world focused and socially relevant programmes that would enable economics graduates to better understand and tackle the economic issues that the world faces today. This movement has accelerated over the last decade, spurred on by the global financial crisis of 2008, the climate crisis and the COVID-19 pandemic.

Under names such as *Rethinking Economics, Netzwerk für Plurale Ökonomik, Institute for New Economic Thinking (INET), International Student Initiative for Pluralist Economics (ISIPE), International Confederation of Associations for Pluralism in Economics (ICAPE), Diversifying and Decolonising Economics, Economists for Future, Reteaching Economics,* and *Oikos International*, these groups come together for dissent, discussion, self-education, action, campaigning, disseminating ideas and engaging with wider audiences.

Research by these groups indicates that many current programmes are not sufficient to prepare students for their future roles in society. They are often organised around the notion of *'thinking like an economist'*: training students to think exclusively from the neoclassical perspective and having skills in econometrics, while neglecting other valuable theoretical approaches and research methods. Furthermore, these analytical tools are taught in an overly abstract way and are presented as being value-free.

These groups and others have also produced a growing amount of innovative teaching material, beyond how economics programmes are traditionally structured. From online educational resources such as the open access CORE project and the bottom-up e-learning platform Exploring Economics, to multiple new pluralist and real-world focused textbooks. Many departments have introduced a wealth of new courses, or even started entirely new programmes.

2 This Book: Purpose and Overview

What has been missing so far in this field is an integral approach for constructing economics curricula and courses. This book aims to fill that gap. We bundle the ideas and materials of renewal and reform into a coherent multi-level vision for economics education: its overarching structure, its goals and its principles. We also provide the concrete building blocks for this in terms of academic content, including detailed overviews of teaching materials and practical suggestions. Finally, we translate these to the level of actual programmes and courses, providing a wide range of practical tools for implementation.

As such, our proposal for a new integral approach to economics education can also be adopted and used partially, rather than being accepted as a whole. Each idea and suggestion can be judged and incorporated independently. You can totally disagree with principle 1 yet support principle 3. Or you might find little value in building block 5 and yet fall in love with building block 9. That's the idea: it's modular. Thus, the book as a whole can be used as a source of inspiration and overview of options for improving and renewing economics education.

The first part of the book, *Foundations*, sets out our philosophy and the three guiding principles that should underpin any economist's education. In contrast to the currently common approach of teaching students to 'think like an economist', the *Economy Studies* approach is this: We envision an education where economics is not centred on a specific method of analysis or thought, but rather centred on a study matter, the economy. Economies can broadly be described as open systems of resource extraction, production, distribution, consumption and waste disposal through which societies provision themselves to sustain life and enhance its quality.

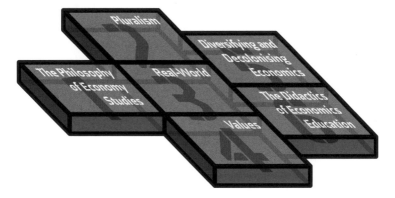

Figure 1: An overview of Part I: Foundations.

Based on this philosophy, we formulate three principles: Pluralism, Real-World and Values.

First, a discipline centred around a single subject matter requires a plurality of theoretical frameworks: one single set of basic assumptions is not enough to understand such a multifaceted subject matter. Here it is important that students learn which ideas are compatible with each other and which are in conflict with each other. Some of these theories fall within the current economic mainstream, others exist on its fringes, and yet others are currently at home in other disciplines. It also implies a plurality of research methods, from basic statistics and regression analysis to interviews, network analysis and survey analysis. Such pluralism means that there is no single dominant framework, which might be more difficult for those receiving economic advice, but is ultimately beneficial for the quality of analysis and the resulting decisions.

Second, the notion of a programme centred on the subject matter of the economy implies a continuous and conscious orientation towards the economy as it exists in the real world. Students benefit from studying practical questions and gaining concrete knowledge, not just abstract analytical tools. For instance: How is the German car industry structured? What hurdles does the global energy transition face? What happens at a central bank? The Real-World principle ranges from studies of economic sectors and key institutions in the local or (inter-)national economy, to the histories of economies and case studies of specific economic challenges.

Third, we draw attention to the wide variety of normative principles and visions that can guide economic decisions and action, and which are often subtly embedded in economic theories. There is little sense in trying to 'solve economics problems' without considering what things exactly are worthwhile or problematic, and what values are at stake. Profits, sustainability, power, equal chances, equal outcomes, job creation, labour conditions, ownership, accountability, GDP growth, wellbeing – what should we focus on?

Economics has historically been, and is still, dominated by upper- and middle-class white men based in the Global North. This has consequences for each of the three principles. In terms of *Real-World*, it is important to pay attention to the lived economic realities of working-class citizens, women, minorities, and those living in the Global South. For *Pluralism*, we need to incorporate often ignored but valuable ideas and contributions of lower class, female, and non-western scholars. For *Values*, it is key to realise that people from different backgrounds have different priorities and values, and work to ensure that these are reflected in the questions we focus on and the theories and methods we use. In sum, we need to *diversify and decolonise economics education*.

The *Foundations* part ends with a chapter on didactics. Improving economics education is not simply a matter of changing *what* is taught, but also *how* it is taught. Various surveys among employers of economists show that more attention for communication and collaboration skills is needed. There are also worrying indications that economics classes often fail to facilitate open, critical, but also respectful, discussions. Finally, to make economics education more lively, interesting for students and connected to the real world, a greater variety of teaching and examination methods could be used. On all these fronts we provide practical suggestions.

The second part of the book is devoted to the *Building Blocks*. Where the *Foundations* part discusses the purpose and principles of economics education in general, the building blocks are more applied: ten thematic areas of knowledge and skills, which form the meat and bones of the *Economy Studies* course design method. Each of the ten building blocks covers an area of knowledge and set of skills that we see as essential for the education of future economists.

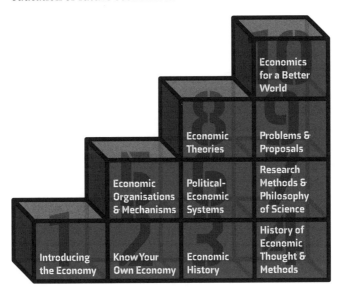

Figure 2: An overview of Part II: Building Blocks.

We start out with two building blocks that focus on acquiring basic economic knowledge, one conceptual and one focused on the real world. *Introducing the Economy* is about getting a feeling for economic matters, discussing what the economy is in the first place, why it is relevant, how it is related to other aspects of the social and natural world, and what societal roles economists have. *Know Your Own Economy*, on the other hand, has a more concrete focus as it is about knowledge of the actual (national and local) economy and its structures, institutions, and sectors.

The third and fourth building blocks deal with history: *History of the Economy* and *History of Economic Thought & Methods*. The fifth and sixth building blocks are more conceptually oriented, dealing with how economies can and have been organised, at micro and meso levels – *Economic Organisations & Mechanisms* – and at the macro level – *Political-Economic Systems*.

The seventh and eighth building blocks provide a broad and diverse analytic toolkit: *Research Methods & Philosophy of Science* and *Economic Theories*. These two, especially the latter, are relatively large. In most programmes, they will require more space than the other building blocks. Finally, building blocks nine and ten deal with practically contributing as an economist: *Problems & Proposals* is about analysing concrete economic challenges and formulating or evaluating proposed policies and actions, and *Economics for a Better World* asks how normative principles and visions can guide action to address the major challenges of our times, and helps students to be reflective of their own role as an economist.

3 Using the Economy Studies Toolkit

These building blocks can be used as templates to create stand-alone courses or modules, or they can be combined in courses. They can be re-ordered, combined or integrated in many ways to suit the specific needs of each programme. For instance, *Building Block 3: Economic History* could be taught as a stand-alone subject, or integrated with the fourth building block into a course *History of Economic Thought and Reality*, or integrated as a minor component in an existing *Labour Economics* course. In our ideal world, these building blocks would be combined to form a wide range of economics programmes. Different contexts and challenges require differently trained economists.

The third part of the book, titled *Tools*, provides material that is directly actionable. It starts with *Pragmatic Pluralism*, a suggested format (including references) for teaching theory in a pluralist manner without drowning students in the enormous diversity of ideas out there. We list thirteen core economic topics and set out for each topic the two main opposing perspectives, a key complementary perspective and additional insights coming from other approaches.

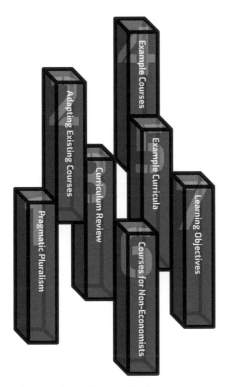

Figure 3: An overview of Part III: Tools.

Often there is no space in programmes for completely new courses but there is room for adjustment in some existing courses. In *Adapting Existing Courses*, we offer ready-to-use sets of suggestions and material to do so, for courses like Micro, Macro, Public Economics and Finance.

The *Curriculum Review Tool* offers a clear starting point for applying our building blocks to an existing programme. This tool helps identify possible blind spots of a programme and suggests ways to strengthen it. The *Example Courses* that follow illustrate how the building blocks can be used to create completely new courses. The next chapter maps out several complete *Example Curricula*, demonstrating how the building blocks might be combined to form a complete bachelor or master programme in Economics.

While this book is primarily oriented towards full economics programmes in academic education, in the chapter *Courses for Non-Economists* we suggest limited packages of core economic ideas that may be useful for secondary school economics programmes, in an academic minor or for self-study. Finally, *Learning Objectives* offers tools for designing the learning objectives behind economics courses, starting not from the question 'what does the teacher know best?' but from 'what do the students need to know, to be prepared for their future societal roles?'.

Economy Studies is more than a book. On the website, we offer an extended version of the *Pragmatic Pluralism* chapter, a broader range of *Adapting Existing Courses* topics, additional *Example Courses, Example Curricula* and programmes for non-economists. We also provide background material on each of the *Economic Approaches* described in this book, as well as neighbouring sub-disciplines such as economic sociology and economic geography. In addition, we provide a more complete overview and discussion of research methods, coordination and allocation mechanisms, and the history of economic thought and methods. Finally, we offer much more extensive lists of teaching materials for each of the building blocks.

Online, we also work together with the INET Education Program, at the Institute for New Economic Thinking. This platform will host free educational resources online, accessible to students, teachers and the general public. This includes video lecture series, syllabi, teaching modules, lecture notes, readings, sample quizzes and exams. The platform will also serve as a center to build up an online community of teachers and learners, working together to improve the way economics is taught and learned. Each of the chapters in this book has a discussion page on that platform.

What kind of graduates would a programme based on these ideas and materials produce? It is important to acknowledge that they would not have all the skills that current-day graduates have. Less mathematical sophistication, less expertise in econometric analysis, less knowledge of neoclassical theory. In exchange for these losses, students gain: a deeper understanding and more concrete knowledge of the economy in which they live and will work. An awareness and understanding of the various ways in which economic processes are organised at the micro, meso and macro levels. Practical skills for investigating and tackling questions of economic policy: understanding the context and choosing the right tools, from a variety of theoretical and methodological approaches. And the ability to argue morally as well as analytically, and to clearly distinguish the two.

With this *creative commons* work, we hope to inspire economists and all students of the economy to rethink how we learn economics. The economic challenges we face as societies are enormous, so we desperately need well-prepared economic experts and a citizenry able to participate in economic discussions. Economics education has the vital task of preparing these people as best as possible.

Foreword
Martin Wolf

What is economics? It is the study of the economy. What then is the economy? It is how we humans *"earn our living"* – how we organise ourselves to wrest the means of individual and collective survival from the world in which we live.

As is true of all other living beings, humans must obtain the resources needed to survive from their environment. Most animals, even other primates, have relatively simple repertoires for finding and taking these resources. This is true even of the social insects, despite the complex division of labour within their nests and hives. Human activities are different in scale and kind. This is because human beings are intensely social *and* individually highly intelligent and adaptable. The complex human economy of today is the result. Moreover, since the human economy is entirely embedded in the natural and social worlds, economics needs to understand the natural and social contexts.

The classical economists did indeed attempt to do this, to the extent that this was possible in the 18th and early 19th centuries. Thinkers like Adam Smith, Thomas Malthus, David Ricardo, and Karl Marx were indeed interested in human motivation, resources, institutions, social classes, and political power. Yet such a wide canvas created problems for a discipline that wished to achieve a high academic status: it was felt to be inadequately scientific. In response, economics adopted the intellectual strategy that had worked so well for the physical sciences: reductionism. Thus, it assumed away many complexities: for it, humans were selfish, rational, and far-sighted, resources abundant, information perfect, externalities insignificant, monopoly irrelevant, interpersonal comparisons of welfare impossible, money neutral and financial markets efficient. Orthodox economics assumed away the complications created by unpriced assets, economies of scale, costs of innovation, uncertainty, stupidity, and the operations of human institutions and social values. It also assumed human beings away, putting robots in their place.

The advantage of this intellectual strategy is that it made it possible to analyse the economy as a simple equilibrium system. The disadvantage is that the assumptions are false. As the education of economists tended to become narrower and more mathematical, the nature and extent of the errors became even less apparent. The inadequacy of economics has also affected the operation of the economy itself. Arguably, it has always done so. This is, after all, the most important way in which a social science is different from a natural one. If we fail to understand the workings of the universe, it will function, though some of the machines that we humans invent may not. If we fail to understand the economy, it may not function well at all, because we in our ignorance will damage it.

A good recent example is the global financial crisis, the biggest purely economic shock of the last few decades. As Adair Turner, the influential British economist, has argued, in the early 2000s, economics came to underpin a *"political ideology"*, namely, *"free market capitalism: the intellectual underpinning was the concept of market completion – the idea that the more market contracts could exist and the more freely, fairly and transparently they could be struck, the closer we could get to the most efficient possible outcome, most favourable to human welfare"* (2010, p. 2). This idea was, to put it mildly, a mistake.

We must not exaggerate the failures of either the economy or of economics. In the broad, the economy has done its job almost miraculously well. By co-operating, human beings could indeed support themselves and their families vastly better than they could have done on their own. Even our hunter-gatherer ancestors were able to combine their efforts (by co-operating in hunting, foraging, and bringing up children), insure themselves (by sharing food), diversify their skills (by specialising), exploit differences in knowledge (by exploring different terrain or foodstuffs on their own or in groups), broaden markets (by trading) and communicate with one another (by talking). Humans massively outcompeted other animals that were individually far stronger and faster than they were.

Humans became masters of the planet. The agricultural revolution was a huge jump. But the industrial revolution was a bigger and, above all, far quicker one. The combination of scientific and technological advance with competition and supportive political and social institutions has created a system of staggering complexity and scale. Today, the human economy supports close to 8bn people, almost all of whom live longer and more prosperous lives than those of the great majority of the mere 1bn people alive two hundred years ago. The inventiveness is no less unbelievable: estimates indicate that today the world economy produces some 10bn different goods and services (Beinhocker, 2006). Today, however, human beings and the livestock they rear for food make up 96 per cent of the mass of all the mammals on the planet (Wolf, 2021).

The human economy is, in sum, a success. But it is also a failure and even a danger: extinction rates are thought to be 100 to 1,000 times higher than their background rate over the past tens of millions of years. Thus, externalities have become far more binding, above all those created by the global environment. Moreover, inequality is pervasive, within and across societies; the financial sector remains a source of instability; corporations are run for the benefit of narrow groups of insiders; monopoly seems to be a pervasive force; new technologies are upending social and political relationships; the media are spreading destructive lies; and the foundations of democracy are corroding.

Economics is itself part of the problem. This is partly because it leaves out so much that matters. It is also because what it assumes about humans is wrong. It does not merely assume *"homo economicus"*, but, some would argue, encourages people to become one: selfish, competitive, and antisocial. This is debated (Girardi et al., 2021). Yet it is at the least clear that if everybody did behave as a rational self-seeker, civilised society, which relies on the unverified or unverifiable trustworthiness of one's fellows, would almost certainly collapse. *Homo economicus* really could not have created Denmark or any prosperous and highly co-operative society.

Economics is not only part of the problem, because of how it simplifies, but also because of what it leaves out. This is true even though it has developed in significant and helpful directions, to include imperfect competition, analyse asymmetric information, recognise endogenous growth, measure creative destruction, discuss multiple equilibria, distinguish happiness from income and analyse actual human behaviour. The discipline has indeed become more empirical and broader, while maintaining its core virtue of rigour. Yet even this is not enough. This book indicates how economics could become better still. It does so by reclaiming economics as the queen of social sciences, the subject that seeks to analyse *all* aspects of the most important thing humans do together, namely, co-operate, in order to deliver flourishing lives to as many people as possible.

If economics is to do this successfully it must embrace broader perspectives. It must be more aware of what it is trying to do and of the wider context in which the economy and economics operate. It must embrace breadth and complexity. The range of knowledge and abilities needed by economists is at the heart of the necessary transformation.

In a celebrated passage, John Maynard Keynes argued that *"the master economist must possess a rare combination of gifts. He must reach a high standard in several different directions and must combine talents not often found together.*

He must be mathematician, historian, statesman, philosopher – in some degree.

He must understand symbols and speak in words.

He must contemplate the particular in terms of the general, and touch abstract and concrete in the same flight of thought.

He must study the present in the light of the past for the purposes of the future.

No part of man's nature or his institutions must lie entirely outside his regard.

He must be purposeful and disinterested in a simultaneous mood; as aloof and incorruptible as an artist, yet sometimes as near the earth as a politician."
(Keynes, 1924, p. 65)

How is such a paragon to be produced? This book offers a good part of the answer. It broadens the foundations of economics, by forcing economists to understand the history of the economy and the subject and so to be aware of what economics tries to do and how it attempts do it. It proposes a practical route towards a better economic education. It provides a wide range of materials on how different schools approach the challenges and opportunities of studying the economy. It is, in sum, a distinguished effort to educate economists to become the sort of people Keynes thought they ought to be: broad intellectuals, not narrow technicians, but at the same time practical guides, not only abstract thinkers.

For many economists, the approach this book recommends will be painful. That is not just for selfish reasons. Those heroic simplifications had virtues. With them will go the old clarity about what economists are supposed to do and how they are supposed to think. Yet the gains from a richer understanding of what the human economy exists to do and how it does and should work will more than compensate.

Do I agree with everything in the book? Absolutely not. That surely is the point. A good book on the teaching and studying of economics should be challenging.

Read. Enjoy. Learn.

Acknowledgements

Only two names appear on the cover of this book, but don't let that fool you. *Economy Studies*, both the book and the accompanying website, is a cooperative effort built with contributions of some 180 people. Sprawling as it is, we simply could not have written it alone, nor would we have wanted to. In this chapter, we want to tell you a bit about the process of this project, and honour the many people who made remarkable contributions to this effort.

1 Building on a Wider Movement

The story of *Economy Studies* is inseparable from the international student movement *Rethinking Economics*. Over the past decade, Rethinkers have pointed out gaps in the curriculum, argued for different material and conducted thorough curriculum reviews. Many staff members and faculties turned out to be quite interested in our proposals. Still, they generally found it hard to implement such requests, being so used to the familiar curriculum. Hence the idea germinated in *Rethinking Economics* meetings to make an example curriculum.

We did not want to reinvent the wheel, but rather assemble the best work from the generations that came before us. So, we reached out to a wide range of seasoned academics around the world, hoping to tap into their collective knowledge and wisdom. Overwhelmed by the breadth and depth of the responses, we have continued this practice throughout the writing process. These economists freed up some of their precious time to respond to one or more of our requests for feedback. Some of them we already knew through classes or conferences, many others had so far just been revered names in our bookcases. Each time, we were honoured and humbled by the many responses, often going in great detail.

Thank you, for many hundreds of valuable comments and suggestions: Maarten Allers, Viviana Asara, Roger Backhouse, Andrea Bernardi, Dirk Bezemer, Olivier Blanchard, Mark Blyth, Peter Boettke, Frank Bohn, Ivan Boldyrev, Wimar Bolhuis, Marcel Boumans, Björn Brügemann, Govert Buijs, Brian Burgoon, Koen Byttebier, Marcel Canoy, Wendy Carlin, Edward Cartwright, Mario Cedrini, Ha-Joon Chang, David Colander, Chris Colvin, Harry Commandeur, Marcella Corsi, Carlo D'Ippoliti, Dirk Damsma, Charlie Dannreuther, Thomas Dark, Marc Davidson, John Davis, Samuel Decker, David Dequech, Giovanni Dosi, Sheila Dow, Robert Dur, Wolfram Elsner, Ewald Engelen, Christian Felber, Thomas Ferguson, Alfredo S. Filho, Ben Fine, Svenja Flechtner, Nancy Folbre, James Galbraith, Pieter Gautier,

James Gerber, Reyer Gerlagh, Teresa Ghilarducci, Neva R. Goodwin, William Greene, Roel Grol, Roelf Haan, Marco Haan, Johan Heilbron, Walter Hulsker, Geoffrey Hodgson, Lex Hoogduin, Brigitte Hoogendoorn, Bas Jacobs, William Janeway, Tae-Hee Jo, Steve Keen, Piet Keizer, Stephanie Kelton, Alan Kirman, Arjo Klamer, Alfred Kleinknecht, Theo Kocken, Ingrid H. Kvangraven, Tony Lawson, William Lazonick, Henry Leveson-Gower, Stefano Lucarelli, Jasper Lukkezen, Bengt-Ake Lundvall, Bart Los, Harro Maas, Senna Maatoug, Olga Mikheeva, William Milberg, Irene Monasterolo, Stephanie Mudge, Daniel Mügge, Felix Munoz-Garcia, Richard Nelson, Bart Nooteboom, Erik Olsen, Sander Onderstal, Carlota Perez, Thomas Piketty, Jan Potters, Menno Pradhan, Pratistha J. Rajkarnikar, Kate Raworth, Jack Reardon, Geert Reuten, Maarten P. Schinkel, Philippe C. Schmitter, Geoff Schneider, Dirk Schoenmaker, Henning Schwardt, Molly Scott Cato, Esther-Mirjam Sent, Anwar Shaikh, Robert Skidelsky, Clive Spash, Joseph Stiglitz, Coen Teulings, Tim Thornton, Rob Timans, Bas van Bavel, Harry van Dalen, Eric van Damme, Hendrik van den Berg, Wypkje van der Heide, Frank van der Salm, Joël van der Weele, Ger van Gils, Charan van Krevel, Hans van Ophem, Jan van Ours, Erwin van Sas, Jarig van Sinderen, Irene van Staveren, Rens van Tilburg, Jacco van Uden, Olav van Vliet, Arjen van Witteloostuijn, Olav Velthuis, Jan Verhoeckx, Koen Vermeylen, Jack Vromen, Robert Went, William White, Randall Wray and Kim Zwitserloot.

In the first round, before starting our own writing process, we simply asked this group of seasoned academics a few open questions. How would they define the economy, what should the core principles of a good economics education be, what courses or programmes did they find inspiring, and what it was that made these courses and programmes so worthwhile? These responses, together with many pages of notes from *Rethinking Economics* gatherings, would form the basis of our new curriculum proposal.

2 A Process of Crowdsourcing

We quickly realised that it would be impossible to write 'the perfect curriculum'. *Rethinking Economics* is at its core a movement for pluralism, and does not intend to replace the current, relatively standardised curriculum with a single alternative. This does not mean that we do not have a coherent view. It just means that it encompasses diversity of theories, methods, values, people, and programmes. We agreed, however, on the major gaps in current programmes, the basic tenets for future programmes, the design principles, and on the general direction we envision for economics education.

This, we decided, would be the form of our curriculum proposals: a modular, open-ended design toolkit built on a clear foundation of guiding principles. The core: teach students to study the economy using a broad and open-ended toolkit, rather than drilling them in a specific manner of thinking about it. Such a modular approach has two advantages. For its writers, it allowed for a collaborative and diverse yet coherent vision to emerge from a broad reform movement. For its users, it offers a menu and a variety of tools, rather than a fully formed 'take it or leave it' alternative structure.

Our first rough draft, just 70 pages long, saw the light of day at a long weekend workshop in January 2019, where it was picked apart and put together again lovingly by Daniel Obst, Eric Sargent, Alexandra Sokolenko, and Sally Svenlen. Special thanks here go to Ross Cathcart, Cameron Fay, and J. Christopher Proctor, who have acted as this project's godfathers from start to finish. We are grateful to the *Independent Social Research Foundation* for funding this workshop. Following this workshop, we took eight months to come to a fuller draft, including much more detailed building blocks, detailed lists of materials and a full version of the *Pragmatic Pluralism* approach.

In September 2019, we went back for more comments. We once again sent out the manuscript, now around 150 pages, to the same group of professors, and again were honoured to receive many pages of valuable feedback. In the year that followed, we processed their comments, additions, critiques and other suggestions to create a new manuscript. We then organised a final round of feedback in the summer of 2020. We went back to the group of seasoned academics mentioned in the list above for a final time, now sending them each one or two relevant chapters to receive more in-depth thematic feedback. At the same time, a group of about twenty rethinkers edited one chapter per week per person for about two months, ensuring that every chapter would pass through many pairs of eyes and hands.

Thank you, to our fellow Rethinkers: Ryan Berelowitz, Elisa Terragno Bogliaccini, Merve Burnazoglu, Charlotte Cator, Michela Ciccotosto, Maeve Cohen, Sebastián Muena Cortés, Eric Decker, Joe Earle, Clara Etchenique, Mads Falkenfleth Jensen, Rita Guimarães, Oliver Hanney, Laurence Jones-Williams, Maarten Kavelaars, Anne Kervers, Liv Anna Lindman, Maria Georgouli Loupi, Cahal Moran, Carles Paré Ogg, Hanna Oosterveen, Ben Pringle, Francis Ostermeijer, Henri Schneider, Vera Veltman, Maarten Vermeir and Tree Watson. Special thanks go to Rethinkers Jamie Barker and Kristin Dilani Nadarajah, for close reading many more of the chapters and sculpting our rough prose into more refined and accurate formulations throughout the book.

3 Constructing the Toolkit: An Iterative Process

Throughout the writing process, we also held some twenty try-out workshops and discussions to broaden and sharpen the work. Many thanks go to the organisers of all these workshops, conferences and gatherings: *the Royal Netherlands Academy of Arts and Sciences (KNAW)*, the *Dutch Ministry of Finance*, the *Oikos* and *Netzwerk Plurale Ökonomik* student movements, *The Hague University of Applied Sciences (THUAS)*, *the Italian Association for the History of Political Economy (STOREP)*, *the Goldschmeding Foundation* and *the Commission for Education, Culture and Science of the Dutch House of Representatives*. We especially wish to thank the *Rethinking Economics* staff team, who have brought together such an extraordinary worldwide network of young academic freethinkers so many times. This book could not have been written without your tireless organising behind the scenes. In addition, the *Vrije Universiteit Amsterdam*, the *Radboud University of Nijmegen, Utrecht University* and *Leiden University* provided inspiring discussions and use cases of early drafts.

The try-out workshops also helped to sharpen another component of the project: course design workshops at economics faculties, using an abbreviated version of the *Economy Studies* toolkit for the initial brainstorming. In November 2020, *Rethinking Economics International* organised an *Economy Studies Expert Training*, where Rethinkers from five different continents came together online for four weeks to discuss the book and how to conduct such workshops in their own region. The feedback from the participants in this series of sessions sharpened the workshop format in many ways.

It was in these workshops that the book grew to take its final size and shape. Through discussions with fellow Rethinkers and many academics, we came to realise that a curriculum proposal or a set of building blocks with guiding principles alone was not enough: it needed a head and a tail. So, we fleshed out the *Foundations* more clearly, and added several more *Tools* chapters to get closer to the practical realities of everyday teaching work, such as *Adapting Existing Courses* and *Learning Objectives*. All this greatly expanded the book's waistline, to the dismay of our publishers. Still, we believe it is worth it, as the project's range is now much more complete: from basic principles to practical application within a single framework.

Throughout this process, we had a steady and warm home at the independent Dutch thinktank *Our New Economy*. We are very grateful for the unwavering support and wide variety of help given by our great crew of colleagues: Sjaak Beirnaert, Peter Mulder, Maarten Nijman, Esther Somers, Martijn Jeroen van der Linden and Danny Verdonk: from brainstorming sessions and feedback to connecting with faculties to organise workshops, and from dissemination strategy to social media. Special thanks go to Charlotte van Dixhoorn, for a close edit of more than half of the book and to Julika Frome for helping us out with communications and organising the book launch. Anne de Kok helped us to build a beautiful website accompanying the book.

At *Amsterdam University Press*, Inge van der Bijl patiently and constructively guided us through every step of the publication process. At *Matterhorn*, Bob van den Berg crafted the wonderful designs for every page of this book. We are also very grateful that Martin Wolf took the time to write such a powerful and incisive foreword – it feels like the missing puzzle piece of the book.

We also want to thank our friends and families for their support. In particular, we want to thank Tane Nieuweboer, Katrien Eisenloeffel and Marion Molliet for putting up with us during this writing process, which was often in the evenings, weekends and holidays, and all the stresses that came with it.

All remaining errors are, of course, our own. In addition, as the main authors of this book are two young white university educated middle-class men from the Netherlands, the book has an inevitable bias towards our own experiences. We hope that you, the reader, will help us to make the next edition sharper and richer, by pointing out errors and omissions and suggesting better teaching materials and techniques.

We also hope you will take the project further. The book and website are Open Access and Creative Commons, which means they can be freely shared and adapted: you may download digital copies of the book for free. You may also copy and redistribute this material in any medium or format, remix, transform, and build upon the material for any purpose, even commercially. We very much hope you will do so.

Introduction

"I don't care who writes a nation's laws, if I can write its economics textbooks."

Paul Samuelson (1990, p. ix)

Economies can broadly be described as open systems of resource extraction, production, distribution, consumption and waste disposal through which societies provision themselves to sustain life and enhance its quality. Their functioning is fundamental for and intertwined with many other human endeavours. Whether it is putting food on the table, providing medical care, ensuring a roof over one's head, fighting a war, running an education system, organising a social outing for a football club or simply getting a coffee, all these actions require interaction with these larger economic systems. Given this importance, good economists are vital for society, at every level. It is their job to investigate the inner workings of the larger systems, help society navigate them, assist in designing parts of them, and monitor their functioning to continuously improve them and avoid unintended consequences or breakdowns.

1 Why Redesign Economics Programmes?

Economists today are in positions of considerable power and influence. Primarily, as key policy experts and advisors in many different policy areas. Under a layer of political supervision, economists are at the head of many of the most powerful public-sector organisations in the world: central banks, ministries of finance, social and economic affairs, and international organisations such as the *International Monetary Foundation (IMF)* and the *World Bank*. Indeed, some argue that we live in an *econocracy*, a society in which improving the economy has become the main purpose of politics (Earle et al., 2016). In the private sector, economists co-direct and influence the behaviour of banks and other large corporations.

Additionally, the economic ideas that are dominant in society exert an influence far beyond the formal advisory of professional economists, guiding decision-making of citizens everywhere. After all, economic dynamics are at the core of many of the aforementioned societal challenges. Anyone grappling with those problems may look towards economic ideas to understand and help solve them: informally, in day-to-day discussions and literature, but also formally through an economic education. In the United States alone, every year two million undergraduates take at least one economics course (Siegfried & Walstad, 2014).

Indeed, as Nobel laureate Friedrich Hayek (1974) noted, the influence of economists and their ideas can sometimes be intimidatingly large. In his acceptance speech, he remarked that *'the Nobel Prize confers on an individual an authority which in economics no man ought to possess'*, particularly because *'the influence of the economist that mainly matters is an influence over laymen: politicians, journalists, civil servants and the public generally.'* The professional authority of economists, often based upon its image of being both more policy-oriented and more *'scientific'* – in the sense of being more like the natural sciences such as physics – than other social sciences, is crucial in understanding the influence of economists in society (Akerlof, 2020; Fourcade et al., 2015).

Today, a clear and systemic understanding of the economy is more important than ever. The 2007-2008 financial crisis yielded widespread unemployment and bankruptcies, only to be worsened recently by the COVID-19 global pandemic. The world remains one of great inequality, where 1% of the world's population owns more wealth than the other 99% combined (Hardoon et al., 2016). The industrial system is simultaneously causing the world's 6th mass extinction (Ceballos et al., 2017), and destabilising the climate, something that has long received too little attention in economics (Butler-Sloss & Beckmann, 2021; Oswald & Stern, 2019). The uncertainty and insecurity resulting from this rapid and frequently threatening change is driving increasing numbers of citizens into the arms of autocratic populists, who promise strength, stability and simplicity (Mounk, 2018).

To face these and coming challenges, we need a comprehensive understanding of our economic system. The COVID-19 pandemic in particular has shown that if we are to effectively manage our economy, we need an all-round, real-world understanding of how economic sectors work, how they are intertwined with each other, what roles various forms of government play versus the market, how citizens economically depend on each other, and how the economy is embedded in our society at large. A single theoretical framework cannot be enough for this. A range of approaches which prioritise different methodologies, assumptions, units of analysis and outcomes will be necessary to gain a more complete understanding, as well as the critical thinking skills to be able to choose the most appropriate approaches for the problem at hand. As well as debating alternative policies, we also need to be able to go deeper and debate the values which underpin our judgement of policies, as well as envisioning, designing and debating alternative policies. In short, economists of the future have a lot of work to do. They will need a thorough and diverse training to prepare them for this.

Fortunately, the discipline has many crucial insights to offer its students. Economists have demonstrated how the pursuit of self-interest may lead to benefits for society at large (Adam Smith), how the capitalist system forces not only workers but also employers to compete and fight for 'survival' (Karl Marx), that we pay not only in money but also in opportunity cost (David Green), how the sum of the actions of many sensible, reasonably-acting individuals may be chaotic and generate explosive irrationality (John Maynard Keynes), how developed countries can enrich themselves at the cost of developing countries even without directly plundering them or extracting resources through military power (Raúl Prebisch), how innovation and economic destruction are part of the same process of turbulent economic development (Joseph Schumpeter), how roughly half the work we do, such as care work, is never paid for (Betsy Warrior), that economic development is not (only) about growth but about capabilities and freedom (Amartya Sen), how communities can be able to sustainably manage vital resources without formal rules and property rights (Elinor Ostrom), and how well-intended actions of human provisioning may wreak havoc on the ecological systems that support all life on this planet (Herman Daly).

We, the authors of this book, chose to study economics because we wanted to understand the powerful dynamics within the economy that lie behind the world's challenges, and to learn ideas that might help to solve them. While we learned much of value in our programmes, we also found that they were not sufficiently broad, open-minded and realistic to help us really get a thorough grasp of how the economy actually works.

For one, the majority of the insights listed above were not part of our programmes. If we had not been informed by curious classmates that the field of economics was much wider than what we were being taught, we would never even have known about them. Neither did we learn to discuss the moral foundations of economic discussions. Why, for instance, are we striving for economic growth? Does this goal still make sense and how does it relate to other goals, such as ecological sustainability and social equity? What is a 'well-functioning market', and when and why do we want one? Nor did we learn much about the economy as it actually exists in the real world: few of us could have listed the main sectors in our home countries, explained how the bargaining processes between workers and employers works in practice, or set out the connection between capitalism and global warming in any more detail than an informed newspaper reader.

Most current programmes are organised around 'thinking like an economist' (see Proctor, 2019, for an overview of curriculum analyses in different countries). That is, they focus on training students to think from the neoclassical perspective and to use econometrics, while disregarding other valuable theoretical approaches and research methods. Furthermore, the approaches that are taught are predominantly abstract, rather than based in real-world practice, and claim to be value-free.

2 Giants on Whose Shoulders We Stand

This movement has produced an extensive literature of proposals and discussions about economics curriculum reform, which we will briefly discuss before setting out the contribution of *Economy Studies* itself and the internal structure of this book. To go directly to the overview of this book's parts and to see reading suggestions for faculty, students and other audiences, skip ahead to the next section of this chapter, *This Book: Structure and Reading Guide*. For more history and detail on the debate about economics education see Butler et al. (2009); Fullbrook (2003); Garnett Jr et al. (2009); Hodgson et al. (1992); Hoyt and McGoldrick (2012); Lee (2009); Reardon (2009); Spiegler and Milberg (2013); Thornton (2016); Tieleman et al. (2017).

For brevity, the literature review starts in 2007, the year the global financial crisis started and as a result the movement for economics curriculum reform received an enormous boost. In this year, *Teaching Pluralism in Economics* (2007) was published; a collection of essays edited by John Groenewegen, which discusses the desirability of pluralism and the different forms it can take, the importance and usefulness of interdisciplinarity, history, and problem-based learning, and differences between an economics education in the United States (US), Germany and the United Kingdom (UK).

Two years later the *Teagle Foundation* report was written by David Colander and KimMarie McGoldrick (2009) about how economics majors in US liberal education could be improved. The report argues programmes should focus more on "big think" questions about highly complex issues as well as the real-world contexts in which economic problems are situated. Colander and McGoldrick also suggest experimenting with new teaching strategies, encouraging active classroom participation and open conversations, and developing teaching commons with openly shared materials and exercises. They also provide organisational suggestions for improvement, such as increasing attention to teaching skills as well as subjects such as economic history, history of economic thought and institutions in PhD programmes so that the next generation of teachers will be better equipped and prepared.

The Teagle report was also the starting point of *Educating Economists: The Teagle Discussion on Re-evaluating the Undergraduate Economics Major* (2010), a collection of essays from a wide variety of perspectives. Among other questions, it discusses whether to deepen and/or broaden the scope of the programmes, how best to teach students to think critically and independently, and the practicalities of organising economics education such as providing the right incentives to stimulate good teaching.

The year 2009, right after the start of the global financial crisis, saw two other important publications on economics education: Robert Garnett, Erik Olsen, and Martha Starr edited the volume *Economic Pluralism* (2009) of which the third part specifically focused on economics education. The volume gives a good overview of the debate surrounding economic pluralism with essays on, among other things, how to manage intellectual diversity to promote knowledge production, whether to base pluralism on Kuhn's concept of incommensurability or Mill's idea of fallibilism, the institutional heterogeneity in real-world economies, and how pluralist teaching can contribute to relevant skill formation among students desired by companies and governments.

Another book on the need for pluralism in economics is *The Handbook of Pluralist Economics Education*, a collection of essays edited by Jack Reardon (2009). It too contains detailed suggestions for teachers on how to reform principles, core theory and advanced economics courses. In this way, it provides fundamental critiques as well as concrete suggestions for how economics courses, from economics 101 and macroeconomics to labour and international economics, can be improved.

In 2011, INET's UK Curriculum Committee wrote a proposal for undergraduate programmes following these principles: a focus on the economy, rather than on a particular methodology of economics; a pluralist 'one-problem-several-solutions' approach; and a focus on the real world and on preparing students to work outside academia, rather than reproducing the skill-sets needed by academic professors.

2011 also saw one of the most extensive publications on economics education with the 850 pages long *International Handbook on Teaching and Learning Economics* edited by Gail M. Hoyt and KimMarie McGoldrick. The book starts out by describing the history of economics education, different teaching and assessment techniques, and research findings on economics education and student performance. Numerous contributors to the book, furthermore, give reflections and suggestions on existing courses, from health economics and game theory to sport and urban economics. It concludes by discussing institutional and administrative aspects of economics education, such as faculty development, student characteristics, teaching enhancement initiatives, and international differences between educational systems.

Two collections of essays followed. 2012 saw the publication of *What's the Use of Economics? Teaching the Dismal Science After the Crisis* edited by Diane Coyle. The book asks how new insights that have become prominent as a result of the financial crisis of 2008 and its aftermath, such as the importance of the financial sector for macroeconomic developments, could be incorporated in economics education. The various authors, including several employers of economists, argue that the following ingredients are too often missing in current curricula: history and real-world context, practical skills for empirical analysis and the importance of inductive reasoning, attention to the limitations of modelling and deductive reasoning, a pluralist approach with multiple perspectives, and communication skills, especially of technical results to non-economists. The book also discusses how UK undergraduate economics programmes, in particular, can be improved, by innovating teaching and testing, and rewarding good teaching rather than letting career success depend solely on publishing in US mainstream journals.

The second collection of essays, edited by Jack Reardon and Maria Alejandra Madi (2014), arrived at a slightly more radical conclusion. According to the various authors of *The Economics Curriculum: Towards a Radical Reformulation*, reforming economics education is not simply a matter of adding some topics to the curriculum, but fundamentally changing its core elements. The book starts out by analysing what is wrong with current programmes and what they are missing. It then moves towards suggestions for how the curriculum could be improved and what such an improved programme could look like. Core ideas are to centre a pluralist approach to theory, to actively discuss methodological issues, and to make real-world and historical knowledge key ingredients of any curriculum.

In that same year, the French student group *Pour un Enseignement Pluraliste dans le Supérieur en Économie* (PEPS, 2014) analysed existing French economic curricula and proposed an alternative curriculum. Rather than organising the programme around techniques, they put real-world problems and questions at the centre of the programme. Furthermore, the programme is characterised by interdisciplinarity, theoretical and methodological pluralism as well as a focus on independent critical thinking. Their research was followed up by a report by the French Ministry of Education (2014), which concluded that economics programmes were indeed insufficient in preparing students for their future societal roles. The report argued curricula should pay more attention to real-world knowledge and interdisciplinarity.

In 2016, the debate further progressed thanks to two books that each in their own way forcefully argued for fundamentally altering economics education. In *From Economics to Political Economy: The problems, promises and solutions of pluralist economics*, Thornton (2016) argues for disciplinary differentiation and institutional independence. Disciplinary differentiation involves reverting back to the original name of the discipline (political economy) and broadening the field by including economic history, history of economic thought, a diversity of theoretical perspectives, economic development, and comparative economic systems. Institutional independence involves operating outside economics departments (for example, in departments of political science or management). In his words, rather than trying to continue a "dialogue with the deaf" inside economics departments, reform-minded students and academics may benefit from more carefully contemplating the full range of available reform strategies. The analysis includes detailed case studies of successful and unsuccessful attempts at change within and outside economics departments.

The other book, called *Econocracy: The perils of leaving economics to the experts* (Earle et al., 2016), was written by three young economics graduates who had been instrumental in the formation of the international student movement *Rethinking Economics*, which we are a part of, in particular by co-founding the *Post-Crash Economics Society* in Manchester. As noted earlier, they argue that we live in an *econocracy*, a society in which improving the economy has become the main purpose of politics. In such a society, the way economists are educated is of paramount importance. Based on an analysis of 174 UK undergraduate economics courses and their course outlines and exam papers, they argue economics education is currently not fit for purpose. The excessive focus on neoclassical theory amounts to a monopoly of thinking that, they argue, can even be defined as indoctrination, as it discourages independent critical thinking and promotes unquestioningly accepting claims and reproducing earlier beliefs. They make the case for economics in the form of a pluralist liberal education with attention to multiple theoretical perspectives, real-world issues, inductive approaches and empirical evidence. Furthermore, they argue for the democratisation of economic policy debates, in order to make sure everyone's interests, values and insights are considered rather than only those of a small group of economic experts.

The most recent contributions to the debate consist of two collections of essays edited by three German economists, Samuel Decker, Wolfram Elsner and Svenja Flechtner: *Advancing Pluralism in Teaching Economics* (2018) and *Principles and Pluralist Approaches in Teaching Economics* (2019). These two books further explore why and how to teach economics in a pluralist way. They discuss how this pluralist approach could be applied to different topics and countries, together with discussions of recent development in economics education in Brazil, India, China, Ghana, Germany and France.

While this book is about education, not about research, our suggestions seem to dovetail with a similar shift in the research arena. A recent survey among nearly 10,000 academic economists, weighted to be a representative sample of all 50,000 scholars who recently published, found that most academic economists want the discipline's research work to be more multidisciplinary, less specialized, riskier, more disruptive and focused on the question's importance rather than on causal identification (Andre & Falk, 2021).

The years since the 2007-2008 financial crisis have also produced a growing amount of new teaching material. This wealth of new (online) materials and textbooks is too extensive to do justice in a brief discussion here. Instead, we provide overviews and descriptions of them in the relevant chapters as well as more extensive online overviews of teaching materials and resources on www.economystudies.com.

Besides textbooks, there are websites such as *Exploring Economics*, an open-access and bottom-up e-learning platform for economic theory with introductions into different perspectives and overviews of online courses. *The School of Political Economy* has also been established to provide university-level courses in pluralist economics from outside of the university system. In addition, INET has created several excellent online courses, such as *How & How NOT to Do Economics* by Robert Skidelsky, *Inequality 101* by Branko Milanovic and Arjun Jayadev, *The Economics of Money & Banking* by Perry Mehrling, *What Money Can't Buy* by Michael Sandel, and *Economics for People* by Ha-Joon Chang, which are freely available on its website. Furthermore, the CORE team, coordinated by Wendy Carlin, Samuel Bowles and Margaret Stevens, has developed online freely available textbooks, such as *The Economy: Economics for a Changing World* and *Economy, Society, and Public Policy*. *The Economics in Context Initiative* has developed a series of textbooks accompanied by online available education materials in which students not only learn about the economy itself but also how it is embedded in social, environmental, historical, institutional and political contexts.

Finally, new economic programmes are being introduced across the world. Over the past years, the initiative *Promoting Economic Pluralism* has developed a platform providing an overview of pluralist economics master programmes around the world. The selection looks, among other things, at whether students are taught a range of theoretical perspectives, taught to reflect on assumptions and values, ecological issues are discussed and real-world knowledge is taught. Since 2005 the online *HED database*, last updated in 2016, also provides a useful overview of (under)graduate programmes with a broader and different theoretical focus (http://heterodoxnews.com/hed/study-programs.html).

3 This Book: Structure and Reading Guide

This book, *Economy Studies*, is neither a textbook, a collection of essays, a course manual, nor a critique of existing programmes. Rather, it is an attempt to take the many specific ideas and materials of renewal and reform and bundle them together into a coherent and complete vision of what a contemporary economics degree could look like. It builds on the above calls for more attention to real-world knowledge, history, institutions, pluralist theory, critical thinking and ethical and methodological reflection in economics education. In doing so, it goes beyond principles and general recommendations. The first part of this book outlines the general vision, the second part provides the building blocks of teaching material and the third part offers a practical toolkit to form and adjust concrete courses and curricula.

Apart from being highly detailed and combining an integral vision with a practical how-to guide, our curriculum proposal differs from others in one important respect: it is open-ended. *Rethinking Economics* was founded to crack open the existing homogeneity in economics education, and we do not intend to replace it with another 'single answer'. We believe society would be best served with a diversity of economists, each having slightly different expertise. Hence, we reject the notion that there could be such a thing as the 'optimal' curriculum.

Instead, we build up the proposal in three steps. The first part of the book, *Foundations*, sets out the philosophy of *Economy Studies*: education organised around studying the subject matter of the economy, rather than learning to think in a certain way. Then, three organising principles: a *pluralism* of theoretical and methodological approaches, a foundational knowledge of the *real-world* economy and a clear understanding of the role of *values* in economics. We discuss the importance of *diversifying and decolonising economics* and changing not only what we teach, but also how we teach with the *didactics* of economics education.

In the second part, *Building Blocks*, the domains of knowledge and skills that economics students should learn about are described. Building blocks can be used as templates to create stand-alone courses, or they can be combined or shaped into different forms, to suit the specifics of each programme. Additional online resources are referred to in the larger building blocks, and can be found on our website: links are provided throughout the book.

While most of this book is a blue-sky proposal, the third part *Tools* takes implementing actual change as its point of departure. It proposes more incremental adjustments and provides ready-to-implement tools: a curriculum review tool, examples of curricula and individual courses designed using this method, as well as ready-to-use sets of material to 'pluralise' existing core courses, also those for secondary schools and academic minor programmes.

As these example curricula and courses show, *Economy Studies* is certainly not something that needs to be swallowed wholesale. It can also very well function as a menu of different options for broadening existing curricula. Readers are encouraged to skip around in the book whilst reading. To facilitate this, we have written the building blocks as independent units. While they form a coherent whole, each building block is also designed to stand alone.

If you are working with an economics curriculum, whether teaching it, learning it or trying to reform it, this book could be for you. The different sections have been designed to be read independently, as they may be of interest to different readers. We suggest all readers start with part one, *Foundations*. Then, if you are currently teaching a course, and would like to expand it with some fresh material, go to part two, *Building Blocks*, and simply dive into the building block that seems most relevant to your course or see the chapter *Adapting Existing Courses* in part three of the book (p. 329). If you are in a position to influence a programme as a whole, whether as a student, a programme coordinator, or in another role, take a look at the *Part II: Building Blocks* (p. 141), *Tool 3: Curriculum Review* (p. 363) and *Tool 5: Example Curricula* (p. 387).

Using the structure of this book, we have also designed workshops that help both students and teachers understand and apply the ideas and tools provided in the book. Throughout the international *Rethinking Economics* network, there are people who have been trained to facilitate these workshops. If you are interested, please get in touch at our website: www.economystudies.com.

Online, we also work with the INET Education Program, a platform hosting free educational resources such as video lecture series, syllabi, teaching modules, lecture notes, readings, sample quizzes and exams. In addition to materials, the platform will host an online community of economics professors. The building blocks and other chapters of this book will be part of that platform.

We hope that the ideas and materials offered in this book will be of use to the students and academics of the worldwide economics community. While our subject often seems dry and intangible to outsiders, it is an absolutely critical field of knowledge for any society, as more and more people are coming to realise. We are thankful to the many passionate scholars, activists, sceptics, philosophers and empiricists who have generously taught us what they knew and reviewed our work. You helped make this book what it is. Any remaining mistakes, which a book of these ambitions is bound to contain, are our own.

Part I:
Foundations

Foundations

Introduction

This part lays the groundwork for the rest of the book. It starts with the central philosophy of the book, explaining the title 'Economy Studies'. From there, we set out three principles that provide a backing structure for the ten building blocks, which form the next part of the book. The next chapter discusses the need to diversify and decolonize our discipline. We end this part with a brief chapter on didactics, suggesting three points of attention regarding the practice of economics teaching.

The Philosophy of Economy Studies

When designing courses in economics, or even an entire programme, there are endless choices to be made: central subject matter, theoretical focus, style of teaching, what materials to use, how to sequence courses and what to test students on. In the chapter *Philosophy*, we start with the question that lies at the foundation of all these choices: what should economics education focus on? We broadly identify two answers to that question. Answer A: organise education around a specific method of analysis or way of thinking. Answer B: organise it around a subject matter.

Answer A implies separate programmes for the neoclassical approach to human life and society, programmes for the institutional approach, others for the Marxian approach, etc. We explain why in this book we instead choose answer B: a programme centred on a specific subject matter. Political science focuses on politics. Biology studies living organisms. Economics, then, focuses on the economy. Subsequently, we define what we mean by 'the economy', discuss where its boundaries lie and how we might deal with its interfaces to other aspects of the world, such as the political, the social and the ecological.

Principles

In the following three chapters of part I, we set out the three main principles of our framework: *Pluralism*, *Real-World* and *Values* respectively.

The first principle, *Pluralism*, focuses on the current dominance of a single approach in mainstream economics education, and our contrasting argument for theoretical and methodological pluralism. Learning to use analytical tools such as theories and research methods is the primary purpose of an academic education. We argue that a truly academic education requires a foundation of pluralism: the side-by-side use of fundamentally different, incommensurate approaches to studying the economy. We set out two basic reasons to support such pluralism: it helps students to gain a richer diversity of insights, and it gives them a clearer perspective on the limitations of any single approach, thus facilitating critical thinking.

The second principle, *Real-World*, concerns the current focus on mathematical abstraction and methodological techniques. We suggest focusing more attention on the real-world economy instead. 'Real-world economics' has long been a core demand of the *Rethinking Economics* movement. It is an ideal that seems self-evident; who would actively reject the real world in their teaching? Still, it is not easy to put into practice. We set out several forms of concrete knowledge about the real world which we believe to be crucial, and provide suggestions on how to implement this in teaching.

The third principle, *Values*, discusses the notion of value-free science. There is a tendency to try to banish normative issues entirely or contain them in an isolated course on ethics. This leaves students blind to the normative aspects of economic topics and unable to articulate moral dilemmas clearly and critically reflect upon them. Values, our moral principles and beliefs, are an integral aspect of economic dynamics, and deserve a central place in economics programmes. In fact, besides sheer curiosity, they are the entire reason we study economics, and the reason that it is the most prominent social science today: economic dynamics matter for almost everything we care about. This principle is about helping students to become aware of the value aspects of economic questions and to be comfortable with discussing them, in their role as an academically trained thinker and researcher. That does not mean making everything normative. It means learning to identify the normative and positive, seeing underlying values when they are relevant and focusing on the normative aspects of concrete economic issues, rather than only discussing general ethical philosophies.

These three principles overlap with the old idea of a tripartite distinction within economics (Colander, 2001; Keynes, 1891). *Real-World* is related to the *art of economics*, also called *applied economics*, which is about concrete actual cases and how to deal with them as economists. *Pluralism* is most closely related to the *science of economics*, sometimes called *positive economics*, which is concerned with analytical tools for understanding how economies work. Finally, the ideas in the chapter *Values* build on the *ethics of economics*, also known as *normative economics*, which is concerned with judgements of importance and value.

The three do not exist in isolation from each other; they are connected in various ways. For instance, the real world cannot be seen directly but only through lenses that allow focus: analytical tools. Using a diversity of lenses helps to understand it better (pluralism). However, even then, we need to be aware that embedded and sometimes hidden inside these different tools, lie different values. We may try hard to be neutral, but what we observe in practice is coloured by our own personal views.

What should be the balance between these three principles in terms of teaching time? Academic tradition tends to focus nearly all of its attention on teaching analytical tools. While we agree that analytical tools deserve the majority of students' attention, we feel a more equal balance is necessary. A good economics education includes explicit discussion of the normative aspects of issues, and is built on a base of knowledge of the real world. In fact, even if pure analysis is all you want to teach, your teaching will be improved by including the other two principles. Students will be more motivated and analytically sharpened by the real-world material, and better able to separate judgements from analysis thanks to the clarity about values.

Diversifying and Decolonising Economics

Following the principles, we discuss the problem of diversity in economics. Our discipline has historically been dominated by white upper- and middle-class men from western Europe and the US, and is still so today. This has led to severe biases in our body of theory and in the teaching practices of our field. The ideas of female, global south, ethnic minority and lower-class scholars have frequently been ignored, both in research and in education. The same applies to their economic realities, values, interests and ways of organising economic processes. In addition, the existing culture and structure of the discipline make it hard for women, ethnic minorities and people from a lower socio-economic class to enter.

In this chapter, we provide a brief overview of the problem. We also discuss several potential causes, weighing the evidence on each of them. Finally, we discuss several paths towards diversifying and decolonising economics. This will not only help marginalised groups, important though that is. It will also make economics education itself better for all students, offering them a broader, more realistic and more relevant set of ideas and realities.

The Didactics of Economics Education

We end the *Foundations* part with a chapter on the didactics of economics education. Improving economics education is not simply a matter of changing what is taught, but also how it is taught. A good course is more than just a good syllabus: it requires effective teaching. The chapter focuses on three didactical issues that are of particular relevance for economics education: communication and collaboration, open and critical discussion, and diversity in teaching techniques.

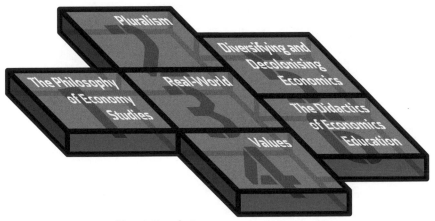

Figure 4: An overview of Part I: Foundations.

Foundation 1
The Philosophy of Economy Studies

Economics should be taught as the study of a subject matter, the economy, using all relevant approaches, rather than as a narrowly defined method of thinking.

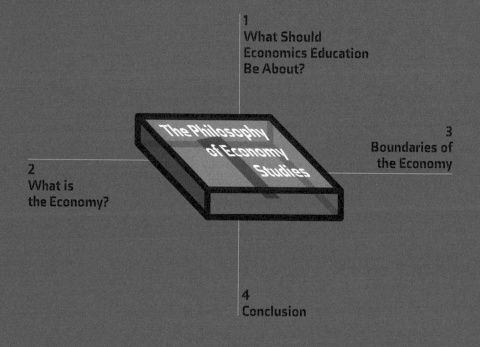

1
What Should
Economics Education
Be About?

The Philosophy
of Economy
Studies

3
Boundaries of
the Economy

2
What is
the Economy?

4
Conclusion

In this chapter, we attempt to answer a fundamental question on economics education: should it be taught as a specific method of thought, which can be applied to any subject matter? Or, should it be taught as a study of a concrete subject matter: the economy, as lawyers study the legal system? We argue the latter, based on the idea that the study of the economy is a vital social function and the primary reason for most students to study economics.

In the second part of the chapter, we define what exactly we mean by 'the economy': economies are open systems of resource extraction, production, distribution, consumption and waste disposal through which societies provision themselves to sustain life and enhance its quality.

We then discuss the question of how the economy is related to other systems: When do we still call something a part of the economy and at what point have we crossed over into other territories? Here we discuss the economy's relation to the natural world, to the social world and its geographical scope, and discuss how to work with these boundaries.

"What do economists study? What do they do? They study the economic system.

Marshall, in the Principles of Economics defined economics thus: 'Political Economy, or Economics, is a study of man's actions in the ordinary business of life; it examines that part of individual and social action which is most closely connected with the attainment and with the use of the material requisites of wellbeing.' A modern economist, Stigler, has phrased it differently: 'Economics is the study of the operation of economic organizations, and economic organizations are social (and rarely individual) arrangements to deal with the production and distribution of economic goods and services.'

Both of these definitions of economics emphasize that economists study certain kinds of activity."

Ronald Coase (1978, p. 206)

1 What Should Economics Education Be About?

The theme of this book is: *how economics education should be organised, to best prepare students for their future roles in society.* In other words, what should economics education be about? There are broadly two potential answers to that question: organising education around a specific method of analysis or organising it around a subject, the economy (Akerlof, 2020).

What would the first answer imply? We would get separate programmes for different theoretical approaches, which subsequently could be applied to different subject matters including for example trade, the labour market, marriage, political party competition, religion, etc. One could imagine a separate programme for the neoclassical approach to human life, another for the institutional approach to human life, programmes for the Marxian approach, etc. Proponents of this view generally claim that while such an approach to the field is by definition limiting, these very limits form its power. Namely, a single, coherent and long-established intellectual framework has the advantage of being more practically useful. Students become experts in a particular method and can communicate effectively and consistently given their shared established syntax, as well as apply and build upon the works of others using the same toolkit.

In economics, this view has become more popular since the 1960s (Backhouse & Medema, 2009a). Before this period, the other view, seeing economics as the study of the economy as subject-matter, was dominant. In fact, the idea that economics is about studying economies has been around in many forms for as long as the field itself has existed (Backhouse & Medema, 2009b). In the classical period, Jean-Baptiste Say (1803, p. 6) described political economy as the *"science"* about *"the production, distribution, and consumption of wealth".* Around the turn of the 20th century, the discipline changed its name from political economy to economics in order to sound more like a modern scientific discipline and to distance itself from its former political image. The core content of the field remained, however, largely unchanged.

In 1932, Lionel Robbins (1932, pp. 15-17) proposed a radically different definition of economics, defining it around a method, rather than a subject-matter, saying: *"Economics is the science which studies human behaviour as a relationship between ends and scarce means which have alternative uses ... any kind of human behaviour falls within the scope of Economic Generalisations. ... There are no limitations on the subject-matter of Economic Science".*

Initially, there was strong resistance to this new definition for economics as being about the rational choice approach to all of human life, or in Backhouse and Medena's (2009a, p. 805) words: *"This definition laid a foundation that could be seen as justifying both the narrowing of economic theory to the theory of constrained maximization or rational choice and economists' ventures into other social science fields. Though often presented as self-evidently correct, both the definition itself and the developments that it has been used to support were keenly contested"*.

Economists, such as Ronald Coase, Frank Knight, James Buchanan, and Kenneth Boulding, argued it was too deductive and anti-empirical, and at the same time too narrow in how topics could be studied and too broad in terms of which topics it concerns (Backhouse & Medema, 2009a). Knight (1933, p. 4) wrote, for example, that it is an *'error'* and *'vice'* to *'look upon life too exclusively under this aspect of scientific rationality [economising]'* and argued instead that economics is about studying *'the social organization of economic activity'*.

Despite these various criticisms, this definition and approach to economics has become more popular since the 1960s. Gary Becker was perhaps its most notable proponent, promoting this approach as 'the economic approach', which he described as follows: *"The combined assumptions of maximizing behavior, market equilibrium, and stable preferences, used relentlessly and unflinchingly, form the heart of the economic approach as I see it."* (Becker, 1976, p. 5). With this 'economic' approach, he proposed we can understand an enormous variety of topics, ranging from traditional economic topics, to topics including marriage, raising kids, education, politics, law, crime, discrimination, and even suicide, as being rational decision making amid scarcity (Becker, 1973, 1976, 2010; Fine & Milonakis, 2009; Grossbard, 1993; Kimenyi & Shughart, 1986).

But while this approach to economics has become more popular, it has by no means become universally accepted. Two of the most popular economics textbooks today, for example, define economics as the study of the economy as subject-matter: Krugman & Wells (2012, p. 12) write *"economics is the social science that studies the production, distribution, and consumption of goods and services"* and the CORE Team (2017, p. 38) defines economics as *"the study of how people interact with each other and with their natural surroundings in providing their livelihoods"*.

While the monistic approach, economics as a method, has some benefits, organising economics education along the lines of one approach creates the risk of replacing the mission with the instrument. The goal of academic programmes is to teach students to understand the world: theories and methods are simply the means to achieve this end. Centring programmes around certain approaches tends to create intellectual silos, where students are taught to be like-minded and adhere to the approach taught in that programme. This approach is therefore often described as teaching students to *"think like an economist"* (Hoyt & McGoldrick, 2012; Siegfried et al., 1991; Tieleman et al., 2017). The danger in this approach is that it *"allows each professor to think of the training that they provide as essentially getting the student to think like him or herself"* (Colander & McGoldrick, 2010, p. 16). As such, the opportunity is lost to help students through open and critical discussions develop their ability to think independently and critically evaluate all the information they are exposed to (on a daily basis) both in their role as future economists and members of society. Or in the words of Raveaud (2009, p. 255):

"While students need to be reassured that their professors know better than they do, they also like to be puzzled. They are students, after all, not guinea pigs! Our role as teachers is not to give them ready-made answers. It is to provide them with the tools and opportunities they need in order to learn to think for themselves about the relative value of competing economic ideas, institutions and policies in the face of genuine uncertainty about which one is 'right'."

In this chapter, we argue for the second answer. That is, to teach economics centred on a specific subject matter: the economy. What would academic education look like in this case? Biologists investigate living things and the ecosystems they form. Sociology is the study of society and social relations. Medical doctors focus on the human body, its health and how to maintain and restore it. Legal scholars study the legal system, rights and obligations. Political scientists investigate politics, the dynamics of power and governance. Economists, then, study the economy. The title of this book, *Economy Studies*, serves to emphasise this point.

2 What is the Economy?

But what exactly is the economy? The term economy originally comes from the ancient Greek word *oikonomía*, meaning *'household management'* (Samuels et al., 2008). The most common modern reformulation of the definition of the economy is the production, distribution and consumption of goods and services. In jargon, it is also known as the *social provisioning process*: the activities, interactions and structures that lead to the provision of the material means of life (Jo, 2016). Furthermore, recent developments and insights concerning ecological issues show that resource extraction and waste disposal are also crucial economic processes, besides production, distribution and consumption (Goodwin et al., 2019). As such, one could say economies are open systems of resource extraction, production, distribution, consumption and waste disposal through which societies provision themselves to sustain life and enhance its quality.

To be clear – political science, sociology, anthropology, law, economics – these are all concerned with human beings and social processes. There is no separate entity called the 'economy', just as there is no isolated thing called 'culture' or 'politics'. Social life is highly complex and consists of many dimensions. But in order to study it effectively, scholars have intellectually distinguished different domains of that larger social life. The social science disciplines each study one of those domains or aspects of society, and for economics that is the material provisioning aspect: the 'economy'.

Before we move on, we need to explain further what we mean by 'the economy', by defining what makes up an economy and subsequently defining its boundaries as well as its relation to neighbouring fields.

The economy can be seen as the sphere in which we carry out practical actions for our needs. We produce things for ourselves and others, we make deals and shake hands and we work together on projects, often in exchange for money. We spend most of our waking hours during adult life working in jobs to 'make a living'. We distribute, and redistribute, resources amongst each other. We do care work for each other, sometimes paid but often unpaid. In short, we do our best to provide for ourselves and each other.

On their own, these interactions seem simple, yet through them we quickly become entangled into larger systems. We engage in all sorts of organisations to coordinate our actions. We form professional associations and labour unions to represent our collective interests. We operate in companies, through which we become involved in supply chains stretching across the globe. We try to ensure that the more vulnerable members of our society, and the natural world on which we depend, are also taken care of. We erect complex structures of government to provide material, legal, educational and other infrastructure. In short, from the simple aim of provisioning for our needs, emerges a complex global system with its own dynamics and tendencies, which nobody has quite 'designed', but which we all influence, and which influences us, in many ways.

These dynamics of human material provisioning, from individual actions, interactions and bonds to larger organisations, institutions, agreements and their emergent dynamics, together form the 'economy'. But what kind of thing does that make the economy? It has been described as a machine, a network, an ecology, a system as well as many other metaphors. Several different analytic approaches conceptualise the economy and its workings differently, each contributing new insights (see *Building Block 8: Economic*

Theories and its online resources). As we explain in more detail in the chapter *Foundation 2: Pluralism*, we argue that students should become familiar with these different ways of looking at economies. Throughout the book we sometimes refer to 'the economic system' as a synonym for the economy. We do not imply any particular conception of the economy by this.

3 Boundaries of the Economy

While there is broad agreement that certain systems and dynamics are clearly part of the economy, there is a lot of debate about the exact definition and the boundaries of the field. We do not pretend to be able to resolve these issues. Instead, we encourage teachers to openly discuss these debates with students (see also *Building Block 1: Introducing the Economy*). Still, for a book called Economy Studies, basing its philosophy on the concept of *the economy*, it is necessary to at least provide a working definition with boundaries. Here we discuss the economy's relation to the natural world, to the social world and its geographical scope.

First, nature. We believe that the interactions between the economy and nature fall, to a large part, within the scope of economics. For example, the extraction of resources and the dumping of refuse are crucial activities in the human material provisioning processes, which often follow economic dynamics. The internal workings of nature, on the other hand, are the domain of the natural sciences. There are at the same time various fields, of rapidly increasing importance, where economists need to cooperate with natural scientists such as in the food industry. We need to better understand how economies are shaped by nature and how economic processes, in turn, influence nature.

For example, throughout most of history, economic cycles could only be understood by taking into account the agricultural cycles (Heilbroner, 1953). While agricultural cycles have lost some of their importance to economic dynamics, natural processes do remain crucial. The growing and harvesting of crops is heavily influenced by topsoil erosion, climate change and the extinction of pollinating insects. Economic dynamics (price competition, the drive for higher short-term efficiency, etc.) systematically affect the natural world, and the consequences in turn limit our ability to grow food to sustain ourselves: economics.

As the man-made ecological challenges of our world multiply, natural processes seem to be regaining their importance for the workings of economies. Even the sector seemingly least connected to the physical world, the financial sector, is increasingly concerned with the effects of climate change (European-Commission, 2021; Wamsley, 2020). Ecological economists have a particular focus on these matters and provide useful teaching material on this. However, the connection with nature goes beyond ecological questions. Health- and technology-related issues are also relevant to the economy, with matters such as aging populations, mechanisation, automation, and, as has become very clear recently, pandemics. In sum, precisely because it is hard to draw an exact boundary between 'nature' and 'economy', the interactions between these two deserve a clear place in economics education.

Secondly, there is a boundary between the economy and the social world, where the latter stretches beyond our actions for practical needs. Here, too, we argue for paying attention to the boundary. Again, this does not mean we are advocating that all social phenomena should be studied by economists. The dynamics of voting behaviour and workings of political parties do still belong to political science; the ways in which information circulates in society to communication studies; the effects of educational practices and policies are still the domain of educational science and the causes of crime and recidivism of criminology – to name but a few. However, we do believe it is important to consider the *interactions* between the two spheres. Politics, information, education and crime are all highly important for our understanding of how economies work, despite being the subject matter of other disciplines. To be sure, economists using the rational choice approach have also contributed to research on many of these topics. While we applaud such interdisciplinary research endeavours, we do not suggest including such insights in economics education. Economics education should focus on understanding the economy, not on a specific method of investigation.

Interdisciplinary cooperation is thus needed to understand how the material provisioning aspect of human societies interacts with other social matters. The economy-oriented sub-disciplines within sociology, anthropology, geography and political science seem to be particularly well-suited to gain knowledge about these interactions. Some economic theoretical approaches, such as institutional and feminist economics, have also paid particular attention to the interactions between the economic and the wider social world. We suggest giving students a brief overview of these fields, so that they will know 'who to talk to' concerning matters spanning various disciplines.

Third and finally, economies have particular geographical boundaries. The term 'the economy' is often used to refer to the national economy. When we use it in this book, we generally do not presume any such specific scale level. Economies can be analysed at any scale of organisation and geography: a household economy, a local economy, a national economy, the global economy. At each level, one can look at bundles of actions (of resource extraction, production, distribution, consumption and waste disposal) as well as the interactions and relations within and between these 'economies'.

We do think it is important to sensitise students to the main differences between these scale levels, and to teach them to pay attention to the ways in which these levels are related to each other. An example could be global value chains, where production facilities around the world interact with households, local economies, national economies, and with the global economy at large. We suggest a flexible geographical approach that allows one to choose and change the level of analysis in order to best understand the matter at hand. This is crucial because the different scale levels also have different relevant theoretical and methodological approaches.

4 Conclusion

To conclude, we argue that the aim of economics education should be to study the economy. The rest of the book is concerned with the 'what' and the 'how' of this general principle, containing building blocks of knowledge, suggestions for teaching material and much more. However, whilst reading the more detailed content of this book, we do hope that you will keep something in mind: these concrete recommendations are not the core of what we are trying to contribute. We are most happy to discuss and question the value of using specific teaching materials, specific theoretical frameworks, and even entire building blocks that we propose. After all, students generally do not retain most of the details, certainly not years after their programme.

What we hope students will retain from a good economics programme is the habit of studying the economy as it is, rather than as an abstract construct, and to think about it in a diversity of ways, independent of fixed theoretical formats. We hope students gain an intuition for various economic dynamics and an appreciation of how deeply the economy is interwoven with the other aspects of our life and world. An ability to see the many different values underlying various economic questions and the confidence that, when faced with a concrete economic problem, they can identify a few different starting points and be able to think through the problem because they know the different places to look, having already practised this during their training. If these basic notions stick, then in our eyes, a programme has been successful, regardless of its exact theoretical and methodological contents.

Foundation 2
Pluralism

Diversity of theories and methods offers students a broader range of insights and helps them see the difference between the map and the territory.

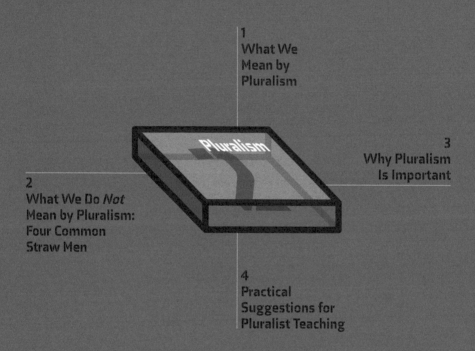

1
What We
Mean by
Pluralism

3
Why Pluralism
Is Important

2
What We Do *Not*
Mean by Pluralism:
Four Common
Straw Men

4
Practical
Suggestions for
Pluralist Teaching

The primary purpose of academic education is learning to dissect important questions with the help of analytical tools. To be able to understand complex economic topics, a diversity of theories and research methods is needed. No single approach is able to fully capture all aspects and dimensions of the economy, so pluralism is not only useful but imperative. We therefore argue that economics education should have a foundation of pluralism: the side-by-side use of fundamentally different approaches to studying the economy.

The economic world is large and complex. To grasp its workings and many elements, we need to use different perspectives and methods as each enables us to better see and understand certain aspects. Furthermore, these different approaches can lead to starkly different insights even when the exact same aspect of the economy is studied. For these reasons, only using one approach can never lead to a full and complete understanding of the economy and using multiple approaches will improve our understanding.

The chapter starts with an overview of what pluralism is, followed by a section describing four common false or 'straw men' versions of pluralism. We then discuss the question whether the latest mainstream is automatically also the best version of a science. Then, we turn to the reasons why teaching in a pluralist manner is important for the intellectual development of students. The chapter ends with some practical notes on how to teach in a pluralist manner and what challenges may occur.

"The world is better served by syncretic economists and policymakers who can hold multiple ideas in their heads than by 'one-handed' economists who promote one big idea regardless of context."

Dani Rodrik (2011, p. 134)

1 What We Mean by Pluralism

Pluralism is about looking at the world from a broad variety of vantage points (Fullbrook, 2008; Garnett Jr et al., 2009). In economics education, this means teaching perspectives that make different assumptions, focus on disparate economic problems, use different units of analysis, apply various methodological approaches, and have distinct ways of reasoning.

The Indian parable of the blind men and the elephant is a beautiful illustration of what pluralism entails. None of the men have ever come across an elephant before, and they can only conceptualise what it is by touching it. The first man's hand lands on the trunk of the elephant, so he thinks it must be a type of snake. The second touches its ear, and says it is a fan. The third places his hands on a leg, and argues that that an elephant must be a kind of tree. The fourth man encounters the side of the elephant like a wall. The fifth man holds the tail and feels a rope. The last man feels the tusk, thinking it to be a spear. Whilst all of their perceptions of the elephant are real, they are incomplete pictures of what an elephant is, and by combining all of these perspectives together, our knowledge is enhanced.

Similarly, all economic theories are incomplete pictures of the world. Any model (whether or not it uses mathematics) is a simplification or an abstraction of the real world. The art of creating a good model or theory is in selecting the most important aspects of the phenomena or process to focus on. However, it is not possible to include an infinite range of variables or concepts in a theory, and even if it was, it would be too unwieldy to use in analysis. Instead, different approaches should be taught and used in tandem, just like the blind men sharing their knowledge about the elephant.

Although one could view the use of a variety of models within the confines of a single theoretical approach as pluralist, we argue that this is not the case. It is as if you would go to a restaurant and get a menu with a wide variety of dishes made up of courgette: roasted courgette, courgette pie, courgette pizza, courgette fritters, courgette soup, stuffed courgette, courgette bread, courgette pasta, courgette pancakes, etc. No one could deny the diversity of dishes, but at a more fundamental level the menu is severely limited in its options. Pluralism requires openness in terms of making fundamentally different theoretical assumptions.

In most contemporary economics programmes, neoclassical economics takes up ⅘ or more of teaching time in theory courses, while all other approaches are largely ignored or marginalised (Proctor, 2019). We suggest that the proportion devoted to neoclassical economics should instead be roughly ⅕.

A proper scientific approach requires us to take seriously relevant ideas about how economies work, irrespective of who developed the idea. There are many important ideas that have been developed outside of academic economics. In particular many other social scientists and philosophers have studied economic topics, leading to the development of the behavioural, feminist and institutional schools of thought.

The subfields of economic history, political economy, economic sociology, economic anthropology, and economic geography have also arisen from the interaction of economics with other social sciences. Various natural scientists, such as biologists and physicists, have also analysed economic topics, contributing to approaches such as econophysics, ecological economics, systems thinking and complexity economics. Ideas from these fields should be taken just as seriously as those developed within economics.

Interdisciplinary Economics provides an overview of five neighbouring subdisciplines, such as economic sociology.
economy.st/interdisciplin

Furthermore, it is not only academics who think about economic matters. Many important economic thinkers worked as policy makers, investors, activists or journalists and were never trained as academic economists. For instance, Karl Marx was a journalist and author. David Ricardo was a stockbroker and then a Member of Parliament. Neither ever held academic positions, but both still had a huge influence on economics. It would be a waste if economics education would ignore all these important contributions simply because these people do not have the label of being an academic economist. Modern-day examples of such thinkers would include journalists such as Rana Foroohar of the *Financial Times*, policy makers such as Andy Haldane of the Bank of England or investors like George Soros.

Finally, pluralism goes beyond theory: diversity in research methods is also required. Time series and other descriptive statistics can provide a quick insight in trends and developments. Interviews or other textual forms of knowledge can provide a richer structural understanding, through the eyes of insiders. Direct observation can highlight different aspects yet again, showing for instance how economic interactions are interwoven with other social dynamics. Geographical overviews can show the physical shape of a sector or supply chain and help students understand the role of practical and political factors. Historical and institutional methods can give valuable understanding of processes and change.

Methods courses in current programmes tend to exclude all the above, focusing instead purely on quantitative data analysis. We suggest spending perhaps ¼ of methods teaching time on this, to make space for some of the above approaches. In addition to including diverse research methods, pluralism means teaching when and why each method should be used, as well as what their underlying assumptions are. Without such diversity, crucial aspects of the world would be ignored, creating collective blind spots. For details, see *Building Block 7: Research Methods & Philosophy of Science*.

2 What We Do *Not* Mean by Pluralism: Four Common Straw Men

Under this heading, we set out four popular straw men versions of pluralism: *relativism, pseudoscience, political diversity*, and *strategic pluralism*. For each of these four, we explain why it is not what we mean by pluralism.

Pluralism, not relativism

We believe that a combination of approaches is required to gain a good understanding of the economy. In the words of Martyn (2017, p. 1): *"[Pluralism] does not reject [neoclassical] economics, it rather suggests that this is only one part of the story. It frees us from both scepticism (nothing goes) and relativism (anything goes)"*.

Diversity and openness in thinking should be disciplined by how they help us understand the real world. Embracing pluralism does not mean embracing relativism. We are not saying that all approaches are always equal, but rather that for different economic questions, it will be different perspectives that are the most useful. For example, when teaching how economic agents make decisions, the neoclassical, behavioural and institutional perspectives could be taught. Whereas for labour economics, the feminist, Marxist and post-Keynesian perspectives could be taught.

The way to decide which approach is superior for a specific case is to compare to what degree different approaches are capable, or incapable, of providing a good explanation of the phenomena in question. This has also been called 'disciplined eclecticism', as it does not rigidly hold on to one single paradigm, but at the same time does not allow for an 'anything goes' approach (INET, 2011).

Scientific diversity, not pseudoscience

While we argue for going beyond the current mainstream, we do support having clear boundaries. Amongst others, pseudoscience, conspiracy theories, climate change denial and creationism have no place in the curriculum.

Where, then, should we draw the line? Distinguishing science from pseudoscience is not as simple as it might look. It has been a core topic of debate within the philosophy of science, referred to as the demarcation problem. There are many ways in which one can conceptualise what the scientific method is. A perspective often referred to by mainstream economists is falsificationism, formulated by Karl Popper in *The Logic of Scientific Discovery* in 1934, which argues one should try to falsify hypotheses, as opposed to trying to verify them. Another influential approach is instrumentalism, proposed by Milton Friedman in *The Methodology of Positive Economics* in 1953, arguing that theories should be judged based on the simplicity and fruitfulness of their predictions, not the realisticness of the theory. These approaches have received substantial criticism since their publication, both for proposing an undesirable principle for demarcation and for not providing an accurate description of what economists actually do (Boumans & Davis, 2015; Maas, 2014; Thornton, 2016). Since then many different methodological ideas have been developed. The following categories outlined by Coates (2005) and Thornton (2016), of the many criteria on the basis of which theories could be evaluated, seem most relevant:

- Explanatory coherence: Internal consistency
- Explanatory power: Fit with evidence and ability to explain or predict real-world phenomena

- Explanatory reach: The scope and depth of explanation, although more is not necessarily better
- Explanatory openness: The flexibility and capacity to absorb new insights and adapt to new circumstances
- Explanatory impact: Influence on the world, ability to help solve real-world problems and the values associated with the theory.

In sum, there is certainly pluralism within the field of philosophy of science (see also *Building Block 7: Research Methods & Philosophy of Science*). However, while the exact definition of 'science' remains contested, we are confident that you will find the vast majority of ideas in this book clearly within the realm of science.

Intellectual diversity, not political diversity

The issue at hand here is teaching students different scientific approaches, not teaching them different political ideas. Of course, it is important that economic programmes are not indoctrinating students into a particular ideology, but that is not the problem we are trying to address here. We don't have the impression that economics programmes are systematically skewed toward left-wing or right-wing ideas. The issue we raise here is that economics education is theoretically homogenous.

The dominant neoclassical approach can be combined with various political beliefs. Research on the political beliefs of economists shows that most economists self-identify as centre-left or (socially) liberal (Berggren et al., 2009; Colander, 2008; Colander & Klamer, 1987; De Benedictis & Di Maio, 2011; Klein & Stern, 2006; van Dalen & Klamer, 1996; van Dalen et al., 2015a). The common critique that most economists are free-market right-wing ideologues is therefore ungrounded. Most programmes today include both new classical and new Keynesian macroeconomics, which respectively typically have right-wing and left-wing policy conclusions. Political diversity is there. Both, however, are based on the neoclassical assumptions of the homo economicus with farsighted rationality, who as an isolated individual is driven by utility maximisation and arrives at equilibria in markets through the price mechanism. Theoretical diversity, then, is lacking.

We argue not for including left-wing or right-wing ideas in economics education, but instead for including ideas that are built on different theoretical assumptions, irrespective of what policy conclusions they might lead to.

Pluralism, not a new dominant paradigm

Advocates of pluralism are sometimes accused of another motive, strategic pluralism (Jackson, 2018; Sent, 2006). That is, they would only be interested in pluralism insofar as this would give their personally favoured approach more room. The true motivation behind the scenes is then to turn their own approach into the new dominant paradigm, thereby undoing pluralism. As such, pluralism would be a temporary stepping-stone towards a new paradigm.

In some cases, this accusation may be correct. Rather than truly believing in pluralism, some might indeed see it as an instrumental tool to promote their own ideas. We are, however, firmly opposed to replacing the current monopoly of ideas with a new monopoly. As we described above, the problem is *not* neoclassical economics. Neoclassical economics is, in fact, a very useful approach to help us understand some economic topics, so we do not want to remove it from economics education. The problem we address in this chapter is that mainstream economics education focuses almost exclusively on one approach, which simply happens to be neoclassical economics. Replacing the old paradigm with a new one or expanding the current paradigm, for example by incorporating behavioural economics, does not solve the problem. A diversity of theories and methods is needed, not another dominant paradigm.

A good example to explain this is the influential and innovative textbook *The Economy* by the CORE team (2017). Their book shares our core philosophy: economics should be defined as the study of economic systems, not the application of a specific method. It also contains many of the concrete topics we call for in our building blocks: history of the economy, prominent treatment of political-economic systems, serious attention for institutions, capstone chapters on major economic challenges of our time, and much more real-world knowledge in general. In short, *The Economy* is a great textbook, which we highly recommend.

However, in terms of pluralism it is important to realise that this textbook replaces the conventional paradigm with a new one, which they call 'the new benchmark'. Bowles and Carlin (2020), the team's lead authors, describe their approach as embracing *'pluralism-by-integration'*, as it builds a synthesis out of insights from *multiple* schools of thought, aiming to create *one* coherent framework. This means that ideas that are complementary to each other are included, while ideas that are in conflict with each other are not included.

While this is a great step in the right direction, *'pluralism-by-integration'* remains somewhat of an oxymoron when it comes to education. Pluralism means including multiple, *plural*, approaches, while integration refers to constructing *one* approach. So, while the new emerging benchmark is much broader than the old neoclassical framework, the risk of *pluralism-by-integration* is that students will still get the impression that the textbook and the teacher simply present 'the truth' about the economy, rather than as presenting one possible synthesis out of a diversity of economic ideas.

In this book, we make the case for a different kind of pluralism: '*pluralism-by-juxtaposition*'. That is, to teach students about multiple contrasting approaches and debates between them. We think this is vital: being able to deal with economic debates and conflicting ideas by making independent and informed judgements and admitting intellectual uncertainty is a core skill for any economist (Denis, 2009; Eliassen, 2016). As long as students are not exposed to the existence of multiple contrasting perspectives and debates, we give them the impression that there is only one way of looking at issues that is relevant enough to learn about. This may hamper their ability and skills in independent and critical thinking, and increasing the risk of groupthink in their later professional lives.

This should not be read as a dismissal or rejection of *The Economy*. The point is rather that we also advocate taking the next step: incorporating conflicting ideas and '*pluralism-by-juxtaposition*'. The textbook is an excellent ingredient for such teaching: it incorporates new ideas and insights, and pays more attention to empirics, history and institutions. We highly recommend using it. And while they do not make this explicit in their textbook, the CORE team also very much encourages *pluralism-by-juxtaposition* programmes, with one ingredient being their textbook (Carlin, 2021).

Sometimes it is argued that teaching students conflicting approaches will lead to inconsistent and incoherent reasoning. We believe the opposite is true. By teaching students how and when ideas are in conflict with each other, they learn to identify contradictions and deal with them. Pluralism in teaching does not mean that students should believe conflicting ideas simultaneously (Courvisanos et al., 2016; de Langhe, 2009). What it means is that students should become aware of the conflicting ideas and acquire the skills to form an independent and informed opinion on issues (Mearman et al., 2011). The key difference is between 'having knowledge of' and 'believing exclusively in'. If one would have to trust one approach without having knowledge of the different ideas and approaches, this would require blind faith in the approach which is scientifically unjustifiable. As such, being able to deal with a diversity of ideas and make informed judgements "*is an intrinsic part of intellectual development*" (Sen, 2005, p. 3).

Whig History:
Is the Mainstream of the Moment Always the Best?

Some economists feel that whatever change the economic discipline has undergone over the years has been for the better, the so-called 'Whig history' interpretation (Samuelson, 1987). The term Whig history was first coined by the English historian Herbert Butterfield in 1931 to describe interpretations of history that saw everything as constantly becoming better, and specifically saw the British constitutional settlement as one of the highest achievements in human history (Butterfield, 1931).

Applied to the development of economics, this implies that knowledge just keeps on accumulating and that the science of economics progresses linearly. In this view, the only cause of change within the discipline is improvement and all of the good ideas of the past have been incorporated in the mainstream. Mainstream as a category, therefore, becomes synonymous with 'the best'. Anything outside it is by definition irrelevant, and the past becomes an imperfect version of the present. From this perspective, it is no problem that mainstream economics in the second half of the 20th century increasingly came to be dominated by neoclassical economics, since its dominance can only be a result of its superiority (A. Freeman et al., 2014).

Such a simplistic view of scientific progress is certainly attractive. However, historians of economic thought and other experts on developments within economics generally view Whig history as incorrect. They view it as overly optimistic regarding the internal workings of science and note that it ignores all external influences on science. In decades of research, they have identified many other important factors that influence the development of economics. The most important among these are the organisational structures within universities and other research institutions, social networks, path dependencies, changes in the economy itself, and the cultural and political context in which economic thinkers operate.

Such institutional factors have prevented relevant ideas from being incorporated within the mainstream, while they also have prevented dominant ideas from being properly scrutinised. Or in W. Arthur Lewis' (1955, p. 174) words: *"Collective judgment of new ideas is so often wrong that it is arguable that progress depends on individuals being free to back their own judgment despite collective disapproval"*. The history of economic thought thus casts serious doubt on the assumption that the current mainstream is always necessarily better (e.g. Akerlof, 2020; Backhouse, 1994; Blaug, 2001; Cedrini & Fontana, 2018; Cedrini & Fontana, 2015; Colander & Landreth, 1998; Davis, 2006; Dequech, 2017; Dow, 2009; Fourcade, 2009; Gans & Shepherd, 1994; Gräbner & Strunk, 2020; Lee, 2009; Morgan & Rutherford, 1998; Samuels et al., 2008; Weintraub, 2002).

> In short, allowing only one approach is problematic, since it can neither be assumed that this dominant approach is the 'best' approach, nor that it has incorporated all of the relevant ideas from other approaches.

3 Why Pluralism Is Important

Pluralism is a critical feature of any economics education. To fully answer any question about an economy, an economist must look at the problem from multiple perspectives that utilise different assumptions, units of analysis and methodological approaches. Economies are such enormously complex systems that they require different perspectives to understand their many elements. In addition, even for the same aspect of the economy, different perspectives often provide startlingly different insights. In the language of philosophy of science, the former point refers to an ontological reason for pluralism and the latter to an epistemological reason (de Langhe, 2009; Lawson, 2012; Salanti & Screpanti, 1997). Hence, no *one* approach provides a full and complete understanding of economies. Or in Chang's (2014, p. 453) words:

> "As the saying goes, 'he who has a hammer sees everything as a nail'. If you approach a problem from a particular theoretical point of view, you will end up asking only certain questions and answering them in particular ways. You might be lucky, and the problem you are facing might be a 'nail' for which your 'hammer' is the most appropriate tool. But, more often than not, you will need to have an array of tools available to you.
>
> You are bound to have your favourite theory. There is nothing wrong with using one or two more than others – we all do. But please don't be a man (or a woman) with a hammer – still less someone unaware that there are other tools available. To extend the analogy, use a Swiss army knife instead, with different tools for different tasks."

To give an example, neoclassical economics takes the individual as its unit of analysis, assumes that humans are rational and relatively independent of their society, and uses mostly quantitative methods to assess formalised hypotheses. In contrast, institutional economics takes institutions and systems as its unit of analysis, assumes that humans are heavily influenced by their social context and uses more qualitative methods and broad reasoning to answer questions. None of these choices are wrong, even though they are very different.

The value of pluralism is that both of these perspectives can be used to answer the same question. The insights that are gained from both perspectives can be combined to give the economist a fuller picture of the problem in front of them, and when they contradict each other help us arrive at sharper analyses. Beyond knowledge of the relevant perspectives, this also requires students to be able to think for themselves. Once the models and theories they have used have yielded their output, an economist must use their own judgement on how much weight to place on the various results obtained, particularly when the results lead to incompatible conclusions.

Not every perspective is equally valuable for any given situation, they all have their points of focus and blind spots. Economics students need to be taught a broad range of perspectives during their education so that they have a bigger toolbox of analytical tools to use in their professional lives. This will allow them to be of far greater value to their future employers and society at large, as Andy Ross (2018, p. 2), former deputy director Government Economic Service in the UK, explains:

> "The need for pluralism is self-evident to practising economists in their day-to-day work, even when, for exposition purposes, such approaches must be played down in final reports to stakeholders. Some economists fear that pluralism equates to 'anything goes' or implies that economics is all just a matter of opinion. Yet the opposite is true. Pluralism demands critical evaluation in order to select the right tools for the job in hand. Most of the mistakes in economics that I encounter have not arisen from technical errors, but from failing to appreciate whether the methods and data used are appropriate."

Beyond the direct benefits of providing budding economists with a broader knowledge base, pluralism also teaches intellectual humility and open-mindedness. When students are being taught only one way of thinking, they may develop the unfortunate idea that this is the best, or the only reasonable way to think about the economy. Such ideas are detrimental to intellectual development and real-world applications. In contrast, an economist trained in the pluralist tradition is used to comparing and combining competing viewpoints, and well aware that even the approach that they are most convinced by personally does not have a monopoly on truth. A good economist is modest and tries to understand other scholars, especially when they have a different point of view. Sometimes it is said that pluralism is undesirable because it is uncomfortable for students when the teacher cannot 'simply tell how the world truly works' and instead has a complicated story about scientific doubt and different possible explanations (Denis, 2009). We would, however, argue that cognitive comfort should never be the goal of academic education. Confronting students with the complex reality and teaching them to question and investigate, rather than to believe and assume, should be central. Or as Max Weber (2009, p. 147) put it: *"The primary task of a useful teacher is to teach his students to recognize 'inconvenient' facts".*

Pluralism encourages creativity and innovation. Indeed, pluralism is more than a worthwhile addition to a programme: it is essential for the training of critical and creative open minds. If everyone is supposed to think in the same way, existing ideas are less likely to be criticised and new ideas are less likely to develop. All ideas and assumptions should be open to questioning. Students should be given the chance to study different schools of thoughts and methodologies, irrespective of whether the idea goes against the status quo or mainstream approach within the field.

Teaching students multiple perspectives on the same issue also allows for the easy integration of critical thinking into any course or programme, something that is normally very difficult to achieve. Pluralism supports students in developing their own critical thinking process; they are forced to consider the potentially contradictory concepts and assumptions that they are being taught. It can be included only in a rudimentary fashion by critiquing the single model or perspective that is presented. Although students might be encouraged to think about what the problems or limitations are, if they have never been taught other perspectives it remains very hard for them to challenge what they learn. Moreover, students can then be encouraged to question the logical soundness of their own interpretations of those ideas. In this way, pluralism, especially when combined with the integration of critical thinking, can lead to improved economic understanding.

Pluralist education, furthermore, helps students learn to effectively communicate with people coming from a different perspective. As their education teaches them that there are multiple perspectives on issues and focuses on developing skills to understand and compare these perspectives, students will be better prepared to work in interdisciplinary teams and communicate with non-economists. However, sometimes it is argued that pluralism will complicate communication among economists, as it means they would use different approaches rather than all adhering to the same approach (Gräbner & Strunk, 2020). If economists would isolate in groups based on economic approach and only have knowledge of their own favoured approach, communication among economists would indeed become more difficult. But what we are proposing here is, however, something else. We are advocating to help students become familiar with the main different economic approaches, so that in their later career they will be better able to effectively communicate with economists who use different approaches than they do.

Finally, teaching only one perspective can have harmful performative effects (Parvin, 1992). Learning only one approach will not only limit the thinking of students, it will also influence their behaviour. One example is how several empirical studies have found that the current dominance of neoclassical theory has caused students to behave more like the homo economicus, calculated and self-interested (Aldred, 2019; Bauman & Rose, 2011; Wang et al., 2011). To prevent such performative effects, it is important to expose students to different ideas about the economy and human nature, and hence a range of counterbalancing influences on their development.

Teaching only one approach will also have consequences at the societal level for outcomes in areas such as human wellbeing, the natural environment, and income, gender and racial inequality. This is because economic thinking has a key influence on policymaking. The way we understand how an economy works – and should work – changes how we behave and how policies and other decisions are advised and made.

4 Practical Suggestions for Pluralist Teaching

A common objection from academic economists to incorporating pluralism into their teaching is that it would be too confusing for their students. However, it is in fact standard practice in every other social science: sociology, geography, political science and so on. In these disciplines, several major schools of thought or individual thinkers are juxtaposed with each other within the same course, often within the same lecture. Students seem to have little trouble with this. The challenge is, however, to change the teaching, as the current monist approach is deeply ingrained in the materials and practices used by most economics educators. This book aims to help broaden these materials and practices.

However valuable and worthwhile pluralism may be, committing to pluralism in educating opens up a thorny and ongoing question. If not all approaches should be taught all the time, then what approaches should be taught, and when? We suggest focusing on the most important ideas and insights on every topic when teaching theories. So, for each topic, one does not try to teach all or just one theory, but one teaches a couple of theories which are most relevant. To assist with this, in the chapter *Tool 1: Pragmatic Pluralism* we have applied this logic to twelve core economic topics. For each topic, we provide suggestions of which approaches are most helpful, including literature references.

Different perspectives can enhance and complement each other, as they concern different aspects of a topic. But approaches can also be in conflict and contradict each other, when they provide opposing explanations of the same phenomenon. We suggest teaching students both about ideas that are in conflict with each other and about ideas that go together.

For instance, the efficient market hypothesis and the financial instability hypothesis are in fundamental contradiction with each other. For any concrete real-world situation, when one of these theories accurately describes it, the other one is bound to be less accurate, or even completely useless – for that particular situation. The credit theory of money and theory of earmarking money, however, are complementary to each other: they can both be true at the same time, describing different facets of the same situation.

Finally, it is important to get students started on pluralism early on. People speaking one language find it very hard to learn a second one, but people who have already learned several languages have the mental apparatus to abstract from "language" and see it in a way that helps them to incorporate the subtle differences of another tongue. Hence, we do not believe that every plausible approach needs to be taught in order to be effectively pluralist: get students started and they will continue on their own. Throughout the building blocks, we suggest both advanced and entry-level teaching materials to get students thinking in open and pluralist ways. In *Building Block 8: Economies Theories*, we focus specifically on ways to teach theoretical pluralism.

Foundation 3
Real-World

Teaching more concrete knowledge about actual economies gives students motivation, helps them to anchor theory to something in the real world, and gives them a basis of knowledge to build on.

1
What We Mean by
Real-World Knowledge

3
Forms of
Real-World
Knowledge

Real-World

2
Why To Teach
Real-World Knowledge

4
Practical Suggestions
for Teaching
Real-World Knowledge

Real-world economics has long been a core demand of the *Rethinking Economics* movement. It is an ideal that you cannot really be against; who would actively reject the real world in their teaching? Still, it is not easy to put into practice. In this chapter, we set out how economics education could be enriched by systematically incorporating real-world knowledge.

By 'real-world knowledge' we mean concrete knowledge about economic sectors, actors, institutions and history. In this way it goes beyond giving 'real-world examples' that illustrate theoretical ideas. Real-world knowledge is a goal in itself, not merely an instrument to help students understand theory. We believe that making space for such knowledge makes an economics programme far more worthwhile, informative, and relevant to almost anything one might do after graduating. It also makes a programme considerably more enjoyable, motivating students and enabling them to relate more actively to the theoretical parts of the programme.

This chapter starts with a more detailed explanation of the term, including the questions: is there such a thing as raw 'real-world' knowledge, what types of real-world knowledge are we referring to, and is this the same as empirics? We then provide an overview of the various reasons for including more real-world knowledge in programmes: motivation, anchoring theory, and professional applicability. Finally, we provide a number of practical suggestions for implementing this principle in economics courses.

"A man who thinks that economics is only a matter for professors forgets that this is the science that has sent men to the barricades. A man who has looked into an economics textbook and concluded that economics is boring, is like a man who has read a primer on logistics and decided that the study of warfare must be dull."

Robert Heilbroner (1953, p. 14)

1   What We Mean By Real-World Knowledge

The notion of real-world knowledge is closely related to the concept of *'idiographic'* knowledge within philosophy of science. It refers to knowledge of the particular, unique, and contingent. It is contrasted with the *'nomothetic'* approach which is about arriving at universal laws through generalisation. For instance, an understanding of the financial instability hypothesis is nomothetic knowledge, whereas familiarity with the main events and dynamics in the 2007-2008 financial crisis is idiographic knowledge.

As economics became more and more focused on the nomothetic approach and general laws, idiographic knowledge has drifted out of sight (Wallerstein et al., 2003). This is problematic, as both idiographic and nomothetic knowledge are required for a good understanding of the world that can then inform actions and decisions. Economics education would greatly benefit from systematically including idiographic knowledge, restoring the balance between the two approaches.

Is there such a thing as pure real-world knowledge?

A frequent objection to the argument for teaching more real-world knowledge is this: *'There is no such thing as real-world knowledge, everything is an interpretation!'* On an abstract epistemological level, we agree with that statement. There is no such thing as a raw presentation of reality. If we want to meaningfully make sense of what we see and hear, we need to interpret. And, this interpretation must be conducted through some sort of assumptions or theory. The kind of real-world knowledge we argue for, however, does not require any sophisticated mathematical models or epistemological discussions.

The theoretical assumptions that one holds shape one's interpretation and framing of real-world developments. A book by a more evolutionary-inclined economic historian will present historical facts differently from an economic historian with more Keynesian inclinations. While both deal with the same reality, they arrive at different interpretations of this reality. This highlights why it is important to combine real-world knowledge with pluralism. Students need to become aware of the multiple ways in which reality can be interpreted and presented. Still, they will agree about *most* of the historical facts. For example, a sustained period of privatisation and marketisation would be seen as an important event by many schools of thought, even if they drew very different conclusions about the consequences.

We are simply arguing for exposing students, as much as possible, to the real world. Let them experience economic processes for themselves. Teach them basic stylised facts about the economy around them. Introduce them to different historical situations. Let them observe directly how organisations work. Give them a basic understanding of the specific institutions shaping the economy. Stimulate them to observe their own behaviour as consumers and workers. In general, just make sure they get some mud on their shoes.

The 'empirical revolution' in research

Is 'real-world economics' the same as 'empirics'? In short: not quite.

Real-world knowledge is about exposing students, as much as possible, to actual economic processes and providing them with a wide variety of factual information. On the other hand, *"Empirical work in positive economics is designed to test and develop theories"* (Davis, 2002, p. 167). So, while real-world knowledge can never be completely theory-free, as discussed above, it is not focused on general theories and explaining causal mechanisms, as empirical research is.

As such, it is also different from the 'empirical revolution' within research. This term is used to refer to the trend among mainstream top journals in recent decades to pay more attention to empirical analyses. This trend is one that we support, but it does not mean that economics has become increasingly a-theoretical. As Cherrier (2016, p. 2) writes, *"economics has not really gone "from theory to data," but has rather experienced a profound redefinition of the relationship of theoretical to empirical work"*. Rather than having rediscovered empirical research, the discipline has further developed the way empirical research is done and how it connects to theory. In Rodrik's (2015, p. 201) words *"The standards of the profession now require much greater attention to the quality of data, to causal inference from evidence and a variety of statistical pitfalls".*

While we applaud doing more, and more careful, statistical analysis, this is not what we are arguing for in this 'real-world' principle. Instead, what we are proposing is more direct observations of the complex and messy real world. Advanced statistical analysis is a different activity: once these messy observations have been transformed into stylised and clean data, statistical analysis might be conducted.

Nor is this principle simply about raw data and statistics. We also suggest that students go out of the classroom to directly observe economic phenomena and speak to the people directly experiencing them. In general, we suggest that a plurality of approaches be used to confront students with the real world. Gathering concrete knowledge of the economic world from as many sources as possible, trying to understand how they fit together. That is what we argue for.

So, while students should also learn how to conduct good economic research combining theory and empirics, this principle focuses on teaching students concrete knowledge about actual economies.

2 Why To Teach Real-World Knowledge

While virtually no one is actively against teaching real-world knowledge, many professors do not prioritise it. We have often heard arguments like: *"Of course, students find it interesting to talk about recent events, but they can read the newspaper in their own time."* ... *"History is fascinating and relevant, of course. But students can read history books in their own time. Now, mathematics, they won't learn by themselves."* ... *"Applying economic theory to the real world? That comes later, at the master or PhD level. First they need to learn the basics."* Many professors see real-world knowledge as an interesting and sometimes even fun addition, but not as a serious and foundational element of economics education because of its specific nature and their tendency to teach at a more abstract level.

We strongly disagree. Real-world knowledge should be at the centre of economics education. Understanding the real-world economy should be the ultimate goal of economics . Luckily, this is a core motivation of students. Many chose to study economics because they wanted to understand the economic and social world around them. Methods and theories are tools to better understand the real world, but they are not the goal itself. While we understand why professors focus on teaching students analytical tools, we think it is vitally important students also learn how to apply and contextualise those tools. The only way for students to grasp the relevance of the tools they are being taught is to see how they relate to reality. Once they do, they will also remember and apply the theory better. It is also key to realise that on average less than 3% of economics bachelor students go on to do a PhD (Colander & McGoldrick, 2010; de Goede et al., 2014). For the other 97%, who go on to become professional, rather than academic, economists, learning pure theory is not a goal in itself as they need to be prepared to apply economics in practice.

Another frequently heard objection is the idea that all real-world knowledge is fleeting, whereas economic theory is timeless. While this is true to an extent, teaching theory only on this basis would be akin to lawyers learning only to think about legal systems in the abstract, but not learn the laws of today. After all, every year new laws are introduced and others are struck from the books, so why bother learning anything about actual laws or landmark cases? A good education combines these two forms of knowledge: theoretical and real-world.

In addition to the question of motivation, a lack of attention to real-world economics greatly increases the risk that students will confuse theory with the real world itself (Clower, 1995; Morgan, 2012). Metaphorically speaking, the map gets mistaken for the territory (Korzybski, 1931). Stepping outside the classroom and engaging with the real economy helps counter such effects. Through real-world knowledge, the contingency of theoretical models is put into a sharper focus.

An example may serve to clarify. If one teaches students different theories and models about unemployment, students might quickly become lost in the equations. The practical concept of unemployment is defined somewhere, but it is not discussed in detail. In such a situation, students often quickly forget the theories once they have passed the exam, as the significance of the ideas never quite reached them. The different models were simply different characters in the equations one had to memorise and work with. Even by the end of the temporary, structural, frictional, cyclical, voluntary, and involuntary unemployment are all too often still just abstract terms. This does not help students to retain the theory, nor will it help them much in recognising these patterns in the real world later on in their working life.

Now let's imagine taking a different approach to teaching these theories on unemployment. The first lesson of a master's course on unemployment is not in a lecture hall, but at the government (un)employment offices. The concept of unemployment is introduced to students through informal conversations they have with actual people who are unemployed. The second lesson is devoted to giving a factual and historical overview of the topic, with the help of readings, videos and statistics on the history of unemployment up to the current day. The third and fourth lesson consist of guest lectures by and discussions with a union organiser and an economist working for the employers' association.

Having focused on the real world in the first four lessons, the class turns to the different theories on unemployment in the fifth lesson. Still, the connection to the real world is kept alive and present. Later on in the course, students are given the exercise to interview different stakeholders: long- and short-term unemployed people, those who were previously unemployed, employers, and people who work at the unemployment office or the ministry of social affairs, in order to better understand how they view the issue. The course then explains the current institutions and policies regarding unemployment. This is done in a guest lecture by a policy economist working at the ministry of social affairs, who also provides real-world case studies and current policy problems as exercises for students to work on in the course.

Through these various ways of incorporating the real world in the course, students will not only have acquired knowledge about the actual economy around them, but will most likely also have learned more about the theories and remember them for longer because they acquire real meaning.

It is not only students who emphasise the significance of real-world knowledge. Professional economists and their employers do so as well. In a recent survey of Dutch economists, the majority ranked 'profound knowledge of the national economy' and 'the ability to place issues within their historical context' among the top five skills a professional economist should have (van Dalen et al., 2015b). Furthermore, a UK study among employers of economics graduates found that one of the top three skills economists need to have is the "application of economic knowledge to real-world problems" (Yurko, 2018). One consultancy employer (anonymously) said:

> "It's important that graduates have had some hands-on experience of trying to work through the use of those [economic] tools for a practical question. So, when the rubber hits the road: how do you go from some sort of perfect way of answering something to the pragmatic way that understands the intricacies of the problems involved, tries to use real world data, understands the human

priorities that are involved there and things like that."
(Yurko, 2018, p. 7)

Another employer, working at a major financial institution, noted that the high degree of abstraction in economics degrees frequently leads to frustrations among graduates, and can hinder them in their careers:

> *"Economics graduates tend to be quite linear in their thinking. Therefore, there is a sort of resilience aspect, a complacency within economics graduates to think that because they've understood something on paper, why is the actual practical application of these things so damn tough? Well, it's partly because what they've learnt is not actually relevant to the much more ambiguous, holistic, 360 thesis. So, I think there's a sort of frustration that an economics graduate may develop in their career, which may hinder their career, which is they feel like they have moved so far away from the nice box of their learning into a very messy place."*
> (Yurko, 2018, p. 10)

Despite its widely recognised relevance and importance, real-world knowledge seems to lack stature within the academic discipline of economics (Fullbrook, 2007). Many have argued that the obsessive focus on the technicalities of analytical tools has made the work of economists less relevant to the world around us (Colander, 2001). Krugman notes how the love for abstraction has led to wrong and damaging policy advice, saying that *"the economics profession went astray because economists, as a group, mistook beauty, clad in impressive-looking mathematics, for truth"* (2009, p. 2).

In sum: real-world knowledge improves understanding of theory and ensures this is retained in the long run rather than forgotten, enabling the application of analytical tools in practice in a responsible and correct manner. The vast majority of undergraduate economics students do not progress to further study and a career in academia, so for undergraduate programmes in particular, prioritisation of technicalities over applications is inappropriate.

3   Forms of Real-World Knowledge

There are many forms of real-world knowledge about the economy. Here we highlight a few important ways in which it could be incorporated into economics education: historical knowledge, basic knowledge of the current economy, and knowledge of the main economic challenges of today.

First, teaching history is a great way of exposing students to the different and changing economic realities that have existed. Think of the various waves of colonisation and globalisation. Think of the rise of capitalism and socialism, and the historical development of monetary systems. Consider the ways that economic organisations have changed throughout history, how industries have evolved through technological progress, how people's lives have changed because of the changing nature of work and consumption, and how government policies have differed over time. Look at the recurrent economic up- and down-swings, from the 19th century and the 1930s Great Depression to the 2008 Great Recession and the economic downturn caused by the COVID-19 pandemic.

Not only are these topics fascinating to learn about, they also expose students to a vast array of facts and events, giving them concrete knowledge about economies. This will allow them to better understand how things evolved and came to be. Additionally, learning about the diversity of economic patterns and forms of organisation throughout history helps students get a better feeling for the wide variety of future possibilities that exist. As such, teaching economic history will help students to better grasp current phenomena and come to realise that economies are ever-changing. Armed with knowledge of the past they become better economists in the present and future. For further discussion, see *Building Block 3: Economy History*.

Second, it is worthwhile for students to gain an understanding of the economy that currently exists around them. That overview could include its central governing institutions, the different sectors and growth poles, as well as basic facts on issues such as growth, income and wealth inequality, carbon footprint, biodiversity, inflation, (un)employment, wages, profit, productivity, investment, current accounts, levels of debt, and the structure of social stratification. A good economist knows the basic shape of the economic landscape around them. Such knowledge allows students to place ideas in context. Institutional knowledge provides insight in the actual structures of economies and the relations between their main sectors and actors. Sectoral overviews provide an entry point into actual economic dynamics, all the while giving students a setting to try out the theories they learn. For further discussion, see *Building Block 2: Know Your Own Economy*.

Third, economists need to be acquainted with the main economic challenges our society faces today. Examples are climate change, financial and economic crises, rising wealth and income inequality, hunger and poverty, pandemics, a lack of education and development of human capital, and gender and ethnic disparities within economic relationships. As well as learning about these problems in a global context, focusing on the problems (and the aspects of those problems) that are most relevant for their own country or region will better equip them to be of use to their societies after they complete their studies. This will also be more engaging for students, as they are more likely to have a personal connection to the problems being discussed in their classes.

Much of economic theory and policy work is concerned with these major challenges. Understanding exactly what is going on comes prior to explaining why it is happening and what should be done about it. We suggest paying explicit and substantial attention to teaching these matters to students in economics programmes, by devoting lectures and readings to such factual information. For further discussion, see *Building Block 1: Introducing the Economy* and *Building Block 9: Problems & Proposals*.

4 Practical Suggestions for Teaching Real-World Knowledge

One fruitful looking glass into real-world economic structures and developments is the traditional or mainstream media. Go beyond the common suggestion to 'start your class with today's newspaper' and for example suggest that students take a (trial) subscription to the *Financial Times*, subscribe to digital newsletters, high-quality blogs, podcasts or video series, or follow any other economics-focused media. Even if their reading is not directly related to the class at hand, this will help students to explore the territory of economics on their own, making them more motivated and knowledgeable students throughout the programme.

Most students will need more than a mention of a few media outlet names to get started. It can help to make these materials an integral part of teaching, at least for some classes, to set the gears in motion. One way to include this in a regular bachelor programme would be assigning one student or group each week to give an update of the recent economic news, and include at least one other stylised economic fact, insight or argument that they personally find fascinating. Another might be to set media materials as required reading or listening, to be debated in a seminar. One way or another, educators need to kick-start their students, to take them by the hand and help them explore the sometimes intimidating world of economic discourse.

For example, climate change may be the predominant societal challenge of our time. Yet we know few students who would, on their own, start reading IPCC reports, evaluations of the European carbon dioxide cap-and-trade system, or research on how climate change will impact the Dutch economy. However, in the rare cases that we have seen professors assign such reading, students were happy to be pushed into this opportunity. This led to lively discussions in class, about both climate change and the economic drivers behind it. Students appeared to learn much more from this than from more abstract readings.

Besides reading, there are many other ways in which students can learn about the real world. Teachers can invite guest lectures from outside academia, whether that may be government employees, entrepreneurs, private sector workers, non-governmental organisations (NGOs), or trade union members. Alternatively, teachers can organise excursions to visit organisations to get a more direct impression of the topic at hand. A course on financial economics could, for example, visit a (central) bank or stock exchange. A longer and more intense version of this would be to allow and stimulate students to do internships at such places.

All this may seem like stating the obvious. After all, nobody is against more inspired students. But there is a tricky bind here which we need to address: lack of time. Most economics professors we know have a strong sense of duty to at least put their students through the essentials of the subject. Again, students can read the newspaper for the rest of their lives, and they might yet dive into the fascinating world of economic history. But they will never practice statistical regression or study pure theory on their own. So, feeling that they have to focus the limited attention of students on the core theory, professors often end up focusing strongly on the types of material that most students find very dry. The students then quickly become tired from this diet of abstraction only, and the professors conclude that they are not motivated.

The problem here is zero-sum thinking. The way out of this double bind is to spend more time on the real-world material. Not as a footnote in the first lecture or a 'case study' box in a textbook, but as an integral part of the programme. It does of course require some time to kick-start students in their explorations, and this may initially feel like a waste of precious teaching time. But it pays off. We are convinced that by helping students to continuously build the bridge between day-to-day events and economic theory and data, professors can engage the long-term interest of many more of their students, thus ensuring themselves of a far more involved audience throughout the programme. When students can see how the theoretical knowledge from their classes helps them to understand the world around them they are also far more likely to internalise this knowledge, to genuinely understand the theories and models that they are taught, rather than merely memorising them. The time spent to get students interested repays itself many times over.

Foundation 4
Values

Value judgements are at the core of economic questions. Students should learn to distinguish between different values and learn to discuss them rather than sweep them under the carpet.

1
Positive vs Normative?

3
Where in Economics
Do Values
Play a Role?

2
Common
Misconceptions:
What We Do *Not* Mean

4
Practical Suggestions
for Teaching to
Understand Values

Economics, at its core, is about sustaining life and enhancing its quality through improving economic systems. What quality of life is, however, depends on value judgements. Values are thus at the core of economics. It is crucial that economics students develop a strong understanding of the role of values in economic systems and in any analysis they make of these systems. From this understanding, they can inform those making decisions on the relevant values at hand, and are aware of any values embedded in their own theories and methods.

An understanding of the values that are at play in economic questions can be gained in part through thought experiments and mental exercises, but ethical philosophy in itself is not enough. Students should be confronted with real-world scenarios, challenges and policy decisions and asked to assess them against a range of value standards to see that contrasting conclusions can be reached by economic analysis when the foundational values are changed. In addition, we believe that economists' work needs to be grounded in the concerns of actual people, through conversations and surveys of them. This habit starts at the undergraduate level.

The chapter starts with an overview of the various reasons for teaching students to understand and highlight values in their economic work. In the next section, we engage with various counter-arguments. The third section sets out three ways in which values play a role in economics: as outcomes of economic processes, as causal factors in economic processes, and as embedded in academic tools. Finally, we provide a number of practical suggestions for implementing this principle in economics courses.

"Economics, as it has emerged, can be made more productive by paying greater and more explicit attention to ethical considerations."

Amartya Sen (1987, p. 9)

Economic problems are never merely intellectual puzzles. At their core, economic problems are problems because they impact people's lives and the Earth's ecosystem more broadly. The ultimate goal of economists' work is to improve economic systems of resource extraction, production, distribution, consumption and waste disposal through which societies provision themselves, so that people can better achieve what they find important. In other words, what they define to be a higher quality of life. To be able to determine what constitutes an *improvement* in the quality of life and thus to the economic system however, we need to make judgments about values (Wilber, 2004). Therefore, it is crucial that economists are able to understand the different values that play a role in an economic issue. Values are an integral aspect of economic dynamics. Keynes, for this reason, wrote that *"Economics is essentially a moral science. That is to say, it employs introspection and judgement of value."* (1938, p. 2). An organising principle of economics education should thus be to teach students to understand the role of values in economies and in economics as a discipline.

By values we refer to *notions of what is important or good*. It is useful here to distinguish between values (abstract concepts about what is good or important) and norms (how one should act in concrete ways). This is also different from the more narrow concept of economic value (Mazzucato, 2018), although the two are related to each other. Ideas about economic value are at the core of economic theories, making them an important aspect of teaching theory. However, in this chapter we focus less on economic theories, and more on the different values that are involved in economic processes.

1 Positive vs. Normative?

Current economics programmes often begin with juxtaposing normative and positive economics. Normative economics, being concerned with the 'what ought to be' questions, is said to be for philosophers and politicians, while economists, as true objective scientists, are said to concern themselves solely with positive economics, the technical 'what is' types of questions (Butler, 2009). Frequently cited in this regard is the following statement in Robert Solow's essay *Science and ideology in economics*, pushing back against those arguing for explicit inclusion of values in economic analysis: *"It is as if we were to discover that it is impossible to render an operating-room perfectly sterile, and conclude that therefore one might as well do surgery in a sewer"* (1994, p. 240). The metaphor in the above quote is frequently presented in class as an argument that values are something filthy and dangerous that are to be kept out at all costs.

If we read on, it becomes clear that Solow did not intend any such thing. His suggestion is rather to try to differentiate between value judgements and scientific analysis, and to show both clearly in their own right. The final sentence of the essay sums it up: *"[T]here is sense in a determined effort to see both that issues of value-conflict do not get smothered in smooth pseudo-science and that conflicts susceptible of a scientific answer not get submerged in a flood of ideology impervious to analysis and evidence"* (Solow, 1994, p. 251). Both are crucial, both deserve the attention of the economic researcher. And it is vital to teach students to see the difference between them.

So why do we frequently hear economists say that their work is non-normative, that they are objectively performing positive analysis? You never hear chemists saying that: it is very hard to imagine such a thing as normative chemistry. Nor do you hear literature reviewers say it, because they are expected to make value judgements. The reason we as economists say this is because our terrain is so intensely normatively charged, and so we attempt to abstract from value judgements, as we explore in more detail later. The outward appearance of positivity and objectivity can be sustained as long as all economists use the same set of normative assumptions to underlie their work (such as that prices reflect value), but that does not make economics value-free.

This is not to say that we economists are consciously cheating everyone. Most economists we know have strongly internalised this professional ethic of the 'technical' advisor: they honestly attempt not to impose their private views. It is merely to say: the fact that many of us pride ourselves on being 'positive' scientists does not mean that normative considerations do not play a large role in our field of expertise. It is rather the reverse: because it involves *so many* thorny normative issues, we try to limit and flag our subjectivity wherever we can.

We agree that economists should try not to let their personal views affect their analysis. But we believe that the best solution is not to blind ourselves to the normative, to treat it as toxic. We should rather put it into the limelight. In other aspects of our society, we have also found that with difficult issues, transparency and active engagement are more effective than burying it and pretending it does not exist.

The idea of the economist as a neutral technical advisor carries within it another danger: advisors generally work for those in power. Most of us do not see ourselves as servants to kings and CEOs, and would rather be seen as serving 'the people'. But the distinction is a fine one. If we do not carefully watch whose interests are being served, but instead focus on limiting our analysis to the technical, rather than the normative, we can easily find ourselves simply reproducing or even exacerbating the existing power relations in society (Roncaglia, 2017).

A productive approach to teaching students to be aware of values is to openly discuss them in class. Through discussing normative issues, students sharpen their analytical skills and critical thinking on the role of values, inside and outside their own minds, when studying economic topics. Doing the opposite, making values into a taboo or relegating them into a single course on ethics, makes students blind to values when doing their analyses. The goal of economics education should not be to train students to quietly or tacitly hide value-judgements. This leaves students unable to discuss and analyse them properly, teaching them at best to play hide and seek with regards to value. Instead, it should be standard practice in economics courses to uncover (potentially difficult to identify) values and openly discuss them. In turn, this transparency and clarity can help society in its economic decision making.

2 Common Misconceptions: What We Do *Not* Mean

To prevent misconceptions, we briefly explain what we do *not* mean by teaching understanding the role of values in economies.

First and foremost, we are not advocating to teach students certain values. Academic education should teach students how to think critically and independently. Trying to instil normative ideas in them would amount to indoctrination (perhaps with the exception of professional codes of ethics). A key difference between education and indoctrination is that the former tries to present a complete picture, with pros and cons, strengths and weaknesses, the status quo and alternatives, while the latter one-sidedly and uncritically presents arguments to convince the audience of something.

When discussing policies, ideas, or ways of organising the economy, it is crucial that teachers do not try to convince students of the superiority of one, but instead present a broad range of evidence, arguments, and alternatives, to allow students to critically assess and evaluate choices for themselves. And perhaps most importantly, students should be allowed to question and examine any assumption and argument.

This is not merely a theoretical notion. Today, there are lobby groups actively working to promote certain political ideas within economics education. To give an example, one of the most important organisations focusing on economics education in the US is the *Foundation for Economic Education* (FEE). It is partially funded by the billionaire brothers Charles and David Koch and promotes according to its own mission statement *"individual liberty, free-market economics, entrepreneurship, private property, high moral character, and limited government"* (FEE, 2021, p. 1). While some of these notions are fairly empty or open to interpretation, such as 'high moral character' (who could be against that?), others form a very specific and politically motivated package of economic thought.

In doing so, the FEE made *"the case against pluralism"* in economics education, arguing only free market ideas should be taught. Using a politically charged Whig history argument, they claim that their favoured ideas are simply scientifically better than other ideas (see also the box *Whig history: Is the mainstream of the moment always the best?* in chapter *Foundation 2: Pluralism*). They stated that left-wing, but theoretically very different economic thinkers, such as Marx and Veblen, were rejected *"not because of political views, ... but rather because their theories were seen as fatally flawed"*, while conceptually distinct but both *"free market economists, like Milton Friedman and Friedrich Hayek, ... rose to prominence by using logic and evidence"* (FEE, 2017, p. 1).

This is just one illustration of an interest group. We equally oppose the monopolisation of economic education by for example Marxian ideas, as was the case in several communist countries. Such politically motivated campaigns to exclude ideas from being taught to students have no legitimacy and should be rejected by any economist, irrespective of their personal political views or theoretical preferences.

Secondly, while we acknowledge that it is impossible to fully separate positive and normative issues, we do not advocate blending the two together. Like Solow (1994), we think it is best to distinguish positive from normative where possible and treat them independently. As such, we firmly oppose treating normative issues as taboo and instead argue for explicitly including them in economics education. When teaching a course on a topic, the values concerned should be treated as a distinct and important element. A course on labour, for example, would be incomplete without explicitly discussing and treating the different values that are involved in labour processes and arrangements such as equity, autonomy and efficiency.

Thirdly, we do not think economists should be the ones making normative decisions for society. In a democratic society such decisions should be made by citizens, either directly or via elected representatives. Therefore, we do not advocate training economics students to make normative decisions and defend them with sophisticated ethical arguments. Instead, students should learn to inform those who make decisions about the values that are relevant for the economic issue at hand. They need to be able to transparently present different economic decisions together with their underlying values and how these might clash.

Clearly revealing and setting out the values concerned also helps economists to avoid imposing their own value-judgements, even if unconsciously, on society's decisions. It is about preventing normative decisions from being hidden inside complex models, so that value-judgements can be made in a transparent and democratic manner.

3 Where in Economics Do Values Play a Role?

We advocate teaching students three complementary angles to understand the role of values in economics. First, values are found in the (intended and unintended) *outcomes* of economic processes. Second, values are *causal factors* in economic processes. Third, values are *embedded in academic tools*. We will discuss these three in turn.

Values regarding outcomes of economic processes

First, we discuss values regarding economic outcomes: to what degree is the resulting situation just, efficient, fair, sustainable etc.? For many economists this will be the most familiar category of the three. When making a decision, a normative valuation is needed. Values determine what is seen as a desired outcome and what is not. In this way a normative judgement can be combined with theoretical reasoning to construct policy recommendations. To be clear, we do not think this entire valuation process should be done by economists, or that our own personal values should determine economic decision making. We think the values of all those involved should be determinative.

The role of economists in policy making, therefore, is to uncover the values concerned and help others understand how they relate to the potential decisions. In economic research and teaching, normative aspects are too frequently smothered, to use Solow's words, in the notion of 'efficiency'. Colander (1992, p. 196) explains that textbooks often give "the impression that discussions of efficiency belong in positive economics", while this is clearly not the case. "[A]chieving economic efficiency is not an end in itself, but is a debatable, normative goal which often will conflict with other normative goals society might have". We always need to ask: efficiency of what? Yes, least input for most output, but what input and output? And when we deal with more than one category of inputs and outputs, we need to determine their relative importance. Often we assume that the market determines this for us, justly. But we know that requires additional moral and analytical arguments, even within a neoclassical framework as there are market imperfections and externalities (Wight, 2017). Inequities, furthermore, can make efficient outcomes be undesirable, because as Sen put it "a society or an economy can be Pareto-optimal and still be perfectly disgusting" (1987, p. 22). For all these various reasons, a good economist needs to see values, name them, and lay them out clearly for the audience, as an integral part of their research and teaching.

A brief example might be helpful here. When the famous pin factory example of Adam Smith is cited, often only the efficiency aspect of the division of labour is discussed. This, however, leaves out the worries Smith had about how the division of labour would degrade and alienate the workers in the pin factory. He wrote that the worker "becomes as stupid and ignorant as it is possible for a human creature to become" because of the extreme focus on one tiny task (Smith, 1776, pp. 178-179). He even argued that the division of labour could cause "the almost entire corruption and degeneracy of the great body of the people. … unless the government takes some pains to prevent it". In other words, Adam Smith identified efficiency as only one of the many values of concern when discussing the division of labour. This is a model for teaching and research in general.

This aspect of values is made more concrete in Building Block 1: Introducing the Economy and Building Block 10: Economics for a Better World.

Values are causal variables in economic processes

The second place of values in economic thinking is as causal variables in economic processes. That is, the values people hold affect their behaviour, and this has systemic consequences. This makes values important drivers of economic action. As such, they cannot remain unstudied if we want to understand how economies work. Recently, this has attracted more attention in economic research and we believe that economics education should follow suit.

Values are also connected to economic forms of organisation. There is, for example, a well-established literature on how values relate to markets: markets can function only when private property is respected and enforced (North, 1990; Robinson & Acemoglu, 2012), and cheating or hiding of defects, because of information asymmetry, is not prevalent (Akerlof, 1978). But the market is also accompanied by the moral logic of *one dollar one vote*, giving rise to debates about whether markets are morally civilising or degrading (Fourcade & Healy, 2007; Hirschman, 1982). It also important to pay attention how power relations are related to values. For instance, ideals regarding the 'proper' role of men and women can make it harder for women to achieve economic independence and success.

When discussing values as drivers of economic processes, it is worthwhile spending time on the question of how people's values are formed and actively shaped into norms or desires by economic actors. Important examples of this are religion, education and the marketing industry. A lot of time, effort and money is being spent to influence what people value, so this cannot be left out of the picture when educating future generations of economists.

This aspect of values is made more concrete in *Building Block 5: Economic Organisations & Mechanisms*, *Building Block 6: Political-Economic Systems* and *Building Block 8: Economic Theories*.

Values are embedded in analytical tools of economists

Finally, the third category of values in economics are those that are embedded in analytical tools. Normative issues do not only arise when choosing between several policy options. They enter at every stage of the research process: choosing which topic to study, which question to ask, which research methods to use, which statistics to create or study, and which theories to use to get a grip on the complexity of the real world. All these choices have consequences for the conclusions reached by economic analysis. This also shows why pluralism of theories, methods and research foci is important: it helps students to see the different sides to the story.

Take for instance the technique of *cost-benefit analysis* (Boardman et al., 2017). It tries to quantitatively estimate costs and benefits which, indeed, makes it a very attractive instrument to policymakers and one that professional economists frequently work with. But it also has serious drawbacks and reasons to be cautious when applying it, to pay explicit attention to its limitations. Perhaps most importantly: it makes normative trade-offs and decisions invisible, especially for non-economists.

Due to the need to monetize or quantify costs and benefits, CBA has to make normative decisions. To arrive at the estimated costs and benefits, CBA touches upon two normative issues. First of all, by looking at overall net benefits, it is not able to deal with the socio-economic distributional effects of the benefits and costs. Secondly, how to measure the unmeasurable? Some things are difficult to qualify in monetary terms, possibly making use of people's willingness-to-pay. For things, such as human life or the loss of biodiversity and animal species, there are important normative debates about whether it makes sense to '*put a price on life and everything else*'. In sum, only by making many, and often highly debatable, normative decisions about how to value things, it becomes possible to come up with seemingly simple numbers that tell us what the "costs and benefits" of policy options are.

What is often neglected is transparency about the moral dilemmas involved in policy decisions and to pay attention to how different value-judgements might lead to different results in terms of the "costs and benefits". Because the CBA process is opaque to non-economists, economists have to make an effort to highlight the value choices they have used and showcase how alternative value choices would have led to different conclusions.

Additionally, certain value-judgements simply cannot be made when using cost-benefit analysis. For instance, the normative decision not to value a human life in terms of dollars is incompatible with cost-benefit analysis: it requires a single, universal unit of measurement to do the calculations. And even if we do decide to monetarily value human life, how do we determine the price of one? The most common method is to look at wage differentials between more and less risky jobs. We personally do not know a better method. But this is based on assumptions about information and calculation that are difficult to confirm, and it leads straight to the cynical suggestion that the lives of people living in rich countries much more valuable than those living in poor countries. A related issue is that certain normative concerns can less easily be translated into costs or benefits. Take the principles of justice and fairness. Does it make sense to put monetary values on just or unjust punishments, protections or violations of human rights, and fair treatment or discrimination in the labour market?

Again, this is a moral choice, often disguised as merely a technical choice. Do we follow the market logic of one dollar one vote? Or the democratic logic of one person one vote? Or another ethical rule altogether? And how do we value the lives of future generations? Do we use financial market interest rates or some rule of thumb to discount the value of the lives of our grandchildren and their grandchildren?

Valuing human life is far from the only moral issue when doing cost-benefit analysis. It is a normative choice to monetarily value everything as if it were a consumption good, ranging from having a park nearby, to spending time with your children and being physically and mentally healthy. The list goes on.

Even for market decisions, a cost-benefit analysis is not value-free. Is the market price paid by the highest bidder the same as something's value? Is the value of a thousand dollars the same to a rich and to a poor person? There are many highly debated normative issues, so we think it is important for economists to lay these out in the open and discuss them explicitly, helping non-economists to see through the technical equations and models.

To be clear, all this is not an argument against such approaches. We think that a cost-benefit analysis is a very useful policy tool. However, what we suggest is to treat the normative aspects explicitly and teach students how to discuss these with non-economists.

Furthermore, normative issues play a role beyond welfare economics. As described above, simply by choosing to include or exclude something in the analysis, we are already making a value judgement. For example, when looking at the effects of a policy, very different conclusions can be reached depending upon whether one only looks at the aggregate GDP figure, or also at the income distribution, or at how the effects of the policy differ between men and women, ethnic groups or regions. Different theoretical frameworks also highlight different values.

For instance, most economic approaches featured in this book focus their lens almost exclusively on values of *human* wellbeing, which itself is understood in different ways by the various approaches. It is not that they explicitly argue that ecological destruction and resource depletion are irrelevant, but these processes are simply not an integral part of the analysis; they can only be tacked on afterwards. Each approach simply has its own focus points and blind spots.

Does that mean theory has a political stance, left or right? Not necessarily. They just help to identify the relevant values more clearly. Based on the same value of allocative efficiency, neoclassical economists have made a wide range of politically conflicting policy recommendations, basing themselves on a wide range of assumptions. One neoclassical economist, focusing on externalities and market imperfections, may suggest government intervention, while in the same real-world situation another neoclassical economist, specialised in government failures, may suggest a laissez-faire approach.

In the below box, *The normative aspects of theoretical approaches*, we briefly discuss the values embedded in various perspectives. Additionally, this aspect of values is made more concrete in *Building Block 8: Economic Theories* and *Building Block 10: Economics for a Better World*.

The Normative Aspects of Theoretical Approaches

In this box, we explore four examples of theoretical approaches: neoclassical, Marxian, Austrian and ecological, and what they strive towards. Each approach aims to understand the economy. At the same time, they all contain elements of *utopia* and *dystopia*. Here we focus specifically on what this says about their ideals and what pitfalls they caution us to avoid. These normative aspects of theories also allow us to understand the motivation of scholars.

Some theories focus more on utopia, such as the neoclassical school. The notion of 'imperfect' markets suggests that although we may never quite reach it, it is worth striving toward such a thing as a 'perfect' market. To do so, we must remove market 'failures', making them function more 'efficiently', and achieve ever more 'optimal' outcomes.

The optimal outcome for society is achieved when each individual is able to freely and in an informed manner choose the bundle of goods that they prefer given the constraints, and the productive resources are allocated in the most efficient manner (Morgan, 2015). In other words, the neoclassical school is about harnessing market mechanisms to maximize the benefits of the consumer side of humanity. The raison-d'être of neoclassical economics seems to be: we should study markets, because they can be a great force for good, if properly harnessed.

Other schools, such as the Marxian approach, tend more toward the *dystopian*. That is, they show us all the horrible places we might end up in if the dynamics work as they are described. Think for a moment how it feels if someone dear to you has created something special for you personally. This is what Marxian thought warns us about losing. It describes the alienation of living in a system where you have no human connection with the people for whose benefit you work all day, producing clothing, food or other things, nor with the people who in turn work for you, the people with whom you work and even yourself. Marx's scholarly motivation was to warn us about what is lost as capitalist production becomes the standard.

This school has other warnings: the gruesome image of capitalism as an unthinking machine that eats up more and more of society and nature. While the bourgeoisie is frequently portrayed as exploitative in Marxian writing, capitalists themselves are also trapped in this war-like market competition. It should, however, also be noted that Marx at times praises capitalism for its strengths. Take, for example, the *Communist Manifesto* in which he and Engels wrote about the enormous economic progress and innovation capitalism causes: *"It has accomplished wonders far surpassing Egyptian pyramids, Roman aqueducts, and Gothic cathedrals"* (1848, p. 6).

The Austrian school also alerts us to a potential dystopia: that of an economic system which is managed too actively, making it a big tangle of bureaucracy. This stifles independent initiative, they say, and does more harm than good. The Austrians also describe utopia. They believe that people themselves know best what is good for them; leave them free to pursue their own goals, and they will creatively organize economic life based on local and tacit knowledge to the benefit of everyone (Schulak & Unterköfler, 2011).

The last example, ecological economics, has a dystopian focus on the vital ecosystem aspects that are at risk of breaking down and also clearly describes the utopian vision of an economy in harmony with nature and focused on broad human wellbeing, rather than material production and consumption. Ecological economists strive to inform how surpassing planetary boundaries wreaks havoc on human society and on planetary life more broadly and simultaneously search for ways to prevent this (Daly & Farley, 2011).

4 Practical Suggestions for Teaching to Understand Values

What are practical ways to integrate thinking about values in economic teaching?

Firstly, it is crucial that values are not only discussed as abstract concepts but discussed in the real world. Students should learn to go out and engage with people to learn what they find important and what concerns them. In this way, students develop the habit of moving beyond armchair philosophy and engaging with the values of the people actually involved in issues. When teaching students to understand values, it can thus be helpful to alternate between teaching different normative principles and visions in class and giving students exercises to find out how citizens think about normative economic dilemmas in the real world.

For instance, when teaching labour economics and discussing the concept of the natural rate of unemployment, or the flexibility of labour markets, it might be informative for students to talk with workers, unemployed people and employers. This will help them to understand the different values that are at stake: in a job we value not only what each month's salary will allow us to buy, but also the dignity of a social identity, a sense of purpose, the community of colleagues, a measure of security, and so on. Conversely, employers care about cost, but also about reliability, long-term continuity, flexibility, workplace relationships, and so on. This is not standard in economics courses today, but sociologists, anthropologists and human geographers are quite used to doing it, starting in year one of their bachelor programmes. One option is to simply ask colleagues from these departments for some practical pointers on how to integrate this in regular economics classes.

Secondly, uncovering values and normative discussions should be integrated into ordinary classes rather than taught separately. Simply ask, when introducing new material on economic dynamics: what values are at play here? Or, when introducing a new theory or research method: what does this tool allow us to see, and what may fall outside our view? Let students think about it for a few minutes, highlight several relevant values yourself, and let the students discuss. And then continue with the analytical and technical aspects. Just as developing methodological skills is best done by both focusing on it in separate methodology lectures and by applying it to specific cases of theoretical and practical interest, ethics should not be an isolated element in economics education but incorporated in the entire programme.

Would such classroom discussions not be a form of indoctrination, by professors forcing their personal values onto their students? We believe the reverse: only by bringing issues of normativity to the fore can students learn to independently think about them. It is a matter of intellectual honesty to openly discuss the values embedded in analytical approaches and economic discussions. By explicitly discussing values, students not only become better able to spot and understand them, they also become better able to articulate them and 'dare' to openly talk about them with each other even when they conflict. This is a particularly important skill because communicating normative concerns and dilemmas involved in economic issues clearly to non-economists is not easy but is nevertheless a crucial aspect of economists' work.

Foundation 5

Diversifying and Decolonising Economics

Respecting women, minority, lower class and Global South economists and taking their contributions seriously will improve everyone's understanding of the economy.

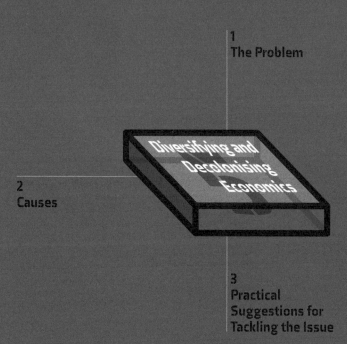

1
The Problem

2
Causes

Diversifying and
Decolonising
Economics

3
Practical
Suggestions for
Tackling the Issue

Economics has historically been, and is still, dominated by white upper and middle class men. This has caused important biases in economic thinking and in the community of our discipline. The ideas of women, Global South, minority and lower class scholars have frequently been ignored, both in research and in education. The same applies to their economic realities, values, interests and ways of organising economic processes. Currently, women and minorities face more hurdles in economics than men and white people do. Causes for this range from subtle but pervasive unconscious biases to outright sexual harassment from colleagues.

We need to diversify and decolonise economics. That includes: working to decrease those additional barriers which women, minorities, Global South and lower class scholars currently face, quite apart from the normal entry requirements of ability and interest. It also includes making the concepts of our global discipline more representative of the worldwide diversity of economic arrangements and ideas.

This will not only help marginalised groups, important though that is. It will also make economics education itself better for all students, offering them a broader, more realistic and more relevant set of ideas and realities.

The chapter starts with a brief overview of the problems of underrepresentation of women and minorities in our discipline and some of the main challenges they are facing. We then discuss a number of potential causes for these problems and evaluate where the fundamental bottlenecks might lie. Third, we discuss several paths towards tackling these issues, from actively acknowledging them to teaching different material and using different didactic techniques.

"We are tired of leaders in the field refusing to see problems happening right under their noses. And we are tired of having these problems distract from what we came here to do: meaningful, high-quality economic research."

An open letter regarding harassment and discrimination in the economics profession signed by hundreds of graduate students and research assistants a few days before the annual meeting of the American Economic Association in 2018

A note before we start. While we are trying to help diversify and decolonise economics, this book only goes so far. Much remains to be done. What's more, as the main authors of this book are two young white university educated middle-class men from the Netherlands, the book has an inevitable bias towards our own experiences. Ideas and suggestions on how to diversify and decolonise economics are therefore very much welcome. With the international movements of *Rethinking Economics* and *Diversifying and Decolonising Economics*, we will keep on working on these matters and are always looking for more people to help in creating change.

1 The Problem

First, we present some basic numbers illustrating which social groups are underrepresented and which are overrepresented within economics. While each of these numbers deserves a more detailed analysis, we go over them rather briefly, to show the general pattern: economics as a discipline is dominated by white men, while other groups are underrepresented. Second, we compare economics to other disciplines to see how much of the problem is specific to the discipline of economics.

Underrepresentation

In the US, UK and Australia, over the last decades roughly one third of undergraduate economics students are women (Tetlow, 2018). In 2014 in the US, 2% of economics doctorate degrees were awarded to racial minority women, 8% to minority men, 29% to white women, and 62% to white men (Bayer & Rouse, 2016). Worldwide, on average 19% of economists are women (Boring & Zignago, 2018). When countries are compared, Thailand

and Eastern European countries, such as Romania, Croatia, Bulgaria and Russia, have relatively high female representation at around 40-50% of economists, while countries such as Saudi Arabia, Ghana, Israel, Japan and Brazil have relatively low representation at around 7-15% (IDEAS, 2021).

In the US, only 6% of tenured and tenure-track economists and 4% of full professors are black or Hispanic (Bayer & Rouse, 2016). There are virtually no black editors at the top economics journals (Casselman & Tankersley, 2020). There is a 20% gender gap in achieving tenure and one of 50% in promotion to full professor (Da Costa, 2017).

The Global South is strongly underrepresented in global economics journals and conferences. Even within the field of development economics, this is true as only 10% of papers published in 2018 were (co-)authored by someone from the Global South (Naritomi et al., 2020).

The most prestigious prize in the discipline, The Sveriges Riksbank Prize in Economic Sciences in Memory of Alfred Nobel, has been awarded to 86 people, as of 2020. Among its winners there are one black man (Arthur Lewis in 1979), two Indian men (Amartya Sen in 1998 and Abhijit Banerjee in 2019), two white women (Elinor Ostrom in 2009 and Esther Duflo in 2019) and 81 white men.

Our discipline has a long way to go towards creating a culture that treats everyone equally and fairly, as the findings of the 2019 'Professional Climate Survey' of the American Economic Association made clear (Allgood et al., 2019). Almost half of all black and half of all female economists experienced discrimination. Only 14% of black economists felt that black people are respected in the discipline and only 45% of all respondents felt that minorities are respected. Economists with a disability or other sexual orientation were also found to experience more discrimination. The survey also showed that about half of female economists declined to present at work or a seminar to avoid disrespectful behaviour.

Perhaps even more alarming, sexual harassment seems to be widespread. 42% of female economists experienced sexual comments or behaviour from colleagues or students, 10% were stalked by a colleague, 7% were threatened if they were not romantically or sexually cooperative, 2% experienced sexual assault: being fondled, kissed or rubbed up against private body parts, had their clothes removed without consent, and/or were penetrated, fingered, or made to have oral sex without consent, 6% experienced attempted sexual assault, and 12% were touched in a different way that made them uncomfortable. The #MeToo movement also brought to light a broader culture of sexist behaviour in economics. Perhaps most famously, Alice Wu showed how misogynistic and toxic the language on economics jobs websites is (Wu, 2017).

The existing underrepresentation of women, minorities, lower class and Global South scholars has many undesirable consequences for the discipline, but perhaps one of the most direct is a lower quality of research. A good example is *Invisible Women* by Caroline Criado-Perez (2019), a data-packed exposition of the many ways in which women are left out of the data and the many ways in which this makes products and policies less than suitable for women, in some cases even dangerous or deadly. As she makes clear, from daily life to workplace organisation, from the design of physical products to the institutions of public life, a more representative group of researchers, designers and managers leads to better outcomes.

The problem is bigger in economics than in other disciplines

Underrepresentation of women and minorities is not exclusively a problem of the economics discipline, but it is relatively large here. Today's societies are characterised by multiple forms of social inequity and discrimination. Solving all problems related to unequal chances and unfair treatment within economics will thus be difficult as long as the larger society remains so unequal. However, the available research indicates that economics is doing worse than other disciplines (Bayer & Rouse, 2016). This is sad news. But it also means that quite some progress can already be made within the discipline without having to do the difficult work of forerunning the rest of society.

Besides outright harassment and bodily violation, there are many more subtle ways in which women face a tougher environment than men do in our discipline. Compared to other math-intensive fields, economics has the largest gender gaps in terms of salaries, job satisfaction, promotion and tenure rates (Bayer & Rouse, 2016; Ceci et al., 2014; Ginther & Kahn, 2004). And rather than displaying progress over time, some inequalities seem to have increased over the last decades (Dolar, 2021; Lundberg & Stearns, 2019). The gender gap in salaries of economics professors has, for example, increased from female salaries being 95% of male salaries in 1995 to 75% in 2010 (Ceci et al., 2014).

2   Causes

Why are women and minorities so badly underrepresented in economics? Is it because women and minorities have less inherent ability or less interest in economics? Or is the discipline somehow biased in favour of white men, making it more likely that they become (highly placed) economists? In other words, is it a supply side or demand side problem?

Is underrepresentation caused by less talent for, or interest in, economics?

First, we discuss the hypothesis that underrepresentation of women and minorities is at least partially a question of talent. The discipline of economics has become heavily mathematised over the last decades. This strong emphasis on mathematical skills is sometimes given as a reason for why there are less women in economics. This is based on the stereotype that men would be better at mathematics than women (Halpern et al., 2007). If the required level of mathematical skill was key, the problem should be similar in other math-intensive disciplines, such as science, technology, engineering and mathematics (STEM). This is, however, not the case. While all of these fields have historically been dominated by white men, in economics in particular the problem seems to be persistent (Varathan, 2017). Related explanations that the lack of role models, or strict grading, within economics would scare women off, are also implausible as this was also the case in other math-intensive fields. Research, furthermore, indicates that the level of math preparation of students does not explain the underrepresentation of women and minorities (Bayer & Rouse, 2016; Crawford et al., 2018). In sum, explaining, or justifying, unequal outcomes based on 'talent' is not convincing.

Second, might the underrepresentation of women and minorities be a matter of research interests? Surveys do indicate that women are less interested in economics (Bayer & Rouse, 2016; Harvey, 2019). But, we must ask, why is this the case? Do women and minorities have a 'natural' lack of interest for the economy? Or is the discipline shaped by the concerns and experiences of white men, thereby seeming less relevant to other social groups? This is also connected to our discussion in the earlier chapter *Philosophy* of what the discipline is, and should be, about.

Men are overrepresented in real and fictional examples in economics textbooks (Stevenson & Zlotnik, 2018). Many parts of mainstream economics focus on what are sometimes described as stereotypical masculine topics, such as impersonal markets and 'the rational man', who cold-heartedly maximizes his own utility (Nelson, 2018). Stereotypically feminine aspects of the economy, on the other hand, are often ignored, whether it is unpaid labour, care or housework, all of which are often described as altruistic, warm and loving.

Similarly, issues related to race and ethnicity are understudied. From 1990 to 2018 only 0.4% of the papers published in the top five economics journals dealt with race or ethnicity (Francis & Opoku-Agyeman, 2020). Economics produces less race-related research than other social sciences (Advani et al., 2021; Bayer, 2018). While economists do seem to know this, they underestimate the differences by overestimating the amount of race-related research that is done in economics. They, furthermore, overestimate the amount of progress that is made over the last decades, as there was only an increase of about 10% in race-related research from 1980-2000 to 2000-2020 while the median estimate by economists was an increase of roughly 40% (Advani et al., 2021).

Geographically, there is a strong bias in favour of the US. From 1985 to 2005, there were more economics papers about the US than the rest of the world combined, as only 1.5% of all papers in the top five economics journals were about other countries than the US (Das et al., 2013). For economics education, it is problematic that most economics textbooks are written from a US perspective, causing many students to learn more about the US than their own country.

But it is also about how we explain certain economic phenomena. If we, for example, want to understand why some people earn more than others do, what theoretical explanations do we give students? Currently, economics courses typically provide answers that are more likely to resonate with (relatively privileged) white men than with women and minorities. As one observer put it (Harvey, 2019, p. 1):

> "The core explanation of the determination of wages in the typical economics classroom centers on the idea that your salary equals some objective measure of your actual contribution (in econ talk, the wage rate is equal to the marginal product of labor). If you earn $5/hour, that's sad but it's what you deserve. And if women earn less than men even in the same profession, then that's simply the objective, scientifically-valid judgement of 'the market'. ... Now stop and think about it: who among the members of an introductory-level economics class is this likely to attract? For whom is 'you get what you deserve' likely to strike a chord? Women? People of colour? White males? I'm sure I don't have to answer that."

The current focus of the discipline, which is on the types of topics and approaches to which the more privileged groups in society have most affinity, could certainly explain why women and minorities feel less drawn towards economics. However, were the discipline redefined to its original definition, as being the science of human provisioning, there need be no reason for a bias towards the interests of white men. This would, however, require a serious reorientation. It would imply bringing in topics that are currently too often neglected, such as discrimination, patriarchy, sexism, racism, imperialism, colonialism, slavery, exploitation and unequal life chances, but also unpaid labour, care, reciprocity, gift economies, commons, and non-western ways of organising economic processes.

Illustrations of Racism and Discrimination in Economics Over Its History

Historically, discrimination was widespread and very explicit in society at large, including within the discipline of economics. Over time, discrimination has become less accepted and is less often expressed openly. Nevertheless, it still exists. So far, we have mainly focused on systematic research to get a better understanding of the issue. But it is important to also look at specific examples that illustrate how hostile economics can be to marginalised groups. Below, we provide a few examples, in chronological order, to help us get a better understanding and feeling for what discrimination in economics is.

The most common nickname of the discipline is the *"dismal science of supply and demand"*. It is worth noting that this term was originally coined by Thomas Carlyle in his essay called *"Occasional Discourse on the Negro Question"* published in 1849 (pp. 530-532). He argued for the reintroduction of slavery in order to restore productivity. While white men should be left free in accordance with classical liberal thinking, the *"idle Black man in the West Indies"* should, instead, be *"compelled to work as he was fit, and to do the Maker's will who had constructed him"*. He based his claim on the economic discipline which he described as *"[n]ot a "gay science","*" but *"a dreary, desolate and, indeed, quite abject and distressing one; what we might call, by way of eminence, the dismal science"*.

Around the turn of the century, the academic discipline began to take shape, under its new name *economics*, rather than the old one, *political economy*. One of the founders of the American Economics Association, Richard Ely, wrote in 1898 (p. 781): *"The problem is to keep the most unfit from reproduction, and to encourage the reproduction of those who are really the superior members of society ... There are classes in every modern community composed of those who are virtually children, and who require paternal and fostering care, the aim of which should be the highest development of which they are capable. We may instance the negros, who are for the most part grownup children, and should be treated as such."*

Half a century later, the economics discipline had grown enormously in size as well as in influence. During the time of the Civil Rights Movement in 1962, one of the white male winners of the The Sveriges Riksbank Prize in Economic Sciences in Memory of Alfred Nobel, George Stigler, wrote a small piece called *'The Problem of the Negro'*. He set to tone of the article by opening with *"The task of our time has been to make the Negro discontented with himself, not with the white man"*. He continued on writing (1962, p. 4): *"Consider the Negro as a neighbor. He is frequently repelled and avoided by the white man, but is it only color prejudice? On the contrary, it is because the Negro family is, on average, a loose, morally lax, group, and brings with its presence a rapid rise in crime and vandalism. No statutes, no sermons, no demonstrations, will obtain for the Negro the liking and respect that sober virtues commend. And the leaders of Negro thought: they blame the crime and immorality upon the slums and the low income- as if individual responsibility could be bought with a thousand dollars a year."*

More recently in the age of Twitter in 2020, the editor of one of the top five economics journals, Harald Uhlig of the Journal of Political Economy, likened the Black Lives Matter protesters to *"flat-earthers and creationists"* as response to the protests following the killing of George Floyd. Again, coming back to the narrative of childishness, he wrote on twitter: *"Oh well. Time for sensible adults to enter back into the room and have serious, earnest, respectful conversations about it all. ... Look: I understand, that some out there still wish to go and protest and say #defundpolice and all kinds of stuff, while you are still young and responsibility does not matter. Enjoy! Express yourself! Just don't break anything, ok? And be back by 8 pm."* Later that week, it became clear that it was not a one-off incident but a recurring pattern for Harald Uhlig. The black economist Bocar A. Ba wrote a few days later to Harald Uhlig, his former teacher: *"I sat in your class in Winter 2014: (1) You talked about scheduling a class on MLK [Martin Luther King] Day (2) You made fun of Dr. King and people honoring him (3) You sarcastically asked me in front of everyone whether I was offended".*

Unintentional biases and discrimination

A third hypothesis: might the underrepresentation of women and minorities be caused by systemic biases? Rather than looking for an explanation on the supply side with the behaviour, decisions, talents or interests of underrepresented groups, here we look at the demand side and the biases that exist within the discipline.

It is important to note here that the majority of these demand side problems are not the result of intentional discrimination, but of unconscious biases. A growing body of psychological evidence indicates that large parts of human behaviour are characterised by unconscious assumptions and decisions. It is important to note here that while having unconscious biases seems to be an inherent part of human nature, the kinds and types of biases we have come from the society and culture we live in. Implicit biases and social stereotypes play important roles in our cognitive processes (Greenwald & Banaji, 1995; Greenwald & Krieger, 2006). Similar patterns are being found by economists who study discrimination on the labour and housing markets (Bertrand & Mullainathan, 2004; Ihlanfeldt & Mayock, 2009). But the fact that a bias is unintentional rather than active malice is no excuse for keeping quiet about it or not trying to solve it. After all, it still has a negative impact for those on the receiving end of discrimination or marginalisation. If anything, it is harder to face unconscious biases: those holding the biases tend to get defensive and deny that there is any problem at all.

Today's pervasive biases generally do not take the form of open and explicit racism or sexism. Instead, biases mainly come from people who do not think they are discriminating, often claiming to be 'colour-blind', fair and objective in their judgements. As such, discrimination does not only come from dominant social groups, but can unfortunately also be internalised and reproduced by members of the marginalised groups themselves. For instance, studies indicate that there is widespread bias in academic hiring in favour of white men. This bias seems to live not only in white men, but also in those minorities who do make it into the discipline: research found *'no evidence that women benefited from contacting female faculty, nor that black or Hispanic students benefited from contacting same-race faculty'* (Bayer & Rouse, 2016, p. 229). Working through such biases takes a lot of effort, and it is understandable if some members of relatively marginalised groups who do make it into the field do not always manage to find the additional energy required to also act as role models or mentors.

The gender bias also shows up in various forms of review, such as publication peer review, credit distribution between co-authors and teaching reviews by students, Female economists face higher publishing standards and longer peer-review processes (Hengel, 2017), are given less credit when they co-author with men (Sarsons et al., 2021), and female teachers systematically receive lower teaching evaluations from male students than male teachers do (Mengel et al., 2019).

Discrimination can also be embedded in procedures, policies, rules, and routines of organisations, often referred to as institutionalised or systemic discrimination (Lopez, 2000). Seemingly neutral practices can disadvantage people based on their gender, ethnicity/race and other supposedly irrelevant background characteristics. Research among the top 50 economics departments, for example, found that 'gender-neutral' policies to stop the tenure clock for new parents had the undesirable effect of increasing tenure rates of men and decreasing those of women (Antecol et al., 2018). Economics, compared to other disciplines, hires more from elite universities and programmes. This seemingly merit-based practice, unfortunately, reproduces social inequalities as the chances for getting into an elite programme are unequally spread (Wu, 2005). Similarly, the practice of only hiring junior job candidates that finished their PhD within six years disproportionately affects racial and ethnic minorities (Bayer & Rouse, 2016).

The culture of the economics discipline

The discipline of economics also has a unique culture. Economics is notorious, also among other disciplines, for being particularly combative, arrogant, authoritarian, and having infamously aggressive seminars (Fourcade et al., 2015; Nelson, 2019). While this relatively harsh culture affects everyone within the discipline, it has a disproportionate impact on women and minorities. Research, for example, shows that female and minority students feel less comfortable asking questions in class, felt less often that the professor cared about whether they were learning the material, and had less frequently the feeling that *'people like me can become economists'* (Bayer et al., 2020).

Behavioural norms are also generally created by the dominant social group, creating often invisible barriers for other social groups. Many first-generation college students, for example, are less likely to approach teachers as they often feel it is not appropriate to 'bother' the teacher with their problems (Strassmann & Starr, 2009). Many teachers, however, perceive this as a lack of commitment, rather than a cultural difference, causing first-generation students to receive less help and worse assessments from teachers. Also, between men and women behaviour differs. Male students have, for example, more intellectual self-confidence than female students, which is related to what is called the impostor syndrome (Carlin et al., 2018).

Furthermore, because white men are generally dominant in the discipline, many people have the impression that their situation and perspectives are the 'normal' ones, while those of other social groups are 'special'. This misconception causes relatively particular interests of white men to be often presented as the general interests, while concerns of large social groups are perceived as 'niche' subjects. Surveys among students show that female and minority students felt more often that important aspects of the studied issues were overlooked and felt less often that examples given by professors were relatable to their lives (Bayer et al., 2020).

In sum, while unconscious biases are a fundamental part of human nature and our societies, there is a clear pattern in economics favouring white people and favouring men, and the skewness is larger than in neighbouring disciplines. Our discipline clearly has work to do.

3 Practical Suggestions for Tackling the Issue

What can we do to tackle the issues of underrepresentation, bias and discrimination in economics education? We suggest three points. Firstly, we need to actively and openly acknowledge the problem. Secondly, we can teach in different ways. Thirdly, we can broaden the content of what we teach.

Acknowledge the problems

The first step in solving any problem is acknowledging its existence. This sounds easier than it is, in particular because one of the main causes of the problem is unintentional bias and discrimination. It is very human to deny the existence of one's wrongdoings and weaknesses, but until we manage to honesty look at ourselves in the mirror it is unlikely that we will be able to change our patterns of behaviour. This does not mean that we are 'bad' people, or that we should see ourselves as such. It just requires us to acknowledge that our behaviour is not morally perfect. We all grow up in societies with biases and discrimination, and if we do not actively work against them, it is likely that we will reproduce and perpetuate them.

Surveys indicate that currently, awareness of the problem is still often lacking. 82% of US economists agreed that when judging a statement, only the content should matter and not the author (Javdani & Chang, 2019). However, when statements are randomly assigned to male and female names, male economists agree significantly more often with a statement if it is assigned to a male, rather than a female, name, which is not the case for female economists. Nevertheless, 72% of male assistant professors and 87% of male professors do not think the profession has a serious gender problem (Javdani, 2019).

In the broader economy, male economists also assume there is less gender inequality than female economists do. Male economists are 42% more likely to think that labour market opportunities are equal for men and women (May et al., 2014). Furthermore, male economists were 26% less likely than female economists to agree with the following statement: *"Unlike most other science and social science disciplines, economics has made little progress in closing its gender gap over the last several decades. Given the field's prominence in determining public policy, this is a serious issue. Whether explicit or more subtle, intentional or not, the hurdles that women face in economics are very real."* (May et al., 2014, p. 33).

So how can we raise more awareness? We can start by educating ourselves and continue with our close colleagues. One example of how this could be done is the open letter *regarding harassment and discrimination in the economics profession* signed by hundreds of graduate students and research assistants a few days before the annual meeting of the American Economic Association in 2018, also cited at the beginning of the chapter. The letter called for the creation and enforcement of department-level standards of conduct and a discipline-wide reporting system to document bad behaviour so that young economists do not have to rely on *whisper networks* to protect themselves, often from senior and established economists.

Furthermore, it is important that we recognize and acknowledge that diversifying and decolonising economics education will not only help marginalised groups (Perry, 2020), but also everyone's understanding of economies and work as an economist as it gives us broader, more realistic and relevant knowledge. We have to realise it is not just a problem of marginalised groups, it is a problem for all of us.

Change how we teach

A popular approach to tackling underrepresentation is training and mentoring of women and minorities (Sandberg, 2013). While this can help build personal alliances and skills, it does not tackle the underlying structural issue in the profession (Zandt, 2013). The international network Diversifying and Decolonising Economics, therefore, argues we should not try to resolve the problem by changing the behaviour of marginalised groups, but instead change the dominant culture and structures that create biases and discrimination. This starts with the way we teach.

Fortunately, studies indicate there are many concrete steps that could be taken to make our teaching more inclusive.

First, make more use of active learning, whether it is with peer instruction, classroom experiments, or open discussions. Economics is still primarily taught in passive ways with traditional lecturing. A meta-analysis of 225 studies among STEM programmes found that all students, but women and minorities in particular, benefit from active learning (S. Freeman et al., 2014). A key reason for this seems to be that active learning activities strengthen a sense of community and self-efficacy among underrepresented groups which often have to deal with stereotype threats and microaggression in the classroom (Theobald et al., 2020). Another cause seems to be that underrepresented groups have often done fewer (quality) active learning activities in their earlier education than overrepresented groups and therefore develop more by engaging in them. Furthermore, it seems that active learning activities combined with a demonstrated commitment to inclusivity is disproportionately more effective in enhancing the performance of underrepresented groups, which brings us to the next point.

Second, explicitly value diversity. Research indicates that giving cues about valuing diversity in terms of social identity improves minorities and women's sense of belonging, while promoting a neutral, or 'colour-blind', philosophy increases experienced identity threats (Bayer & Rouse, 2016; Purdie-Vaughns et al., 2008). A basic way to do this is to pay attention to representation of women and minorities in examples and materials that are used. While many textbooks are shifting towards a more gender- and ethnic-balanced distribution of examples, the standard human in most quantitative work still appears to be a white male (Perez, 2019). If more balanced materials of the right type and quality are not available, a first step is to mention this in class when presenting or assigning them, to make students more aware.

Third, debias teaching and assessing, as well as hiring and admissions, practices. If we organize our activities in specific ways, we can minimize the effect of biases that are some inherent human behaviour (Soll et al., 2014). We can, for example, make evaluations less-biased by 'removing identifiers, minimizing time pressure and distractions, discrediting feelings of connection or chemistry, committing to fair and relevant admissions or hiring criteria before learning applicants' race or gender, collecting more evidence on candidates' competencies, creating accountability, and strategically setting default options and other nudges' (Bayer & Rouse, 2016, p. 237). And regarding hiring, it helps not to make use of referrals from traditional networks, elite programmes and test score cut-offs.

Finally, it is important to be aware of potential unintended consequences and dilemmas. Research, for example, indicates that the desire to have equal gender representation on university committees, while having fewer female than male faculty members, causes female academics to spend more time on service and less on research on which academic success is (largely) based (Bayer & Rouse, 2016). To improve equal chances, white men can more often take on 'less promotable' tasks, which are necessary for the organisation but irrelevant for one's career advancement such as serving on a committee, writing a report or organising an event, as these are often disproportionately performed by women and minorities (Babcock et al., 2017).

Change what we teach

Last but not least, we need to rethink the contents of economics education. This means recognising contributions of economists from marginalised groups and making students aware of them. But it also means paying more attention to the lived experiences and concerns of marginalised societal groups. As such, it has implications for virtually every economics course. Below, we briefly discuss these implications, for each of our three organising principles: real-world, pluralism, values.

First, real-world. When studying, we always have to make choices in terms of what topic and aspects to focus on. In these choices, we need to become less biased and pay more attention to currently understudied and under-taught topics, such as discrimination, patriarchy, sexism, racism, imperialism, colonialism, slavery, exploitation, unpaid labour, care, reciprocity, gift economies, commons, and non-western ways of organising economic processes. So when we teach a course on an economic topic, theory, empirical analysis, policy, institutions, or history, we need to bring in the experiences of women, minorities, lower classes, and the Global South. This is especially important when mainly relying on standard US textbooks, which are generally written by white middle or upper class men. Try to also make use of studies and material created by women, local, minority and/or lower class economists. Decolonize teaching materials (Basole & Jayadev, 2018; Chelwa, 2016). This is not only important for these groups themselves, but also for all economics students as it gives them a better, less biased and broader understanding of the economy.

Second, pluralism. This chapter shows that the issue of diversity in economics relates not only to ideas and tools, but also to people and identities. While thoughts can theoretically be separated from thinkers, in practice they often go together. For example, the theories advanced by privileged white men have historically often ignored issues of power imbalances, discrimination and exploitation, because they less often experienced or observed the negative impacts of these phenomena in their own personal lives. So when teaching economic theories, we need to bring in ideas from the Global South, women, minority, and lower class economists. Again, this is not to please these groups but to open and decolonize all of our economic thinking and broaden the domain of considered knowledge. Two recent examples of ideas from the Global South may serve to illustrate. Comaroff and Comaroff (2012) argue that the Global North can learn from theories developed in the Global South as it is increasingly experiencing similar phenomena such as economic informality, rising inequality, and austerity. To understand dynamics and (core-periphery) relationships within the eurozone, dependency theory and structuralist economics, which are mainly developed by Latin American economists, seem particularly useful (Kvangraven et al., 2017).

Third, values. As we explained in the previous chapter, it is important to pay attention and explicitly discuss normative assumptions and aspects. Assuming to be neutral, universal or objective, in practice often means being blind to one's own position. Therefore, it is important to actively ask and investigate what other people's and groups' concerns, values and interests are, rather than assuming to know them. Research shows, for example, that male and female economists, also when controlled for PhD attainment and job position, have different normative views related to government regulation, income distribution, and linking labour standards to import openness (May et al., 2014). The underrepresentation of women and minorities in economics causes their concerns and views to also be underrepresented. Therefore, it is critical that we bring in normative ideas and concerns from different groups when teaching.

In terms of values, it is also important to help students realise that many of the concepts in economic theory, whether mainstream or heterodox, are grounded in western ideas and value concepts. For instance, the autonomous individual, whether selfish or not, plays a large role in our theories. But the western culture of individualism is much less self-evident or even accepted in many other parts of the world. Other value concepts exist in every language or culture, yet carry other connotations: the average Thai, Englishman or Burundian might mean something quite different when they use words like freedom, fairness or wellbeing.

The worldwide diversity of economically relevant concepts goes beyond the matter of value judgements or cultural norms of what is worthwhile. Seemingly neutral and factual economic entities and relationships like a household, a company, an employer-employee relationship and a business deal can also have very different structures and implications from one place to another. Unfortunately, we have few ready-to-implement suggestions as to how to get this point across. One possibility would be to ask an anthropologist, sociologist or historian, for a guest lecture or workshop, just to briefly expose students to the diversity of cultures, social inequalities, and the diversity of economic relationships and forms that exist today or have existed in the past.

Resources

In this chapter, we hope to have flagged some important issues, but we fully recognize that more is needed to diversify and decolonize economics education. Fortunately, there is a growing body of well-designed resources that can help with this. Here, we provide a brief overview of a few useful books, articles and chapters.

- *Reclaiming Economics for Future Generations* by Nicola Scott, Lucy Ambler, and Joe Earle, forthcoming. A book about the need to diversify, decolonize and democratize economics education written by active members of the international *Rethinking Economics* movement, based in the UK.
- *Valuing Us All: Feminist Pedagogy and Economics* by April Laskey Aerni and KimMarie McGoldrick, from 1999. A collection of essays discussing both changing what is taught and how it is taught in order to make economics education more inclusive.
- *A User's Guide to Debiasing* in *The Wiley Blackwell Handbook of Judgment and Decision Making* by Jack B. Soll, Katherine L. Milkman, and John W. Payne, from 2015. A chapter on strategies to reduce the biases in our cognitive processes.
- *A Better Economics for the Indian Context* by Amit Basole and Arjun Jayadev, from 2018. This article reflects on using the new textbook *The Economy* by the CORE team in undergraduate education in India and discusses the need for a different version of the book that would better fit the Indian context.
- *Decolonising SOAS Learning and Teaching Toolkit for Programme and Module Convenors* by the Decolonising SOAS Working Group, from 2018. This report provides practical suggestions on how to decolonize courses by using inclusive pedagogies and tackling colonial and racialised discrimination and privilege.
- *Decolonizing the university* by Gurminder K. Bhambra, Dalia Gebrial, Kerem Nişancıoğlu, from 2018. This collection of essays provides critical reflections and practical suggestions by academics, students and activists, and was inspired by student protests in South Africa which in turn triggered a global discussion about decolonising universities.
- *Decolonisation in Universities: The politics of knowledge* by Jonathan Jansen, from 2019. This collection of essays discusses what decolonisation is, why it is important, its difficulties and problems, practical cases and examples of decolonising programmes in universities located in Africa, and ideas for how to move forward.
- *Postcolonialism Meets Economics* by S. Charusheela, Eiman Zein-Elabdin, from 2004. A collection of essays exploring colonial and hegemonic aspects of classical and contemporary economics and how a postcolonial economics would look.
- *How to Be an Antiracist* by Ibram X. Kendi, from 2019. A popular and controversial book arguing we should look at racism from a consequentialist perspective, meaning that we should not care about whether intentions are 'racist' and instead focus on whether policies create inequitable outcomes between social groups.

Foundation 6
The Didactics of Economics Education

Improving economics education is not only a matter of changing what is taught, but also how it is taught.

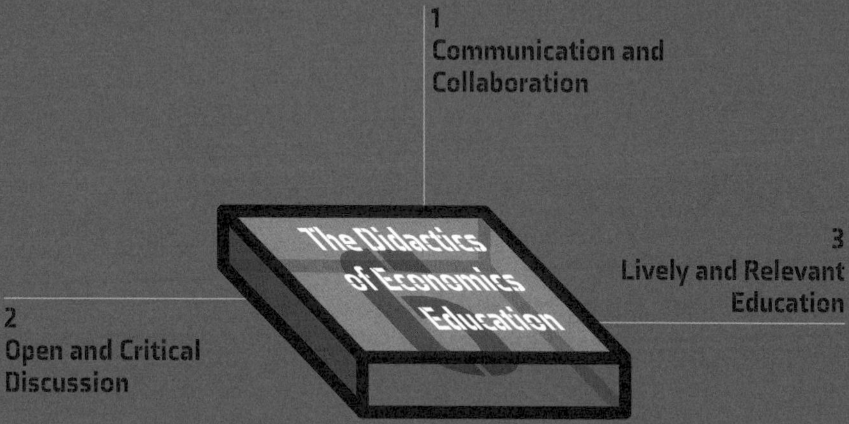

1
Communication and
Collaboration

3
Lively and Relevant
Education

The Didactics
of Economics
Education

2
Open and Critical
Discussion

Improving economics education is not only a matter of changing what is taught, but also how it is taught. A good course is more than just a good syllabus: it requires effective teaching. Most students will remember a good teacher making a horrible subject interesting or even fun to study, and vice versa.

There are many ways of teaching economics and we do not claim nor believe that there is one single best approach. While different situations and aspects of learning call for different techniques, there are three didactical issues that seem to be of particular relevance throughout economics education.

First, many studies have indicated that economics education could be improved by paying more attention to teaching students to communicate and collaborate. In addition, there have been worrying indications that economics education often fails to facilitate open, critical, but also respectful, discussions. Finally, more diverse and relevant formats of teaching and examining could be used to make economics education more lively and connected to the real world. Towards the end of the chapter, we also suggest useful resources that relate more specifically to varying the ways in which we teach, even if the content often remains the same.

"We make a crucial distinction between formal literacy, where the subject matter is a fixed body of knowledge which participants are encouraged to learn unquestioningly, and substantive literacy, where participants are encouraged to interrogate and critique the subject matter and develop their own independent judgements."

Joe Earle, Cahal Moran & Zach Ward-Perkins (2016, pp. 156-157)

We start this chapter with two non-specialist skills, communication and collaboration, which we believe deserve more attention in the curriculum. We then turn to the culture of our classrooms, arguing for a more open, less hierarchical style of teaching, which stimulates students to start thinking for themselves. Finally, we discuss the need to make the programme content more relevant for the students, and offer a variety of teaching and assessment techniques that help students to better master and retain the material.

1 Communication and Collaboration

Firstly, communication and collaboration skills are a crucial part of becoming an effective economist, as well as growing as a human being. A survey among Dutch professional economists found that being able to make economics simple and understandable is the second most important skill for a professional economist (van Dalen et al., 2015b). Multiple studies among UK employers also found that good communication and working well in teams are both vital skills for economists (O'Doherty et al., 2007; Pomorina, 2012; The Economics Network, 2015; Yurko, 2018).

Noting their importance, research also indicates that there is room for improvement in economics education in these areas. A study among UK employers of economics graduates summarised the need for better communication skills as follows (Yurko, 2018, p. 4):

"Although data analysis and IT abilities fared relatively well in terms of employer satisfaction, employers across all of the aforementioned surveys believed economics

graduates' communication and application skills needed further development. For example, 40% of the employers surveyed in 2012 believed economics graduate appointees had 'not very high' critical self-awareness, followed by inadequate written communication skills and the ability to apply what had been learned in a wider context.

While the prominence of these skills broadly reflects the priority given to generic competencies within the entire graduate employer population, the technical nature of economic analyses requires a particularly demanding set of communication abilities. This is illustrated by employers' focus on the communication of economic concepts and analyses to non-economist audiences, a requirement that emerged regardless of occupational sector, organisational size, or type of graduate job provided by their organisations."

This lack of communication skills can have severe consequences as it can lead to misunderstandings, misinformed decision makers and citizens, and a distrust of economists. A survey among UK citizens found that only 12% felt that *"politicians and the media talk about economics in a way that is accessible and easy to understand"* (Rethinking Economics & Ecnmy, 2018). Furthermore, only 25% of the UK public trusts economists, while 71% trusts scientists.

So what does this mean for the didactics of economics education? On a very basic level it simply means that students should learn how to communicate and collaborate, and practise this wherever possible. On a more detailed level, we suggest the following: written communication, oral communication, and practice.

Written communication

In a survey among employers of economics graduates, several respondents also emphasised the value of learning to communicate economic ideas to different audiences and in various styles of communication (Yurko, 2018). Economists frequently communicate in written form, so it is useful to learn how to write for different audiences. Currently, many programmes spend most attention on writing academic research articles. This is great, but it can also overshadow other forms of written communication that may be even more important for students, as most of them will go on to be professional economists rather than academic economists.

A better balance between various styles of writing might be found by assigning students to write practical reports that are commonly published by and within public and private organisations. Students could also be tasked to write pieces for the general public, like blogs, newspaper articles or columns. The goal here is not so much to learn how to write amazing stories, but rather to communicate to non-economists in a clear and accessible manner.

Oral communication

Besides written communication, oral communication is another very useful skill, also contributing to students' general cooperation skills. Again, there are various styles here: presenting for other economists, but also communicating with non-economists. Besides giving presentations, learning how to productively debate can be very useful. This is not only for those aspiring to go into politics: in virtually every field people discuss with each other what they could best do.

In general, it is important that students learn to communicate with different audiences, such as fellow economists, hands-on policy makers or private sector workers, and the general public. These groups require different styles and forms of communication with different levels of complexity and different foci. Policy makers and private sector workers may be mainly interested in practical applications and implications, while academic economists might be more interested in the analytical arguments and empirical procedures. As such, one has to change what one discusses when addressing an audience. Framing and choice of words are crucial here, as one British consultancy employer explained (Yurko, 2018, p. 8): *"...in particular [we're] looking for the ability to be able to explain economics to people who aren't economists. It's the ability to explain economics concepts without relying on economics jargon, using plain English, and being able to explain the intuition behind economic theory."*

Practise, practise, practise

A final suggestion. We believe that the best way to learn something is by actually doing it. In this case, it means actually communicating with different audiences. Of course, the teacher still plays an important role in this and the first times practicing can be in class with students among each other. But it can be very helpful for students to go out and actually communicate with policy makers, private sector workers, and of course members of the general public.

The latter is probably most easily achieved. An assignment might be to write or present something for some of their friends or family members. This allows the student to practise communicating about economic concepts with non-experts. A way to practise interaction with policy makers and private sector workers might be through exercises on actual cases the professional is currently working on. This way the students can actually help the professional, who in turn can be asked to assess and give feedback to the students, both on the content and way of communicating it. *Building Block 9, Problems & Proposals*, goes into this in more detail.

2 Open and Critical Discussions

Most economics professors are in favour of open and critical discussions. Nonetheless many have argued economics education could be more open and critical by allowing for more reflection and questioning of assumptions and arguments. As a British government employer argued (Yurko, 2018, p. 10): *"...it's that sense of critical thinking which doesn't always come through in economics degrees because, and I know I'm generalising, but there's a lot of assumptions or knowledge that aren't necessarily challenged quite early on in the economics degree. Which, I think, does make a better government economist if you're able to critically think through, for example, whether that neoclassical welfare framework is appropriate or not."*

Whenever an economic theory, model or perspective is being taught, the content should be presented critically. This means that instead of merely listing the assumptions of a theory, they should be discussed and challenged. When might these assumptions hold and when is the theory likely to be useful? This also means discussing the limitations of a model as well as how to solve the algebraic equations within it. How could students combine the outputs of the model with the context of the economy that they are studying?

Is it worth the time invested?

Because time available in class is normally fixed, we appreciate that more time spent being critical means less time available to teach technicalities and let students memorise content. For two main reasons we think the gains of this change are worth the cost. Firstly, learning is a process where knowledge is internalised and not only memorised. Critical thinking is a crucial part of this internalisation, as well as being vital to understand the logical connections between different ideas. This means that even though less time may be spent directly teaching content, students will still understand that content better by the end of the course. Second, critical thinking is necessary for students to actively use their newly acquired knowledge, by applying it to the real world. To make useful recommendations to decision-makers, economists need to be able to choose between competing ways of understanding the world, know how to contextualise the output of their chosen model(s) and understand the limitations of the methods that they have used.

However, there does not need to be a direct trade-off between time spent learning content and learning critical thinking. There are also ways to expand the time available for learning. Students should be encouraged to read material in advance of classes, so that their thinking and learning processes have already started. By the time they reach university, students should be capable of learning much of the core content of their studies through readings, videos and other media on their own. This means that contact hours with staff such as lectures and tutorials can be reserved for the more complicated content, and for the development of critical thinking.

Another important aspect of being critical is being able to reflect and examine our own ideas and assumptions. A critical mind brings modesty through a better understanding of the limitations of theoretical and methodological tools. Students should be able to challenge and critically reflect on the topics that are being taught; and to think critically about their own understanding and opinions. Critical thinking skills are vital in order to arm students against biases and manipulation. These skills will empower the students to be more independent and creative in their thinking, the rewards of which will be greater success later on in their work life.

Classroom culture: authoritarian or open?

In our experience, it is powerful when teaching staff not only allow open discussions, but actively encourage them – allowing students to raise points, including those that run counter to the professor's personal beliefs. A crucial factor in this is awareness of hierarchical relations. The students are subordinate to the teacher and have (almost by definition) less knowledge and experience of the topics. Thus, unsurprisingly, many students are cautious to speak out and share their thoughts. This hesitation can be remedied by treating students with respect, especially when they dare to challenge the teacher's views. A more horizontal teaching dynamic will open up the space for students to be more proactive and critical towards the material they are being taught.

Unfortunately, the fairly harsh and direct debating style that seems to characterise the research side of the discipline can sometimes seep into teaching, resulting in a dismissive and authoritarian classroom style. It is a dangerous situation when a teacher uses the fact that they know best as justification to brush off counter arguments or critiques from their class. While the teacher will almost by definition know more about the topic at hand, this patently fails to create a suitable environment for students to query, interrogate and, by extension, understand what they are being taught. A telling example of this was given by Prof. Stephanie Kelton (2018, min 26-28), recounting an experience from her student days:

> "When I was at [the University of] Cambridge and I was taking a graduate macro theory course ... Willem Buiter is the professor, he is teaching IS-LM theory. So I am sitting there in this big class and there is nothing critical at all being said about this model ... So I raised my hand and I posed some questions regarding loanable funds and money. And he [Willem Buiter] turned red in

the face. That was not welcome and he looked at me and made an example of me in the class. He pointed at me and said: "If you are the type of person who thinks money is important, you are probably the same type of person who would enjoy beating yourself with the rubber hose." It was meant to put me in my place and to tell me there are things one does not talk about."

The point here is not this specific example, but rather how it reflects a broader concern about the classroom, and by extension the discipline; that it is not a space for open, engaged discussion (Fourcade et al., 2015; Wu, 2017). In a welcome development, various associations of economists have recently adopted professional codes of conduct to prevent such behaviour. And we hope this will also help prevent such behaviour in economics education.

It is important that teachers stimulate and facilitate discussions, rather than suppress them. And in such discussions it is key that everyone has a chance to speak up, so that they are not dominated by a handful of loud students. Diversity is often a challenge here: white people and men are often more comfortable being vocal than other groups. Students often feel that the bar for questioning the material being taught in economics is set very high. At many universities, it is extremely rare for economics students to raise their hands in a class, where many go through an entire degree without actively participating.

Teaching techniques that stimulate independent thinking

This is also related to how the subject is taught. Instead of teaching economics as a set of scientific facts, teachers could aim to bring up arguments that can be debated, encouraging students to participate in their own learning. Here it is vital that teachers ask open-ended questions that can open up the space for students to share their analytical reflections. In this way, teachers can work towards creating an open space for active discussion and joint learning.

A final dimension specific to economics is that one's mathematical skills are taken as a proxy for general intelligence. To be sure, mathematics is a very useful skill for economists: crucial in some corners of the profession, a useful adjunct in others. But rather than being treated as one of many kinds of knowledge students have to learn, it is often used as a selection mechanism, painting any student less talented in mathematics as unfit to be an economist and not to be taken as seriously in discussions. This is not right. The ability to think clearly is not by a long stretch the same as the ability to solve a mathematical equation.

3 Lively and Relevant Education

It is very important that economics is taught in a lively way with room for creativity and imagination, and which makes clear why its contents are so relevant. It is important to motivate and stimulate students to become engaged and interested in the topics that are discussed. This is especially important given the life stage people generally are in while studying.

Teaching a difficult audience

Academic students can be a challenging audience. Most students are fairly young when they start studying economics, between the age of 18 and 20. Frequently having moved to a new city, an unfamiliar world, they try to make friends, often already before the first day of the programme through introduction weeks and sometimes even more ritualised initiations. While entering this new environment, they slowly learn to become more independent, frequently living on their own for the first time.

In this stage of life between adolescence and adulthood, many students are strongly distracted by the freedom of student life, partying, drinking, and having fun with friends. For some, this leads to a minimum-effort policy in terms of studying. It can take great effort from academic teaching staff to get these students to study and focus on their programme. Teachers just have to hope that they have given these young people some valuable insights, knowledge and skills that will stay with them for (a bit) longer than until the exam.

Against this background, it helps when the teaching of economics is done in as lively, creative and clearly relevant a manner as possible. Below we give a number of suggestions on how to do so: make it relevant, and use diverse teaching and assessment methods.

Relevance

It is crucial that students understand why the material being taught is worth learning. If this is lost on them, motivation will quickly slip away. Unfortunately, it is no trivial matter to get students to grasp the relevance of every aspect of economics programmes. So how can we ensure that students realise why the material at hand is worth learning?

A first step is simply explaining: why are you teaching something? The first lecture of a course is a good time to do so: set out the various reasons why the contents of the course are relevant for the students to learn. Second, make frequent links to the real world. In *Foundation 3: Real-World* we suggest ways to do this, including the use of newspapers, blogs, guest lectures, visits to economic organisations, policy reports, and case studies.

Third, it helps when students develop a better understanding of how their professional future might look, and how this material would be useful then. This can be done by facilitating career orientation and personal self-reflection. Another way to help in this regard is making them more familiar with the roles economists play in society, through guest lectures, visits, and perhaps even more effective internships. Such an internship could be very big, being full time for half a year. But it could also be quite brief and small, for example being only one day a week lasting for a couple of months. These smaller internships are probably more suitable for earlier on in economics programmes, while the more extensive ones fit better at the end.

Diverse teaching and assessment methods

Besides helping students understand the relevance of what they are learning, it can help to experiment with different teaching and assessment methods, creatively using a broad range of different and active learning strategies and tools.

Research shows that active learning strategies, such as cooperative learning exercises, classroom experiments, and case studies, result in better learning outcomes, higher test scores and longer retention, especially when there is repetition in the content (Hoyt & McGoldrick, 2012, p. 331). So far, however, economics remains taught mainly through traditional lectures in which students are largely passive (Watts & Schaur, 2011).

As for different active learning strategies, well established approaches one might make use of are differentiated learning, vicarious or observational learning, problem-based learning, and blended learning. Each having different ideas about how differentiated or universal the teaching material should be, how active or passive students should be in class, how to use digital or physical experiences, and whether to focus on individual or group exercises. Differentiated learning, as the term suggests, believes in differentiation, meaning that students in the same class get different assignments, explanations and/or materials based on their personal interests, preferred learning styles, abilities and levels. Vicarious and observational learning focus on learning from the experiences of others and observing their behaviour, and can be done through guest lectures, field trips and exercises, and internships. Problem-based learning is about working through the processes of solving open-ended problems in small groups. Blended learning is about effectively combining online and in-person classroom education, enabling teachers to benefit from both their strengths. And there are many other useful approaches that teachers could benefit from, some of which are also covered in the resources described below.

It is also an option to involve students, particularly in more advanced courses, in the selection of the material. One could, for example, ask the students to select one piece, chapter or paper, on the economy, or specific topic at hand, that they find good or insightful and let them write and present a short introduction into the text for the rest of the class (Dow, 2009). Besides letting students participate in selecting teaching material, one can also ask them to come up with real-world examples that can help illustrate theoretical concepts. One could do this in class but also as an assignment, grading students based on how unique, well-chosen and explained the example is. And this brings us to the next point: assessment methods.

For assessment there are also many methods. A useful distinction is between formative and summative assessment, the former focusing on monitoring students' progress and the latter focusing on evaluating students' knowledge or skills. Examples of formative assessment methods are: rubrics, (active) participation in class, handing in weekly notes on readings, peer- and self-assessment. And summative assessment is often done with the help of written and oral exams, projects, and presentations.

It is important that assessment methods complement the students' learning process and their understanding of the economy. Examination methods where students are encouraged to cram are more likely to result in students forgetting the material they have been taught. Examples of this are time-constrained exams and non-open ended questions, frequently used in the UK (Earle et al., 2016). Assessment design should be made in such a way that fosters cognition and critical thinking, enabling students to apply their newly acquired knowledge in the real world. Moreover, this will contribute to rewarding the students that have spent time reflecting on the subject and demonstrates a better understanding of the material. We should see assessments as an integral part of the learning process, not only as a means in itself. They are a chance for students to spend time to think independently about what they have been taught.

Once you start redesigning the educational process, a wide field of unexpected possibilities opens up. Three interesting examples are service learning programmes, the Cusanus Hochschule and the Schumacher College. Service learning, as described in *Putting the invisible hand to work* by McGoldrick and Ziegert, is about using service activities in local communities to help students better understand the economy and develop their skills at applying this knowledge. An added benefit of this approach is that not only the students learn from their service activities, the local communities can also be strengthened by it and it makes economics more accessible and connected to citizens. Cusanus is a young and independent academic institution in a small German town where most students live on campus only part-time, to attend the intensive block seminars which form the heart of its program. In these week-long sessions, topics are treated in context, including extensive exchanges between teachers and students and active group work. Schumacher students live on the (UK) campus full time, working together in other ways besides studying, such as growing 50% of their own food. Both of these institutions have economic questions at the core of their programmes, but actively interweave these with a broader set of social and ecological questions.

Resources

In this chapter, we hope to have flagged some important issues, but we fully recognize that more is needed to improve the didactics of economics education. Fortunately, there are many good resources that can help with this. Here we provide a short overview of useful books, journals, and online resources and communities.

Books

- *International Handbook on Teaching and Learning Economics* by Gail M. Hoyt and KimMarie McGoldrick, from 2012. A rich and useful collection of essays both on the content and didactics of economics education with chapters on case use, context-rich problems, cooperative learning exercises, improving classroom discussion, classroom experiments, interactive lecture demonstrations, just-in-time teaching, Socratic teaching, feminist pedagogy, economic blogs, integrating media and response systems, distance education, and using literature, novels, and poetry.
- *Teaching Economics: More Alternatives to Chalk and Talk* by William E. Becker, Michael Watts, and Suzanne R. Becker, from 2006. Another useful collection of essays focusing on moving away from traditional lecture and textbook based teaching with chapters on classroom experiments, cooperative learning, case studies, active learning techniques in large lecture classes, using digital technologies, team term papers and presentations, and, in our opinion very important and inspiring, having fun in the classroom.
- *Teaching Economics: Perspectives on Innovative Economics Education*, by Joshua Hall and Kerianne Lawson, from 2019. This more recent book on how economics can be taught is filled with concrete examples and exercises, explores new opportunities like using video games, music and medical experiences when teaching economics.
- *Putting the invisible hand to work: Concepts and models for service learning in economics*, by KimMarie McGoldrick and Andrea L. Ziegert, from 2002. This collection of essays introduces the reader to what service learning

is, explains why it can be useful, provides guidelines and resources, and gives examples of applications with chapters on land economics, forensic economics, access to health care, non-profit organisations, volunteer work, and a statistics course.

Journals

Besides these books, there are also useful academic journals containing a broad literature on the different ways of teaching economics. A useful literature review to start with could be 'Research on teaching economics to undergraduates' by Allgood, Walstad and Siegfried, from 2015.

Examples of journals on economics education are:

- The *Journal of Economic Education (JEE)* was founded in 1969 and is to this day an important journal for research on how economics is, and should be, taught.
- The *International Review of Economics Education (IREE)* was launched in 2003 by the Economics Network of the UK's Higher Education Academy and has since 2013 been published by Elsevier.
- The *Australasian Journal of Economics Education (AJEE)*, founded in 2004, has ten objectives, including improving the pedagogy of economics, the relation between teaching and research, and paying more attention to interdisciplinary issues, history, economic philosophy and implicit assumptions.
- The *International Journal of Pluralism and Economics Education (IJPEE)* was launched just after the start of the global financial crisis in 2009 to bring together a diverse community of scholars to investigate and share knowledge about how economics could be taught in a pluralist way.
- The *Journal of Economics Teaching (JET)* was founded in 2015 and focuses on innovating economics pedagogy and sharing insights to economics teachers at all educational levels.
- *Perspectives on Economic Education Research (PEER)* was launched in 2005 and has a strong tradition of research on active learning activities, such as experiments and case studies.
- The *Journal of Economics and Economic Education Research (JEEER)* was founded in 2000 and covers a broad range of issues, from micro- and macroeconomics to normative, environmental and financial economics.
- *Citizenship, Social and Economics Education (CSEE)* started in 1996 and has a broad focus on the role of social and economics education in society.
- The *Journal for Economics Educators (JEE)* was founded in the 1990s and is published online by the Tennessee Economics Association.
- The *Computers in Higher Education Economics Review (CHEER)* existed from 1987 to 2011, when it was incorporated into the IREE.

Online resources and communities

It can also be helpful to learn directly from other teachers and share experiences and insights with each other. Many countries have multiple didactical organisations as well as associations for economics teachers, especially on high school level.

- The American Economic Association, for example, provides an useful overview of teaching resources, ideas for classroom experiences and giving examples to illustrate concepts: https://www.aeaweb.org/resources/teachers
- Another useful source might be the UK-based Economics Network, which offers an enormous amount of sessions, advice and materials, such as the Handbook for Economics Lecturers: https://www.economicsnetwork.ac.uk/
- The Institute for New Economic Thinking offers a platform for exchange of academic teaching materials, discussion and peer-to-peer exchange at https://ineted.org
- Exploring Economics is an open access, e-learning platform on pluralist economics. Here you can discover and study a variety of economic theories, methods and topics. https://www.exploring-economics.org
- Economics Education offers a range of materials and links on the movement to make economics education more diverse and socially relevant: https://www.economicseducation.org
- Finally, using games and experiments to teach students about microeconomics, industrial organisation, game theory, behavioural economics and coordination and allocation mechanisms has become increasingly popular. A useful and interesting tool for learning more about this is Economics Games: https://economics-games.com/

Part II:
Building
Blocks

Building Blocks

Introduction

This part of the book contains the meat and bones of our curriculum design method: ten thematic areas of knowledge and skills in economics. Each of the ten building blocks covers an area of knowledge or a skill that we see as essential for the education of future economists. These 'building blocks' can be used as templates to create courses, of generally six to ten weeks each. One can also pick and choose elements of the different building blocks to combine them into a broader course, or split up a building block into several courses.

This book is designed to help construct a curriculum that fits your specific situation, rather than to advocate one 'ideal' curriculum. Hence we have designed the building blocks to be useful for constructing anything from a single course to an entire bachelor programme. They can be shortened, lengthened, combined or altered according to the needs of the programme. We strongly believe that any full economics programme should touch on all ten of these building blocks in some form or other. Shorter programmes, like individual courses or semester-long minor programmes, might do better to pick and choose the most relevant blocks for their particular purpose.

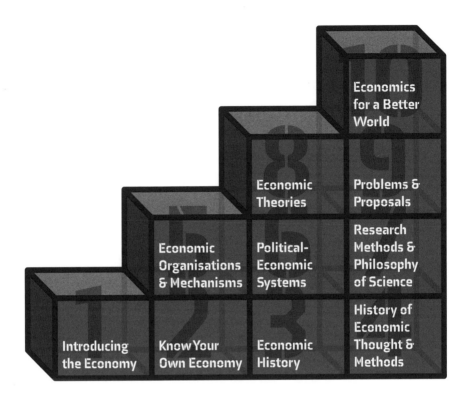

Figure 5: The ten building blocks that form the core of this book. The order of the numbers is not necessarily the order in which they should be taught. Their relative size varies, with building blocks 7 and 8 generally taking up much more space than the others. Programmes may also combine various building blocks into a single course, or split a single building block up over a number of courses. See the chapter Tool 5: Example Curricula for how this can look in practice.

The first two building blocks focus on helping students to develop a feeling for economic matters and teaching them basic conceptual and real-world economic knowledge. *Building Block 1: Introducing the Economy* discusses the definition and relevance of 'the economy' and how it is related to other aspects of the social and physical world. *Building Block 2: Know Your Own Economy*, explores actual national and local economies and their structures, institutions and sectors.

With this basic knowledge in hand, we explore the history of economic thought and of the real-world economy. *Building Block 3: Economic History* explores the fascinating and diverse history of economic events and developments. *Building Block 4: History of Economic Thought & Methods*, in contrast, is about the remarkable and complex history of ideas about the economy. Together, these chapters provide a crucial foundation for students' further education.

Besides knowing basic economic concepts, facts and history, it is key that economics students learn how economies can and have been organised, at micro-, meso- and macro-levels. *Building Block 5: Economic Organisations & Mechanisms* investigates the different forms of economic interaction and organisation that operate at each level and together make up an economy. *Building Block 6: Political-Economic Systems* reviews the complex structures, institutions and power relations that form the overarching structure of an economy.

Another core element of a good economics education is a broad and diverse analytic toolkit, filled with relevant methods and theories. *Building Block 7: Research Methods & Philosophy of Science* is about both quantitative and qualitative data collection and analysis methods. In *Building Block 8: Economic Theories* we propose a 'pragmatic pluralist' approach to teaching theories by focusing on only the most important insights for every topic. These two building blocks will likely take more space in most programmes than the others, as the centre of gravity of an academic education lies in methods and theories.

The last two building blocks are largely concerned with the productive application of economic ideas in the real world. Economics education should be preparing the economic experts of tomorrow for their future roles in society. *Building Block 9: Problems & Proposals* deals with the practical skills necessary for the work of almost all economists: analysing real-world problems and working on proposals to address them, whether in a company, government agency, think tank or academic department. *Building Block 10: Economics for a Better World* deals with the values involved in decision making, asking what normative principles and visions can guide actions to address the major challenges of our times.

Finally, a note on how the building blocks are related to the three principles as illustrated in the figure below. While the principles are present throughout the book, some building blocks are more strongly linked to certain principles than to others. The principle *Values* shows up most clearly in: *Building Block 10: Economics for a Better World*. The *Real-World* principle is most strongly expressed in *Building Block 2: Know Your Own Economy* and *Building Block 3: Economic History*, as well as *Building Block 9: Problems & Proposals*. As for Pluralism, it comes through most distinctly in *Building Block 4: History of Economic Thought & Methods, Building Block 7: Research Methods & Philosophy of Science* and *Building Block 8: Economic Theories*. As to combinations of principles, *Building Block 5: Economic Organisations & Mechanisms* and *Building Block 6: Political-Economic Systems* combine pluralist analytical tools with real-world knowledge. And finally, *Building Block 1: Introducing the Economy* combines all three principles.

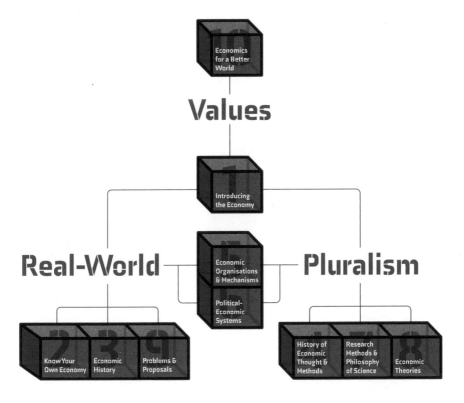

Figure 6: An overview linking each of the ten building blocks to the principles that are most relevant for them.

Building Block 1

Introducing the Economy

Getting a feeling for economic matters. What is the economy, why is it important, how is it embedded in the larger social and natural world, what are the main current societal challenges, and what roles do its experts, economists, have?

1
What is the
Economy?

2
Ecological
and Social
Embeddedness
of the Economy

3
Reasons to
Study the
Economy

**Introducing
the Economy**

4
The Main
Current Societal
Challenges

5
The Role of
Economists in
Society

What

Economics education is about preparing the next generation of economists for their future roles in society. Therefore, it is crucial that economics programmes help students to develop their understanding of how the economy is embedded in the wider social and ecological world. It is about asking seemingly simple questions that go to the core of what economists are concerned about: What is the subject-matter of the study, why is it relevant, how does this relate to other fields, and what does it mean to become an economist?

Why

Introducing the subject-matter of the economy and its relevance is foundational for any economics programme. This basis informs the entire programme and every course students will take. Clearly introducing students to the subject-matter of their study allows them to see the bigger picture and put the different elements of the programme in context. Furthermore, it motivates students and helps them understand why studying economics is worthwhile. In contrast, failure to properly introduce and contextualise the general subject matter will lead to demotivated students and fundamental misunderstandings throughout the programme.

Contrast with current programmes

Currently, economics programmes usually begin with teaching mathematics or highly abstract models. As such, an introduction to the field as a whole is often missing. When a more general introduction is given, it often focuses on *thinking like an economist*, that is, thinking in neoclassical models, which is described as 'the correct way'. We believe that instead of convincing students to follow a particular point of view or study methodology (see also *Foundation 1: The Philosophy of Economy Studies*), an economics education should start by introducing the field of study more broadly and in particular the topic of study: 'the economy'.

Let's start at the very beginning

A very good place to start

When you read, you begin with A-B-C

When you sing, you begin with do-re-mi

Maria von Trapp – The Sound of Music

In economics, models play an important role. However, before studying a conceptual model of something, it is important to clearly scope and define what exactly it is that one is studying as also outlined in the chapter *Foundation 1: The Philosophy of Economy Studies*. This first building block therefore introduces the subject-matter of economics: the economy. It helps students to grasp what it is they are studying, why it is such an important topic, and how the economy is interrelated with other aspects of our world. Furthermore, in this building block, students explore the question of what we seek in our economy, are introduced to the most important challenges of today, and take a look in the mirror: what does it mean to be an economist and what do and don't they do?

This building block primarily aims to raise questions, rather than provide answers. Before delving into various forms of knowledge, theories and methods, students need to be motivated, to feel grounded in the field, and to have a basic delineation of what it is they will be doing. We therefore suggest using this building block early on in programmes. It touches on many subjects which are covered in more depth in other building blocks, and does so intentionally as a high-level introduction to gain a good overview; to understand 'the big picture'.

1 What is the Economy?

When we personally started our studies in economics, we had a rather vague idea of what the field entailed. We were aware that it had something to do with money, companies and politics, and that it was crucially important for the functioning of society. That was about it. Such a deep lack of awareness, we think, is fairly standard for beginning students, as high-school economic programmes often focus more on business topics. Therefore, it is crucial to introduce students to the thing they are supposed to become experts on. Without such an introduction, students would, and do, learn about specific topics and methods, without understanding why they learn these things and of what larger whole these are part. A shared understanding of the subject-matter should therefore be built, as soon as the programme begins.

An important first step in economics programmes is to introduce the core concepts defining what the economy is: the systems of resource extraction, production, distribution, consumption and waste disposal through which societies provision themselves to sustain life and enhance its quality. To develop a feeling for how these processes can be organised, it can be useful to discuss the major actors and institutions of an economy. That is, the government, big and small private companies, cooperatives, labour unions and employers associations, households, banks, regulatory and civil society organisations. Other aspects of the economy one can introduce to students are the primary, secondary, tertiary, quaternary and quinary sectors, as well as the formal and informal sectors. There is no need here to go deeply into theory or empirics, it is much more important that students begin to understand how these various entities and concepts relate to each other and form a larger system.

Economics programmes should start by helping students to get a feeling for economic matters. This can, for example, be done by taking the economic sections of newspapers and discussing recent economic events. A more conceptual introduction into what the economy is can be given with the material listed below. A useful material could be 'Economics: The User's Guide' by Chang, as it provides an accessible bird-eye overview of the economy.

A valuable exercise in economic awareness is the following: let students analyse and describe the provisioning processes they engage in and encounter in the course of a single day. For instance, students might realise that they perform a lot of unpaid work to take care of themselves, such as preparing food, cleaning, washing, and that such work is also performed by family members and friends. When they go to a shop to buy something, they would have to ask themselves how that company operates and where it gets its inputs from. If the student pays by card, the bank also plays a role in his or her economic activity and becomes part of the exercise.

Another aspect might be that these daily provisioning processes are embedded in an institutional framework of standards, labels and regulation by government or consumer associations which play a role in economic coordination. When the student comes to class for a lecture, for example, various questions arise: how is education organised, who performs what work and how is it financed? A link can then be made with other processes, as the education is (partially and indirectly) financed through the taxes paid on the product that was bought earlier in the shop.

If the student goes to a local sports club, which runs a competition as a volunteer-based association, this provides another type of economic setting to analyse. In terms of exercises, this could be coupled with a weekly assignment to analyse a student's own economic daily life, making use of the concepts introduced that week.

In general, we suggest briefly touching upon the various constituent elements of economies, but saving the details for building blocks 2, 5, 6 and 8. This first building block should provide a bird's eye overview of the system as a whole.

2 Ecological and Social Embeddedness of the Economy

The economy does not exist in a vacuum. It is embedded in the ecological and social world with much (and ever-changing) overlap and interaction. Without understanding what this embedding looks like, it is very hard to understand the economy itself. In addition, an understanding of this embedding greatly facilitates the application of economic knowledge. Finally, it helps motivate students, who often come to the programme carrying concerns about larger societal and environmental issues (such as international development, climate change, pandemics, and human well-being or happiness). They know that economic dynamics greatly determine such issues, and hope to gain an understanding of how, exactly, these systems are related and what can be changed.

Since this first building block can only provide a brief vista on the embeddedness of the economy, its main goal is to get students thinking and questioning. More detailed answers will come later in the programme. Several of the theoretical approaches discussed in *Building Block 8: Economies Theories*, and *Tool 1: Pragmatic Pluralism* offer useful starting points to stimulate students' questions.

For instance, institutional economics provides insights into the ways economic dynamics are interrelated with social and legal systems. Feminist economics has important insights on not only economic gender dynamics, but also care work and unpaid work in general. And ecological economics provides easily grasped theoretical models to show how economic activity is situated within life-supporting ecosystems. In terms of the interface between economy and ecology, there are several other emerging fields, of which industrial ecology seems particularly promising.

Economic sociology studies the social processes within the economy and how the latter is embedded in larger societal structures. Political economy focuses on the interaction and connections between politics and the economy. Economic anthropology analyses how people understand and make sense of economic life and how this is connected to larger cultural and meaning-making processes in human societies.

In discussions on the embeddedness of the economy, the question of boundaries may arise: what do we still consider 'the economy'? As in every field, the exact boundaries are widely debated, as discussed in the chapter *Foundation 1: The Philosophy of Economy Studies*. While exploring these debates could be interesting, it is more important that students develop a rough understanding of the interfaces between the ecological, social and economic realm. For example, care work, institutions and ecosystems are essential for the workings of economies, but cannot be reduced to being simply economic phenomena. We suggest that economics education focuses on how these things shape the functioning of the economy, leaving the entire ecological and social realm to other scholars to study.

A good start is basic instruction in the economic strands of ecological, feminist and institutional economics as well as related fields such as economic sociology and political economy. If the lecturer does not have training in these fields, we suggest using introductory chapters of the respective textbooks and recorded lectures. In addition, it can be useful to have scholars from these fields give guest lectures: biologists, sociologists and political scientists. This is generally most productive when these lecturers have experience with working on interdisciplinary teams with economists, so that they can also explain how the economists can contribute to better understanding the world.

Interdisciplinary Economics provides an overview of five neighbouring sub-disciplines, such as economic sociology. economy.st/interdisciplin

Again, it can also be very fruitful to ask students to debate these matters for themselves: how is the economy related to the social and ecological world? Getting students to develop their thinking on this simple question will most certainly make for lively workshop classes, and lead to increased motivation and curiosity later in the programme.

3 Reasons to Study the Economy

Why do we study the economy, other than as a purely intellectual pursuit? What makes this field of knowledge such a socially vital one? Many economics programmes fail to discuss their own *raisons d'être*. We believe this is a serious omission. Students will be far more motivated if they are prompted to think about the possible purpose(s) of their work, and consequently about their own place in society.

Here, a useful distinction is between goals, more broadly, and measurements, more specifically. As for goals, we try to understand the economy, *so that* we can alter economic resource extraction, production, distribution, consumption and waste disposal processes such that societies are better able to provision themselves to sustain life and enhance its quality. Where 'better' can be more abundant, fair, reliable, sustainable, healthy, fun, or meaningful, or so that we or our family, company, town, or country, can gain more relative wealth, security, independence, power or social cohesion. In chapter *Foundation 4: Values* we discuss these different interpretations of goals of an economy in more detail. Subsequently, to see whether we are attaining those goals, we need measurement tools, such as Gross Domestic Product, the Human Development Index, the Gross National Happiness Index, the Better Life Index, and the Genuine Progress Indicators.

Self-evident as these 'goals' of economic policy may seem, they need to be determined by societies at different levels and may conflict or at least vary so much that universal measuring sticks do not suffice. If we leave this undiscussed, it will be difficult for students to realise when they are giving normative advice, and how to chart their own course in these waters. Rather than teaching general ethical theory (for example utilitarianism, deontology and virtue ethics), we propose to directly focus the philosophical lens on economic questions. Presenting and confronting students with concrete cases in which normative goals conflict with each other can be very useful in developing professional skills. In this way, besides becoming familiar with normative debates and arguments, students learn how economic decisions are often about considering multiple goals and finding the best compromise.

It may be useful to teach this section of the building block in conjunction with the previous one, on ecological and social embeddedness of the economy. We encourage teachers to also use their personal passions and interests to convey to students why the economy is so important. Another approach could be to let students debate among themselves why the economy is important and what economic outcomes they think are crucial.

It is important here to clarify the relationship between goals and measures: we need measures, but for some goals, this is trickier than for others. Monetary indicators, such as GDP and profits, have been further developed than social and ecological indicators. However, given the increasing relevance of the latter, it is important to introduce students to newly developed measurements of economic success.

The point of this building block is not to be exhaustive, showing or discussing *all* possible economic goals. Rather, it is to open students up to thinking consciously about them, to name and discuss them explicitly, and to learn to recognize (and step beyond) their personal values. For instance, deep ecology enthusiasts should learn why global competitiveness may be worth striving for, and vice versa. The textbook *Principles of economics in context* could be particularly useful to give students an idea of the different reasons why studying the economy is relevant.

4 The Main Current Societal Challenges

An important role for economists is to help society understand and deal with many of its most difficult challenges. While the 'goals of the economy' discussed above are more or less timeless, the challenges in this section are specific to this generation. If future generations of economists are to fulfil this role, they need to be well acquainted with these challenges. In addition, knowing the various challenges our world is facing will help motivate students to apply themselves to more theoretical material, such as research methods and the details of theory. It will give them concrete issues to which they can apply these methods and theories and also guide them in their choice of electives and their own research subjects, further into the programme.

We distinguish two major societal challenges that students should understand, which are increasingly interrelated: human wellbeing and ecological preservation. Starting with the former, many traditional economic concerns are social and still highly relevant today such as poverty and hunger. Keynes (1930) termed this *'the economic problem'*: freeing us up from material worries, to focus humanity's energies on more interesting pursuits. This *'economic problem'* goes beyond mere productivity. There are growing concerns about inequality and social polarisation, financial and economic instability, psychological and health issues, unemployment, automation, digitalisation, market concentration and concentration of political power, political anger, populism, nationalism and migration.

The other set of challenges is ecological. According to many scientists, we live in the 'Anthropocene', a time when humanity has the power to change the physical world at a systemic scale (Lewis & Maslin, 2015). We are running an increasingly grave risk of undermining the ecological foundations of our life world. Economists need to play a large role in determining how we can prevent catastrophic climate change and slow or preferably stop the rapid destruction of biodiversity, poisoning of the oceans and so forth – problems that are caused by our increasingly powerful production technology, unceasing growth of material consumption and detrimental waste disposal. Students should have basic knowledge of such issues.

We suggest presenting a broad fact-based overview of both types of challenges: covering where the world currently stands and what the key influencing variables and uncertainties are. For this, reports, such as the *Sustainable Development Goals Reports*, *World Development Reports*, and *World Happiness Reports* could be of use, but more engaging material, such as documentaries, and materials on domestic issues can also be helpful.

We believe it is crucial to introduce students in the beginning of the programme to these issues and advise linking them to discussion on the goals and visions for the economy. Emphasis should be placed on broad and concrete knowledge of the current problems, to motivate students and to help them to put information they later acquire in context. As with other aspects of this building block, the point is not to provide a complete overview or to go far in depth, but rather to introduce students to a new way of thinking and a strand of knowledge that they can later deepen.

5   The Role of Economists in Society

"... do not let us overestimate the importance of the economic problem, or sacrifice to its supposed necessities other matters of greater and more permanent significance. It should be a matter for specialists-like dentistry. If economists could manage to get themselves thought of as humble, competent people on a level with dentists, that would be splendid."
John Maynard Keynes (1930, p. 7)

We mentioned a number of times already that economists have an important role to play in achieving the goals of the economy and dealing with the challenges of society; how do we do so? Sometimes economists seem passive commentators to the developments in the world. At other moments, they seem to be the ones calling the shots and determining the direction of actions. This started perhaps with the Physiocrats in 18th century France, and has not abated since, with the prime examples being the central planners of the USSR economy and the free market zealots that led deregulations in the 1980s. While the role of economists in society is a complex and sometimes indirect one, it is clear that we are a highly influential professional group especially in today's world where economic considerations have come to determine so much of our political decision-making.

This is not to say that economists should stick to their personal square millimetre of research territory. Economists have valuable knowledge and insights and can contribute importantly to a healthy public debate and smart policy. However, there are limits to an economic understanding of the world, and limits to the amount of (social) engineering possible. Therefore, it is important that students learn early on to reflect on their societal roles as social scientists, policy makers and educators.

Humility and a focus on the real world are a crucial part of this. 97% of economics students will never go on to the finesse and accompanying modesty of detailed research work within academia, but rather become practitioners (Colander & McGoldrick, 2010; de Goede et al., 2014). This majority needs to be trained in the limitations of their perspective for when they staff many of the country's most important institutions, such as the central bank and the ministries of finance, economic and social affairs. Visiting these institutions where economists work or inviting employees for guest lectures can help provide a realistic understanding of the role of economists in the real world. A better idea of the kind of professional activities they will experience in the future also allows students to better understand the relevance of what they are being taught.

Presenting and reflecting on literature can help students deepen their understanding. This is also an excellent opportunity to encourage students to develop their essay-writing and debating skills. Below are a number of suggestions for book chapters and papers which could form the readings for such exercises.

Teaching Materials

- *Economics: The User's Guide* by Ha-Joon Chang, from 2014, chapters 1 & 2. Perhaps the most accessible and yet insightful introduction book into economics, with particular attention to why it is relevant to learn economics and what economics is in the first place.

- *Introducing a New Economics* by Jack Reardon, Molly S. Cato, Maria A. C. Madi, from 2018, chapters 1, 3, 4, & 5. An accessible textbook which introduces students to what economics is, how it is embedded in society and the environment, and major societal challenges, such as climate change, poverty, financial instability, and inequality.

- *Principles of economics in context* by Neva Goodwin, Jonathan M. Harris, Julie A. Nelson, Brian Roach, Mariano Torras, most recent edition from 2019, chapters 0, 1, 20, and 21. This economics textbook covers many of the traditional economic topics, but pays more attention to why studying the economy is relevant and concerns, such as human wellbeing, ecological sustainability, distributional equity, and the quality of employment.

- To help students get an idea of the main societal challenges of today, it can be useful to have them take a look at reports, such as the *Sustainable Development Goals Reports*, *World Development Reports*, and *World Happiness Reports*. It can also be useful to use more engaging types of materials, such as documentaries and coverage of political protests and debates. Furthermore, it can be interesting and useful for students to also be exposed to material on the key issues in the domestic, rather than global, economy.

- *Economists and Societies* by Marion Fourcade, from 2009. This book presents a great historical overview of the societal role economists have had in the United States, Britain and France. For students of one of these countries, reading the introduction, conclusion and chapter devoted to their country can be very insightful in better understanding the role of economists in their society. For courses taught in other countries, it would help to find similar material on their own country. For us as Dutch citizens, for example, a useful additional resource would be the book *Telgen van Tinbergen: Het verhaal van de Nederlandse economen* by Harry van Dalen and Arjo Klamer, from 1996.

Visit the website for a wider range of teaching materials, to provide feedback, and to exchange ideas and ask support from colleagues worldwide.
economy.st/bb1

Building Block 2
Know Your Own Economy

The basic structure of the national economy, its most important institutions, its basic statistics, its economic class composition, its dominant economic sectors, and students' own economic position in the world.

1
Key
Indicators

2
Institutions

3
Sectors

Know Your
Own Economy

4
Practical
Suggestions

What

This second building block, *Know Your Own Economy*, introduces the structure and state of the economy today. Students should become familiar, even if only at a basic level, with the economy in which they live. The building block focuses on three fields of concrete knowledge: key indicators, institutions and sectors. For each of these, it suggests a more detailed overview of how to structure this knowledge in a manageable form.

Why

An economist who does not have basic knowledge of her own economy is an armchair academic. Given that more than 97% of all economics students do not continue into a PhD trajectory but rather work as professional economists, this is impractical. Gaining real-world knowledge is also highly motivating for students. This concrete knowledge allows them to see how the more abstract economic ideas they are learning can be appropriately applied to help them understand and solve these real-world problems. Finally, comparing abstract theory to an existing economy will also help students to be more reflective of the theory they are taught and become conscious of their position within the economy.

Contrast with current programmes

Current programmes focus on theoretical models and quantitative research methods, which allows students to develop certain analytical skills. We argue that, whilst very useful, this is not enough. An economics education should also teach students concrete knowledge and give them a practical understanding of existing economic institutions and sectors.

"If economists wished to study the horse,

they wouldn't go and look at horses.

They'd sit in their studies and say to themselves,

'What would I do if I were a horse?'"

Ronald Coase (1999, p. 1)

Most economics programmes contain at least some information about the real economy. This generally appears in the form of an example, illustrating a certain theory. For example, 'duopolies work so and so, here is an example about Boeing and Airbus'. This building block goes beyond that approach. We suggest making a factual overview of an actual economic system the core aim of at least one course. There are three main reasons why this is important.

The first reason is that focusing on a real-world case study motivates students. An excessive focus on mathematical models and other abstractions can demotivate students who came to learn about how the economy works. It may also discourage them from pursuing further studies or a career in economics, despite their curiosity and initial motivation to do so, because their education failed to demonstrate its value.

The second reason is that students need a mental image of the general structure and components and dynamics of the real economy in order to properly understand the urgency and application of the theoretical and methodological tools learned throughout the programme. While the type of knowledge we describe below might be assumed to be common knowledge, or easily gained from reading newspapers, this is often not the case. Media provide, as it were, the derivative of the economy. They tell us what changes, not what the whole system looks like. Students need a basic systemic overview first. If a small investment is made early on in the programme, it will create a positive feedback loop, making it increasingly easy and enjoyable for students to learn more on their own.

Third and finally, this type of concrete knowledge helps to guide students' critical thinking. A central skill for economists is to judge which theoretical ideas fit and can help us understand a specific case, 'choosing the right model'. Whether it is theory on inflation, competition, or international trade, students should have a basic factual overview of the world these models help to explain, in order for them to be able to judge the usefulness of a certain theory. This building block provides students with basic knowledge of this kind, as well as the tools, familiarity, and confidence necessary to go out and acquire more of it.

It might seem that this eats into the time available for teaching theories and methods, and in the short run, this is true. However, the teaching of theories and methods is also greatly helped by connecting them to the actual economy and basic facts. An example is when we teach the IS-LM model in a macroeconomics 101 course. It is much more interesting for students to discuss how recent developments can be understood through this model, rather than just discussing it in abstract and applying it to imaginary textbook examples. This will activate the theories in their minds, helping them understand and retain the knowledge, rather than just pushing through the exam and forgetting it all again.

After this introduction, we discuss several categories of basic facts that any expert of an economy should be acquainted with. Secondly, we suggest various economic institutions that seem worthwhile spending some time on. Thirdly, we present sectors as a useful object of study, in order to get a better understanding of an economy. Finally, we explore how these various elements could be taught within a limited timeframe and in a sensible combination, offering some practical teaching tools as well.

Scope: Time & Geographical Scale

What are the temporal and geographic limits of 'your own economy'? Any answer to this question will be somewhat arbitrary. Still, this building block requires at least a working delineation, which this box provides.

In terms of a geographic scope, we generally suggest taking the national level as a point of departure for most of this material. Many – perhaps even most – key economic institutions are organised at that level. However, where aspects of economic systems are primarily organised at a local or a global level, that should be the point of departure.

It is also valuable to help students understand how the various geographical scales interact with each other through complex networks. In order to understand how the food provisioning of a small town works, one will likely end up analysing several global value chains that stretch far beyond the national borders. Hence, our proposal is, in sum: start at the national level, and make excursions to smaller and larger scales where this seems fitting.

In terms of the temporal scope, this building block focuses explicitly on the current state of the economy. The next building block, *Economic History*, looks into the past, whereas the final two building blocks of this book, *Problems & Proposals* and *Economics for a Better World*, are more future-oriented. As noted in the introduction, each of these building blocks is not necessarily a separate course: they can be fruitfully woven together, as the needs and circumstances of the programme require.

1 Key Indicators

Any expert should be familiar with the basic facts of their field. This also applies to economists: basic facts should be part of their training. When discussing such facts, it is important to help students understand how they are measured and constructed, and what applications and limitations they thus have. As different measurements are insightful for different problems, providing students information on various forms of basic economic data can help them interpret the presented 'facts' in any given discussion. Besides learning about key indicators, students should also develop a basic understanding of what things statistics generally leave out (for example by using material from the book *The Uncounted* by Cobham). This will allow them to develop a better understanding of the meaning and relevance of the indicators discussed below. It will also show students something of the power structures that are implicit in the type of statistics that we collectively choose to gather and the importance we assign to each of them.

So, what basic facts should be taught? We suggest six categories: Production, Finance, Wellbeing, Inequality, Nature & Resources, and Demography.

Production

This category covers the most typical economic statistics and national accounts, such as GDP, inflation, unemployment, exports and imports, and government income and expenditure. But there are many more statistics of interest, including levels of productivity, consumption, investment, profits and wages. To get a better understanding of how the labour market is organised, one could also take a look at the amounts of full-time versus part-time workers, permanent versus temporary contracts, and self-employed workers. Another interesting aspect to look at is the size of the informal economy and the amount of unpaid labour in an economy. In many countries, data on this can be fairly easily found in concise reports and datasets of national or international bureaux of statistics.

Finance

Since the global financial crisis of 2007-2008, it has become increasingly clear that financial metrics are not only interesting in themselves, but also crucial for the larger economy. Along with the aforementioned traditional statistics, it can thus be helpful to look at key financial data, such as household, corporate and public debt levels, gold, land and housing prices, sectoral financial balances, the money supply, and net and gross capital flows.

Wellbeing

While the aforementioned economic and financial statistics are important, there are increasingly strong arguments that we should pay more attention to the broader wellbeing of people, rather than solely their position in relation to the market. Most notably, GDP is often criticised for not being a satisfactory measure or proxy for economic success. As a result, new measurements have been developed to better capture this. One approach is to ask people how happy they are in order to capture their subjective well-being, or life-satisfaction (see for example the United Nations' World Happiness Reports). Another increasingly prominent approach is to create a broad dashboard of indicators capturing different aspects of human wellbeing, from the prevalence of crime and life expectancy, to leisure time, educational attainment and the level of social support (see for example the OECD Better Life Index).

Inequality

While all of the above statistics deal with aggregates, differences are just as important. Economic inequality, in income as well as in wealth, significantly shapes economic dynamics in a society. Inequality also materialises based on gender, ethnicity, education, age and in many countries, location. What different socio-economic classes could be distinguished, and what are the proportional sizes of the upper, middle and working classes? How many (children) live in poverty? In the UK, the Great British Class Survey provides a good starting point for such questions.

Information on financial inequality becomes increasingly relevant when coupled with information on its real world impacts. Discuss with students: in your society, what is for sale, besides the usual consumer goods? Quality education? Healthcare? Political influence? Physical safety? To what degree does economic purchasing power equal social or political power? In some countries, millionaires can buy all the goods they want, while quality of life and effective civil rights are still fairly equally distributed. In other countries, personal wealth can make the difference between life or death, between standing above the law or being crushed by the system.

Nature & Resources

This category is relevant for understanding both the physical requirements and the ecological implications of economic growth. Core data include levels of biodiversity, nitrogen and phosphorus loading, and water quality. Carbon footprint statistics provide a useful proxy for economic impacts on the environment. Furthermore, there is an increasing set of indicators which used to be mainly of environmental interest, but which are now gaining increasing economic relevance. For instance, the rapid degradation of the fertile soil layer on farmland worldwide is acutely relevant for the production of basic goods such as paper, clothing and nearly every type of food. Likewise, information on veins of mineable metals and other minerals, including their locations and remaining stocks, is becoming more and more important. Industrial Ecology programmes and journals provide useful data and analytical tools to engage with such questions. The Planetary Boundaries reports of the Stockholm Resilience Center form another good teaching tool, as do materials from the national ministry of the environment.

Demography

Finally, demography is a well-developed field that deals with statistics on the core of any society and economy: populations of human beings. Knowledge about this is foundational for understanding how groups of people organise economic life. Giving students a basic understanding of the following aspects can be particularly informative: population size, degree of urbanisation, migration, household structures, and the age structure of the population.

A more general point: all the aforementioned statistics only become meaningful when they are placed in context and compared. They may be compared across geographies: for example, between countries or regions, between sectors, or over time so that developments, changes and trends can be identified. They can be placed in context by comparing them to targets, such as the international climate goals. In addition, it is particularly useful to expose students to the different metrics and measurements used for these topics. For example, comparing wellbeing indicators and GDP or the different ways to measure inequality. Finally, these topics are also very well-suited to introducing different theoretical perspectives and the debates amongst them. See for example the topic *Money* in the chapter *Tool 1: Pragmatic Pluralism* for different perspectives on the role of debt and money in the economy.

We are well aware that this is a long list of basic knowledge. Please keep in mind that it is provided as inspiration, not as something that needs to be taught in full, nor as a comprehensive list. We suggest selecting from this list only those statistics that seem most relevant to the particular focus of your programme. Another way to save time is the *pars pro toto* approach. That is: introduce a certain field of knowledge – say, *nature* – and then zoom in on only one or two datasets from that field. Students are then aware of the existence of the wider field, and know their way to factual overviews when they need them.

One may question, to conclude this section, is all this not common knowledge? While we might expect economics students (or professors) to know most of these things, we encourage you to hold a brief quiz in class or among colleagues to clear any doubt. The results may be quite surprising.

2 Institutions

Understanding how an actual economy functions, requires a basic overview of its most important institutions: public and private. In the below overview, we focus on the legal and official frameworks, main roles and activities of key organisations, how they work internally, how they interact with other organisations and how influential they are. In this section, it is worthwhile to also spend some time on the question of economic power structures: which groups within society are relatively powerful, and what mechanisms or structures form the basis of their power?

The public sector will have different forms in different countries, and materials from politics courses may be helpful to give a brief overview of how the various forms of government function in your own economy. Generally, important roles are played at the national level by ministries such as the Treasury/Finance, Economy/Commerce, Social Affairs, Infrastructure, Agriculture and Foreign Affairs. Subsequently there are different ways in which the country is divided and governed, for example at the state, province or city level. At all these levels there will be various public institutions such as the central bank and executive institutions such as the tax authorities.

Another important set of organisations are national policy institutes that influence and shape public policies and the discussions surrounding them. Every country has different policy institutions, ranging from governmental policy bureaux, such as *the Bureau for Economic Policy Analysis* in the Netherlands and *the Council of Economic Advisors* in the US, to private think tanks, such as *the New Economics Foundation* in the UK and *the Brookings Institute* in the US.

Other key non-state institutions are the so-called 'corporatist' institutions, such as labour unions and employers associations. Around them we find various bodies which help these parties come to agreements, local, national and international such as *the Social Economic Council* in the Netherlands and *the European Economic and Social Committee* in the *European Union*. At the global level, *the World Trade Organisation, International Monetary Fund, Bank for International Settlements*, and *World Bank*, for example, play an important role.

Another important set of institutions close to, but separate from the state is the civil society, which includes consumer organisations and professional associations. In many countries of the global south, the (foreign) NGO sector similarly plays a key role.

The structure of the private sector is fundamentally influenced by the state through the legal frameworks it sets. Details of the tax system and corporate law are arguably too vast to be taught in economics courses; however, a basic overview of the various forms that private entities can take, such as the corporation, general partnerships and self-employment, and their legal rights and obligations, can help students to better understand the economic playing field. Besides these foundational legal aspects, it can be helpful to give a basic overview of how the state structures the economy through its social security system, regulatory system, research and innovation policy, the provisioning of healthcare and education, and the monetary policy by central banks.

We suggest keeping this overview rather basic and factual, leaving much of the deeper theoretical insights and implications to *Building Block 5: Economic Organisations & Mechanisms, Building Block 6: Political-Economic Systems* and *Building Block 8: Economic Theories*. Alternatively, those two building blocks can be integrated with this one in a longer or more advanced course. Nevertheless, the basics of such an overview are part of this early building block, as a minimal overview of at least (supra-) government agencies and legal and corporatist frameworks helps students to gain a fuller picture of what an actual economy looks like.

3 Sectors

Before embarking on a wide range of theoretical and methodological abstraction, as set out in the following building blocks, students might start with gaining a concrete image of at least one economic sector, as a tangible point of reference. This could be coupled with a broad grasp of the other sectors making up the economy as a whole. In this section, we take the energy sector as an example and provide several perspectives from which to analyse sectors: physical, institutional, technological, and (geo-)political and ethical.

The physical structure of a sector can provide a practical and tangible first analysis. For example, in the energy sector households and firms are connected to large networks of electricity and gas lines, which are fed by major power plants and mining sites inside and outside the country.

Subsequently, the institutional arrangement may be considered: both locally and internationally. For example, in the Netherlands, the network is state-run, and the supply companies are a few large private firms, albeit heavily regulated. There is also a growing sector of smaller non-profit, self-sufficient producers, such as local energy cooperatives. At the same time, the sector is embedded in global value chains. For energy, we find this in mining, extraction and refinement, which is mostly done by globally operating firms. This takes physical shape in drilling sites, connected by giant gas and oil sea vessels and a global network of large pipelines to refineries.

In turn, we can analyse the sector from a technological perspective: what are the main technologies used, and how (un-)evenly is this technological know-how distributed across the globe?

This naturally yields a final discussion of (geo-)political and ethical issues at play in the sector. For example, if gas is found in, say, Ivory Coast, it is likely that French, American, Dutch and British companies compete to dig it up, since these are at the technological forefront in that sector. Is that fair? For energy, other critical points are climate change and geopolitical conflicts, such as the tug-of-war between Russia and the EU around the supply of Russian gas.

With such concrete knowledge of various economic sectors, the more abstract theoretical models taught in the economics programme will both be much more interesting and useful to students. After all, it is the central mechanisms and structures of such economic sectors that these models are designed to capture and to summarise.

For inspiration on other sectors that could be covered, a useful overview is the International Standard Industrial Classification. One interesting exercise might be to divide students in groups among several of these sectors, let each group investigate its own sector, and then present their findings in class to each other.

4 Practical Suggestions

A well-known teaching technique that can be applied is to bring the material closer to the everyday experiences of students. This is especially useful for our discipline, as it is often deemed a very abstract field – unjustly so, in our eyes. For example, what does it mean to earn $20 a month compared to say $20.000? This is not merely a matter of learning some statistics, it is about developing an appropriate perception and sense of economic concepts (in this case a low versus high income) and how they impact people's lives.

An excellent tool for this is the Dollar Street: a highly graphical, beautifully designed comparison between levels of material welfare in countries worldwide, developed by the Gapminder Foundation. On this website, you can digitally visit the homes of families in sixty countries around the world with monthly incomes between $20 and $20.000 per month, to experience their standard of living and the astounding reality of contemporary globalisation. We would very much recommend having a look at this as it is one of the most tangible visualisations of economics out there.

A more straightforward statistical approach, but nevertheless also highly informative, would be to let students check where they, or their parents, fall within the national and global income and wealth distributions. As human beings, we all have the tendency to think of our own situation as normal and average. For most economics students, especially in the Western world, this will, however, not be the case. Doing such an exercise can thus give students a better understanding of their own position in the world and of how their economic experiences relate to those of others.

The same can be done for a personal ecological footprint, using an online footprint calculator. For a more involved exercise, students could be asked to map and compare their opportunities for future life and career, access to education, personal network, cultural and social capital, and so forth.

Besides reading and number-crunching, students could get in contact with actual people in the economy. This can be done by sending students to firms and organisations to talk to the people who work there, or asking non-academic experts or practitioners to give a guest lecture. Such interactions give students a much richer picture of the economy, as it allows for a transfer of practical, tacit and insider knowledge, which statistics are unable to capture.

In general, we suggest varying between focusing on in-depth knowledge about a particular institution or sector, and focusing on developing a rough understanding and overview. The former allows for detailed knowledge on how actual processes work, while the latter gives one an understanding of how the bigger picture looks. Which sectors or institutions will be analysed is not of major importance. The main thing is that students learn how to analyse a metric, an institution or a sector, and acquire some points of entry.

To recap, this building block should be seen as a general invitation to pay considerable attention to how actual economic systems look in their concrete forms. We have suggested a couple of specific ways to go about it, just to make our suggestions more tangible and concrete. But we are under no illusions that these would be the only or even the best ways to teach such material. Our suggestions should rather function as inspiration to develop a program and a locally grounded approach to teaching economics students about the real world.

Teaching Materials

It is hard to suggest specific teaching material for this building block, as its contents will vary so much between different regions and countries. To give some idea of what kind of materials could be used to teach students about their own economy, we provide some example materials on the Dutch economy.

The following three books seem to be most useful when teaching students about the Dutch economy:

- *De Economie in Nederland: Theorie en Werkelijkheid [The Economy in the Netherlands: Theory and Reality]* by Hans Buunk, most recent edition from 2011. A highly informative and accessible introduction into the Dutch economy as well as basic economic concepts, covering topics such as Dutch capitalist history, market competition, finance, industrial and social policy, and labour relations.
- *Sociale Kaart van Nederland: Over Instituties en Organisaties [The Social Map of the Netherlands: About Institutions and Organizations]* by Jan W. Duyvendak, Carolien Bouw, Klarita Gërxhani, and Olav Velthuis, most recent edition from 2013. An unique and accessible overview of Dutch society that introduces students to its many different domains and how they are structured, from education, healthcare, and housing, to business, labour and social security.
- *Varieties of Capitalism and Business History: The Dutch Case* by Keetie E. Sluyterman, from 2015. This collection of essays explores the Dutch variety of capitalism and institutions, with special attention to its labour relations, corporate governance, inter-firm relations, knowledge infrastructure, and its famous corporatist consultative *'polder model'*.

Besides books, it can be useful for students to look up statistics and read reports on economic sectors and issues. Naturally, national statistical authorities are a good place to look for these, but economic ministries, central banks, and policy research institutions, can also be helpful for finding useful material. For the Netherlands, one could have a look at the websites of *Centraal Bureau voor de Statistiek [Central Agency for Statistics]*, *De Nederlandsche Bank [Dutch Central Bank]*, *Centraal Planbureau [Bureau for Economic Policy Analysis]*, *Planbureau voor de Leefomgeving [Netherlands Environmental Assessment Agency]*, *Sociaal en Cultureel Planbureau [Netherlands Institute for Social Research]*, and *Wetenschappelijke Raad voor het Regeringsbeleid [Scientific Council for Government Policy]*.

Furthermore, domestic journals can often be useful as they frequently do not only publish general academic work but also research describing particularities of the national economy and its issues. For the Netherlands, the following three journals have plenty of interesting and helpful material: *Economisch Statistische Berichten [Economic Statistical Messages]*, *MeJudice*, and *Tijdschrift voor Politieke Ekonomie [Journal for Political Economy]*.

Depending on the program, one could also look for more specialised material that does not cover the economy in general, but focuses on a specific element or aspect of it. In a master programme on public economics in the Netherlands, the following two books could, for example, be of use:

- *Overheidsfinanciën [Public finance]* by Flip de Kam, Wimar Bolhuis en Jasper Lukkezen, from 2021.
- *De rekenmeesters van de politiek [The math masters of politics]* by Wimar Bolhuis, from 2017.

Finally, one could also use more opinionated but still informative materials on the economy or an economic issue. For the Netherlands, the following recent books, and chapters from it, could, for example, serve this purpose:

- *Over de dijken [Over the dikes]* by Coen Teulings, from 2018.
- *Een land van kleine buffers [A country of small reserves]* by Dirk Bezemer, from 2020.
- *Fantoomgroei [Phantom growth]* by Sander Heijne en Hendrik Noten, from 2020.
- *Met ons gaat het nog altijd goed [We are still doing well]* by Peter Hein van Mulligen, 2020.
- *Ontspoord Kapitalisme [Derailed Capitalism]* by Bert de Vries, from 2020.

Building Block 3
Economic History

The history of how the economy evolved over time, from the physical aspects of technology and nature to the social aspects of organisations, institutions and political-economic systems.

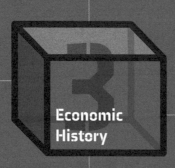

1
Scope:
Time &
Geographical Scale

2
Physical Aspects
of History:
Technological
Change & Nature

3
Social Aspects
of History:
Organisations,
Institutions &
Political-Economic
Systems

Economic
History

4
Practical
Suggestions

What

Economic history is about the evolution of real-world economies, rather than the history of economic thought (see for this *Building Block 4: History of Economic Thought & Methods*). This building block focuses on what happened, how, and what effects it had. It helps students gain a basic understanding of the histories of different real-world economies and to learn from the past.

Why

The evolution of economies throughout history is a fascinating and motivating field, full of drama and action. It is also highly valuable for anyone trying to understand the current economy: history can provide great insight into how economic processes work and how today has come about. Finally, a good understanding of what has happened in the past can also help us understand what may happen in the future.

Economists have claimed, repeatedly, to have solved the economic problems of the past, such as booms and busts. Recent history, however, shows us that this is far from the truth. Many of the key issues of our time – financial instability, trade wars, economic inequality – are far from new. So, let us learn from the past to help us better understand how we can tackle the problems of today.

Contrast with current programmes

Currently, the history of the economy is often not taught in programmes. Some even argue that past events and structures are relevant only to historians, while economists should focus on the present. Consequently, economists lack historical knowledge. We propose teaching future generations of economists the basics of how economies have evolved and avoiding the (over)use of abstract models and econometric techniques.

"Nobody can hope to understand the economic phenomena of any, including the present, epoch who has not an adequate command of the historical facts and an adequate amount of historical sense."

Joseph Schumpeter (1954, pp. 12-13)

On August 13, 2007, as Goldman Sachs was making unprecedented losses, David Alan Viniar said "We were seeing things that were 25 standard deviation moves, several days in a row" (Conti-Brown, 2009). As the chief financial officer and executive vice president of Goldman Sachs at the time, Viniar used this statistical jargon to describe the ongoing events. His statement reflects, however, a severe lack of historical knowledge, leaving him unable to comprehend the economic phenomena he was part of.

His statement was based on an econometric model which Goldman Sachs used to analyse developments on financial markets. The model's estimate that the events of that week were *"25 standard deviation moves, several days in a row"*, suggested they were supposed to happen only once every 1.3×10^{136} years (Conti-Brown, 2009). To put this into perspective, the universe is estimated to be some 13 billion years old, 1.3×10^{10}. Viniar's workhorse model told him that what he was witnessing day after day was not supposed to happen in many lives of this universe.

A basic historical awareness of the fact that financial crises are periodically recurring would have helped this chief financial officer to comprehend the events he was witnessing. In general, a basic grasp of history is crucial to developing a sense of what is possible. Hence, we propose including economic history into economics programmes.

In this building block, we suggest a few dimensions to consider when designing courses on the history of economies. Different programmes will require different things in this regard, and the interests and personal expertise of the lecturer also make a big difference. Here, we hope to help lay out several options and to highlight the potential benefits and drawbacks of various choices. In *Tool 4: Example Curricula*, we provide illustrations of how one could use some of these options to create separate courses, or combine them with other building blocks to create new courses.

1 Scope: Time & Geographical Scale

When teaching history, it is important to first delineate a clear geographical and temporal scope. Geographically, the global, regional and national scales can provide useful delineations. Temporally, one might look either at the entirety of human history, at the last few centuries or at very recent developments. These various scopes can of course also be combined or taught in sequence. This is, after all, just a framework for course design.

Naturally, the larger the scale, the less room there is for detail. So, while students would benefit much from developing a basic understanding of world history, we would not advise spending equal time on each period of history. Instead, we suggest alternating between discussing very big topics in broad terms and treating smaller episodes in more detail. It is a balancing act, between having an historical overview of economies and understanding the complexity and nuance of changes in economies.

A brief note on teaching very recent developments. It is a misconception that history is only about long-gone days. History means concrete events and phenomena in the past, whether they occurred a long time ago or recently. Recent history, too, can be very useful for economists, as it helps them understand the situations they find themselves in today.

An important example of this for the current generation of economics students would be the history of the financial and economic crisis of the last decade. While most of us have kept track of major events in our lives, very few have a good understanding of precisely what happened in that crisis. Therefore, it could be useful to discuss in detail the events and developments of the last decade, using for example 'Crashed' by Adam Tooze.

Such recent histories are very important because they provide sophisticated and rich analyses of what happened, as opposed to the often simplistic and partial accounts that are prevalent in many debates around even the most recent events. As future economic experts, this can teach students how crucial it is to have a factual overview and contextualisation of phenomena in order to be able to grasp them. Furthermore, recent histories can show students how multidimensional economic events are and how useful a multidisciplinary approach is, as it also takes political, social and cultural factors into consideration.

We are aware that the advice above is quite general while this building block is, by nature, rather location- and time-specific. Exactly which aspects of history are most relevant also depends on the focus of each programme. We hope that the framework offered here can still prove useful in terms of selecting an appropriate scope and relevant historical episodes.

2 Physical Aspects of History: Technological Change & Nature

Having chosen a temporal and geographical scope, we suggest course designers split up the material into two aspects of history, and deal with them both explicitly: the physical and the social. The physical aspect refers to how human beings interact with their natural environment and the technologies they use. The social aspect, on the other hand, refers to how people together organise their economic lives through work, organisations, economic mechanisms, institutions and political-economic systems. The two are clearly related to each other and could very well be combined into a single storyline. Nevertheless, we think it is important to focus on both sides, as each captures different elements of history.

In terms of the physical aspect of the history of economies, there are three angles that seem particularly relevant: dominant forms of production, technological innovation, and relationship with nature.

Firstly, the dominant forms of production. Technologies have fundamentally changed economies, and with them, human life multiple times in history. The main story, in this regard, is that human societies moved from hunter-gathering, to horticulture, to agriculture and finally into industrial production. Many places, however, retained fishing, herding and maritime societies, which also played important roles in the world history of the economy. It is therefore important to teach students about how these different economies functioned. A useful book on this is *Human societies* by Nolan and Lenski.

Secondly, technological innovation. Given that technological change has often been a driving force of economic change, it is worthwhile to give students an idea of how technologies have developed over time. Which waves of innovation have characterised the last centuries and how did they alter economic processes? How did these innovations come about and how did the knowledge of them spread? To discuss these matters, a helpful and accessible book is *A Short History of Technology* by Thomas Kingston Derry and Trevor Illtyd Williams.

Finally, nature. Throughout most of human history, human societies and, in particular, their economies were largely shaped by their natural surroundings. Today, this relationship has become a two-way street, as human beings are having an enormous impact on natural ecosystems and Earth's geology. It is crucial that students develop an understanding of how this happened. One could discuss questions such as: How have energy consumption and land use changed over time? Which countries and organisations have contributed most to these developments? How has the use of different energy sources changed throughout history, including recent development related to renewable energy? What policy measures have been taken over the last decades to tackle environmental and ecological problems? Who has historically paid the biggest economic and social price for humans' extractive use of nature? Useful books to discuss these issues are *Energy and Civilization: A History* by Vaclav Smil and *Climate Change: A Very Short Introduction* by Mark Maslin.

3 Social Aspects of History: Organisations, Institutions & Political-Economic Systems

Having considered the physical aspects of economic history, it is important to also teach the social aspects. Here we suggest looking at the differing ways in which humans have socially organised economic processes: through different organisational forms, institutions and political-economic systems. For an overview of these, see building blocks 5 and 6: respectively *Economic Organisations & Mechanisms* and *Political-Economic Systems*. Knowing how societies moved from one political-economic system to another is imperative. Yet, it is also valuable to develop an understanding of how political-economic systems themselves changed. So, for example, one could discuss how capitalism was deeply intertwined with colonialism, slavery, patriarchy, and imperialism – but later on became associated with the welfare state and representative democracy. These are all complicated issues that deserve attention in courses on the history of the economy. For this one can use different teaching materials, from academic readings to documentaries such the DW documentary *Slavery routes – a short history of human trafficking*.

Recent history is again of particular importance here. How have political-economic systems changed over the last decades? How have the social structures and power relations of the economy changed with developments such as globalisation, neoliberalism, financialization, and digitisation? To give an example, one could look at the history of markets as Bas van Bavel (2016) did in *The Invisible Hand?: How Market Economies have Emerged and Declined Since AD 500*. Van Bavel documents how markets became more dominant in various societies at points in history, but also how markets over time lost their importance in determining how economies were run. In this book, he analysed how different economic mechanisms interacted with each other and how power relations in societies changed.

4 Practical Suggestions

More concretely, how can this subject best be fitted into a curriculum? One way is to devote entire courses to the subject, but it can also be incorporated into existing courses along with other subjects.

An economic history course could, for example, mainly focus on the physical and social history of the global economy, while connecting it to the history of the national economy of the country where the course is taught. In a specialised graduate programme, it makes sense to focus specifically on the topic of the programme. For instance, in a graduate degree on financial economics the scope might be narrower, zooming in on financial history, rather than treating the history of the economy more broadly.

Besides teaching it as a stand-alone course, some historical background can add value to other courses. For example, a course on labour economics would be enriched by starting with an overview of labour history before delving into specific theories. Such an introduction into a course gives students a clear idea of the real-world phenomena they will be studying in that course. That is, history is not simply used to illustrate theory, but to provide students with a basic understanding of the actual phenomena that the theories try to wrestle with.

Introducing a topic through its historical background will also increase students' motivation, especially when recent history is discussed. Virtually every course, whether it focuses upon economic development, firms, public policy or markets, could benefit from devoting some space to the history of the topic.

Teaching Materials

- *Capitalism: A Short History* by Jürgen Kocka, from 2016. A concise and yet broad-ranging account of how capitalism developed from early merchants, colonialism and slavery to the recent wave of globalisation and financialisation, accompanied by discussions of capitalism's key thinkers, such as Smith, Marx, Weber, and Schumpeter.
- *Economics: The User's Guide* by Ha-Joon Chang, from 2014, chapters 2 & 3. Two short and well written chapters on how the economy has changed over the last centuries and how capitalism evolved.

- *Global Economic History: A Very Short Introduction* by Robert C. Allen, from 2011. A brief but insightful introduction into the economic history of the world with chapters on industrialisation, the rise of the West, great empires, the Americas and Africa.
- *An Economist's Guide to Economic History* by Matthias Blum and Christopher L. Colvin, from 2018. A useful collection of short essays on the economic histories of many different regions, periods, methods and topics, from globalisation and labour markets to the environment and children.
- *A History of the Global Economy: 1500 to the Present* by Joerg Baten, from 2016. A broad collection of essays on the histories of the different regions in the world, with chapters on the economic consequences of independence in Latin America, US business history and the workings and impact of colonial empires in Africa and Asia.
- Besides these global histories, it can be particularly useful to look up materials on national economic history. For the Netherlands, for example, this book would be useful: *The Economic History of The Netherlands 1914-1995: A Small Open Economy in the 'Long' Twentieth Century* by Jan L. van Zanden, from 1997.

Visit the website for a wider range of teaching materials, to provide feedback, and to exchange ideas and ask support from colleagues worldwide.
economy.st/bb3

Building Block 4
History of Economic Thought & Methods

The history of ideas about the economy, from theories to methods, from mainstream and heterodox economics to other disciplines studying the economy.

1
The Discipline
of Economics

2
Interdisciplinary
Economics

History of
Economic
Thought &
Methods

3
Methods

4
Practical
Suggestions

What

This building block lays out the history of ideas about the economy. This includes the history of economics as a discipline, both mainstream and heterodox, as well as how other disciplines have analysed the economy over time. It also covers the different methods used throughout the history of the discipline. Since intellectual developments never take place in a vacuum, we suggest coupling this history of ideas with the historical contexts in which they evolved as described in *Building Block 3: Economic History*.

Why

History of thought about the economy is a crucial element in the training of future economists, for two reasons. First, it helps to structure and understand current ideas. It enables students to organise and group the various insights they gain, by giving them an overview of their shared roots. This helps students to develop a more direct or personal relationship to economic ideas and theories, as well as prominent (economic) thinkers. Second, it shows that the current paradigm is not the only way to think about the economy and that ideas about the economy change over time. This encourages critical thinking and provides students with fresh insights from a broad set of ideas, old and new.

Contrast with current programmes

Generally, economic programmes today hardly include any history of economic thought, and where they do, we propose a broader history of economic thought than is usually taught. The scope we suggest is the history of ideas around the economy, rather than the history of how today's mainstream academic discipline (economics) came to be. That includes ideas from both orthodox and heterodox economics, as well as from other social science sub-disciplines such as economic sociology, economic anthropology and economic geography.

"We cannot help living in history.
We can only fail to be aware of it."

Robert Heilbroner (1960, p. 209)

Throughout most of his study programme, one of the authors of this book experienced economic theory largely as an unstructured cloud of individual models, papers, names and methods. He perfectly well understood each of these on its own, and was well aware that they all dealt with similar types of subject matter. But he found it difficult to see how it all connected to each other.

It was only when he followed a (relatively short) online course in history of economic thought, that this amorphous mass of ideas and techniques began to take a defined shape. Central principles emerged. Ideas began to group themselves. As the fog lifted, a clear structure became visible: all those unconnected models and names turned out to be the many branches of a few large trees, connected at the base in their common roots.

In our view, this is the main purpose of teaching history of economic thought: to give students an overview of the larger structure, a coat rack upon which to hang the ideas presented throughout the programme. It is also an excellent opportunity to include critical thinking, as different perspectives can be compared and contrasted.

The purpose of a course on economic history is not to teach 'forgotten theories'. If they were unjustly forgotten, we suggest teaching them in theory and topic courses based on their contemporary value, not as historical relics. Nor is it to show how history inexorably leads up to the current set of mainstream ideas, as the best incarnation of economic thinking to date.

If anything, we propose a history of economic thought that shows how ideas clash, how schools of thought compete and how the winner is not always the most useful or insightful one. Politics, power, personalities and pure luck play a large role in this, as any good historian of economic thought will make abundantly clear.

We thus simply propose to expose students to this diverse and complex history, rather than trying to present some simple linear story of progress which leaves out many crucial and fascinating parts of the history. In this way, a history of economic thought can help students to understand what lies behind different economic ideas and debates, enabling them to make their own judgments as economists.

Such a genealogy of ideas is useful for all students, a structure in which they can house the various individual tools gained throughout the programme. But there is one group for whom it is especially valuable: those going into research roles themselves. An economist who only reads current publications and is ignorant of the economic ideas developed before them, is awkwardly at risk to spend enormous amounts of time and energy to reinvent the wheel. In addition, they are far more likely to lack crucial critical thinking skills. Understanding the ideas and their contexts will on the other hand give students a broader perspective of economic ideas and allow them to see it in a more holistic manner. This is crucial in the making of future economists, where they are better equipped to make judgement of current economic ideas and debates. A financial employer of UK economists argued economics programmes should start with the history of economic thought as the great economists of the past *"have a large amount to tell us about how economies are run"* (Yurko, 2018, p. 11).

For conceptual convenience, we divide the historical material into three different sections in this chapter. We start with the discipline of economics. The next section highlights several valuable ways of studying the economy, which currently have a home in other social disciplines. The third section deals with the history of methods. However, we do not necessarily advocate using these categories to organise a course. They are simply heuristic devices. In the last section of the building block, we do discuss various ways to structure courses.

1 The Discipline of Economics

When teaching students about the history of the discipline of economics, it is important to expose students to the diversity by which it is characterised. We will emphasise two different expressions of diversity here: diversity in terms of people and diversity in terms of ideas.

Firstly, it is important to recognise the diversity in terms of people in the history of economic thought. Since most societies were, and still are, dominated by white males, it is perhaps no surprise that the same applies to economics. Therefore, it is important to ensure that the many relevant contributions of female and non-white thinkers are not ignored. In terms of including schools of thought, for this reason it seems particularly important to include approaches such as feminist and structuralist economics. But the point goes beyond this. There have been many important contributions from female and non-white thinkers in almost every approach. Thus, we need to actively include a larger diversity of thinkers into curricula, and go beyond the old, limited, set of white male economists.

This already starts at the roots of the discipline: do we teach Adam Smith (1776) as the founder of the discipline, or Ibn Khaldun (1377), who outlined early theories of division of labour, taxes, scarcity, economic growth, and the origins and causes of poverty? Subsequently we find that histories are currently often presented as exclusively male. This is not quite accurate. Ursula Webb Hicks and Vera Smith Lutz, for example, made highly influential contributions to neoclassical economics throughout the twentieth century, in particular with regards to the role of banking in economic development (Brillant, 2018). There are also important more recent thinkers, male and female, from the Global North and Global South, such as Jayati Ghosh and Thandika Mkandawire, who are critical of the neoclassical approach to economic development, international economics and macroeconomic policy. It is imperative that we include such examples in the story of economic thinking that we tell students.

Besides discovering the diversity of voices, students should become familiar with the diversity of economic theory. We suggest not to focus exclusively on one school of thought or the mainstream of the discipline, but rather to showcase debates between different points of view and include discussions of dissent thinkers as well as the dominant paradigms at points in time. As such, it does not suffice to tell the typical story, starting from the classical political economists, moving to the birth of neoclassical economics, the Keynesian revolution and finally to the formation of the modern discipline after the second world war. While each of these episodes are important in the history of the discipline, this story leaves out many crucial elements.

Students would, for example, miss the fact that the historical school, in particular its German branch, was highly influential during the 19th century. Not only in terms of theoretical and empirical work, but also in terms of influencing actual policies of countries; by placing the state at the centre of its analysis. This strand of thought, in turn, was crucial for the emergence of institutional economics in the United States. This approach also significantly contributed to the theoretical, empirical and policy work that economists engage in. These are just two examples. It would also ignore the long history of Marxian and Austrian economic thought, and more recent history of structuralist, ecological, behavioural, evolutionary, feminist and complexity economics.

A course cannot practically cover every approach in detail; rather, the goal should be to make clear to students that there exist many different and sometimes conflicting ways of thinking about the economy. It is crucial to explicitly discuss these debates and intellectual conflicts that have shaped the history of the discipline. This helps students get a sharp understanding of how approaches differ from each other, place theoretical ideas into perspective and think independently.

One way to do this would be to examine a limited number of intellectual conflicts in a bit more detail. This can help students understand how economic debates work, from the construction of arguments to the importance of institutional power. For example, one could discuss the so-called *Cambridge Capital Controversy* (Cohen & Harcourt, 2003). This was a debate in the 1950's and 1960's between the post-Keynesian economists such as Nicholas Kaldor, Joan Robinson and Piero Sraffa at the University of Cambridge (UK) and the neoclassical economists such as Paul Samuelson, Robert Solow and Franco Modigliani at MIT (US Cambridge, Massachusetts) on whether it makes sense to define capital, as an input of production processes, by its monetary price. Though technical, the debate had far-reaching consequences. For one, the post-Keynesian economists argued that the neoclassical mathematical models of economic growth were internally inconsistent. Although this was admitted to indeed be the case by leading neoclassical economists such as Paul Samuelson, those models did remain in use as they defended them based on their practical usefulness.

Descriptions of such historical skirmishes provide students a view behind the curtain of the discipline, showing how even the most widespread ideas can be fruitfully questioned. To be sure, the point here is not to choose sides when discussing these debates. Students should be given a fair presentation of the different sides of the debates and they should make up their own mind as to which arguments they find more convincing. Learning how to make these kinds of judgments is a key skill economists need to learn that they will require for their future work, so we should help and trigger students to do so, rather than just trying to convince them of one point of view.

2 Interdisciplinary Economics

Economists are not the only ones who have thought about the economy. Many valuable insights into how economic processes work have been developed by other social scientists. If we would solely focus on the ideas of economists, we would thus miss out on important insights. Therefore, it is key that courses on the history of economic thought also include ideas on the economy developed in other disciplines.

There are a number of fields that are of particular importance here: economic sociology, economic geography, economic history, economic anthropology and political economy. These are all sub-disciplines that (typically) exist outside the field of economics but are nevertheless organised around studying the economy. As such, they form important traditions and fields in the history of economic thought and should be taught as such.

Interdisciplinary Economics provides an overview of five neighbouring subdisciplines, such as economic sociology.
economy.st/interdisciplin

Rethinking the History of Economic Thought & Methods provides a more inclusive history of the field, including teaching materials.
economy.st/rethinkinghistory

One way to include these neighbouring disciplines is again by examining a single concept from different perspectives. For example, the meaning of money and value (creation) is one of the economic discipline's main concepts but perceived very differently in the various other fields that study it. Disciplines such as anthropology and sociology, for example, contributed a lot to our understanding of money and value, paying particular attention to social networks, culture and power relations (Carruthers & Ariovich, 2010; Graeber, 2005; Hart, 2005).

Another concept to explore from the perspective of different disciplines is the market. For instance, economic sociologists using a cultural approach have found that market devices, which refer to cognitive tools, technologies and rules of thumb, fundamentally alter economic outcomes, such as prices, rather than only facilitating economic life to be more efficient (MacKenzie et al., 2007). By taking a different approach to the economy, new insights are generated.

A key part of the literature on these market devices focuses on the ideas and mathematical models of economists, which turn out to be crucial market devices that shape economic processes. A good example is how the Black-Scholes-Merton model shaped how derivatives traders priced options (MacKenzie, 2008; MacKenzie & Millo, 2003). While in the beginning the model was fairly weak at empirically describing or predicting how option markets behaved, slowly more and more traders began to use the model. In doing so, it created its own reality as it strongly began to structure option markets and as a result became fairly good at predicting market behaviour for a while. And as such, the market device *performed*, rather than simply described, economic life. Thus, this literature also illustrates the performativity of economics: the study of economics does not simply (try to) reflect the world, but influences and performs upon the world it studies through its methodology.

If the history of economic thought is confined to the ideas of economists, students would not experience these alternative perspectives nor grasp as easily the performativity of economics. Therefore, we advise to include interdisciplinary insights into how economies work in courses on the history of economic thought.

3   Methods

Finally, methods are a crucial aspect of the history of human beings and their understandings of economies. Economic thought is strongly shaped by the methodological tools used to study the economy and, as such, methods are a key aspect of teaching history of economic thought.

Just as with the history of theories, the history of methods is both diverse and complex. Therefore, again, instead of focussing on the technical details, students should acquire a rough understanding of how different methodological approaches developed, evolved over time and in particular conflicted. Exposing students to these debates helps them to think critically about methodological choices made in literature as well as their own.

Students should learn about how the different methods evolved over time and shaped economic thought as a result. A key part of this history is how statistics slowly developed as the economists' method of choice during the 19th and early 20th century. Throughout this period, many different forms of statistical analysis developed and competed with each other as well as other methods, such as interviews and qualitative historical analysis. After the Second World War in particular, a strongly mathematical approach to economics became more and more dominant, and still today skills in mathematics are seen as crucial for success. Students have much to gain by learning about this complicated and fascinating history.

There have been many other clashes of methodological views that one could discuss with students. For example, the *Methodenstreit* during the late 19th century between Austrian economists, such as Carl Menger, who argued for using deductive reasoning, and German economists favouring historical and comparative statistical approaches. Alternatively, there have been many debates about how to best study business cycles throughout the twentieth century between economists such as Wesley Clair Mitchell, Jan Tinbergen, John Maynard Keynes, Milton Friedman and Lawrence Klein. And many recent discussions have been about the use of experimentation and simulation in economics (Maas, 2014).

4   Practical Suggestions

Given the large scope of history, we first advise to focus on particular examples and be selective in terms of geographic or temporal scope. Second we discuss organising the content effectively depending on your goal: either by theoretical approach or chronologically, and in a standalone course or lectures that are part of a broader course. And finally, we consider the need to include the contexts in which ideas developed.

Firstly, it is important to realise that one can never be completely comprehensive. No course will have enough teaching time to discuss all relevant economic thinkers in history. So, how then to focus and select ideas and thinkers to teach? As stated in the introduction of this chapter, we think the history of economic thought can be very useful to help students organise their thinking and be able to place specific ideas in a larger intellectual tree of economic thought. As such, it is important to allow students to develop an understanding of the different branches of this tree. We would therefore advise to make students familiar with the various branches, without necessarily going into great detail into all of them. Next to giving such a broad overview of the history, one could go into more detail into specific debates and ideas to also give students more concrete knowledge and a feeling of the history, rather than studying it as if history was a concatenation of isolated events. Independently of this, one could focus on the history of thought in the country the university is located in. The history of economic thought is often dominated by the UK and US; however, for a programme situated in Brazil, for example, it makes sense to pay particular attention to how economic thinking has evolved there. In general, we should make the history of economic thought less Eurocentric; for instance, why should we teach about Adam Smith as 'the father of economics' while ignoring many others, such as Chanakya and Ibn Khaldun, who wrote about the same topics centuries earlier?

Secondly, there are a number of ways in which courses can be structured. A course can be entirely dedicated to the history of economic thought, but the topic can also be a small part of a broader course (Dow, 2009). In a course on micro or financial economics one could, for example, devote one lecture to the history of the ideas that will be discussed in more detail throughout the course. When teaching a course on the history of economic thought one could organise it by theoretical approaches. One would thus discuss the history of Marxian political economy, followed by the history of neoclassical economics, followed by the history of complexity economics, etc. Another way to organise such a course is to structure it chronologically: first discussing the early history of dispersed individual economic thinkers, subsequently the formation of the discipline and ending with its recent developments.

Thirdly, it can be very helpful to take time to discuss the contexts in which ideas emerged: history of economic thought can be fruitfully combined with economic history as well as broader social, cultural and political history. For instance, Adam Smith's notion of the *division of labour* becomes a more insightful story when coupled with his visit to a proto-factory for pins, one of many small firms arising in that age of early industrialisation. It becomes even more interesting when we add a description of the general economic circumstances of the time; the growing class of landless peasants looking for paid jobs following the enclosures of their commons, and in the background a growing tide of political liberalism.

An interesting teaching technique might be to let students assume the positions of various historical thinkers or schools of thought, and then debate from those positions, in written or spoken form. This can help students practice understanding others and placing themselves in others' shoes, which stimulates active reflection on the topic. Besides teaching them the mental flexibility of understanding and taking on various positions, this also helps to develop their faculties of writing and public speaking.

In addition, students can learn a lot from reading (parts of) original texts, whether it is *The Communist Manifesto* of Marx and Engels (1848), the *Economic Possibilities for our Grandchildren* of Keynes (1930), *The Use of Knowledge in Society* by Hayek (1945), *Equality of What?* by Sen (1979), *How Did Economists Get It So Wrong?* by Krugman (2009) or *Beyond Markets and States: Polycentric Governance of Complex Economic Systems* by Ostrom (2010). This gives students a direct impression of economic debates and helps them understand and reflect upon them. Reading classics is, however, a time intensive task, so it is important not to assign too much text. How much is too much, of course, depends on the teaching level and available teaching time. Our advice is to let students read (small) parts of original texts accompanied with secondary literature and teaching materials on the ideas and history. Besides reading old texts, it can also be insightful for students to watch or listen to old debates and presentations. The two classic television series *The Age of Uncertainty* by John Kenneth Galbraith, originally broadcasted in 1977, and *Free to Choose* by Milton Friedman, originally broadcasted in 1980, for example, give an informative view on the economic debates of the time.

Teaching Materials

- *The Worldly Philosophers: The Lives, Times and Ideas of the Great Economic Thinkers* by Robert Heilbroner, most recent edition from 1999. While first published in 1953, it remains perhaps the best introduction into the history of economic thought to this day. In a remarkably well-written and accessible manner it discusses the ideas of key economists and puts them into historical context.
- *Grand Pursuit: The Story of Economic Genius* by Sylvia Naser, from 2012. Another very accessible but more recent book introducing the history of economic thought through captivating narratives.
- *Economic Methodology: A Historical Introduction* by Harro Maas, from 2014. A well-written and useful book on the history of economic methodology from debates about deduction and induction, statistics, modelling, and experiments in economics.
- *The History of Economic Thought Website* made by INET: http://www.hetwebsite.net/het/. A useful collection of material and discussions of different schools of thought, historical periods and institutions.
- *A Companion to the History of Economic Thought* by Warren J. Samuels, Jeff E. Biddle, and John B. Davis, from 2003. An extensive and detailed collection of contributions covering many periods and developments in the history of economic thought, as well as covering historiography and different ways of approaching that history.
- *Routledge Handbook of the History of Women's Economic Thought* by Kirsten Madden and Robert W. Dimand, from 2019. A unique history of economic thought book focusing on the too often ignored contributions of women around the world.

If one is looking for more standardised textbooks, these three other options might be useful.

- *History of Economic Thought* by David Colander and Harry Landreth, from 2001, is accessible and transparently opinionated, triggering students to think for themselves and form their own opinion.
- *History of Economic Thought* by E. K. Hunt and Mark Lautzenheiser, most recent edition from 2015, is written from an explicitly critical

perspective on the current mainstream profession and reflects upon great thinkers of the past, how today's dominant approach developed and approaches that have been pursued at the margins of the discipline.

- *A History of Economic Theory & Method* by Robert B. Ekelund and Robert F. Hébert, most recent edition from 2016, is the most extensive of the three and covers the classics as well as more innovative topics such as economics' relation to art, religion, archaeology, technology and ideology.

- As with economic history, national history is always particularly relevant. *The Routledge History of Economic Thought* book series can be useful for this, as it contains books on many countries, such as *A History of Indian Economic Thought* by Ajit K. Dasgupta from 2015, *The History of Swedish Economic Thought* by Bo Sandelin, most recent edition from 2012, and *Studies in the History of Latin American Economic Thought* by Oreste Popescu, from 2014.

Visit the website for a wider range of teaching materials, to provide feedback, and to exchange ideas and ask support from colleagues worldwide.
economy.st/bb4

Building Block 5

Economic Organisations & Mechanisms

The different economic organisations and mechanisms – how market, hierarchical, communal, associational, familial and cooperative forms together make up the economy.

1
Forms of
Economic
Organisation

2
Coordination
& Allocation
Mechanisms

Economic
Organisations
& Mechanisms

3
Practical
Suggestions

What

This building block discusses the different ways in which economic processes can be organised. These are the different ways in which people determine how to allocate the limited time and resources available, how to work together to create economic value and subsequently how to distribute it. The focus of this building block is on making students familiar with the variety of organisational forms and ways of interacting with each other that shape how our economies work.

Why

Without an understanding of the variety in the organisations and mechanisms that exist it is very difficult to grasp how an economy works and misunderstandings arise easily. A better grasp of the different ways in which economies are organised will also enable students to think openly, accurately and critically about any proposal to reshape economies.

Contrast with current programmes

Many academic programmes currently focus on markets. Additionally, even when the topic of study is not a market, it is often understood as if it were a market. This causes students to find it hard to think in ways that do not follow market principles. Upon studying a problem, the natural inclination of many economists is to introduce a market or correct a market failure. However, this causes (policy) recommendations to have a *one-size fits all* tendency, and causes many parts of the economy to be unstudied or misunderstood. We therefore encourage introducing and defining a wider range of economic organisations from the start, as well as the different coordination and allocation mechanisms that exist between and within them, examining where they occur, how they differ from each other and how they interrelate.

"The economy is much bigger than the market."

Ha-Joon Chang (2014, p. 456)

Economies consist of many different types of organisations, ranging from multinational corporations to groups of volunteers caring for the elderly, and from small cooperatives to state-run infrastructure companies. Within and between these organisational structures, we find different coordination and allocation mechanisms, such as market transactions, hierarchies, commons, networks and reciprocity. These are all different ways in which people organise themselves to create value – whether monetised or not. Differences in both aspects, the organisational forms as well as the different coordination and allocation mechanisms, yield micro and meso level variations in how an economy is structured and functions.

Among all these economic forms, most contemporary economics programmes focus almost exclusively on market mechanisms. We suggest widening the scope, to include the large real-world variety of economic organisations and mechanisms. Without knowledge of how economic activities are organised, it is virtually impossible to understand how economies work or to give good advice for economic decisions. To be sure, we are not suggesting taxonomy or classification for its own sake. We argue for a better understanding of economic processes by conceptualising the wide diversity in forms.

This building block is closely linked to the next, *Building Block 6: Political-Economic Systems*, as they both focus on the different ways in which economies are organised. However, the current building block focuses more on micro and meso patterns, looking at the various ways in which specific processes can be organised, coordinated and allocated. The next building block has a more macro focus on economies as full systems with complex networks of organisations and mechanisms.

1 Forms of Economic Organisation

Economic systems, like natural ecosystems, are made up of many different forms. Looking around us, we see a large variety of private businesses, cooperatives, governmental organisations, households and forms of non-profit organisations, most of which also exist in informal varieties. These social constructs vary amongst others on the following aspects, which in turn will vary by country:

- Legal form (as defined by the state);
- Main motive or purpose (profit or non-profit);
- Type and number of owners and transferability of ownership (tradable shares, private owners or state);
- Funding (sales, taxation, donations);
- Power structure (centralised or decentralised);
- Size (individual, small, medium, large);
- Geographic scope (local, national, international).

The universal system of taxonomy that biologists use to identify the different species of the natural world does not have an equally well-structured counterpart in economics. Fortunately, becoming familiar with this diversity does not always require much analysis, but it does require looking with an open perspective. To grasp the different forms of economic organisation that exist, students can simply look at the world around them, perhaps using something like the above list of variables. This list is not an existing theoretical framework; we put it together for this building block, and the relevant variables would differ depending on the purpose of the investigation. We will now briefly review the main categories of economic organisations that can be distinguished.

Private businesses are perhaps the most visible type of economic organisations and come in all shapes and forms depending on amongst others ownership (who is the owner and how easily is ownership transferable such as on the stock exchange), their size and whether they act locally, nationally or internationally. *Corporate businesses* for example are large complex legal entities, owned by shareholders (often anonymous underneath a certain threshold and whose shares are freely tradeable) and run by managers. Their employees may be organised through *trade unions* in order to increase their bargaining power and have a voice in how the company is run. In many countries, large corporations are also required by law to have worker representation on corporate boards. Next to corporate businesses, there are various other forms of private businesses. Many companies are privately owned by a *family*, a *partnership* or a *sole proprietor*. It should be noted that family firms are not always small: the ALDI supermarkets, Tata Steel, Koch Industries and Dell are all majority-held by their founding families.

Cooperatives are run in a more direct democratic manner: not by shareholders but by their workers, customers, consumers and/or other stakeholders. These too come in many forms and sizes, ranging from small grocery stores to the Basque giant Mondragon. In *worker cooperatives*, such as Mondragon, the people who work at the company determine how it is run. *Consumer cooperatives*, on the other hand, are owned and managed by customers. These have been especially important in retail and finance such as The UK Co-operative Group and the Swiss Migros. *Producer cooperatives* have been particularly prevalent in agriculture, as they allow relatively small farmers to achieve economies of scale together. Recently, the idea of *multi-stakeholder cooperatives* has become more popular, with the aim to give all relevant groups a voice and seat at the table: from consumers and workers, to producers, investors and members of the local community.

Next to such formal forms of economic organisation exists a large variety of *informal organisations*, which together are generally referred to as the 'informal economy'. This includes all economic activity that is not fully grounded in the legal structures of the state. In the western world, this is relatively limited to particular sectors such as unregistered housekeepers and illegal drug trade networks. In many developing countries, on the other hand, the informal economy covers vast parts of economies. There are various myths surrounding the term, as it is often associated with 'black' markets and 'underground' activities. One should, however, realise that the majority of workers in the world, 61% in 2018, earn their living in the informal economy (ILO). It is not some backwater shadow world, but rather says something about how far the formal systems of state reach.

Most textbooks discuss government mainly as a rule maker, an arbiter and a mechanism of redistribution. While the formal regulations of the state cover only a relatively limited part of the economy in much of the developing world, states are in virtually every country highly important economic producers themselves. The public sector often contributes around half of GDP and *government agencies* conduct massive amounts of economic activity themselves: running hospitals and clinics, schools and universities, the military and police, infrastructure, energy and water systems, and state-owned enterprises in many other sectors.

Another core form of economic organisation is the *household*. While individually, households are fairly small, in sum they are an enormous part of economies. Think of all the unpaid labour, such as care work and housekeeping, that is coordinated and performed inside households. Estimates suggest that household activity may even amount to about half of all economic activities (OECD, 2018). Students should note that the structures and functions of households are different from place to place and from time to time, from the stereotypical *nuclear family* to *single-parent* but also *extended families*. A look at the current situation in terms of household structures in the country can be useful and interesting for students.

Finally, there are also various *civic non-profit organisations*, such as *charities, foundations, community groups*, and *voluntary associations*, which receive donations to work on some cause and/or function on the basis of voluntary unpaid work. Recently, the line between non-profit and for-profit has become more complicated with the rise of *social enterprises*, which in varying complex ways combine social and commercial goals. There are also many *civil society organisations*, or *non-governmental organisations* (NGOs), trying to influence governmental policies. Commercial corporations are again key here, as private business through employers' and trade associations are the most powerful interest groups in many countries.

All the above descriptions refer to very large categories and there are many differences within them. Letting students choose more than one case of each category to look at or analyse can therefore be very useful, as it will show them how companies can be legally very similar yet function very differently in practice. Useful materials to teach about economic organisations in an accessible way are: *Introducing a New Economics, Economics: The User's Guide* and *Organisations: A Very Short Introduction*.

The study of these different organisational forms is not merely an intellectual pastime. The same product or service can be produced by very different types of economic organisations, and this often has far-reaching consequences for all stakeholders, from workers and investors to suppliers and consumers, as well as broader society and the natural environment. A concrete example from the Netherlands: when private equity started buying up child care organisations and transforming their internal organisation, from their services, labour arrangements and scheduling practices to their real estate ownership and lease structuring, this had serious consequences for the way they functioned, sparking societal and academic debate (Dutch Government, 2020; Dutch Parliament, 2019; Roosenboom, 2020; Van Bussel, 2020; Van de Weijenberg, 2018).

2 Coordination & Allocation Mechanisms

The previous section discussed fairly straightforward typologies of economic organisations: forms into which people organise themselves. This section focuses on the more complex underlying coordination and allocation mechanisms between and inside these organisation forms, which decide how people and organisations allocate their time and resources. The two most known of these are market transactions and hierarchical redistribution. There are, however, multiple other mechanisms that, despite their importance in real-world economies, have received less academic and popular attention. These include commons, networks and reciprocity. Students should become familiar with these different ways in which people interact economically with each other in order to understand how economies work.

Markets and Hierarchies

Markets are currently at the core of economics education, and for a good reason, as markets are highly important for how economies operate today. However, due to an abstract theoretical and mathematical approach, relatively little attention is paid to the exact forms that markets take in the real world. Not every market is the same, as markets are made out of social rules and practices that vary from place to place and from time to time. The economic sociology of markets and game theoretical field of mechanism design, in particular, have focused on the concrete ways in which markets are and can be structured. Markets allocate time and resources based on price, money, competition and individual gain. We suggest letting students study examples of different real-world markets in different contexts, identifying the actors, how they are organised and how they interact, so that they can better understand how markets function.

Hierarchical distribution allocates time and resources based on fixed roles and formalised lines of command. It is typically associated with public sector and state entities, but it is also the way in which many organisations within the private sector are organised internally. Although the number of self-employed people has increased over the last decades, most economic activity in the private sector still takes place within hierarchical organisations: private bureaucracies. This form is not restricted to large organisations. Small organisations can also function on the basis of hierarchical distribution. The key differentiating factor from the market is that decisions within such an organisation are made between people based on hierarchical interactions and not based on the price mechanism.

Similarly, entrepreneurship exists both within the private and public sector and small and big organisations. Change and innovation do not only come from small private start-ups. Big organisations, public and private, often play key roles in creatively developing new products and processes, and changing economic structures.

The interactions between markets and hierarchies are many and complex, as we already noted that many market actors, such as private businesses, are internally organised as hierarchies. Indeed there are various combinations and variations between hierarchical bureaucracies and markets which make the study of organisations so fascinating and important. Simplistic dichotomic notions of *public versus private* and *big versus small* are not likely to improve our understanding of how these dynamics play out in reality. Therefore, we suggest exposing students to this wide variety of hierarchies and how they can function.

Other Mechanisms: Commons and More

Besides the mechanisms of the market and hierarchy, there are various others that often get less attention than they deserve, given their importance in real-world economies. There are multiple theoretical conceptualisations of these other coordination and allocation mechanisms amongst which commons, reciprocity, gift economies, associations, networks and householding. The coordination and allocation may be done based on social relationships, trust, group identity, norms or shared practices. Compared to markets and hierarchy, these mechanisms are often somewhat more symmetrical and norm- or culture-driven. *Contemporary Capitalism: The Embeddedness of Institutions* gives a useful overview and introduction into a wide variety of economic mechanisms, from markets and public and private hierarchies, to communities, associations and networks.

How do these coordination and allocation mechanisms function? Here we take one example: the *commons*. In the online resources we provide a brief literature overview of other mechanisms, such as reciprocity, gift economies, associations, networks and householding, accompanied with suggestions and teaching materials for more in-depth courses on economic mechanisms.

Over the last decade the commons have received increasing attention. The term describes situations where resources are held in common by a community which governs them through informal norms and social practices. Traditionally, the concept has been associated with natural resources such as grasslands, fisheries, forests and irrigation systems. Recently, the concepts of the digital, urban, cultural and knowledge commons have gained prominence.

There are two main academic approaches to the commons. First, commons are analysed to determine why and how they can fail, centred on the idea of *The Tragedy of the Commons* popularised by Garrett Hardin in a paper in 1968. A second strand focuses on how they can succeed, centred on Elinor Ostrom's empirical body of work. Ostrom (1990) found that institutional arrangements largely determine the success of shared resource management resources, requiring the following:

1 Clear boundaries regarding users and non-users and which resources are concerned
2 Appropriation and provision rules are adapted to local conditions
3 Most people affected by the arrangements are able to participate in creating and changing its rules
4 The appropriation and provisioning, as well as the conditions of the resources, are monitored
5 Sanctions for rule violations start very low but become stronger if a user repeatedly violates a rule
6 Mechanisms allow conflicts among users or with officials to be quickly and locally resolved at low costs
7 Higher-level authorities recognize the rights of local users to make their own rules
8 When connected to a larger economic system, governance is organised in multiple nested layers

Going beyond the notion that resources necessarily need to be managed by either the state or the market, Ostrom points out multiple other possible solutions that rely on voluntary self-governing. The point here is not that markets and states are not important, it simply means they are both part of larger governance structures, which she calls *polycentric*, in which commons also play important roles.

Rather than debating which mechanism in general is superior, she argues we should be more open-minded and consider the diversity in ways in which decisions about time and resources are made. We should look at specific cases with their own characteristics and contexts and analyse which (combinations of) mechanisms, and especially which design rules, lead to successes. In other words, rather than trying to simplify the world, we should recognise its complexity and learn about the many ways in which economies can be (more and less successfully) organised.

Coordination & Allocation Mechanisms elaborates upon this overview of the commons as well as the other mechanisms of coordination and allocation by examining them from three perspectives: economic anthropology, social systems of production and new institutional economics. We show how these three are connected, how their focus differs and offer suggestions on how to use them in teaching this material.
economy.st/backgroundbb5

3 Practical Suggestions

Below we describe four suggestions to consider when teaching economic organisations and mechanisms. First, treat forms both as analytical concepts and in their real-world expressions: always use examples. Second, start with basic explanations of individual static forms and move towards discussions of dynamic and interacting forms. Third, in specialised courses, showcase the different ways of organising surrounding that topic, such as different labour, financial or tax systems. Fourth, distinguish analytical description from normative evaluation of forms.

First, treat economic organisations and mechanisms both as concepts and as real-world phenomena. Forms of economic organisation (companies, non-profits, etc.) are easily spotted in the real world, and this can make for interesting student assignments. As for the different coordination and allocation mechanisms (hierarchy, the commons, market mechanisms, etc.), they can be quite difficult to grasp. So it might be useful to first discuss the concepts with the help of some clear examples of different mechanisms with students. Nevertheless, it is also important for students to learn how to see these forms in the complex real world around them.

An exercise for this could be to let students record the different mechanisms they themselves engage in on a day. A student might wake up and first make breakfast for him- or herself, an example of householding. Subsequently, they might go on public transport to university which is organised through hierarchical organisations of the state, partially funded by taxation. On their way, they might look up the topic of today's class on Wikipedia, a commons. In class, they might help out a friend by lending him or her a pen – reciprocity. For lunch, they buy a meal at a local cafeteria, a market transaction with a formal private business. In the end of the afternoon, they might go to the student sports club, a voluntary association. As a side job, in the evenings they tutor their neighbour's son in mathematics, an informal private business.

A more extreme exercise to make students understand the roles of these mechanisms in economies, would be to give them the assignment to avoid using one mechanism for a day. This could be done once, or multiple times to let students experience it with different mechanisms. How would a day look without being able to buy or sell anything? Not following any instructions from a superior or giving them yourself (please, only on the weekend). Or without being able to reciprocally receive and return favours (not for too long, or everyone will hate you)? And perhaps most impossible of all, without doing any householding and self-care activities? The goal here is not that students strictly adhere to the exercise, but that they realise the prevalence of each of these different economic mechanisms.

For a less extreme exercise, let students describe what life would look like *if* they were to avoid one particular type of economic coordination mechanism. Different groups could be assigned different mechanisms, and afterwards, groups could debate what mechanisms are most vital to our economic organisation.

Our second suggestion: start simple and move to more complexity. To help students get an idea of the different organisations and mechanisms, it might be useful to start with isolated and static descriptions: *"This is the concept of a multinational, and here is an example. This is the concept of a commons, and here is an example."*

Reality is, however, of course more complex. In the real world, organisations and mechanisms do not exist in isolation from each other but do interact in various complex ways. They might strengthen each other but they might as well undermine each other. Furthermore, things change over time. For example, elderly care might first be organised through households and religions organisations, but later through various state organisations and, after that, privatised to for-profit companies.

Understanding how some economic activities and resources move from one form to another is at the core of understanding economic change. Our advice is to start with isolated static mechanisms and, when possible, move to more complex discussions about how they interact with each other and change over time.

Our third suggestion: when teaching a specific topic, such as finance, labour or fiscal policy, use the same logic. Showcase different ways of structuring economic life. Say you are teaching a course on financial economics. This could include an overview of the highly different kinds of financial *organisations*: such as commercial and investment banks, public investment banks, credit unions, hedge funds and green banks. It could also include an overview of various *mechanisms*. For instance, the different financial systems such as a gold standard, fiat money, the international Bretton Woods system and, recently getting more attention, crypto-currencies, full reserve banking and central bank digital currency. The same could be done for various labour arrangements in labour economics courses, or for tax and government systems in public economics, etc.

Fourth and finally, it is important to distinguish normative evaluation as much as possible from the analytical description of organisations and mechanisms. Both are relevant for students to learn about, but mixing them can be very dangerous, so we suggest being explicit to students about whether the focus is on description or normative evaluation. Furthermore, we think it is helpful to start by giving students an analytical and real-world understanding of the different ways of organising, before going into the normative judgements about them (which is at the core of the final building block of this book, *Building Block 10: Economics for a Better World*).

This approach is somewhat opposite from the currently prevalent approach, which starts from a normative assumption and subsequently goes into analytical descriptions. How so? Many current programmes start by explaining to students that markets, if they are *'perfect'*, lead to *optimal* outcomes. Much of the subsequent programme then consists of learning analytically how these optimal outcomes, sometimes also referred to as 'competitive equilibria', do or do not come about, with the help of neoclassical models. Later, the state often comes in as a possible solution for market imperfections, although students are also taught to look out for government failures in such cases.

While this approach teaches students many valuable lessons, it can give students the impression that markets (sometimes accompanied by an interventionist state) are a priori desirable and superior compared to other mechanisms. We firmly believe that learning to think independently and critically is at the core of academic education. Therefore, we think it is important that programmes expose students to a wide variety of positions and analytical ideas, as opposed to teaching a single main perspective or starting point, with the danger of (unintentionally) instilling normative beliefs into students.

The point is not that the neoclassical answers to questions about economic mechanisms are false. It is rather that they are only one set of possible answers to complex normative and analytical questions. We therefore advise to expose students to these different sets of answers and help them to critically scrutinize the philosophical arguments and empirical evidence that underline them.

Furthermore, we think it is important to pay attention to the complex and often nuanced nature of arguments and positions. We would not suggest assigning students to write an essay or debate about which mechanism they think is superior. Rather, students might be given specific cases to analyse and argue about how they can best be tackled. This could require students to suggest combinations of mechanisms and organisational forms to address the real-world problem. The degree of nuance and complexity of such an assignment would depend on the level of the student or class.

Teaching Materials

- *Introducing a New Economics* by Jack Reardon, Molly S. Cato, Maria A. C. Madi, from 2018, chapters 10, 11 & 12. Three accessible and brief chapters, with accompanying classroom activities and questions, introducing students to what public goods, commons and firms are and how they can be governed, for example as a corporation owned by shareholders or as a cooperative owned by its workers or consumers.

- *Economics: The User's Guide* by Ha-Joon Chang, from 2014, chapter 5. A short well-written chapter on different economic actors and organisational forms, from multinational corporations, cooperatives, and labour unions, to governments and a variety of international organisations.

- *Organisations: A Very Short Introduction* by Mary Jo Hatch, from 2011. A brief, accessible and yet highly informative book full with scientific theories and ideas on what organisations are, how they can be structured, how they change, and their internal dynamics and interaction with markets and society.

- *Governing the Commons: The Evolution of Institutions for Collective Action* by Elinor Ostrom, most recent edition from 2015, chapters 1, 2 & 3. A sharp and rigorous discussion of commons, how they are different from markets and hierarchies, how we should theorize them and real-world examples that help us better understand how they can be successful.

- *Contemporary Capitalism: The Embeddedness of Institutions* by J. Rogers Hollingsworth and Robert Boyer, most recent edition from 2012, chapter 1. An instructive analytical introduction and overview of different coordination and allocation mechanisms, such as markets, public and private hierarchies, networks, communities and associations.

Visit the website for a wider range of teaching materials, to provide feedback, and to exchange ideas and ask support from colleagues worldwide.
economy.st/bb5

Building Block 6
Political-Economic Systems

The macro-structures of economies – how economies are organised, which institutions they have and what their power relations look like.

1
Political-Economic
Systems as Concepts

2
Political-Economic
Systems in the
Real World

Political-
Economic
Systems

3
Practical
Suggestions

What

This building block is concerned with the macro-structures of economies. It focuses on how economies are organised, which institutions they have and what their power relations look like. Economies are highly complex configurations of structures and institutions. Throughout history, there have been a number of evolutions and revolutions that have fundamentally changed how economies are organised. Furthermore, there is huge variety in how economies function across geographies.

Why

The ways in which the production and distribution of goods and services are organised shapes people's lives. Therefore, it is crucial that students learn about the different macro political-economic systems, both as concepts and as their real-world manifestations. This will help them think about how economies as a whole might function and what dynamics they might have. It will also help them better understand how the different parts operate and interact with one another.

Contrast with current programmes

Currently, political-economic systems are rarely discussed. Instead, the focus is on models of markets. While knowledge of the workings of markets is very important, it is also important to understand the larger systems which those markets are part of as these interact and influence each other. Furthermore, economies consist of more than markets as discussed in *Building Block 5: Economic Organisations & Mechanisms*. How these various parts are combined and interact with political systems is the subject of this building block.

"[As an old Polish joke goes:]

Under capitalism, man exploits man.

Under communism, it is just the reverse."

John Kenneth Galbraith (1981, p. 306)

A political-economic system is the institutional configuration and social structure of an economy. To put it another way, it is the overarching way an economy is organised: combinations of and interactions between the different organisational forms and mechanisms as described in *Building Block 5: Economic Organisations & Mechanisms*. How are goods and services produced, distributed, consumed and disposed of? How are the factors of production, land, labour and capital allocated and coordinated? What do power relations look like and how do they function?

In the real world, political-economic systems are highly complex, with many different (and possibly even contradictory) elements and aspects. Therefore, it is useful to teach students abstract concepts that enable them to think more clearly about actual political-economic systems. As such, this building block consists of two main elements: theoretical concepts and real-world knowledge.

1 Political-Economic Systems as Concepts

There are many ways of conceptualising political-economic systems. A prominent dichotomy is that of capitalism versus socialism, which in the form of the Cold War defined much of the 20th century. While these two concepts are still highly useful, it is crucial not to fall into a Cold War mindset, painting 'the other side' as essentially evil while maintaining that your side is good and only has strengths (irrespective of which side you would be on).

The goal here is to be more analytical and to give students the tools to systematically analyse and think about political-economic systems. For this reason, it is important to stay away from straw men which idealise or demonise particular systems. Students need to learn to see the complex and more nuanced nature of political-economic systems, each with blurred boundaries and both strengths and weaknesses. We therefore also advise refraining from using mainly ideological notions, such as *(un)just, (un) free* or *(un)fair*, as analytical concepts to describe economies. This is not to say that normative evaluation is not relevant. In fact, *Building Block 10: Economics for a Better World* is largely devoted to this. It is, however, important to do so explicitly and not mispresent normative evaluation as analytical description.

The universe of political-economic systems is larger than the dichotomy between capitalism and socialism would suggest. These two concepts mainly characterise recent history. How to best conceptualise these other systems can be debated, but Wolf (1982) and Chase-Dunn & Hall (1997) offer a useful conceptual framework. Their framework attempts to understand the different kinds of economies that have existed throughout human history, rather than focusing only on the recent history of the Global North.

The typology for political-economic systems developed by Wolf and Chase-Dunn & Hall is connected to the more micro-focused concepts of the coordination and allocation mechanisms (see also *Building Block 5: Economic Organisations & Mechanisms*). All political-economic systems consist of multiple mechanisms, but generally one mechanism is dominant. Here the way factors of production (land, labour and capital) are allocated and coordinated is particularly important. When the market mechanism is dominant, people generally describe the political-economic system as *capitalist*. Alternatively, when hierarchical redistribution is dominant, the political-economic system can be described as *tributary*. Contexts in which reciprocity is the dominant mechanism, can be described as *kin-ordered* (family and community-based) political economies. We address *socialism* later, as it is hotly debated, including the question of what mechanism is dominant in socialist systems.

This framework partially overlaps with the common division in market, planned and traditional economies. This classification is, however, largely based on recent western history, and the category *traditional* economies is somewhat of a leftover category: it simply refers to all kinds of economies that are neither market nor planned, despite their many differences. The concepts are ideal types of economic systems which are assumed to function according to only one coordination and allocation mechanism, be it the market, hierarchical distribution or more traditional mechanisms such as reciprocity. The literature does, however, recognise that real economies exhibit more than one mechanism and, therefore, are often referred to as *mixed* economies. While many studies using these concepts contain valuable insights, we think it might be more helpful to use the more nuanced concepts described above, as they offer students a better understanding of the structures and institutions that make up economies.

At the same time, it is critical to emphasise to students that these are merely classifications. They are not exhaustive nor mutually exclusive. Rather than memorising the different categories, it is most important for students to think about what variables differentiate the categories and what the implications of this are.

In the section below, we discuss each type of political-economic system briefly. We dedicate most attention to capitalism, as most countries today could be best described as such.

Kin-ordered Political Economies

Most early human societies can be described as kin-ordered political economies. In these economies, processes are mainly structured by the mechanisms of reciprocity, trust due to family and community relations, and moral norms and obligations. Inequality was generally limited in such economies. Differences between people were mainly based on their personal behaviour, relation to the group, and successes and failures, as inheritance and accumulation of vast riches played a very limited role in these economies.

Although it is true that many of these economies had limited technological capabilities, practising hunting, gathering and horticulture, it cannot be said that living conditions were always bad. They were heavily dependent on nature and the seasons. Some economies were plagued by uncertainty and shortages, others knew stability and abundance. There are also indications that working days were frequently relatively short, spending substantial amounts of time on leisure activities, as well as communal rituals and feasts (Chase-Dunn & Hall, 1997; Nolan & Lenski, 2003).

While very few political-economic systems today could be described as being kin-ordered, this has been the main form of economic organisation throughout most of human history. In addition, learning about these concepts does help us to think more flexibly about what kind of economic arrangements are possible. As such, teaching students about them is less about understanding the realities that directly surround them, and more about enabling students to think outside of today's structures and understand what economic options exist.

Tributary Political Economies

Tributary political-economic systems are dominated by hierarchical redistribution, generally based on legal systems and organised military power. In many cases, most of the population is engaged in subsistence farming, while elites extract surpluses with the help of political and military means. As most of written history is characterised by tributary systems, there have been many varieties of it. European feudalism, for example, was a politically fragmented version of a tributary system, while most Chinese dynasties were more centralised versions of tributary systems with stronger imperial bureaucracies.

While one specific mechanism dominated these systems, they did also contain several others. Trade, for example, has a long history and the market mechanism was also well present in many primarily tributary systems. The crucial difference with capitalist economies is that those markets were mainly focused on products, and luxury goods in particular (Chase-Dunn & Hall, 1997). These consumer markets did not play a dominant role in the allocation of land, labour and capital. So while merchants definitely did exist in these societies, they had a rather limited position. Besides hierarchies and markets, these economies were also often organised through commons and associative arrangements. Natural resources in particular have historically been mainly organised through the commons. The associative arrangements were frequently found to structure occupational, religious, communal and neighbourhood organisations (Van Bavel, 2016).

Capitalist Political Economies

Capitalism describes a political-economic system in which market mechanisms are dominant, as not only goods and services, but also land, labour, and capital are bought and sold on markets. The political-economic system derives its name from the fact that capital goods, also called 'the means of production', are largely privately owned, by a class of individuals known as the capitalists. Capitalists aim for profit and accumulate capital by hiring workers and selling the produced products to consumers. Given the importance of capitalism for the current world economy, it is important for students to develop an accurate and deep understanding of capitalism as a concept, including its main institutions and varieties.

What should students be taught about this topic? This question has been at the centre of entrenched economic debates since Bernard Mandeville's *The Fable of the Bees* (1705) and later Smith's foundational text *The Wealth of Nations* (1776). Most authors agree on what the core dynamics of the capitalist system are. The central profit motive, endless accumulation of capital and drive for economic growth, private ownership of the means of production, wage labour, ever higher levels of specialisation, relentless competition for market dominance, continuous expansion into new sectors and new markets, increasing commodification of natural and social life, recurrent financial and economic crises, and rapid mass-marketing of innovations, are all generally recognised properties of capitalism (Ingham, 2013; Keynes, 1936; Marx, 1867; Schumpeter, 1942; Shaikh, 2016).

Great economic thinkers, whether they are perceived as being left- or right-wing, from Smith and Marx to Keynes and Schumpeter, did not confine their analyses to ideological comfort zones and instead focused on understanding capitalism with both its strengths and weaknesses.

This is not to say that there is just one way of viewing capitalism. Various thinkers understand these core properties in very different ways. For instance, although almost every economic thinker recognises the importance of market competition as a core feature of the system, neoclassical economists understand this in a radically different way to classical, Marxian and evolutionary economists. Neoclassical economics views market competition as a harmonious outcome and optimal equilibrium, while the other three approaches see it as a ruthless process (see *Building Block 8: Economic Theories* for more detail). Needless to say, we propose that the various thinkers should be taught in conversation with one another.

To give students a good understanding of what capitalism is, it is useful to discuss its core institutions as also discussed in the useful introduction book *Capitalism* by Ingham. We suggest starting with the following four: *private property, factor markets, capitalist firms,* and *credit-based banking systems*. Here, we discuss each briefly.

While the concept of owning your own things might be as old as humanity, private property as we know it today is far more recent. In contrast to what is often called *personal* property, *private* property does not only refer to items people use frequently in their daily lives, but can practically refer to everything, ranging from a piece of land on the other side of the world to an idea about how to produce something more efficiently. In both cases you have exclusive ownership and it is illegal for others to use it.

These private property rights do not exist without being actively protected (ultimately through violence). This is one of the crucial roles of the state in capitalism. It is worthwhile to spend some time on the specific rules around property, as these can differ substantially. A useful concept here is *bundles of rights*: ownership gives you certain rights, but not others. You might own a house, but not be allowed to run a factory there. More generally, all sorts of complicated contracts, combinations and separations of rights are possible.

One of these rights is generally to sell the item. This brings us to the second core institution: markets. Markets for goods and services have existed throughout much of history. The historical innovation of capitalism was that it allowed for the large-scale buying and selling of land, labour and capital through markets. These three *factors of production* have unique characteristics compared to goods and services. Karl Polanyi (1944), for example, deemed these 'fictitious' commodities because, in contrast to goods and services, land, labour and money are not, and cannot be, produced for the market.

The third core institution of capitalism has given it its name: the fact that the dominant economic organisations are *capitalist* firms. A firm is capitalist when the owners of the capital, the capitalists or shareholders, have the power to make the decisions and direct the organisation. The typical capitalist firm is run through wage labourers, supervised in a hierarchical structure by managers. The products that are produced by the firm are the sole property of the capitalists, as the workers and managers only have the right to their wages. These commodities are sold on markets in order to make a monetary profit for the capitalists, thus putting the profit motive at the core of these economic organisations.

Fourth, while capitalism did not invent money, in a way the system puts it at the centre of societal life. Credit-based bank systems in particular are a distinctive feature of capitalism. In these systems, debt is transferable in the sense that money, nothing more than an IOU (referring to *"I Owe U [You]"*), can be used as means of payment to third parties. This money takes various forms, but the lion's share is actively created by banks by issuing credit, thereby injecting the economy with new purchasing power. According to Schumpeter (1911), it is precisely this characteristic of capitalism that makes it so dynamic.

Capitalism touches more than just the economic aspect: it is an important component of a society's overarching political-economic system. This should be part of the classroom discussion. For instance, there is the frequent misconception that capitalism and democracy are the same thing. While they *can* go together, history shows that they often exist without each other. In fact, there is a long history of thought that argued the two are incompatible, both by proponents and opponents of capitalism (Almond, 1991; Bowles & Gintis, 2012; Friedman, 1962; Lindblom, 1982; Schumpeter, 1942). The reason for this is that democracy is based on the principle of political equality, while capitalism, left unchecked, can yield large economic inequalities, which over time translate into political inequalities as well (Bartels, 2016; Gilens, 2012; Gilens & Page, 2014; Schakel et al., 2020). Similarly, the complex relationships between capitalism and slavery, capitalism and colonialism, and capitalism and patriarchy are important to discuss with students.

Finally, this is also connected to a larger point: there are many varieties of capitalism. Students should learn about the contrasting way in which capitalist systems have been structured. For instance, think of the differences between the early modern Dutch economy and the current day Indian economy. Both, however, are capitalist political economies. The literature on the varieties of capitalism was initially centred around the concepts of *liberal* and *coordinated* market economies, to respectively describe Anglo-Saxon and north-western European countries based on their differences in industrial relations, vocational training and education, relations with employees, corporate governance and inter-firm relations. Recently, researchers have tried to expand the number of concepts to also capture Asian and Latin American varieties of capitalism, with concepts such as *hierarchical* market economies. These concepts could be useful to link to material focusing on comparative discussions of political-economic systems in the real world.

Socialist Political Economies

Socialism is generally understood in opposition to capitalism, as an economy that is collectively run and in which the means of production are in social ownership. In the real world, capitalism and socialism are, however, not necessarily each other's opposites as there are also complex combinations of the two, such as in China or Scandinavia. The main misconception about socialist economies is that they are necessarily highly centralised state economies. Socialist economies can also take decentralised forms, such as through autonomous cooperatives. As such, it is important not to fall for the strawman image of socialism as necessarily a completely dictatorial-run bureaucracy in which everything is centrally planned: that is *state socialism* or *totalitarian socialism*.

Just as it is important that students are aware of the varieties of capitalism, students should become familiar with the varieties of socialism. The economy of the Soviet Union had a different structure from the Yugoslav economy with its powerful worker councils, which was once again different from the Chinese or Cuban economy. Comparative case studies are an excellent way to help students see this.

There is a lot of debate on whether these so-called socialist economies are truly a different type of political-economic system. Some people contend that, although the goal of these systems was to break free from capitalism, they in fact remained stuck in the capitalist world system, and simply instituted a state-controlled version of capitalism (Howard & King, 2001). Others argue that these socialist economies are fundamentally different from capitalism, but that the systems in effect are tributary as they see hierarchical redistribution as the dominant mechanism (Chase-Dunn &

Hall, 1997). Others yet argue that the logic of these systems is different from both capitalist and tributary systems, as socialist structures (should) have their own dynamics to them (Wolff, 2012). One such variant is the definition of socialist systems as economies in which allocation and coordination decisions are made democratically by the people they affect, for example through self-managed worker cooperatives.

Giacomo Corneo in *Is Capitalism Obsolete? A Journey Through Alternative Economic Systems* provides an useful and systematic overview of the different socialist economic systems, such as associationalism, planning, self-management, market socialism and shareholder socialism. While the book has some limitations as it is written from a neoclassical perspective, it provides a good overview of arguments for and against the various economic systems and as such can be informative for students.

Our point here is not to take a position in this debate, but rather to point out that it is helpful to expose students to this debate, so they can make up their own mind as to how they think socialist economies can be best understood.

Normative Debates on Political-Economic Systems

Beyond a technical understanding of the main structures and dynamics of various political-economic systems, students need to learn to navigate the main normative arguments for and against them. In this box, we will set out a brief overview of these debates regarding capitalism, as an example. We discuss both capitalism in general and particular varieties of capitalism.

Similarly to debates surrounding climate change, a simple dichotomy is not likely to properly capture the full debate. Hirschman (1982), and updated in 2007 by Fourcade and Healy, identified the following three fundamentally different moral positions, respectively arguing capitalism is (1) civilising; (2) destructive; and (3) feeble.

The *civilising* view is very important in the liberal tradition. It claims that capitalism not only leads to economic growth and efficient outcomes, it also causes people to behave more rationally, cooperatively, freely, creatively and morally. Thus, capitalism is more than a way of organising economic systems: it changes the social morality of a society away from armed power struggles and towards more productive and harmonious forms of competition.

Those that are more critical of capitalism, on the other hand, argue that capitalism is *destructive*: it causes people to behave hedonistically, selfishly, short-sightedly and wastefully. Instead of creating a harmonious world as the civilising view argues, the destructive view argues capitalism creates alienation, exclusion, coercion, subordination, deception, inequality and exploitation. Note, however, that both the civilising and destructive view assume that capitalism is a very powerful political-economic system which fundamentally shapes the societies it manifests itself in.

The *feeble* view argues, instead, that capitalism is not inherently good or bad. Rather, its effects depend on the kind of social and cultural institutions within which it is embedded. Some, for example, argue that capitalism only creates positive outcomes in certain cultures, in this case amongst Protestants, while it creates negative outcomes in other cultures, for instance Catholics. Others argue it is about choosing the right policy mix, such as fair and enforced property rights, and thus think it is quite possible to move from a negative version of capitalism to a positive version. Finally, there is also a more differentiated view, which argues that there are multiple successful varieties of capitalism. While the Anglo-Saxon liberal and European continental coordinated market economies, for example, function differently in terms of flexibility of labour markets and patience of corporate governance, they can both lead to economic success. In each case, whether they emphasize cultural legacies, having good political institutions, or having a prospering variety of capitalism, the point is that capitalism in itself is not desirable or undesirable, but that it depends on which forms of economic organisation and mechanisms of coordination and allocation are dominant where, and what institutions these are embedded in.

2 Political-Economic Systems in the Real World

Theoretical concepts are useful tools to understand political economic systems, but learning about how they manifest themselves in the real world is what really matters. While the theoretical concepts of kin-ordered, tributary, capitalism and socialism are clearly differentiated from each other, actual political-economic systems are usually diverse and complex combinations.

Comparative economics is of great value here, as it explores how different economies are structured, generally at the national or regional level. Besides such knowledge of how various economies are organised, it is important to take a global perspective too and examine how different national and regional political-economic systems interact with one another and with international institutions to form, for instance, transnational structures of capitalism.

Comparative Economics

Comparative economics is the study of political-economic systems in the real world, as opposed to the ideal types of theory. This approach will not only allow students to see that every situation is different, but will also teach them to see similarities between different cases. When studying different economies, we suggest choosing a mixture of economies with various degrees of development and in various parts of the world.

Rosser & Rosser (2018) is a suitable book for this as it discusses multiple countries of each category. First, the authors give an overview of comparative economics and theories about different economic systems. Second, they discuss the varieties of advanced capitalism with the cases of the US, Japan, France, Sweden and Germany. Third, they explore the varieties of transition among socialist economies with the cases of Russia, Poland, China, and North and South Korea. Finally, they analyse alternative paths among developing economies, in particular India, Iran, South Africa, Mexico and Brazil. In doing so, the reader becomes familiar both with different economic systems and with the varieties of each of those economic systems. The particular histories and traditions of economies are of crucial importance for what political-economic systems look like – this broad overview can give students an idea of the various forms they can take.

The Global Economy

Besides looking at specific countries and their political-economic systems, it is also useful for students to become familiar with the concrete institutions and structures of the global economy. Naturally, the global economy consists of the countries that are studied in the comparative approach, so we propose to build on this knowledge in courses. A basic understanding of the political-economic systems of China and the US, for example, makes it a lot easier to understand how these two countries interact in the global economy and how this influences other countries.

It is also valuable to look at more and less intensive collaborations and coalitions of countries and how they work internally and interact. Two key international coalitions are the Organization for Economic Cooperation and Development (OECD) and the Organization of the Petroleum Exporting Countries (OPEC). There are also multiple regional collaborations, such as the European Union and its Eurozone, the Association of Southeast Asian Nations (ASEAN), the Community of Latin American and Caribbean States (CELAC), and the African Union. Finally, more loose collaborations between countries, such as the G7 and G20, are also of importance for the global economy.

When discussing such international collaborations, it is also important to pay attention to the power relations between countries. While outright colonialism and imperialism are largely phenomena of the past, international power imbalances and struggles are still highly relevant. Students should develop, at least, a basic understanding of these. They can, for example, be found by comparing foreign aid flows with other financial flows (United Nations, Economic Commission for Africa, 2015).

Furthermore, international institutions are important actors to analyse, each with their own dynamics and affecting specific aspects of the economy. In particular, it is useful to discuss intergovernmental organisations, such as the United Nations (UN), World Trade Organization (WTO), International Monetary Fund (IMF), and International Chamber of Commerce (ICC). Public banks such as the World Bank, Bank for International Settlements (BIS), Asian Development Bank (ADB), and the China Construction Bank (CCB), also play a key role in the global economy that needs to be understood.

When discussing these institutions, it is valuable to focus not only on their formal structure and mission, but also to look at the power relations upon which they are built, and to discuss which ideas are dominant within them. For example, presenting the history of the dominant ideas within the IMF, including recent changes as a result of the Global Financial Crisis, helps students' understanding of how the world economy functions. Similarly, the growing importance of China, Russia and Brazil in the global economy has changed the functioning of the UN and WTO.

Economic power lies not only with countries and their political institutions. Private companies in the form of multinational corporations are key actors in the global economy. Of particular interest are the financial firms operating at a global level, making the financial dynamics of different countries and currency areas strongly interrelated, as has become particularly clear since the Global Financial Crisis of 2007-2008. Therefore, it would be worthwhile to make students familiar with the most important global financial centres, such as Wall Street in New York, The City of London, Hong Kong, Tokyo and Singapore.

3 Practical Suggestions

When teaching students about political-economic systems, it can be helpful to keep the following things in mind: the level of difficulty and the different ways to learn about political-economic systems.

In terms of the level of difficulty, political-economic systems are by nature highly complex entities and there is a virtually endless amount of material on them. As such, they might seem to be a topic only for the more advanced levels. We believe this is not necessarily so. There is a great amount of accessible written, as well visual, material on political-economic systems, and capitalism in particular.

One could, for example, use the brief book *Capitalism: A Very Short Introduction* by James Fulcher and let students watch some documentaries to give them an idea of the concept and of what different kinds of economies around the world look like. There are many documentaries on political-economic systems, and on capitalism in particular, such as *Capitalism: A six-part series* by Ilan Ziv, but also the old classics *Age of Uncertainty* by Galbraith and *Free to Choose* by Friedman. Globalisation, particularly the role of China, has also received a lot of attention with documentaries such as *The New Silk Road* by Deutsche Welle and *China: Power and Prosperity* by the US Public Broadcasting Service. These are just some suggestions, but there is a wide variety of documentaries that can be used in courses.

In more advanced courses, one could go in more detail and look at various economic processes that work differently in different (varieties of) political-economic systems. Examples and case studies are very useful here. For instance, discussing how countries and economies reacted to the COVID-19 virus and how this relates to their political-economic systems can be an interesting and enlightening exercise.

In terms of the different ways to learn about political-economic systems, students will benefit most from making connections between the world around them and the things they learn in class. This can be done by connecting topics to recent developments and the news, going on field trips with the class and by bringing them in contact with people living in different political-economic systems.

In addition to direct experiences and academic material, it can be helpful to expose students to popular material. There is a vast catalogue of art, literature, movies and music that deals with political-economic systems. From the classic novels of Charles Dickens, Leo Tolstoy, George Orwell and

Hannah Arendt to the more recent visual street art *Shop Until You Drop* by Banksy and the film *Margin Call*. These are likely to enhance students' understanding of political-economic systems in different ways and speak differently to them than textbook materials do. At the same time, especially for the analytical side of political-economic systems, more traditional ways of teaching such as assigning readings and lectures are irreplaceable. The most promising way of teaching seems to combine these various aspects, bringing together analytical work, experiences and art.

Teaching Materials

- *Capitalism* by Geoffrey Ingham, from 2008. A highly insightful introduction into capitalism with chapters on key ideas from Smith, Marx, Weber, Schumpeter and Keynes, and core institutions, such as market exchange, the enterprise, money, capital, financial markets and the state.
- *Capitalism: A Very Short Introduction* by James Fulcher, most recent edition from 2015. A brief and yet useful book on capitalism's definition, historical evolution, varieties, global networks, and recurring crises.
- *Socialism: A Very Short Introduction* by Michael Newman, most recent edition from 2020. A similarly brief and yet useful book, but then on capitalism's main rival socialism, with chapters on its varieties around the world, historical traditions and more recent developments.
- *Is Capitalism Obsolete? A Journey Through Alternative Economic Systems* by Giacomo Corneo, from 2017. A systematic and sharp overview of different (mainly socialist) economic systems that helps students think analytically about their allocation and coordination mechanisms and informs them about the possible ways of organising economies and the arguments for and against the various options.
- *Comparative economics in a transforming world economy* by J. Barkley Rosser, Jr. and Marina V. Rosser, most recent edition from 2018. A highly useful and broad book describing many varieties of advanced market capitalism, varieties of transition among socialist economies, and alternative paths among developing economies, with chapters on many countries, such as the United States, Russia, Sweden, China, India, Iran, South Africa, Mexico, and Brazil. It is particularly useful for students to learn about their own country. If this country is not included in the book, as is the case for us as Dutch citizens, it can be useful to supplement the book with teaching material on the national political-economic system.
- *Rise and Demise: Comparing World-Systems* by Christopher Chase-Dunn and Thomas D. Hall, most recent edition from 2018. A concise analytical overview of the political-economic systems that have characterised

human history, with chapters on concepts and definitions, theories of change, cases and periods.

- *International Organizations: Politics, Law, Practice* by Ian Hurd, most recent edition from 2020, chapters 1, 5, 6 & 7. A leading textbook on international organisations with chapters on various key economic international organisations, such as the World Trade Organization (WTO), the International Monetary Fund (IMF), the World Bank, and the International Labor Organization (ILO).

Visit the website for a wider range of teaching materials, to provide feedback, and to exchange ideas and ask support from colleagues worldwide.
economy.st/bb6

Research Methods & Philosophy of Science

A broad methodological toolkit with quantitative and qualitative data collection and analysis methods, and reflection upon them.

1
Philosophy
of Science

3
Quantitative
Data Analysis:
Descriptive Statistics,
Regression Analysis
& Network Analysis

2
Research
Methods: A
Broad Overview

**Research
Methods &
Philosophy
of Science**

4
Quantitative
Data Collection:
Experiments &
Survey Research

5
Qualitative Data
Analysis:
Case Studies

6
Qualitative
Data Collection:
Interviews

7
Practical
Suggestions

What

The philosophy of science provides an important foundation for evaluating research methods. We encourage discussing ontology, epistemology, and ethics with students. This helps them choose suitable methodologies for their own research projects and develop their critical thinking when encountering research results. Research methods are a vital element in the modern economist's toolkit. This includes quantitative analysis methods, such as descriptive statistics, regression analysis and network analysis. It also includes qualitative analysis methods, such as case studies. Besides such data analysis tools, students should also gain experience with quantitative and qualitative data collection: designing and conducting experiments, survey research and interviews. This will give them a feel for data quality and put them in touch with the actual context that they are studying, beyond only the numbers.

Why

Economists are knowledge workers. Much of our work, both inside and outside academia, consists of working with – more or less formalised – research methods. Hence, we need a broad range of methodological skills and knowledge, as well as the ability to reflect upon our methodological choices and explain the implications for the interpretation of our findings. These are unique skills that make economists valuable members of teams and organisations.

Contrast with current programmes

Methods courses in current undergraduate programmes are generally limited to mathematics and various forms of regression analysis. These are useful tools for proving and testing economic theories, and crucial for publishing in today's academic journals. For a lot of work, however, it is essential to have a broader range of methodological tools available. The main purpose of most economists' work is generally guiding action, rather than developing and improving theories. Hence, students need to learn how to apply various quantitative and qualitative data collection and analysis methods to real data.

"Research is formalized curiosity.
It is poking and prying with a purpose."

Zora Neale Hurston (1942, p. 91)

Quantitative data *analysis* methods are important. In economics however, they do not require much defending: they are already the established status quo. Quantitative data *collection* methods, however, are rarely taught to economics students, despite the fact that students do learn how to analyse this data once it is collected. Philosophy of science, too, is largely accepted as a necessary component of academic programmes, even if it is still too often banished to the fringes of the programme. We believe it could be taught in a more integral and applied manner, as we discuss in the first section of this chapter.

The most unusual of our suggestions must be the inclusion of *qualitative* methods in the economist's toolkit. Hence, we will start by briefly making the case for methods like interviews and case studies. A good example is found in Karen Ho's work on Wall Street. Financial institutions, which are at the heart of the economy, are so quantitatively oriented that they generally prefer hiring physicists and mathematicians over economists and other social scientists. But when the curtain came crashing down in 2007, numbers were not enough to understand what had happened. In *Liquidated*, Karen Ho investigates financial instability by conducting over a hundred interviews and engaging in participant observation during her work as a consultant in various investment banks on Wall Street during multiple years (2009).

Her findings indicate how investment banks export their own insecure workplace labour arrangements to other sections of the economy. She identified a Wall Street culture that has distinct fads and fashions in its approach to business management. In the years before the crisis, this culture had come to focus relentlessly on downsizing and the flexibility of labour arrangements. Thereby, it had contributed both to the practices that led to the crisis throughout the broader economy, and to a banking landscape unable to withstand the shock, once it came.

Most students will not go on to extensively study topics such as the driving forces of Wall Street, nor will they have time for ethnographic research. Yet interviewing, absorbing and understanding bits of culture, and analysing case studies are skills that go beyond analysing pre-existing statistical data sets. They complement these data sets by providing context and new insights into mechanisms which can help to explain observable phenomena, and are crucial for any economist, regardless of their area of expertise.

Qualitative methods are particularly important for understanding institutions and culture, crucial in economic dynamics. They also allow us to gain insight into the nature of different kinds of economic relationships, such as employment, transactions, buyer-supplier relationships and competition. Qualitative methods can also inform us about unexpected developments within the economy. For example, interviews and participant observations have provided new insights into how the financial sector works and why financial instability arises. Qualitative research methods can be very helpful in understanding the context of a specific case and acquiring an overview of how those involved perceive the situation. These various skills are particularly useful when working on concrete problems as professional economists. In short, qualitative methods can contribute both to the development of theory and to practical, concrete understanding.

It can also be very useful and productive to combine quantitative and qualitative research methods, often called mixed methods research. We discuss this on our website.

Research Methods & Philosophy of Science provides a practical discussion of teaching mixed methods research, as applied to economic topics.
economy.st/backgroundbb7

We start this building block with the philosophy of science and a broad overview of available methods, from quantitative to qualitative and from data collection to data analysis. We then explore quantitative methods in more depth, first discussing data collection methods, then discussing various techniques for data analysis. We subsequently do the same for qualitative methods. The chapter ends with suggestions on how to teach and effectively combine these various aspects of research methods, and a list of useful reading and teaching materials.

1   Philosophy of Science

The aim of teaching philosophy of science is not to teach students 'the best way to do research'. Rather, it is to teach students how to make informed methodological choices and to be reflective on those choices. This requires explicit attention for the limitations of methods and the trade-offs involved in the process of making methodological decisions.

The two aspects of philosophy of science that are of particular importance are those that relate to the ontology and epistemology of economics. Here we only mention a few of important questions and approaches students should be exposed to; our website discusses further details.

Ontology is the study of the nature of the world. It asks questions such as: is there a world 'out there' that we can study objectively, or do we actively construct reality? Does the world consist of individual parts that relate to one another, or is it a systemic whole? It also questions whether the economic world fundamentally differs from the natural world.

Epistemology is about how we can or cannot know things. It asks whether we can objectively observe reality, or whether "knowledge" is always the result of our own interpretation and experience. It also considers the different ways in which we can or should acquire knowledge. For example, should we start from empirical observations or from logic? These questions are answered differently by different methodological traditions, such as positivism, interpretivism, (critical) realism, and pragmatism.

The goal here is not to convince students to choose one particular approach. Instead students should understand the different approaches, and in particular which arguments they make, so that they can make informed methodological decisions when studying a topic.

The *ethics* related to doing research are also an important aspect of the philosophy of science. Most universities have ethics committees to review the moral acceptability of studies, whether experiments, surveys or interviews. It is important to introduce students to ideas and debates surrounding these issues.

Philosophy of science does not have to be overly complicated or abstract. The easiest way to ensure this is to integrate it with other aspects of research methodology, which is why we combine them into this single building block. Philosophical issues can be discussed with the help of specific studies and concrete applications of methods, rather than only discussing the concepts in the abstract. When, for example, teaching students about the technicalities of regression analysis, it is important to discuss ideas about what statistical significance really tells us about the world (Ziliak & McCloskey, 2008).

Research Methods & Philosophy of Science discusses additional aspects of the philosophy of science, comparing different ontological and epistemological perspectives.
economy.st/backgroundbb7

2 Research Methods: A Broad Overview

Now we turn to the research methods. In figure 7 below, we present an overview of qualitative and quantitative data collection and analysis methods. This is meant to illustrate the wide variety of options there are when teaching research methods to economics students. But as teaching time is always limited, we allocate the methods in two categories, *essential* and *additional*. We suggest the methods in the 'essential' box are most relevant for all economists to become familiar with.

The additional methods can, however, be crucial for students specialising in certain directions. If a student, for example, decides to specialise in qualitative research, it is key that he or she also learns about doing observations and how to apply content analysis and grounded theory to qualitatively analysing data. On the other hand, a student focused on quantitative methods would, for example, be helped by learning about automated data collection, and mathematical and agent-based modelling. As such, there are many relevant methods that are often too much to teach to all economics students, but are of great importance for those specialising in a certain direction.

We are very aware that this categorisation is likely to be contested and we advise teachers to change it according to their own views. At the same time, we recommend keeping the list of essential methods short, in order to keep it practically feasible to teach in a programme.

The methods categorised as essential are elaborated upon in the headings 3-6 of this chapter, below. In the online resources, we discuss the additional methods mentioned in the table.

	Qualitative	**Quantitative**
Data Collection	Essential: • Interviews Additional: • Non-participant observation • Document collection • Participant observation • Focus groups	Essential: • Experiments • Survey research Additional: • Structured observation • Automated data collection
Data Analysis	Essential: • Case studies Additional: • Content analysis • Grounded theory • Discourse analysis • Qualitative comparative analysis • Analytic induction • Framework analysis • Ethnomethodology • Phenomenology • Thematic analysis • Property space analysis	Essential: • Descriptive statistics • Regression analysis • Network analysis Additional: • Mathematical modelling • Principal component analysis • Factor analysis • (Multiple) Correspondence analysis • Cluster analysis • Geospatial information systems • Automated content analysis • Structural equation modelling • Simultaneous equation models • Vector autoregression • Agent-based modelling

Figure 7: An overview of research methods.

Research Methods & Philosophy of Science discusses the methods listed under 'Additional' in the above table.
economy.st/backgroundbb7

Part II

3 Quantitative Data Analysis: Descriptive Statistics, Regression Analysis & Network Analysis

Statistics can provide very helpful insights into economic systems and dynamics. For this reason, we think it is important that economics students acquire a good basis in quantitative data analysis in their programmes. When teaching quantitative data analysis methods more diversity can also enrich economics education. Current programmes focus predominantly on regression analyses. Students could benefit from learning a broader set of statistical techniques, and in particular network analysis. It is becoming increasingly clear how such new methods can help us understand economic dynamics, such as the Global Financial Crisis of 2007-2008 and its build-up with massive international financial flows, or the COVID-19 crisis with the global spread of the virus.

More generally, we encourage putting less emphasis on mathematical modelling in compulsory economics courses. Surveys among employers of economists indicate that professional economists rarely need sophisticated mathematical or econometric skills (Yurko, 2018). What is generally needed in practice, is being able to work, make sense of and communicate relatively basic statistical analyses. As such, economics programmes can better prepare students for their future roles by putting less emphasis on mathematical skills. As Robert Frank, professor at Cornell University (2011, p. 408) writes:

"Most introductory courses (and my own was no exception in the early days) make little use of narrative. Instead, they inundated students with equations and graphs. Mathematical formalism has been an enormously important source of intellectual progress in economics, but it has not proved an effective vehicle for introducing newcomers to our subject. Except for engineering students and a handful of others with extensive prior training in math, most students who attempt to learn economics primarily through equations and graphs never really grasp [it]."

This is not to say that mathematical modelling has no use. For those students with interest or talent for mathematics, like ourselves, it should be possible to specialise in this area through elective courses. In this way, the students who would later like to publish papers in mainstream economics journals have the opportunity to learn the research methods generally required there. At the same time, those less inclined towards mathematics are not prevented from becoming economists. In this way, economists, as a group, will be better able to fulfil their societal role as they will be able to apply a broader range of methods.

When mathematics is taught, we advise to mainly teach it mainly through tutorials and assigned homework as these allow for more differentiation and personal attention. Even more so than for other parts of economics education, students follow mathematics at different speeds and learn it in different ways. The traditional lecture teaching style, with a single professor standing at the front of the class writing out equations on the blackboard, therefore, does not seem to be the best way to enable students to develop their mathematical skills.

4 Quantitative Data Collection: Experiments & Survey Research

Beyond these techniques of analysis, we suggest that students gain hands-on experience with data collection methods, and in particular experiments and survey research. This will give them a feel for how datasets should be interpreted, but also help them gauge the reliability and limitations that come with any dataset. Let students design their own questionnaire and go out and gather a small dataset by themselves, and then work with that dataset on the aforementioned analytical techniques.

More and more programmes are incorporating behavioural economics and experimental methods. We applaud this development and encourage it, but we do think that learning how to collect quantitative data through surveys is even more critical. The main reason for this is that most data used by economists, both in academic and policy circles, still comes from surveys or processed government and tax files.

As Chang put it (2012, p. 1): *"Some economists say [numbers] are like sausages: you don't know what they really are until you cut into them."* If students do not learn how datasets are constructed during their education, they are likely to never really understand the numbers they will be intensively working with for the rest of their careers. Just as with statistics, it is important that students not only learn how to do the techniques, but are also taught how to reflect upon the advantages and disadvantages of methodological choices.

5 Qualitative Data Analysis: Case Studies

There are many different forms of qualitative data *analysis*, but case study research seems most essential for any economist. This is a useful approach to finding and describing essential information, and has the additional advantage that it almost automatically provides students with knowledge about the actual economy. Like interviewing, case study research is often applied by professionals working outside of academia. For this reason, it is useful to focus on teaching students to apply the method in practice and what aspects to be conscious of. Academic research is generally done more carefully in a longer time span and puts more emphasis on methodology. Practical applications of methods are often more concerned with the substance and conclusions. Students should therefore learn how to be able to acquire practically useful insights but in a methodologically proper manner.

For the systematic analysis of qualitative data, there are many other methods as outlined in the table above, such as content analysis, grounded theory, qualitative comparative analysis, and analytic induction. And like with quantitative analysis, it is useful for students to learn to work with software for analysis. However, while these methods are of great importance for students specialising in qualitative analyses, they seem to be less important for the average professional economist. Therefore, we recommend offering these qualitative data analysis methods in elective, rather than compulsory, courses. More details on these other techniques can be found in the online resources.

6 Qualitative Data Collection: Interviews

In addition to the large variety of qualitative data collection methods mentioned in the table above, we believe the most foundational method is interviewing. A key example of the usefulness of interviewing to economics is the study of Bewley into wage rigidity (1999). Rather than theorising about human behaviour in the abstract, he realised more insight into the matter could be gained by empirically investigating why both employers and employees are reluctant to let wages fall during recessions, creating a widely cited breakthrough study by using interviews.. Interviews are not only used by academic researchers. Many professionals in different types of organisations often use interviews to collect data, as it is a uniquely useful method for systematically acquiring knowledge about processes and people's experiences and thoughts.

Students can easily start working with this method, just as running a regression analysis on a computer can be done with the push of a button. The challenge is, however, to do it well and to make students conscious of methodological issues and trade-offs, and helping them acquire skills and experience by practising the method. It is, for example, important to pay attention to issues such as the structure of an interview, the phrasing of the questions, the non-verbal communication during the interview, and the context in which the interview takes place.

7 Practical Suggestions

We have three suggestions for how to teach these methods: be as hands-on as possible, use up-to-date software and teach specific approaches as part of a broader overview of the methods field.

First, ask students to apply the methods you teach them. Students find it much more interesting that way, and much more memorable. Perhaps most importantly, it prepares them for how they will use the methods in the future in their careers, as most students will become practical – rather than academic – economists. Another possibility is to teach methods in the context of a larger research project, which includes reading and evaluating existing research as well as letting students conduct empirical research themselves.

We understand that, for didactical reasons, it can sometimes be helpful to use fictional data to introduce students to the basics. However, we think it is important that this practice is kept to a minimum and students learn to work with real data as much as possible. The importance of this was expressed by a UK public sector manager who said (Yurko, 2018, p. 11):

"I'd basically make a lot of it more applied. I'm always slightly astonished you can go through three years of an undergrad learning macroeconomics without really knowing what GDP is or even knowing where to look on the internet to get GDP data. ... It would be useful if they had a bit more of how to actually use econometrics rather than the technical, basic how to do econometric proofs."

To collect quantitative data students could design their own survey to investigate a particular research or policy question. Going door to door to conduct those surveys and finding respondents online will teach them much about the messy nature of statistical data, and it is a valuable personal experience that they will not forget easily. In addition, it breaks the school-like monotony of lectures and working groups. Once collected, the data can be analysed using the various descriptive and inferential statistical techniques mentioned above.

Teaching the qualitative data *collection* method of interviewing is an excellent opportunity to send students out to do fieldwork. For instance, students could be tasked to find a company, government institution, a bank or any other economic environment to do observations and conduct (brief) interviews with a number of employees. This data could then be analysed using qualitative data *analysis* techniques, such as content analysis and case study.

Second, we advise to use state-of-the-art software, both for quantitative and qualitative data analysis. Being able to work with up-to-date software is often a highly rewarded skill in employment and thus important to teach in economics programmes. We do recognise that this might sound easier than it is, as it requires continuous time investment from the teacher to be acquainted with recent developments in software. To find the right software, ask employers and academics at the research frontier, or search online.

Third and finally, we suggest it is useful to teach students to understand and be able to evaluate a broader set of methods, which students will not learn to actively apply themselves. Such overviews of the methods field will enable students to grasp more advanced work and other types of research, and to know what things to pay attention to. Approach the methods in an integrated way and connect the different aspects to each other. Instead of teaching and reflecting on the techniques (only) separately, discuss them together. An assignment could be to read a certain set of papers or research reports, and reflect upon the main methodological choices and steps, and explain how the results should be interpreted. Properly reading and summarising literature is a skill in itself, not only a preparation phase for conducting new research projects.

Unfortunately, there are limitations on how many methods students can be taught in up to three-year programmes. It is practically impossible to try to teach them all relevant methods. It is, however, possible to give them an overview and basic understanding of them, and to give them the skills required to learn new methods quicker and more thoroughly. We would therefore advise teaching students a wide range of methods relatively briefly, and select a few research methods for hands-on training, in more detail. This gives students both a rough idea of different methods as well as the experience of working more in-depth with some of them.

Teaching Materials

- *Economic Methodology: Understanding economics as a science* by Marcel Boumans and John B. Davis, most recent edition from 2015. A sharp and accessible introduction into economic methodology and philosophy of science with explanations of different views on science and key debates on how economics should be practiced.

- *Social Research Methods* by Alan Bryman, most recent edition from 2015. A prominent textbook that introduces a wide variety of quantitative and qualitative research methods, such as interviews, structured and participant observation, content analysis, and survey research.

- *The SAGE Handbook of Applied Social Research Methods* by Leonard Bickman and Debra J. Rog, most recent edition from 2009. A leading textbook on applied research with attention to choosing the right method for the question at hand, practical considerations, and how to make informed methodological decisions for a variety of quantitative and qualitative methods.

- *Handbook of Research Methods and Applications in Heterodox Economics* by Frederic Lee and Bruce Cronin, from 2016. An instructive collection of essays with explanations, reflections on and applications of innovative research methods that deviate from the standard econometric approach usually taught in economics programmes, such as survey research, network analysis, experiments, ethnography, and agent-based computational modelling.

- *Qualitative Research Practice A Guide for Social Science Students and Researchers* by Jane Ritchie, Jane Lewis, Carol McNaughton Nicholls, and Rachel Ormston, most recent edition from 2013. A useful introduction into how to do rigorous and reflective quantitative research with chapters on interviews, focus groups, observation, research design, ethical considerations, and data analysis.

Visit the website for a wider range of teaching materials, to provide feedback, and to exchange ideas and ask support from colleagues worldwide.
economy.st/bb7

Part II

Building Block 8
Economic Theories

A pragmatic pluralist approach to theory, focusing on the most important insights for every topic.

1
Introducing
Economic
Perspectives

2
Interdisciplinary
Economics

3
Pragmatic
Pluralism

**Economic
Theories**

4
Practical
Suggestions

What

This building block provides a map through the complex jungle of economic theories. There are many schools of thought and each aspect of the economy has been analysed by a number of different schools. However, it is neither feasible nor productive for students to engage with every possible angle for every topic. Hence, this building block sets out an alternative approach: pragmatic pluralism. That is, make a selection of the most relevant theoretical approaches for the topic that is taught. Furthermore, before going into specific theories, teach students about the core assumptions that approaches make.

Why

Teaching theory in social sciences is important because it allows one to understand the components, processes and causal mechanisms characterising various social phenomena in a more structured and systematic manner. However, every topic can be understood from various theoretical perspectives, which can complement or contradict each other. It is essential to teach students a variety of approaches in order to give them a rich and broad understanding of the topic as well as the debate around it. This also helps them learn how to think critically and not take things as absolute truths.

Contrast with current programmes

Most contemporary economics programmes focus almost exclusively on neoclassical theory. In opposition to this, some argue to focus entirely on another perspective. We believe, in contrast to both, that there is no single 'correct' or 'best' way to understand the economy as a whole. It is too large and complex to be captured by a single point of view. Hence, we propose a fundamentally pluralist approach to teaching theory. Approaches should be judged on their merits, topic by topic: thinking critically and reflectively to decide which theoretical points of departure help us best to understand this particular corner of the economic system.

> *"Scientific knowledge is as much an understanding of the diversity of situations for which a theory or its models are relevant as an understanding of its limits."*

Elinor Ostrom (1990, p. 24)

The goal of teaching economic theory is to familiarise students with the most relevant ideas about how economies work. Given that there are many such important insights, what should students be taught in the short time available for a course? What will help them most to understand the economic world around them? One answer to this question is to follow a standard economics textbook. Polished, well-structured and widely recognised, it is no wonder most teachers choose this option. Unfortunately, most textbooks available today cover only the relatively narrow theoretical space of neoclassical economics. While this school of thought has much to offer, using solely a neoclassical textbook means students miss out on all other economic insights, and do not learn to compare different ideas and choose the one most valuable for the question at hand.

There are many reasons for making programmes more pluralist. First, no single theoretical framework explains everything: theories complement each other in many ways and are thus required to obtain a more complete understanding of the economy. Second, there are conflicting points of view and debates about virtually any economic topic. A pluralist education helps students to realise that they always have a choice as to how to approach issues, that there is no single 'right' answer nor one 'correct' method that is always superior. An education that leaves out such discussion, does not prepare students for the real world in which there is also often debate about what is the right way to understand an issue. Third, a pluralist programme introduces students to a wider range of economic wisdom collected throughout the past centuries, much of which regains its relevance time and again. These and other reasons for choosing theoretical pluralism are set out in more detail in *Foundation 2: Pluralism*, earlier in this book. In that chapter, we also discuss several of the most frequent objections to theoretical pluralism.

In practical terms pluralism might not look attractive at first sight. If we teach a plurality of theories, where does it stop? It would be impossible to cover all of the theoretical approaches when teaching on a concrete topic, such as the financial system. 'Indiscriminate' pluralism is impossible in practice.

In this building block we therefore present a more pragmatic way to teach theory in a pluralist way, focusing on the most important insights for every topic. Among all our building blocks, this one has by far the most content to discuss. For this reason, it is the largest of our ten building blocks and has a more complex internal structure.

This building block is structured as follows. In the first section, we discuss the need to introduce the main assumptions underlying different economic perspectives, before presenting their specific insights and more sophisticated theoretical work. Next we discuss interdisciplinary economics, which reveals that many key economic ideas and research do not stem from academic economists. In the third section we set out the general pragmatic pluralist approach: focus on the theoretical perspectives that seem most relevant in the specific thematic area one teaches about. The final section provides practical suggestions on teaching economic theory in a pragmatic pluralist way.

1 Introducing Economic Perspectives

Before delving into the specific insights that economic perspectives provide, it is important that students become familiar with their basic assumptions. What assumptions are made about what the economy is made up of, how it changes and how human beings act? What methodological preferences and normative ideas are typical? Without such basic knowledge, it is likely that students will perceive theory classes as one big blur with endless random insights. Armed with a basic understanding of what differentiates perspectives, students are able to situate and contextualise the insights that the perspectives have on specific topics. In other words, it allows them to see the bigger picture and connect the dots.

To keep such an introduction manageable, we suggest focusing on the core intuitions of perspectives, rather than presenting students with fully fleshed out models or mathematical representations. Furthermore, the core perspectives in the programme can be selected so that not too many perspectives are included within a single course. When introducing perspectives, the history of an approach can be of great use: it provides context and a broader understanding of its contribution to economic thinking.

The theoretical perspectives that we cover in this book are:

- Austrian School
- Behavioural Economics
- Classical Political Economy
- Complexity Economics
- Cultural Approach
- Ecological Economics
- Evolutionary Economics
- Feminist Economics
- Field Theory
- Historical School
- Institutional Economics
- Marxian Political Economy
- Neoclassical Economics
- Post-Keynesian Economics
- Social Network Analysis
- Structuralist Economics

For each of these approaches, we start with the key assumptions and aspects, followed by a brief history of the approach and some suggested low-threshold teaching materials to introduce students to the approach. There is no space in this book for sixteen such overviews, but to demonstrate what can be found on our website, we have included two examples below. The first is neoclassical economics and the second post-Keynesian economics.

Economic Approaches describes the core assumptions and history of the sixteen different economic approaches included in this book, and offers useful teaching materials. These brief descriptions form a practical starting point for introducing different theoretical approaches to students.
economy.st/approaches

Neoclassical Economics

Key assumptions and aspects:

- *Main concern*: Efficient allocation of scarce resources that maximises consumer welfare
- *Economies are made up of*: Individuals
- *Human beings are*: (Hyper)rational, self-interested and atomistic individuals with fixed and given preferences, also called 'homo economicus' and 'economic man'
- *Economies change through*: Individuals optimising decisions

- *Favoured methods*: Equilibrium models and econometrics
- *Typical policy recommendations*: Free market or government intervention, depending on assessment of market and government failures

Neoclassical economics arose out of the marginalist revolution, during the long depression which started in the 1870s. Neoclassical economics was largely a reaction against Marxian political economy as it argued that markets create harmony, not conflict. Human beings were assumed to be rational and selfish, as their decisions are solely motivated by expected utility maximisation based on their given and stable preferences. Mathematically deduced from these assumptions about individuals, an analysis of market equilibria arises. These markets work mainly through price mechanisms; their efficiency as well as their potential failures are analysed.

Neoclassical economics quickly became an important school of thought after its birth in the late 19th century, and after the Second World War it became the dominant theoretical approach in most countries. The increase in its practitioners gave rise to many different sub-branches of neoclassical economics, such as general equilibrium theory and neoclassical growth theory. Sometimes neoclassical economics is mistakenly equated to neoliberalism. While there is overlap between neoliberal thought and neoclassical sub-branches, such as monetarism and new classical macroeconomics, the two are not the same. Many economists, among which neo-Keynesians, for example, use and build on neoclassical (microeconomic) models to oppose neoliberal ideas.

To this day, neoclassical economics remains a highly influential approach, in research, policy making and especially education. At the same time many have been arguing for, or predicting, its demise for a couple of decades already (Colander, 2000). New approaches, such as behavioural, evolutionary and complexity economics, are often thought to replace neoclassical economics as core of the mainstream discipline. Whether this will indeed be the future remains to be seen.

Post-Keynesian Economics

Key assumptions and aspects:
- *Main concern*: Full employment
- *Economies are made up of*: Individuals and classes
- *Human beings are*: Following rules of thumb and habits because of fundamental uncertainty
- *Economies change through*: Animal spirits and government intervention
- *Favoured methods*: Stock-flow consistent models and econometrics
- *Typical policy recommendations*: Stabilisation of effective demand through active fiscal policy

Building on older underconsumption theories, Keynesian economics arose during the 1930s in order to explain and develop ideas to solve the economic depression. In doing so, it considerably overlaps with the Stockholm school. Keynesian economics argues that people compare themselves to others and build their decisions partly on rules of thumb and habits, because of psychological reasons and fundamental uncertainty. Effective demand, consumption and investment, therefore, depends to a large extent on animal spirits and herd behaviour. In the post-war period until the stagflation of the 1970s, it was highly influential. This was especially the case for its *neo-Keynesian* branch, sometimes also called old Keynesian, which synthesised Keynes's ideas with neoclassical microeconomics and this neoclassical synthesis forms the core of introductory (macro)economics education to this day.

After the 1970s, *post-Keynesians* (sometimes also called Cambridge Keynesians), who radically broke with neoclassical economics as they constructed a fundamentally new approach to economics with Keynes as main inspiration, became formally organised as a distinctive heterodox approach. At the same time, *new Keynesians* introduced imperfections in then influential neoclassical (DSGE) models of new classical macroeconomics, and in doing so came to Keynesian (pro-government intervention) rather than new classical (free-market) conclusions. Theoretically, however, they are furthest removed from Keynes' own work and thinking.

Economic Approaches provides teaching materials and offers the same as the above section does for neoclassical and post-Keynesian economics, for the following approaches: Classical Political Economy, the Historical School, Marxian Political Economy, the Austrian School, Institutional Economics, Behavioural Economics, Ecological Economics, Evolutionary Economics, Feminist Economics, Complexity Economics, Structuralist Economics, Social Network Analysis, Field Theory and the Cultural Approach.
economy.st/approaches

2 Interdisciplinary Economics

The economy is not only studied by economists; other disciplines also have much to contribute. While this may seem strange at first, it is good to realise that academic disciplines have historically been the field of power struggles between different groups of scientists. Often, the ones who were forced out of the discipline, often for personal, practical or worldly reasons, have found a home elsewhere. For instance, some economic perspectives mentioned above, such as social network analysis and field theory, were developed by economic sociologists rather than economists and are currently also mainly practised by these academics.

In the online resource *Interdisciplinary Economics*, we provide an overview of the most relevant economic approaches found in other disciplines. We briefly discuss the histories of and different approaches practised in the following economic subdisciplines:
- Economic Sociology
- Economic Anthropology
- Economic Geography
- Political Economy
- Economic History

Teaching students the basics of these economic subdisciplines and their approaches has two advantages. First, students gain valuable intellectual tools. Second, these approaches often form a natural bridge between the disciplines, helping students to communicate and collaborate more easily with other social scientists. Due to space restrictions we are only able to provide one example here: economic sociology. On our website, we offer the other four: economic geography, economic history, economic anthropology and political economy. We also provide more suggestions on interdisciplinary teaching, using the subdisciplines of neighbouring fields.

Economic Sociology

Economic sociology has been an important part of sociology since its origins. Many of its founders, such as Auguste Comte, Karl Marx, Émile Durkheim, Max Weber, Georg Simmel and Vilfredo Pareto, wrote extensively on the economy. In fact, most of them can be regarded as both a sociologist and economist (and often philosopher, historian and political scientist as well). After the formation of the discipline of sociology, most sociologists, however, ceased studying the economy, causing the subdiscipline of economic sociology to move to the background.

This rigid division between the two fields came about as a sort of truce, where both economists and sociologists agreed not to study each other's fields. The origins of this truce are associated with Talcott Parsons and Lionel Robbins in the 1930s (Velthuis, 1999). Economists would solely focus on the means to achieve given ends, while sociologists studied those ends and the values people have. According to this logic, institutional economics was no longer considered to be proper economics, and economic topics should no longer be studied by sociologists. However, with the partial disappearance of institutional economics and economic sociology, large parts of the economy fell outside the scope of any field of study.

This changed again in the 1980s (Granovetter, 1985; Smelser & Swedberg, 2010). The truce to not study each other's fields was broken because of a revival of economic sociology and the rise of the imperialism of neoclassical economics. Since then, economic sociology has emerged as one of the main fields within sociology and as such it has produced multiple new approaches and insights. The main approaches stemming from economic sociology are social network analysis, the neo-institutional approach, field theory, cultural approaches, and performativity theory. These different approaches have in common that they all analyse how markets are socially constructed with the help of state structures, social relations and cultural norms. In other words: how they are embedded in society. There is, for example, a strand of research that investigates how the lifestyles and morals of people shape what they do, and do not, buy (see online).

Interdisciplinary Economics provides teaching materials and a similar overview for the subdisciplines Economic Geography, Economic History, Economic Anthropology, Political Economy.
economy.st/interdisciplin

3 Pragmatic Pluralism

This building block is coupled with *Tool 1: Pragmatic Pluralism*, which further fleshes out the approach by suggesting which ideas and insights seem to us most relevant to teach in specific courses, such as Labour or Financial Economics. The core of that resources chapter is a table connecting theoretical approaches to thematic areas, followed by a few pages describing the various ideas and insights by the most relevant perspectives for every topic.

Overview

As noted in the introduction to this building block, 'indiscriminate' pluralism, teaching every perspective on every topic, is neither feasible nor desirable. Fortunately, different theoretical perspectives have different focal areas. Some have crucial ideas about consumption, others focus on the state, yet others concentrate their explanatory power on finance and business cycles, and so on. These differences form the foundation of our approach. Figure 8 shows an overview of these thematic focal areas of the major theoretical perspectives in economics.

	Governments	Business Cycles	Consumption	Economic Development	Finance	Firms	Households	Inequality	International Trade	Labour	Markets	Money	Nature
Austrian School	+	■						+			+	■	
Behavioural Economics	+			+	+			+			+		
Classical Political Economy	+			■		+					■		□
Complexity Economics	+				□			+					
Cultural Approach					+		□			□	□	□	□
Ecological Economics			□	+									■
Evolutionary Economics	□			+		□							
Feminist Economics							■	□		+			
Field Theory						■					+		
Historical School	+			■								+	
Institutional Economics			■	□		■							+
Marxian Political Economy	+	+		+			+	■		■			
Neoclassical Economics	■	□	■	+	■	+	■	■	■	■	■		■
Post-Keynesian Economics	■	■			■			+	■			■	
Social Network Analysis					+					+			
Structuralist Economics				+					□				
Other	+		+			+		+	+				+

- ■   Main opposing perspective
- □   Main complementary perspective
- +   Additional perspective

Figure 8: An overview of the pragmatic pluralist approach to teaching economic theories.

To construct such an overview requires three levels of selection: thematic areas, theoretical perspectives and the most fruitful combinations of these. We will discuss each of these in turn.

First, what are the main thematic areas in economics? Here we stay close to the existing categories in economics education, academic fields and policy areas to create an overview of the core fields of study in the wider economic system. This results in a list of thirteen thematic areas, ranging from markets to development, households and nature, which are shown on the x-axis of the table above.

Second, which theoretical perspectives to include? We decided to include only theoretical perspectives which had a relatively established body of research and ideas and have made crucial contributions to at least two of the thematic areas. Since we see *economics* as centred on an object of study, the economy, rather than something defined by its current mainstream, we included some approaches which are practised more widely outside economic faculties than inside them. The vast majority, however, falls within the economic discipline. This resulted in a list of sixteen theoretical perspectives, which are shown on the y-axis of the table.

In theory, this could result in an overview of 13x16 topic-approach combinations. However, as stated above, different approaches focus on different topics. This brings us to the third level of selection: which schools to teach on which topics? Building on a wide-ranging literature review and the advice of many experts, we selected the approaches that had the most original and relevant ideas and insights on each of the thematic areas. The functionality of a theory was central in this choice.

For each topic, this resulted in two main opposing perspectives, one complementary perspective and a short summary of other useful insights and perspectives. In this way, one could start a course by discussing the debate between the two conflicting approaches in the first half of the course. The third quarter of the course could be devoted to the additional complementary perspective. Finally, in the last quarter, other useful perspectives and insights could be discussed.

With this pragmatic pluralist approach to teaching economic theory, no single approach is dominant but there is also not an impractical excess of theories. Here it is important to note that following our suggestions would imply reducing the teaching time devoted to neoclassical theory. Studies indicate that currently roughly 4/5 or more of economic theory courses are devoted to neoclassical economics (Proctor, 2019). With this pragmatic pluralist approach about 1/5 of teaching time would be devoted to neoclassical economics. This means that there will be more need to focus on the most relevant and important insights of neoclassical theory, and to in turn spend less time on the technicalities of its models.

Cautionary notes

The table previewed above has a number of important limitations to keep in mind. This section sets out three cautionary notes. Firstly, our table should be seen as a starting point. It leaves much room for improvement and will change over time. Secondly, we have presented a limited overview, but it could easily be expanded by adding additional topics and theoretical approaches. Thirdly, the boundaries between various topics and various approaches are heuristics only: the field is interconnected in many ways.

On our first point, as far as we know, this is the first attempt at trying to systematically identify the most relevant ideas and insights on the different economic thematic areas (with a pluralist approach). Combined with our limited knowledge of the various topics and approaches, it is likely to be rough and imperfect. It should not be seen as a complete overview, but rather as a starting point and an illustration of how such a pragmatic pluralist approach might look in practice. Suggestions for improvement are most welcome. Furthermore, such an overview should never be set in stone as the discipline itself is always subject to change. When new important insights are gained, they should be integrated in education as well. Twenty years from now, the table should look different from how it looks now.

It should also be noted that some topics and theories have more ideas and insights listed than others. Some thematic areas have traditionally received much attention, such as economic development. This results in a larger amount of insights than on less studied areas, such as households, but it is not a judgement on the importance of the topic itself. Equally, some approaches have historically had the benefit of a large research community, such as neoclassical economics, Marxian political economy and the cultural approach. These have thus been further developed and are better represented in the table. Again, this is not to be taken as an endorsement of those schools in general and it could also very well change over the coming decades, as some approaches will be further developed while others will be done less so.

Following on our second point, the table could be expanded to allow for more nuance and detail, and cover more ground. A table of 13x16 is admittedly already quite large, but for trying to compress the entirety of economic thinking into it, it is bound to be too small. Expansion could come from adding topics and approaches as well as from combining the current ones and differentiating within them.

On the x-axis, many other topics could be added, such as health economics, the economics of education and transport economics. Topics like finance and nature could be combined to create new topics like green finance. Within topics like public economics, differentiation could be made between the economics of taxation and the economics of government spending.

The same applies to the y-axis, which lists theoretical perspectives. The regulation school and neo-Ricardian or Sraffian economics could, for example, be added. Combinations between neoclassical and Keynesian approaches could, for example, be made to identify neo- and new Keynesian economics. And further distinctions between original and new institutional economics as well as original and new behavioural economics could be made.

Furthermore, the table could cover more ground by simply adding more insights into the empty spaces in the current 13x16 structure. As said, we intentionally tried to keep it as empty as possible, while capturing the most relevant insights. Where to precisely draw the line between inclusion and exclusion? This is a difficult matter and to a certain degree will always be arbitrary. One could easily imagine including more ideas and insights in the table than we did, or fewer.

Finally, it is important to keep in mind that these categories are only heuristic tools to help our thinking. It would be a misunderstanding to suggest that they exist in isolation. The topics and perspectives are fundamentally linked to each other and sometimes the boundaries between them are unclear. Where does the topic 'firms' end and 'labour' begin? How exactly should we separate 'money' from 'finance'?

While we suggest focusing on specific topics and approaches in different courses, we think it is also important to pay attention to how they are connected and together make up a larger economic whole. These fields do not exist in isolation of each other, nor do their associated insights. To take an example: the new insights in finance from Hyman Minsky had important consequences for those studying business cycles. His core insight was that financial markets had their own dynamics. Rather than simply following developments in the real economy, financial markets could cause huge changes in the real economy. His ideas on the mechanisms surrounding debt accumulation by private sector businesses, financial actors and households proved to be crucial in understanding the financial crisis of 2008 and its causes. In other words, the topic of finance is important to understand for the related field of business cycles.

Just as topics are often connected and difficult to separate, perspectives at times are also strongly linked to each other. Some ideas can even be attributed to multiple perspectives at the same time. So while perspectives sometimes might be in conflict with each other, they also often agree with each other. For brevity and clarity, we included every idea only once in the table. However, in the explanations below the table we discuss when an idea is shared by multiple perspectives.

An example: Finance

To show how this table works in practice we consider the topic of finance as an example. As shown in the table, the following perspectives seem to have made the most relevant contributions:

Main opposing perspectives
- Post-Keynesian economics: Animal spirits shape market movements
- Neoclassical economics: Banks are rational intermediators

Main complementary perspective
☐ Complexity economics: Systemic risk

Additional perspectives and insights
+ Behavioural economics: Systematic irrationality
+ Cultural economics: Analytical constructs shape the market

Post-Keynesian and neoclassical economics represent two long-standing perspectives on the role of finance within the economy. The first approach, currently strongly linked to post-Keynesian economics, is more inductive in nature and makes use of accounting, or stock-flow consistent, models, which strive for completeness in capturing all flows (transactions) and stocks (balance sheets). The second approach, associated with neoclassical economics, is more deductive and uses equilibrium models, which only include variables that are theoretically deemed to be important in an economy defined by optimal outcomes (equilibria). The latter approach sees the non-financial economy and rational individual behaviour as key, arguing that money is primarily a unit of account and that finance can be excluded from standard macroeconomic models. The financial sector is a passive rational intermediary between savers and investors that enables efficient capital allocation. The former approach, in contrast, emphasises the importance of monetary flows in modern economies and dynamics at the system, rather than individual, level. It argues finance has an active and innovative role and that financial decisions depend on animal spirits because of fundamental, or Knightian, uncertainty that makes it impossible to calculate probabilities for future events.

In the main complementary perspective, complexity economics, financial booms and busts are understood as self-reinforcing asset-price changes, which are prevalent but unpredictable as the decisions and forecasts of many individual agents in complex networks go through phases because of their interactions and feedback effects. An important topic is therefore systemic risk, which is the risk associated with the financial system as a whole, as opposed to individual banks, companies or firms, and thus is concerned with interlinkages and interdependencies. Countering earlier popular ideas that diversification and deregulation are generally desirable, this line of research focuses on the risks associated with interconnectedness and ever more sophisticated financial instruments.

Finally, behavioural and cultural economics provide additional insights into how finance works by focusing on psychological, cognitive and social processes. Behavioural economics, or rather behavioural finance, focuses on how people systematically make errors because of their limited cognitive capabilities and how this influences financial markets. The cultural approach, as practiced by various economic sociologists and anthropologists, focuses on how economic ideas can be *performative* in the sense that they can shape the phenomena they describe and thereby bring reality closer to their theory. One example of this, is how the neoclassical Black-Scholes-Merton model of option pricing initially poorly described pricing patterns, but later on became empirically successful as market participants began to use the model to trade (MacKenzie, 2008).

4   Practical Suggestions

How can this pragmatic pluralist approach be implemented in practice? In this section we discuss the choice between organising courses around topics or around perspectives.

Courses on topics or perspectives

Within the pragmatic pluralist approach, there are the two options: to organise the key insights by topic or by perspective. 'By topic' means that a programme might have separate courses on labour economics, financial economics, public economics, and so on. 'By perspective' implies a programme built out of courses on institutional economics, neoclassical economics, Keynesian economics, and so on. In theory, both of these programmes could cover exactly the same ideas and material. Still, there are some important differences between the two options.

Firstly, the two options have different consequences to students' learning trajectories and their subsequent ability to see the connections between approaches and topics. Placing perspectives at the centre of courses emphasises the theory, while organising courses around topics focuses on the real-world topic as daily life is organised around topics. When a full course is devoted to a perspective, it is likely that this way of thinking will stick with students. If a course is organised around a topic, on the other hand, it is more likely that specific knowledge concerning that topic will be remembered. Focusing on topics also allows us to more easily incorporate real-world knowledge. As such, the choice seems between placing emphasis on understanding a way of looking at the economy or understanding a part of the economy.

There is, however, also another dimension to this choice. When courses are organised around theoretical frameworks, the links between topics are clearer. If topics are put at the centre of courses, it becomes clearer how perspectives complement and contradict each other. The choice is thus between putting emphasis on understanding the topics and seeing links between perspectives or focusing on perspectives and seeing connections between topics.

Secondly, there are practical choices to make. There is a functional advantage to organising courses around topics: it requires less change in existing course structures. Current programmes generally do provide education on a broad range of topics, but focus almost exclusively on the neoclassical perspective. As such, courses are generally already organised around topics. To implement a pragmatic pluralist approach would thus entail pluralising existing courses. If, on the other hand, one chooses to organise courses around perspectives, current courses would have to be replaced by new courses each focused on a different approach.

However, there is also a practical advantage for organising courses around perspectives. Often, it is easier to find academic staff who are knowledgeable in one perspective, who can then apply their perspective to different topics. It can be harder to find teachers who have broad knowledge of a topic and the different perspectives on them. When this is indeed the case, then teachers specialised in certain approaches could be hired to teach courses on them. The reverse, pluralising existing courses organised around topics, would require current teachers to become knowledgeable of the different approaches to topics they teach about. An alternative is to invite academics from other departments or universities to teach a few guest lectures on the perspectives in which they have specialised.

Finally, there is also a danger in organising courses around perspectives, especially if this is implemented piecemeal. The impression can arise that all perspectives, except for the currently dominant neoclassical one, are just 'nice extras' that can be taught all together in one additional course, possibly as an elective for those who happen to be interested in it. In an extreme case, the programme would thus change from being exclusively neoclassical to one in which everything is still neoclassical except for one course on "*alternative*" or "*heterodox*" approaches.

The point is, however, that these other approaches are not some enjoyable, exotic add-ons. They are crucial for students to learn about as they contribute key insights into how economies work. Without them, students lack important knowledge and remain blind to crucial aspects of economies. In sum, having one course on *other* perspectives, can give the false impression that they are 'covered'. Much more attention is needed to properly teach the various important insights – just as substantial time is needed to teach the relevant neoclassical insights.

Teaching Materials

Especially since the Global Financial Crisis of 2007-2008, a wide variety of textbooks has been published to facilitate topic-based pluralist economic teaching. Following every topic-summary in the online resources for this book (finance, labour, nature, etc.), we suggest literature for that specific topic. A few of these textbooks deserve specific mention, because they are useful in teaching several of the topics and approaches. We will introduce them in order from introductory to advanced.

- *Economics: The User's Guide* by Ha-Joon Chang, from 2014. This book provides a brief and accessible pluralist introduction to a broad range of theoretical insights the discipline has to offer. While theoretical, this book is never dry. It is clearly written and has a very succinct style.
- *Rethinking Economics: An Introduction to Pluralist Economics* by Liliann Fischer, Joe Hasell, J. Christopher Proctor, David Uwakwe, Zach Ward Perkins, Catriona Watson, from 2017. This collection of essays provides an accessible introduction into post-Keynesian, Marxian, Austrian, institutional, feminist, behavioural, complexity and ecological economics.
- *Exploring Economics*: www.exploring-economics.org/en/. This website provides sharp and helpful introductions into the different economic perspectives and furthermore gives many useful overviews of related teaching materials, videos and existing (online) courses.
- *Principles of Economics in Context* by Jonathan Harris, Julie A. Nelson and Neva Goodwin, most recent edition from 2020. A useful textbook that treats much of the traditional content, but also consistently discusses the social and environmental challenges inherent in economic questions.
- *Economics After The Crisis* by Irene van Staveren, from 2015. This well-written textbook describes twelve central topics in economics at an introductory level, each from four different perspectives: the neoclassical, institutional, social and post-Keynesian perspectives.
- *The Economy* by the CORE Team, from 2017. This highly successful textbook, freely available online with additional resources, provides a treasure trove of empirical data, context and recent research.
- *Introducing a New Economics* by Jack Reardon, Maria A. Madi, and Molly S. Cato, from 2017. This ground-breaking textbook introduces many of the core issues in economics today and weaves together pluralist theory and real-world knowledge in an eminently readable way.
- *Political Economy: The Contest of Economic Ideas* by Frank Stilwell, most recent edition from 2011. This well-written textbook provides a good introduction to economic ideas from multiple perspectives, with particular attention to classical, Marxist, neoclassical, institutional,

Keynesian and more recent insights related to capitalism.

- *Foundations of Real-World Economics* by John Komlos, from 2019. This textbook is perhaps the most critical of this list, providing a sharp criticism of the neoclassical school as well as providing a wealth of empirical data and findings.
- *Capitalism: Competition, Conflict, Crises* by Anwar Shaikh, from 2016. This impressive and extensive book covers many traditional economic topics and compares multiple perspectives on each including classical, Marxian, neoclassical, Austrian, Keynesian, complexity and several others, as well as testing them against empirical data. Not light reading, but very much worth it.
- *The Routledge Handbook of Heterodox Economics: Theorizing, Analyzing, and Transforming Capitalism* by Tae-Hee Jo, Lynne Chester, and Carlo D'Ippoliti, from 2017. This collection of essays discusses a great variety of economic topics and theories, from theories of production, value and prices, to theories of finance, the environment, and the state.
- *The Microeconomics of Complex Economies: Evolutionary, Institutional, Neoclassical and Complexity Perspectives* by Wolfram Elsner, Torsten Heinrich, and Henning Schwardt, from 2014. This innovative textbook makes readers familiar with new insights coming from frontier mainstream economic research, with particular attention to game theory, agent-based modelling, system dynamics, and empirical realities.
- *Macroeconomics* by William Mitchell, L. Randall Wray, Martin Watts, from 2019. This ground-breaking and much-discussed textbook written by three leaders of Modern Monetary Theory (MMT), describes in detail the history of economic thinking about the state and macroeconomy as well as recent theoretical and policy debates.

Visit the website for a wider range of teaching materials, to provide feedback, and to exchange ideas and ask support from colleagues worldwide.
economy.st/bb8

Building Block 9
Problems & Proposals

Practical skills to critically and constructively analyse real-world problems, with a focus on the economic aspects, and work on proposals to address them.

1
Sector or
Topic Scan

2
Problem
Analysis

3
Proposals

**Problems &
Proposals**

4
Practical
Suggestions

What

This building block is about investigating specific economic issues and proposing or evaluating ideas that aim to solve them. Students should gain experience with the full process: from acquiring an overview of the problem and the field it is located in, to various ways of evaluating possible solutions and presenting those solutions to decision-makers. Students should learn both practical and analytical skills to give good advice on how to address issues, based on a variety of values and analysis techniques.

Why

Practical economic analyses, like cost benefit analyses of proposed public investments, are a core aspect of most economics students' future work. While more sector- and role-specific techniques and skills can be learned on the job after graduation, academic education should teach skills beyond the purely academic. It is vital that students are trained to think through real-world economic questions in a systematic, analytical and thorough way.

Contrast with current programmes

Most current programmes mainly focus on theory and statistical testing of universal economic laws. This is a very useful skill set to develop scientific knowledge. Professional economists, however, need a number of different skills, which are associated with the work before and after the typical 'academic' research. Before working through a specific theoretical model and applying statistical tests, one needs to analyse the context: the sector or topic, and subsequently define the problem at hand. This involves exploring different perspectives, using systems thinking to map the structure of the relevant economic sector(s) and topic(s), locating and understanding stakeholders, values and interests, and getting an overview of available data and information. Then, after performing data analysis, one needs to outline possible future directions, formulate concrete proposals – to make the conducted analysis policy- or decision-relevant, and communicate the analysis to internal and external stakeholders.

"Blackboard economics is undoubtedly an exercise requiring great intellectual ability, and it may have a role in developing the skills of an economist, but it misdirects our attention when thinking about economic policy."

Ronald Coase (2012, p. 19)

Economists are often employed in the role of advisers and policy designers: whether working as a consultant, as a policy-maker, in the non-profit domain or in the commercial or financial sector, our job is frequently to provide a framework for strategic decisions and policy-making. In this building block, we discuss how students can get basic training in this key aspect of working as an economist: evaluating practical problems and coming up with potential solutions. We have divided the process in three parts: first the sector or topic scan to build context, then the problem analysis and finally the concrete proposal.

A good way to learn to work on practical challenges is through case studies. Throughout this building block, we use an example case study to make our proposals more concrete and tangible: the problem of increasing numbers of people with debt problems.

1   Sector or Topic Scan

A good analysis starts with context. This generally requires forming an overview of the sector or topic at hand. *Building Block 2: Know Your Own Economy* suggests various angles to gain an understanding of national economies. Those methods may again be useful here, when applied to a specific topic or sector rather than an economy-wide scan. Sector analyses are often used in investment banking to analyse profitability. We propose here to go beyond this specific focus in order to prepare students to also be able to conduct sector analyses for a public or civil society organisation which can have different and broader priorities.

A sector or topic scan could include analysing relevant documentation, such as policy reports, media coverage and annual reports, as well as gathering basic statistics and talking to experts and stakeholders. Such practical literature research requires somewhat different skills from writing an academic literature review, so it is important that students gain experience with this. Some historical background knowledge of the sector is also very helpful when trying to set a new direction, and can be gained through expert interviews and reading. Using these and other sources, students can start to outline their own overview of the relevant organisations, groups, relationships and pressures around the topic in question.

One useful analytical tool for sketching such an overview is *systems thinking*, as it helps students connect different aspects and help them better understand how they interact with each other. Systems thinking enables us to think in terms of networks and relations between various groups and organisations, in terms of stocks and flows, and in terms of processes, rather than static situations. Systems may spiral out of control as certain dynamics can enter self-strengthening (positive) feedback loops. At other times its forces and pressures, whether for good or for ill, may fizzle out through balancing negative feedback loops. Systems can be any size and have numerous integrations and connections to other systems. They can be as small as the economic dynamics in a single shopping street, as shops enter and exit and retail culture changes over time, or as large as international financial systems. Two useful books to learn about systems thinking are: *Thinking in Systems: A Primer* and *Systems Thinking For Social Change*.

Taking the example of increasing prevalence of chronic personal debt, the sector and topic scan might include any of the following components:
- Gathering statistics on chronic debt prevalence and duration;
- Exploring the legal frameworks on personal indebtedness and bankruptcy;
- Taking stock of governmental practice on the issue;
- Interviewing debtors to explore their experiences and to create an overview of typical trajectories into and out of chronic debt problems;
- Creating an overview of the types of commercial parties involved and their business models;
- Writing up an overview of any other governmental and non-profit organisations that work in the area;
- Mapping all these actors and factors together using systems thinking.

It is unrealistic to expect students to have the perfect overview of a sector or topic. However, teaching them a technique to analyse the context will help them to approach concrete problems with confidence. This is particularly useful and important because in their later career they will often have to do similar exercises, although often in a more quick and dirty way.

2 Problem Analysis

After exploring the context in a broad-ranging, structured and systematic way, it is time to start defining the problem itself more precisely. Colander (2001) provides six common sense methodological rules for what he calls 'the art of economics', that is, applied and practical economics:

- Take in all dimensions of the problem;
- Use whatever empirical work sheds light on the issue at hand;
- Do not be falsely scientific and present only empirical tests that are convincing to you;
- Do not violate the law of significant digits;
- Use the reasonable person criterion to judge policy;
- Use the best economic theory available.

Applying the most suitable theory requires gathering an overview of potential theoretical approaches to the problem, and from those, 'choosing the right model' (Rodrik, 2015). Any model, whether mathematical or based on another language, is a simplification of the world. The main criterion for choice is this: does the model capture the most relevant mechanisms and elements for this specific problem and set of values? For details on choosing between theoretical approaches, we refer to *Building Block 8: Economic Theories* and the accompanying online resources.

In terms of practical tools, a useful technique for defining the problem is *stakeholder mapping*. Stakeholders can range from well-defined interest groups such as employers' organisations and labour unions, to often less organised stakeholders such as citizens and consumers.

This is not merely a technical exercise. When deciding what the problem is, normative questions inevitably come into play. A problem, after all, can be defined as a negative deviation from the desired situation. And in defining the desired state of affairs, we are acting normatively. The tricky part is this: it is not the role of the economist to make normative decisions. But it is the job of the economist to clearly lay out the normative concerns involved.

This is only possible if economists are *aware* of the normative issues surrounding the topic. It is not enough to assume the various stakeholders have certain interests or preferences. Actual empirical research is needed to find out what they find important and worrisome. In this process, students should learn to be aware of power differentials between various stakeholders and to repeatedly ask themselves: *whose* problem are we talking about? Which groups might be adversely affected by potential solutions?

Systematically mapping concerns and normative ideas of people requires skills, so this course could well be combined with methods courses focusing on teaching students how to conduct interviews and survey research. Furthermore, they need to be able to conceptualise normative concerns in a coherent and clear manner. Here, questions of values and economic goals will inevitably play up, which are respectively discussed in *Foundation 4: Values* and *Building Block 1: Introducing the Economy*.

To return to the example of increasing prevalence of chronic personal debt, the problem analysis might include any or all of the following aspects:

- The moral obligation to stick to contracts and agreements, to pay one's due;
- The societal cost of an expensive judiciary system dealing with debt default;
- The various psychological burdens of living with chronic debt, such as guilt, fear and loss of self-esteem;
- The notion of fairness: the current system is penalising poverty and widening existing inequalities;
- The financial problems of companies whose goods and services go unpaid;
- The societal loss of the active and unburdened social contributions of chronic debt sufferers.

Ideally, a problem analysis would also include some overview of the upsides of the current situation, so that in solving a problem, we realise what positive elements might be worth considering, and what parties might be opposed to certain solutions. In our case study, these might be some of the following: the economic benefit of additional jobs at debt collector agencies, the extra income for public coffers brought in by interests and penalties on late-paid fines, the decrease in negotiating costs resulting from having strongly enforceable contracts backed up by a credible threat.

Some of these are easily expressed in monetary terms, others not as they primarily exist in other dimensions. While a policy solution may require comparing pears and apples and translating everything to monetary values, we suggest expressing each of these problem factors first in their own terms. This is especially important because translating everything to monetary values requires making normative trade-offs. It is not the job of the economist to make these normative decisions, so it is important that students learn how to communicate the normative trade-offs to non-economists (DeMartino & McCloskey, 2016).

3 Proposals

Writing proposals

Having mapped the context and analysed the problem, it is time to think about solutions. Choosing which solution is most desirable is often not up to economists. However, we do need to be knowledgeable about the different normative principles that can guide decisions. This is an important element of *Building Block 10: Economics for a Better World*. This section is rather about how to analyse the different options to choose from. What are relevant and good suggestions to address the issue at hand?

Coming up with innovative solutions has a creative element to it which is difficult to plan and teach. Nevertheless, students can be stimulated to engage in open brainstorm sessions triggering them to look at the matter in different ways. While creativity is useful, it is also important that students learn not to reinvent the wheel. Rather than coming up with entirely new ideas, most often good potential solutions come about from further developing and building on earlier ideas and applying them to the specific situation. History does not repeat itself exactly, but it does follow certain patterns. A crucial skill to teach students is therefore to find such ideas and examine similar cases.

Economic theory is also key here. How one theoretically understands the problems also for a large part determines what one comes up with as a solution. If over-indebtedness is theorised to come about because of individual cognitive mistakes and miscalculations, one might come up with the idea to give people more and better information, and nudge them to be more aware of the risks of borrowing money. If one, on the other hand, theorises that over indebtedness is caused by certain characteristics of the larger economic system, one might come up with ideas to reform elements of that system. For instance, one might look at regulation of lending practices and addressing underlying trends such as stagnating wages and rising housing prices.

This example demonstrates not only the link between theory and solutions, it also shows how difficult it can be to separate theoretical and normative assessments of issues. Pluralism is thus not only a matter of better understanding a topic, but also of bringing out underlying normative assumptions.

Once several potential solutions have been identified and developed, a useful technique to analyse and compare them is *scenario thinking*. Scenario thinking is a structured process of thinking ahead and anticipating. The objective is to examine possible future developments that could impact individuals, organisations or societies, in order to find directions for decisions that stand a good chance to pass the test of time. Scenario thinking always includes a number of possible future scenarios, thus preparing for many possible future events. This tool can be fruitfully combined with systems thinking. Students could ask: of which system is the problem or proposed solution part? What feedback loops could this policy initiate? With what other processes might it interact with? Are there relevant tipping points? Are there strong countervailing forces preventing change?

It is also important to think about what unintended consequences a potential solution might have. Besides solving the problem, it might create or worsen other problems. Therefore it is important that students learn to think through what the effects of a policy or action might be. And finally, a key element that should not be forgotten is the implementation. An idea is not of much use if it only works well in theory, but is highly unlikely to ever be implemented because of practical issues or power pressures.

To systematically take these various factors into consideration, various practical policy tools have been developed that professional economists frequently use in their work. The most well-known of these is cost-benefit analysis (Boardman et al., 2017), based on neoclassical economics. Newer policy tools include risk-opportunity analysis, based on complexity economics (Mercure et al., 2020), and participatory evaluation (Cousins & Chouinard, 2012), inspired by the cultural approach. To prepare students for their future work, we advise devoting teaching time to these policy tools and expose them to recent developments in the field.

These practical policy tools are also connected to larger perspectives on how one should think and approach policy making. Examples of these perspectives are the positivist approach aiming for evidence-based policy making (Davies & Nutley, 2000), the constructivist approach aiming to include different conceptions of social reality in policy making (Guba & Lincoln, 1989), and the (critical) realist approach, which aims to synthesise the other two approaches making use of theory-based evaluation (Pawson, 2002; Pawson & Tilley, 2001; Stame, 2004).

Evaluating proposals

At this stage, we also suggest providing students with the tools to evaluate and compare proposals. In their careers, students will often have to assess proposals and arguments put forward by others, so it is important to prepare them for this.

Evaluating proposals takes many of the same skills as writing proposals, but there are also a couple of important differences. Evaluating proposals written by others takes less time. Rather than experiencing the entire process of writing a proposal, one reads only the final outcome. As such, it is important to learn how to quickly develop an understanding for an issue at hand. This requires knowing what to focus on and what not, which in turn rests on the ability to spot and identify the crucial steps and elements in proposals. Students need to learn to see the line of reasoning and identify the core theoretical and normative ideas underlying the arguments. They should learn to weigh empirical evidence that is presented to support claims and know how to rather quickly assess the methodologies of studies.

4 Practical Suggestions

These are skills that are best learned by doing. The best way to teach this type of practical skills is not using textbooks, but through concrete case studies. These might be historical as well as current. For students, it is often more interesting to work for a real-world organisation, so it is great if companies, government agencies or NGOs can bring in the case studies. If a practitioner from one of these organisations can be found to help teach the course, even better. Alternatively, cases can be drawn up by the professor.

More generally, students need to go out into the world and talk to stakeholders. Problem analysis assignments might be bigger projects, up to several months long, but could also very well be structured as smaller tasks. Training students to evaluate existing proposals can be done by giving them reports from academics, NGOs, political parties, government agencies, lobby groups and firms. They could analyse these in smaller groups, discuss them, write summaries, criticisms or evaluations of them, or compare them to other proposals on the same topic. In general, we would recommend doing this on topics that students already know a lot about: it saves time on reading up. However, it can also be a valuable exercise to do this on topics they know less of, as this frequently happens in real world jobs as well.

Finally, this building block is also particularly well suited for teaching students communication skills. They could be given assignments to argue for proposals as well as problem analyses, both in written and spoken forms. This could be done through essays, debates, or letting students give pitches. The goal here is not only being as convincing as possible, but also being understandable and transparent about limitations and underlying assumptions.

Teaching Materials

- To introduce the policy tools, reading materials can be of use, but they will probably have the most lasting impact when combined with practical exercises in which students have to apply the tools themselves.
  - For cost-benefit analysis, a useful book is: *Cost-Benefit Analysis: Concepts and Practice* by Anthony E. Boardman, David H. Greenberg, Aidan R. Vining, David L. Weimer, most recent edition from 2018.
  - For participatory evaluation, the following book can be of help: *Participatory Evaluation Up Close: An Integration of Research Based Knowledge* by J. Bradley Cousins and Jill A. Chouinard, from 2012.
  - Risk-opportunity analysis is newer and has yet to be explained in a textbook, but a useful working paper explaining the tool and providing examples of applications is: *Risk-opportunity analysis for transformative policy design and appraisal* by Jean-Francois Mercure, Simon Sharpe, Jorge Vinuales, Matthew Ives, Michael Grubb, Hector Pollitt, Florian Knobloch and Femke Nijsse, from 2020.
- A useful and accessible book about systems thinking is: *Thinking in Systems: A Primer* by Donella H. Meadows and Diana Wright, most recent edition from 2015. Another helpful book is *Systems Thinking For Social Change* by David P. Stroh, from 2015. A website providing an overview and links to explanation texts and courses is: http://learningforsustainability.net/systems-thinking/
- *The Oxford Handbook of Public Policy* by Robert E. Goodin, Michael Moran, and Martin Rein, from 2008. An extensive book, which provides a useful overview of different aspects of public policy, such as the role of economic policy tools, engagement of stakeholders, and producing and evaluating policy.
- *Handbook of Policy Formulation* by Michael Howlett and Ishani Mukherjee, from 2017. Another extensive book, which focuses on how policy is made with its different aspects, such as choosing policy goals and instruments, policy appraisal techniques, and the politics of defining and resolving policy problems.

Visit the website for a wider range of teaching materials, to provide feedback, and to exchange ideas and ask support from colleagues worldwide.
economy.st/bb9

Building Block 10
Economics for a Better World

What normative principles and visions can guide action to make the world a better place and address the major challenges of our times?

1
Normative
Principles
for Decision

2
Visions for
the Economy

Economics
for a Better
World

3
Practical
Suggestions

What

This building block is about normative ideas in economics. That is, the underlying ideals guiding economic thinking and decisions, such as equity, efficiency, liberty and solidarity. It also includes visions for how the economy could and should look, ranging from concrete policy proposals to visions of differently organised economic systems.

Why

It is crucial that students are taught about the normative aspects of economic thinking. It helps them deal with normative issues in a more conscious and sophisticated way. This is especially important because it prepares them for their later work in which they will have to inform non-economists on the normative dilemmas of economic decisions. If they are never taught to think about and explain these issues, it is very likely that as graduates they will be blind to them. Or that if they do address them, they will likely do so in an inconsistent and haphazard manner. Students thus have to gain experience with normativity during their education.

Contrast with current programmes

Current programmes generally have two approaches to normativity. Some try to ignore it, along the lines of: *'There is normative economics, and there is positive economics; here we only deal with positive science'*. We think this is an unrealistic and damaging approach, as it in no way prepares students for their future roles in advising others to make decisions. The other frequently found approach is to tuck away all normative aspects in a separate course on ethics. Though more helpful, this is not enough. Besides learning general ethical philosophy, students need to understand its role in economic questions. We suggest teaching normative aspects in a more integrated and applied way, making students aware of normative aspects of theories when they learn them and teaching them to spot the more normative elements of policy advice.

"The choice between different social arrangements for the solution of economic problems should be carried out in broader terms than this [comparisons of market values] and that the total effect of these arrangements in all spheres of life should be taken into account. As Frank H. Knight has so often emphasized, problems of welfare economics must ultimately dissolve into a study of morals."

Ronald Coase (1960, p. 43)

The ultimate goal of economics, apart from sheer fascination, is to contribute to a better world. How such a better world looks however, is hotly debated. In fact, normative discussions about economic questions are often at the centre of political debates. Economic questions are thus not simply a matter of intellectual curiosity or academic interest, they are key societal issues. Economists have the vital role of supporting society in making decisions and taking actions concerning these economic questions.

As explained in *Foundation 4: Values*, it is not the job of the economists to make these decisions, but it is our job to inform and support others in making economic decisions, shedding light on their normative and analytical aspects, as well as their implications in the real world. This requires that economics students learn about the normative aspects of economic questions, the focus of this building block.

In other words, in contrast to many of the other building blocks which focus mainly on *descriptive* or *analytical* ideas and knowledge, this building block focuses on *normative* ideas. It is about teaching students to identify the underlying values and moral dilemmas involved in economic issues and to explain these clearly to non-economists. These skills enable economists to minimise their own normative biases in their work and identify weak points in normative arguments and reasoning.

This chapter starts with a section on teaching students to spot and critically assess the normative elements embedded in analytical tools, such as models and measurements. The next two sections are more applied and focus on ideas that can guide action. The second section has a more short-term focus and looks at normative principles on which decisions can be based. The third section has a more long-term perspective focusing on visions of how the economy should look.

1 Normative Principles for Decisions

To be able to make a decision, one has to apply normative principles, be it consciously or not. Since the ultimate goal of economics is to help the world make better economic decisions, it is important that students become familiar with the normative aspects of decisions. By being able to uncover relevant normative principles and clearly articulate how they relate to the issue at hand, economists can inform others to better understand the decisions they have to make.

These normative principles are often called 'welfare criteria' in economics. It is, however, important to note that maximising the welfare or utility of individuals is only one such normative principle. The different economic approaches described in the online resource *Economic Approaches* (economy.st/approaches) provides an overview of the assumptions underlying different economic theories. Other principles than welfare include fairness, legitimacy, security, stability, and reciprocity. These principles differ in their translatability into mathematical form and their applicability in practice.

Of particular importance is how normative principles deal with the pros and cons of decisions. Within welfare economics, the principles of Pareto efficiency, *'do no harm'*, and Kaldor-Hicks efficiency, *'hypothetical compensation'*, are well known. These are only two among many principles on which normative assessments can be based. Solely within the utilitarian tradition already, there are, for example, also those who argue the average or minimum utility should be maximised.

Besides utilitarian principles there are also other ideas about how to deal with moral dilemmas, such as the precautionary principle and inalienable rights and liberties. Students need to become familiar with these different ways of approaching normative trade-offs, as they are relevant for many real-world problems.

The goal here is not to teach students how they should independently make value judgments, but to learn how to identify underlying normative assumptions and trade-offs and clearly communicate them to non-economists. Or in Huei-chun Su's words (2012, pp. 378-379): *"Normative economics in this sense is primarily concerned with exploring the way of making an evaluation, but it does not have to commit to endorsing the evaluation. In this way, normative economics only relates to value judgements but does not make value judgements."* It is not about teaching students 'what is right', it is about teaching them how to clearly see where and how value judgments are being made throughout the analysis.

Since it is not economists themselves who should make normative decisions, students should learn how the general population sees certain central normative trade-offs. This can be done by looking at interviews and surveys of citizens, or letting students conduct new ones. Of course, it is not a matter of learning survey data by heart, nor should students internalise majority opinions on a certain issue as 'the right view'. Rather, learning the habit of looking at the normative choices of people can help students to realise the range of value-judgements that may exist beyond the 'common sense' they personally are used to or automatically adopting the values or interests of their employers – looking outside their own values bubble, as it were.

How can this be done? A course on labour economics, for example, generally covers the topic of unemployment and frequently also discusses the related policy options. When discussing these different social policies, one could explicitly identify the normative questions involved in the different aspects of those policies. Kuhn et al. (2020) and Nicoli et al. (2020), two papers related to one research project, identified the following six questions as main normative issues concerning EU social policy:

1 How generous should the unemployment benefit levels be?
2 Should there be training and education opportunities for unemployed citizens?
3 How much between-country redistribution should there be?
4 How much tax are you willing to pay and should there be progressive, proportional or regressive taxation?
5 Should it be centrally administered by the EU or decentrally by national governments?
6 How much job search effort do unemployed citizens need to do to be able to get benefits?

Surprisingly they found that the majority of the EU population is in favour of such an EU unemployment scheme. But citizens' support depends heavily on the choices made concerning the normative issues mentioned above. Most EU citizens prefer decentralised implementation, more generous programmes, requiring education and training opportunities as well as job search effort conditions, and low as well as progressive taxation. The point here is not that these are the 'right' moral positions, but rather that these are simply the normative choices most EU citizens would make. By looking at the results of such surveys students become aware of the normative choices citizens prefer and develop a feeling for what is generally considered important.

2 Visions for the Economy

Next to the normative elements embedded in analytical tools and normative principles for decisions, normative visions and ideas on economies are relevant for economics education. Such economic visions are often at the core of political ideologies and the directions in which societies develop. These visions can range from short-term concrete policy proposals to idealistic visions of utopian economic systems. These ideas about how to structure and organise an economy are thus crucial for any economist to be familiar with. Again, this should not be aimed at turning economics students into believers of those visions. Instead, the goal should be to make students knowledgeable about the wide variety of visions, so they can develop a good understanding of them and are able to inform non-economists about them.

The central challenges of an age generally define its normative discussions. The main societal challenges of our time seem to be climate change, pandemics, rising levels of public and private debt, cultural clashes between nationalism and cosmopolitanism, growing inequality and a concentration of economic power. It is key to teach students something about the range of economic visions on these topics.

Taking climate change as an example, it would be useful to expose students to debates between the ideas of green growth, degrowth as well as growth agnosticism. *Green growth* is based on a future vision in which ecological sustainability is accompanied with a further rise in GDP, often linked to a strong belief in technological progress (Allan & Meckling, 2021; Meckling & Allan, 2020; OECD, 2021). Opposing this idea, the *degrowth* perspective envisions a sustainable future in which GDP has declined, because they argue it will not be possible to fully decouple GDP growth from resource use and carbon emissions (Haberl et al., 2020; Hickel, 2020; Hickel & Kallis, 2020). Then there are those who want to shift the focus of the debate because they argue GDP is not a particularly relevant topic or economic goal. Instead, they argue that human wellbeing should be the goal of economic activity, making them focus on the relationship of sustainability with wellbeing, rather than with GDP (Van den Bergh, 2011; Van den Bergh & Kallis, 2012). As such, they are growth *agnostic*, being indifferent to GDP's development and focusing instead on human wellbeing.

These economic visions are likely to shape the coming future as they are already influencing political movements and policy decisions. Students need to learn at least their outlines. Besides having strong links to societal challenges, these economic visions are also deeply connected to economic organisations and mechanisms (Building Block 5) and political-economic systems (Building Block 6). Therefore, it is important that students become familiar with the various moral views on ways of organising economies. Given that most economies are currently mainly organised along capitalist lines, it is perhaps no surprise that normative discussions about capitalism are particularly relevant. However, in a master's programme specialising in labour economics for example, it would be particularly important to expose students to the different normative visions on how labour should be organised and rewarded.

In sum, students should learn about the different visions that exist about how the economy could or should look. In addition, it seems particularly promising to connect these discussions about normative ideas to societal challenges as well as ways of organising economies.

3 Practical Suggestions

Firstly, meaningful normative discussions require shared reference points: a solid grounding in analytical and real-world knowledge. For instance, when discussing the different visions on the future concerning climate change, it pays to first discuss with students what climate change is and how it has evolved so far.

- What are the main causes of climate change?
- How far are we from reaching the various planetary boundaries (and by how much have we already exceeded some of them)?
- How much of our natural resources have already been depleted and how much is left?
- What are the future scenarios climate scientists think are likely?
- Which sectors and countries have been mainly responsible for the emissions?
- What is the state of the different sources of energy?

etc.

Without such knowledge, students would not learn how to form informed, rather than purely ideology-driven, opinions.

Secondly, we think this building block provides the perfect opportunity to let students practise their communication skills, both in written and spoken form. The most direct method would be to ask students to write essays and debate about the normative positions they believe in. Additionally, it can be very useful to make students defend normative positions that are not their own. This forces them to consider the strengths of positions that they personally disagree with, and the weaknesses of the position they hold themselves. It is a particularly relevant skill for their careers, as being able to understand others' normative ideas is often a lot more important than convincing others of yours.

Another way to do this could be to give students the assignment to prepare a written argumentation on a normative question and hand this in. Based on their answers, every student is linked to another student who views the issue from a different perspective and arrives at another conclusion. Thereafter, every couple gets a limited timeslot, for example one hour, to explain to each other their argumentation and reasoning. Directly after this, students have to write down the argumentation of the other as best as they can, thereby testing how well they understand their opponents' reasoning. Finally, the teacher compares the original assignments with the written recounts, assessing how many of the key arguments match. Each couple receives one grade so that both their explaining and listening skills are rewarded and teamwork between (intellectual) opponents is stimulated.

Some interesting questions to discuss could be the following:

- Is material consumption the goal of the economy?
- What level of inequality is justifiable if it contributes to economic growth?
- Is alienation a justifiable side effect if the work creates economic growth?
- Do owners or shareholders have the sole moral right to make decisions in firms or should other stakeholders, such as workers and consumers, have a say on decisions as well?
- What should be commodified, and what do we find too sacred or too dangerous to trade or manage commercially? Consider for example, organs, humans, human time, education, housing, citizenship, mind-altering substances, weapons, land, medicine, ideas, techniques, prisons, the right to pollute, or political office.
- Should trade in these items be forbidden, regulated through limiting rules or market mechanisms, or left free? Sandel's *What Money Can Buy* provides great material for such discussions.

Furthermore, taking controversial positions should not be punished, but nor should students be pushed to choose an ideology to believe in. It should be perfectly fine if students take nuanced and complex positions that are not easily put in ideological boxes. So when giving such randomly assigned normative positions, we think it is important to not only assign ideologically stereotypical positions.

Finally, and connected to the point above, it can help to link such exercises to real historical or recent cases to ground them in reality and link them to specific contexts. This is also what they will be doing in their careers, so it only makes sense to give them experience in doing so.

Teaching Materials

- *The Oxford Handbook of Ethics and Economics* by Mark D. White, from 2019. This extensive collection of essays explores the many moral dimensions of economics, from different ethical theories and the ethics in schools of thought, to the ethics of money, labour markets, risk, law, civil rights and ecological sustainability.
- *Economic Analysis, Moral Philosophy, and Public Policy* by Daniel Hausman, Michael McPherson, and Debra Satz, most recent edition from 2016. A great introduction into normative economics, covering its many areas and topics from welfare economics and utility theory to liberty, equality and justice.
- *A Guide to Ethics and Public Policy: Finding Our Way* by D. Don Welch, from 2014. A brief but insightful book providing a broad framework for evaluating policy proposals and outcomes, organised around five moral principles: benefit, effectiveness, fairness, fidelity, and legitimacy.
- *The Oxford Handbook of Professional Economic Ethics* by George F. DeMartino and Deirdre McCloskey, from 2016. This insightful collection of essays explores the different aspects of ethics in economics, with special attention to ethical issues related to economic theory, research and policy advice.
- *Political Ideologies: An Introduction* by Andrew Heywood, most recent edition from 2021. A useful and accessible introduction into a wide variety of political ideologies, from liberalism, socialism, and conservatism to feminism, nationalism, and green ideology, that shape much of our normative thinking on the economy.
- *Moral Views on Market Society* by Marion Fourcade and Kieran Healy, from 2007. An insightful overview paper on the key different normative perspectives on capitalism, enabling readers to better understand and place ideas and arguments prevalent in many debates about the economy.
- *Is Capitalism Obsolete? A Journey Through Alternative Economic Systems* by Giacomo Corneo, from 2017. A systematic and sharp overview of different (mainly socialist) economic systems that helps students think analytically about their allocation and coordination mechanisms and

informs them about the possible ways of organising economies and the arguments for and against the various options.

- *What Money Can't Buy: The Moral Limits* of Markets by Michael J. Sandel, most recent edition from 2012. A highly influential and well-written book reflecting on the moral place of markets in society and asking the key question whether everything should be up for sale. The Institute for New Economic Thinking has also launched a video series on the book and topic: https://www.ineteconomics.org/perspectives/videos/what-money-cant-buy

Visit the website for a wider range of teaching materials, to provide feedback, and to exchange ideas and ask support from colleagues worldwide.
economy.st/bb10

Part III:
Tools

Tools

Introduction

While the rest of this book mixes practical advice with elements of philosophy, ideas, topics, teaching materials, considerations and overviews, this section is exclusively about putting everything into practice.

If you find the prospect of pluralism daunting, because there is so much material out there, start with *Tool 1: Pragmatic Pluralism*. That chapter provides key insights and ideas for thirteen core topics in economics, organised by selecting the most relevant theoretical approaches per topic and contrasting them with each other. It also suggests teaching materials.

If you are looking to modify an existing course, see *Tool 2: Adapting Existing Courses*, where we offer ready-to-use sets of material to broaden courses such as Micro, Macro, Public Economics or Finance.

Are you working with an existing curriculum and do you want to quickly identify potential gaps and come to concrete recommendations for improvement? *Tool 3: Curriculum Review* may be useful.

Do you want to see some examples of courses, or even complete programmes, that have been designed using the *Economy Studies* building blocks and principles? See *Tool 4: Example Courses* and *Tool 5: Example Curricula*.

Whilst the focus of this book is on educating future economists through academic programmes, *Tool 6: Courses for Non-Economists* provides a limited package of core economic ideas that may be useful for secondary school economics programmes, professional education or in an academic minor for students of other disciplines.

If you are working to rethink an economics programme from the ground up, based on the question *'What do the students need to know to be prepared for their future societal roles?'* turn to *Tool 7: Learning Objectives*.

Since a physical book has only limited space, and we are trying to cover a wide field, significant parts of these chapters are presented through our website www.economystudies.com. This is noted in each chapter, including a description of what exactly can be found online, and examples of those materials. So it is easiest to just turn to the most relevant book chapter first, and go online after reading that.

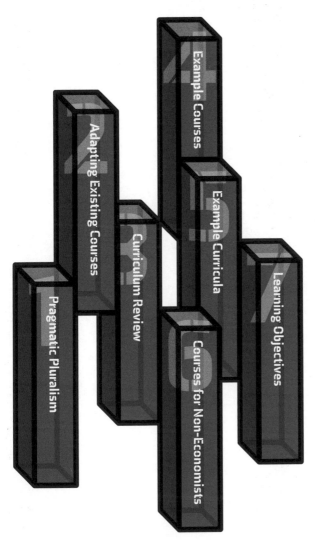

Figure 9: An overview of Part III: Tools.

Tool 1
Pragmatic Pluralism

Key insights and ideas for thirteen core topics in economics, organised by selecting the most relevant theoretical approaches per topic and contrasting them with each other.

1
Governments

Pragmatic Pluralism

Online:
Extended Version

This chapter provides a map through the complex jungle of economic theories. There are many different theoretical approaches, and each aspect of the economy has been analysed by a number of different ones. However, it is neither feasible nor productive for students to engage with every possible angle for every topic. Hence, this chapter, together with *Building Block 8: Economic Theories*, sets out an alternative approach: pragmatic pluralism. That is, make a selection of the most relevant theoretical approaches for the topic that is taught.

While the building block chapter set out the general approach, in this chapter we instead focus on the content, applying the pragmatic pluralism approach to thirteen core topics in economics:

To reiterate, the core logic of this approach to teaching economic theory is that whilst pluralism is an essential aspect of academia, we also need to be pragmatic to successfully apply it in practice. Rather than pursuing the extreme of either only focusing on one approach, or including every possible strand of thought for every topic, we propose a pragmatic middle ground: teaching a select number of approaches for each topic. In this way, it is possible to introduce students to the variety and diversity of economic thinking, whilst still having enough time and space to properly discuss each of the insights in detail with them.

"Reasonable people may have different theories of the way the economy works – different pictures in their heads of what connects one thing with another in the economic system."

Robert Solow (1983, p. 67)

Theory is the beating heart of all social sciences, including economics. It allows one to understand the components, processes and causal mechanisms characterising various social phenomena in a more structured and systematic manner. However, every topic can be understood from various theoretical perspectives, which can both complement and contradict each other.

Most contemporary economics programmes focus almost exclusively on neoclassical theory. In opposition, some other programmes choose to focus entirely on another perspective. We believe, in contrast to both, that there is no single 'correct' or 'best' way to understand the economy as a whole. It is too large and complex to be captured by a single point of view.

Hence, we propose a fundamentally pluralist approach to teaching theory. It is essential to teach students a variety of approaches to give them a rich and broad understanding of the topic, the debate around it and learn to think critically and not to take things as absolute truths. Approaches should be judged on their merits, topic by topic: thinking critically and reflectively to decide which theoretical points of departure help us best to understand this particular corner of the economic system.

Including this pluralist discussion is crucial for the development of students' vital critical thinking skills, through the investigation of links and contradictions between the insights learnt. For a pluralist economics education to be truly valuable, students must graduate not just with strong knowledge of a range of perspectives and methods, but also with a critical understanding of the limitations and blind spots of those tools. Without this, they will struggle to select the most relevant approaches to the task at hand, and to judge how much confidence to have in the conclusions that they reach. Active discussion also has the additional benefit of making sure that students are genuinely understanding the content taught to them, rather than just temporarily memorising it for an exam.

Pragmatic pluralism in practice

So how does this approach work when applied to a topic?

Each topic is subject to debate between alternative views. To make students familiar with these competing theories, for every topic the two main opposing perspectives are selected. However, not all differing ideas and theories are necessarily in conflict with each other. There are also approaches which can supplement one, or both, of the main opposing perspectives, contributing to a richer understanding of the topic. Therefore, each topic also contains one main complementary perspective. On top of these three main theoretical approaches, there are many other useful ideas that students could benefit from by learning about. For this reason, we provide a short summary of other useful insights and ideas that could be included for each topic. In addition, we suggest a few particularly useful teaching materials. In the online version, we provide longer lists of suggestions.

The topics presented below could be, and often already are, taught in individual courses. They can also be combined, especially when there is significant overlap as is the case for the topics of *Finance* and *Money* for example, although this does of course shorten the teaching time that can be devoted to each topic and its insights. As to determining the relative teaching time to the various perspectives, the following rule of thumb could be useful: devote the first half of the course to the two main opposing approaches, the third quarter to the complementary perspective and the last quarter to the other useful insights. As with every rule of thumb, the specific case and context should be considered and we advise teachers to determine the relative teaching time devoted to each insight taking the local situation into account.

Cautionary notes

Before we go into the specific ideas and insights, we want to provide a short recap of the cautionary notes, which are described in full in *Building Block 8: Economic Theories*.

Firstly, the following overview should be viewed as only one possible example of a pragmatic pluralist approach to teaching economic theory. An overview such as this one should never be set in stone, as the discipline itself is also constantly evolving. While some approaches, such as complexity economics, currently have relatively few insights listed in the overview, this might change over the coming years as more scholars will further develop this approach and apply it to different topics.

Secondly, the overview could easily be expanded to allow for more detail and nuance or a wider range of perspectives or topics. The examples have been written to suit the time constraints of an individual course. The framework could be adapted for a relatively brief programme, such as an economics major in a liberal arts programme, by selecting fewer perspectives for each topic and including fewer topics and possibly combining them into courses. Equally, if the available teaching time is greater, for example with a theory-oriented four-year undergraduate economics programme, more topics, insights and a greater range of perspectives could be included.

Thirdly, our economics education and own reading have shaped the topics and perspectives that are presented below. This is greatly influenced by living and studying in the Netherlands, and Europe more broadly, and the strong bias in the discipline as a whole towards economic thinking from the Global North. We strongly believe that economics curricula need to be decolonised and with this book we try to contribute to this. To help us do so, we have asked students and professors from all over the world, as well as organisations active on this issue, such as *Diversifying and Decolonising Economics*, for advice. Nevertheless, it is important to say that this is not an area that we personally have particularly strong knowledge of and feel that more could, and should, be done in this regard. We therefore welcome all suggestions on how the content in this chapter, and the rest of the book, could be enriched and improved by including other topics, perspectives and insights.

Finally, this technique of putting approaches as well as topics in separate boxes is only a heuristic for identifying the most important ideas and insights to teach. Many of these approaches and topics are strongly interlinked and can be difficult, or even impossible, to truly separate from each other. As a result, individual thinkers and their ideas can be difficult to put into a single box. For instance, Joseph Schumpeter built on classical, historical, Marxian, Austrian and neoclassical ideas, and is often seen as a key inspiration for evolutionary economics, which is therefore also sometimes called Schumpeterian economics. It is important that students learn about these links and become familiar with how both the ideas and the topics are connected.

With these cautionary notes in mind, we hope this overview can be of some help in putting the pragmatic pluralist approach in practice and adapting economic theory courses.

Core theoretical approaches on 13 topics

Below we have put the thirteen economic topics (along the top) and sixteen theoretical perspectives (down the side) in a table to give an overview of how our pragmatic pluralist approach works.

It would be possible to fill in every box (representing a combination between a topic and an approach) to create what could be described as 'indiscriminate' pluralism. We think that for research purposes, such an approach could be very useful as it could generate new insights by utilising approaches previously not applied to a topic. However, for education we would not advise such an approach, as it would be impossible to teach every possible perspective on a given topic in a meaningful way, given the limited teaching time available.

Instead, we advise teachers to focus on the main insights into their chosen topic. In other words, when teaching an economics course, they should focus on the combinations of the topic and perspectives that are most important. For every topic, we have noted to the two main opposing perspectives with ∎, the main complementary perspective with ☐, and the perspectives that can provide smaller but still valuable additional insights with +. In this way, many boxes stay empty. This does not mean that the perspective has nothing to say on the topic. However, economics education requires us to make choices as to what to teach and what not. In this overview, below we have presented an attempt at making such choices, asking which insights help us understand the world the most. Sometimes there are cases in which perspectives share a certain insight. This is discussed in the explanations of the insights, but for brevity each insight is attributed to a single perspective in the table.

	Governments	Business Cycles	Consumption	Economic Development	Finance	Firms	Households	Inequality	International Trade	Labour	Markets	Money	Nature
Austrian School	+	■						+			+	■	
Behavioural Economics	+			+	+			+			+		
Classical Political Economy	+			■	+						■		□
Complexity Economics	+			□				+					
Cultural Approach					+		□		□	□	□		
Ecological Economics			□	+									■
Evolutionary Economics	□			+		□							
Feminist Economics							■	□		+			
Field Theory						■					+		
Historical School	+			■								+	
Institutional Economics			■	□		■							+
Marxian Political Economy	+	+		+			+	■		■			
Neoclassical Economics	■	□	■	+	■	+	■	■	■	■	■		■
Post-Keynesian Economics	■	■			■			+	■			■	
Social Network Analysis					+					+			
Structuralist Economics				+					□				
Other	+		+		+			+	+				+

■   Main opposing perspective
□   Main complementary perspective
+   Additional perspective

Figure 10: An overview of the pragmatic pluralist approach to teaching economic theories.

1   Governments

The state is often at the heart of public and intellectual debates about the economy, as the amount of contrasting perspectives below shows. This should be no surprise: governments are the biggest single actors in the economy, whether measured in employment or in total budget. How should these economic giants behave? Should they sit back and allow the economy to unfold on its own, merely providing an efficient level playing field for private actors through rule-based policy? Or should the state play a more active role to stabilise the economy, take an entrepreneurial role to spur innovation, and/or pursue social policies to ensure the wellbeing of its citizens?

Main opposing perspectives
- Post-Keynesian economics: Discretionary policy works best
- Neoclassical economics: Rule-bound policy works even better

Main complementary perspective
- ☐ Evolutionary economics: The entrepreneurial state

Additional perspectives and insights
- + Behavioural economics: Nudging
- + Complexity economics: Modern economies require diverse and flexible policy tools
- + Historical school: Social policy takes the sharp edge off capitalism
- + Marxian political economy: Class struggles play out through the state
- + Classical political economy: Night-watchman state
- + Austrian school: Dispersed knowledge precludes effective government intervention
- + Other: The economic dimension of governments in political science

Main opposing perspectives: Post-Keynesian and neoclassical economics

A key debate concerning the state is between (post-)Keynesian economists, who argue for discretion in economic policy, and neoclassical economists, who argue for rule-bound policy. Keynesian economists argued the state has a role to fulfil in the economy because it is the only actor that can successfully solve economic problems such as mass unemployment. The state can provide stability and freedom by creating and adjusting policies in a discretionary manner, mainly with regard to fiscal policy to influence effective demand.

Neoclassical economists, on the other hand, often argue that the state should focus on providing a framework in which private actors can operate. Policy should be rule-bound, also known as commitment policy. Instead of relying on expert and political judgement of the specific situation, a prescribed mathematical model should be ollowed (i.e. the Taylor rule). As such, only the factors included in the model have an influence on decisions. This is important because neoclassical economists, and more specifically public choice theorists, warn us about government failures, which are assumed to derive from self-interested behaviour of voters, politicians and bureaucrats and/or imperfect information.

A core idea in the neoclassical framework is what is often called 'sound finance'. Simply put, it means governments should run balanced budgets, with revenues equalling expenditures. This stands in opposition to the Keynesian idea of 'functional finance', which argues public finance should not be a goal in itself but merely a means through which to achieve economic and social goals. The latter idea is also associated with Modern Monetary Theory, which combines functional finance with the chartalist state theory of money, to argue that (monetary sovereign) governments face no inherent financial restrictions on their finances, although they do face important limits in the real economy. While neoclassical economists favour central bank independence and a disconnect between fiscal and monetary policy, modern monetary theorists argue for using fiscal and monetary policy in harmony to create desired economic outcomes.

Main complementary perspective: Evolutionary economics

Another insight that has gained greater attention recently is that the state is crucial for innovation. Contrary to the myth that prosperity is the result of new technologies developed and funded purely by private companies operating in a free market, Mariana Mazzucato and others have used an evolutionary approach to show how economic success is largely the result of state-funded investments in innovation. Mazzucato argues that the dominant neoclassical view of the state as an actor that is only there to address market failures and provide public goods is fatally limited. She points out that governments create, shape and guide markets, and also should embrace this ability to give direction to the economy. For this reason, she has advocated mission-oriented policy in which a clear goal is formulated, experimentation and risk-taking are encouraged, dynamic capabilities are cherished, budgets are based on (achieving) outcomes, collective value creation is recognised, risks and rewards are shared, the public, private and civic organisations partner in a symbiotic rather than parasitic way, and democratic participation in decision-making is central. In this way, a mix between top-down guidance and facilitation, and bottom-up initiatives and participation, is created to solve the big problems of the day.

Additional perspectives and insights

Classical political economy: The discipline of economics is often said to have started with the arguments of classical political economists against mercantilist ideas and policies, which aimed at increasing national economic power through running a trade surplus. Classical political economy argued, instead, that the state should have the limited role of a night-watchman, which secures external defence and the rule of law, in particular the protection of property rights and enforcement of contracts. Today, many people and economists still advocate this. Many classical political economists, however, also recognise that the state should provide services which the market is not well-suited to deliver, such as infrastructure, postal services, standard weights and measures, and a stable currency. A key logic behind the night-watchman state is to eliminate the rents that various powerful special interest groups were able to acquire through the mercantilist state.

Marxian political economists built on classical political economic ideas but came to a starkly different conclusion and argued against the idea that the state can be a neutral passive organisation that ensures that private individuals can flourish in a fair economy. Marxian scholars see the state as an indispensable tool for class domination, which protects the wealth of the rich and punishes the poor if they do not accept the inequalities. The similarities with classical political economists in this regard are surprising. Adam Smith (1776, p. 299), for example, wrote *"Civil government, so far as it is instituted for the security of property, is in reality instituted for the defense of the rich against the poor, or of those who have some property against those who have none at all."* Instead of advocating for free trade and *laissez-faire* as classical political economists do, Marxian political economists argue that in order to end the exploitation and suppression of the working class, the working class has to seize control over the state and undue class domination.

Historical school: Largely in reaction to the problems associated with the industrial revolution, such as child labour, poor working conditions and low standards of living, historical economists argued that the state should ensure through social policy that the national community was flourishing, instead of falling apart. As such, they oppose both laissez-faire liberals, who viewed society as the total sum of individuals and favoured a night-watchman state, and socialists, who emphasised class conflict and aimed to overthrow the capitalist economic system. Although social policy was initially conceived in this way, largely thanks to the innovative work of the Verein für Socialpolitik in Germany during the late 19th and early 20th century, it has since been argued for and thought of in many different ways. Within Germany after the second world war, for example, ordoliberal thinking and the concept of the social market economy were influential. In this line of thinking, both planning and free markets are rejected, in favour of the combination of a capitalist economy with a strong state that ensures fair market competition as well as a social welfare system. More recent research indicates that government spending on social policies not only enhances the wellbeing of citizens, but also stimulates the economy and productivity.

Austrian school builds on the classical idea of the minimalist night-watchman state and argues that if governments go beyond this limited role, they will cause, rather than solve, problems. A key reason for this is that knowledge is necessarily dispersed, leaving central authorities with a lack of information needed for effective action. Instead, 'free' markets are seen as the best way to communicate the local knowledge of individuals to create efficient economic outcomes. Austrian economists thus embrace the classical liberal idea of protecting "negative liberty" and ensuring freedom from government intervention, while they reject the social liberal idea that the government should guarantee people's "positive liberty" and enable them to be able to act upon their free will.

More recent contributions to thinking about government policy come from behavioural and complexity economics.

Behavioural economics sees people as susceptible to manipulation in their decision-making. People's bounded rationality causes suboptimal choices that do not maximize their welfare, thus creating 'internalities'. To tackle this issue, governments can nudge people towards more 'rational', or desirable, behaviour by making use of behavioural insights into social proof heuristics, default bias, salience, positive reinforcement, and indirect suggestions. The underlying political philosophy of this policy approach is often called *libertarian paternalism*, as it pushes people in a direction that is deemed as desirable by the authorities, without hurting the freedom of choice of individuals.

Complexity economics, on the other hand, focuses on the fact that policy tries to influence complex and dynamic systems, and therefore argues that governments should pay more attention to the unexpected consequences of policies. Complexity economists believe that policy tools need to be diverse and flexible enough for the systems that they try to control, so that adaptation and the learning process can work more effectively.

Other: Quite naturally, political economists and political scientists have extensively studied governments and their economic roles. In doing so, many important approaches within political science, such as realism and constructivism, have also played a major role in analysing the economic dimension of governments. An important topic here is to what extent companies are in practice regulated by the state, and the influence that companies have on the rules and regulation that they are subject to. Furthermore, political economists study economic policy more broadly, from how the dynamics of political competition influence policy decisions, to the influence of experts and the internal structures of government institutions.

Teaching Materials

- Chapters
  - *Economics: The User's Guide* by Ha-Joon Chang, from 2014, chapter 11. This brief and accessible pluralist book contains a useful introductory chapter on the role of the state.
  - *Economics After The Crisis* by Irene van Staveren, from 2015, chapter 6. This well-written textbook sets out the neoclassical, post-Keynesian, social economic and institutional perspectives on the state.
  - *The Economy* by The CORE Team, from 2017, chapters 14, 15 and 22. This successful textbook provides an introduction into mainstream ideas and empirical findings on fiscal, monetary and public policy.
  - *Principles of Economics in Context* by Jonathan Harris, Julie A. Nelson and Neva Goodwin, most recent edition from 2020, chapter 12 and 25. This useful textbook, which pays particular attention to social and environmental challenges, devotes two chapters to tax and fiscal policy in specific.
  - *The Microeconomics of Complex Economies: Evolutionary, Institutional, Neoclassical and Complexity Perspectives* by Wolfram Elsner, Torsten Heinrich, and Henning Schwardt, from 2014, chapter 17. This innovative textbook makes readers familiar with new insights coming from frontier mainstream economic research, with one chapter devoted to the policy implications of the findings discussed in the book.
  - *Macroeconomics* by William Mitchell, L. Randall Wray, Martin Watts, from 2019, chapters 20, 21, 22 and 23. This ground-breaking and much-discussed textbook written by three leaders of Modern Monetary Theory (MMT), describes in detail the history of economic thinking about the state and macroeconomy as well as recent theoretical and policy debates.
  - *The Handbook of Economic Sociology* by Neil J. Smelser and Richard Swedberg, from 2005, chapters 22, 23 and 24. This extensive and yet accessible book for non-sociologists provides an impressive and useful overview of the field of economic sociology, including three chapters on the role of the state in the economy.

- Books
  - *The Entrepreneurial State: Debunking Public vs. Private Sector Myths* by Mariana Mazzucato, from 2013. An influential and well-written book, inspired chiefly by evolutionary economics, on the role of the state in innovation.
  - *Alternative Theories of the State* by S. Pressman, from 2006. A useful and informative collection of essays which introduces readers to the institutional, Marxist, post-Keynesian, feminist and behavioural perspectives on the state.
  - *Money and Government: The Past and Future of Economics* by Robert Skidelsky, from 2018. This well-written and insightful book introduces readers to historical and current debates about the state, with particular attention to neoclassical and Keynesian ideas.
  - *Political Economy: The Contest of Economic Ideas* by Frank Stilwell, most recent edition from 2011. A well-written textbook, with parts devoted to classical, Marxist, neoclassical, institutional, and Keynesian economics and particular attention to ideas surrounding the state, reform, policy and economic systems.
  - *Routledge Handbook of International Political Economy* by Mark Blyth, from 2009. A useful and extensive book which provides an overview of the wide field of international political economy with particular attention to its North American, British, and Asian branches.
  - *Frontiers of Heterodox Macroeconomics* by Philip Arestis and Malcolm Sawyer, from 2019. A useful collection of essays on recent insights coming from unconventional thinkers, and in particular post-Keynesian economists.
  - *Handbook of Public Economics, Volume 5* by Alan J. Auerbach, Raj Chetty, Martin Feldstein, and Emmanuel Saez, from 2013. Another useful collection of recent insights coming from mainstream economists on topics, such social insurance, charitable giving, urban public finance, and taxing labour, wealth and profits.

2 Business Cycles

"The central problem of depression-prevention [has] been solved for all practical purposes."

Robert Lucas (incoming address to the American Economic Association, 2003)

Booms and busts, academically known as 'business cycles', have been part of the economic system for a long time. Contrary to Lucas' optimistic statement, they also remain one of the most central problems both to economic theory and policy. Old questions are still hotly debated. How do business cycles work? What causes the economy to sometimes crash or slump into recession, while at other times it cranks into the highest gear? What can be done to prevent crises and what should be done once the economy is in a depression or recession? An important debate in this field is whether the government is the solution or the problem, and whether the emphasis should be placed on the demand or supply side of the economy. Besides this, economists have analysed the impact of external shocks on the economy.

Main opposing perspectives
- Post-Keynesian Economics: Effective demand is the crucial driver
- Austrian School: Malinvestment is the crucial driver

Main complementary perspective
- ☐ Neoclassical Economics: Crises happen because of external shocks

Additional perspectives and insights
- \+ Marxian Political Economy: Crises are inevitable and inherent to capitalism

For the full version of *Pragmatic Pluralism* on *Business Cycles*, see online.
economy.st/cycles

3 Consumption

One of the purposes of our economy is to produce and distribute goods for consumption. It is one of the main activities that humans in an economy undertake. But there are many questions on the source and nature of various forms of this activity. A core point of contention is what determines buying choices: are people entirely independent, or are they influenced by their environments? Is consumption the highest goal? Or should we see it merely as a means to other ends, such as human wellbeing?

Main opposing perspectives
- Institutional economics: Preferences are culturally and socially constructed
- Neoclassical economics: Humans have insatiable and innate preferences

Main complementary perspective
- ☐ Ecological economics: Material consumption ≠ human wellbeing

Additional perspectives and insights
- **+** Other: Surveillance capitalism

For the full version of *Pragmatic Pluralism* on *Consumption*, see online.
economy.st/consumption

4 Economic Development

The economic discipline was born out of the question why certain places become rich and others don't. Ever since the 1776 publication of Adam Smith's classic *An Inquiry into the Nature and Causes of the Wealth of Nations*, the question of what economic development is and what causes it has been at the centre of the discipline. Big issues within this field are: Should we have protectionism, or free trade? What is the role of cultural, political and legal institutions in economic development?

Main opposing perspectives
- Classical political economy: Free trade and *laissez-faire*
- Historical school: Infant industry protection

Main complementary perspective
- ☐ Institutional economics: Laws and politics are crucial

Additional perspectives and insights
- + Ecological economics: Consumption growth shouldn't be the goal
- + Evolutionary economics: Creative destruction
- + Marxian political economy: Technology and class conflict drive history
- + Structuralist economics: Development as international power struggle
- + Neoclassical economics: Modelling economic growth
- + Behavioural economics: Experimentally tested micro-interventions

For the full version of *Pragmatic Pluralism* on *Economic Development*, see online.
economy.st/development

5 Finance

We are living in a financialised age. More and more aspects of our lives are governed by financial flows and assets, as the financial sector has grown enormously over the last decades. In addition, non-financial firms have become more financialised. But what is finance, and what is its function in the economy? Is it a place where risk and opportunities lead to rational pricing, or is it a place of herd behaviour and speculation in a fundamentally uncertain world? And how can we see whether the financial system is robust or fragile?

Main opposing perspectives
- Post-Keynesian economics: Animal spirits shape market movements
- Neoclassical economics: Banks are rational intermediators

Main complementary perspective
- ☐ Complexity economics: Systemic risk

Additional perspectives and insights
- ✛ Behavioural economics: Systematic irrationality
- ✛ Cultural economics: Analytical constructs shape the market

For the full version of *Pragmatic Pluralism* on *Finance*, see online.
economy.st/finance

6 Firms

In our economies most production is organised through firms, from enormous multinational corporations to small family shops and independent contractors. Given their importance, many scholars have thought about and analysed firms. Core questions in the field: why do firms exist in the first place, and how do they work? Are firms social structures that help stabilise and control power relations, or are firms better understood as a technical solution to organize the economy efficiently? What makes one firm successful while another one fails?

Main opposing perspectives

- Field theory: Firms stabilise and shape power relations
- Institutional economics: Firms are a way to minimize transaction costs

Main complementary perspective

- ☐ Evolutionary economics: Entrepreneurship and innovation drive success

Additional perspectives and insights

- ✛ Classical political economy: Firms are drivers of the division of labour
- ✛ Neoclassical economics: Firms maximize profit
- ✛ Social network analysis: Firms largely consist of informal networks
- ✛ Other: Business and organisational studies

For the full version of *Pragmatic Pluralism* on *Firms*, see online. economy.st/firms

7   Households

"From the homicidal bitchin' / that goes down in every kitchen / to determine who will serve and who will eat".

Leonard Cohen knew it: the household is the locus of complex economic struggles. Much of our economic life plays out inside households as we care for ourselves and each other, decide how to live, what to consume, how to relax but also do the housekeeping. Are gender relations and cultural roles a main driver of these decisions, or is it best understood as utility maximisation?

Main opposing perspectives
- Feminist economics: Unequal division of unpaid labour
- Neoclassical economics: Rational utility maximisation within the household

Main complementary perspective
□ Cultural approach: Household relations vary strongly between cultures

Additional perspectives and insights
+ Marxian political economy: Class fundamentally changes the meaning of gender

For the full version of *Pragmatic Pluralism* on *Households*, see online.
economy.st/households

8 Inequality

Inequality is a hotly debated topic both within economics as well as outside it in other academic disciplines, in politics and in society at large. As such, there are also many dimensions and aspects of inequality to which various thinkers and activists have drawn attention, from economic inequality based on class to gender and ethnicity, or race. A key question is: inequality in what? Market or disposable income, wealth, power, influence, opportunities, happiness or health, to just name a few dimensions. Another key question in the field is whether people are fairly rewarded for their work, or whether power differences prevent equitable remuneration. In short, whether market inequalities are fair or not. And how do different forms of inequality relate and interact with each other? Is being a black woman, for example, simply about adding up the effects of being black and female, or do combinations have their own unique characteristics?

Main opposing perspectives
- Marxian political economy: Exploitation
- Neoclassical economics: You get what you deserve

Main complementary perspective
☐ Feminist economics: Intersectionality is crucial to understand inequalities

Additional perspectives and insights
+ Post-Keynesian economics: Equity generally promotes efficiency
+ Austrian school: Social justice is a nonsensical idea
+ Behavioural economics: Inequality is relative, and mostly disliked
+ Complexity economics: Marx was right – there are two classes
+ Other: Even merit-driven inequality can be socially undesirable; Piketty's 'r>g'

For the full version of *Pragmatic Pluralism* on *Inequality*, see online.
economy.st/inequality

9 International Trade

We live in a globalised world in which many products are produced in global value chains and shipped overseas to be sold to customers all around the world. What drives globalisation, what forces counter it? And why are electronics produced in East Asia and many raw foodstuffs grown in Africa? Does everyone benefit from trade or does it systematically favour some at the cost of others?

Main opposing perspectives
- Post-Keynesian economics: Absolute advantage
- Neoclassical economics: Comparative advantage

Main complementary perspective
☐ Structuralist economics: Unequal terms of trade

Additional perspectives and insights
✛ Other: International trilemmas (you can't have everything)

For the full version of *Pragmatic Pluralism* on *International Trade*, see online.
economy.st/trade

---

10 Labour

Labour forms a crucial part of our lives. Besides sleeping, we spend most of our time working. Labour is also the backbone of the economy as a whole. Understanding the role of labour in society is therefore important for any economist. A key question in the field is: should work be understood as a process of self-realisation, having value in itself? Or should we see it as a disutility that is necessary because it allows us to produce the consumption products we want? A key insight in this field: our cultural understandings of work shape how the economy functions.

Main opposing perspectives
- Marxian political economy: Alienation and exploitation
- Neoclassical economics: Labour as necessary disutility

Main complementary perspective
- ☐ Cultural approach: Your work gives you dignity and identity

Additional perspectives and insights
- ✛ Feminist economics: Unpaid labour is everywhere
- ✛ Social network analysis: It is not what you know but who you know

For the full version of *Pragmatic Pluralism* on *Labour*, see online.
economy.st/labour

11 Markets

Markets make up much of contemporary economies, organising more and more aspects of our lives. But how do markets function? Is competition between firms more like a gentle process of balancing, or a ruthless war of attrition? Do markets facilitate rational allocation, or are they more often defined by manipulation, norms, and power struggles? And how do markets relate to broader society?

Main opposing perspectives
- Classical political economy: Competition as a ruthless process
- Neoclassical economics: Competition as an optimal outcome

Main complementary perspective
- Cultural approach: Markets are embedded in social structures

Additional perspectives and insights
- **+** Behavioural economics: People can be manipulated
- **+** Austrian school: Markets excel at spreading information
- **+** Field theory: Market stabilisation through social and formal rules

For the full version of *Pragmatic Pluralism* on *Markets*, see online.
economy.st/markets

12 Money

Money rules the world, or at least it often seems to. We all use it every day, so we often assume that we know it very well. But what is money in the first place? This seemingly easy question has triggered countless debates for many centuries. At the core of these debates is the question whether money is something purely technical and instrumental, or whether it fundamentally shapes, and is shaped, by social and power relationships. A key insight: cultural practices influence how we see and use money.

Main opposing perspectives
- Post-Keynesian economics: Credit theory of money
- Austrian school: Commodity theory of money

Main complementary perspective
☐ Cultural approach: Earmarking money

Additional perspectives and insights
+ Historical school: State theory of money

For the full version of *Pragmatic Pluralism* on *Money*, see online.
economy.st/money

13 Nature

As human beings we are only one form of life living on this planet. In the early history of humankind this meant that we had to adapt to our environment. Later, we learned how to adjust our environment to serve our needs. This process has gone so far that many scientists have proposed naming the current ecological era the *Anthropocene*, implying that human beings are currently the main cause of changes in the Earth's natural systems. But how can we best understand the relationship between humans, their economic activities and the natural world around them? How does nature influence the economy and what role do natural resources and land play in the economy? And increasingly important: how does the economy influence nature , for instance through climate change?

Main opposing perspectives
- Ecological economics: The economy is embedded in nature
- Neoclassical economics: Natural resources are key inputs for production

Main complementary perspective
☐ Classical political economy: Land and natural resources generate rent

Additional perspectives and insights
+ Institutional economics: The tragedy of the commons can be overcome
+ Other: Policy ideas to tackle climate change

For the full version of *Pragmatic Pluralism* on *Nature*, see online.
economy.st/nature

Tool 2
Adapting Existing Courses

Suggestions for incremental change to existing economics courses, drawn from the ten building blocks of Economy Studies.

1
Microeconomics

2
Macroeconomics

3
Public Economics

4
Finance

Online: **5**
Economics 101

Online: **6**
Environmental economics

Online: **7**
Industrial Organisation

Online: **8**
Development Economics

Online: **9**
Econometrics

Online: **10**
Labour Economics

Online: **11**
Monetary Economics

Online: **12**
International Economics

Adapting Existing Courses

Online: **13**
**Game
Theory**

Online: **14**
**Behavioural
Economics**

Change often happens incrementally and slowly. In the economics textbook market, for example, there is an unwritten rule that new textbooks cannot differ more than roughly 15% from the standard textbook in order to be 'acceptable' (Colander, 2003).

While our book clearly breaks this rule and proposes more far-reaching and fundamental changes in most chapters, in this chapter we focus instead on how existing courses could be adjusted incrementally. By doing so, we hope to assist educators in improving and adapting the courses they teach without needing to rip them up and start again, as well as helping students make suggestions for how this could be done.

We do so by proposing additional contents to the standard set of economics courses. For every course, we start with a short discussion of what is currently included in typical courses on that topic. Secondly, we provide suggestions for what could be included by making use of the building blocks. As in other chapters, we provide a concise set of teaching materials here and a more extensive overview of suggested resources in the online resource Teaching Materials.

The suggestions and descriptions in this chapter are quite brief. For more details, we recommend turning to the building blocks noted above each paragraph.

For the sake of brevity, in the physical book we provide suggestions for four of the most common core courses: Microeconomics, Macroeconomics, Public Economics, and Finance. On our website, we provide the same for the courses Economics 101, Environmental Economics, Industrial Organisation, Development Economics, Econometrics, Labour Economics, Monetary Economics, International Economics, Game Theory and Behavioural Economics. The website also offers more details and teaching materials for the four courses included in this physical book. Hosted by the Institute for New Economic Thinking, we provide an online forum where you can discuss these materials with other educators.

For each of the standard courses, we first provide an overview of the typical contents of current courses and the most frequently used textbooks. We then offer suggestions for additions and changes to this standard content. Within each course, our suggestions are grouped into five categories, each consisting of two building blocks:

- Practical skills and real-world knowledge: *Building Block 2: Know Your Own Economy* and *Building Block 9: Problems & Proposals*.
- A diversity of analytical tools and approaches: *Building Block 7: Research Methods & Philosophy of Science* and *Building Block 8: Economic Theories*.
- Institutions and different ways of organising the economy: *Building Block 5: Economic Organisations & Mechanisms* and *Building Block 6: Political-Economic Systems*.
- Societal relevance and normative aspects: *Building Block 1: Introducing the Economy* and *Building Block 10: Economics for a Better World*.
- History: *Building Block 3: Economic History* and *Building Block 4: History of Economic Thought & Methods*.

Coupled with these suggestions, we offer various options for potential teaching materials. Finally, we briefly discuss how to make space for this additional course content. After all, simply cramming more material into existing courses without freeing up space is not likely to serve students well, except perhaps the most prodigious students.

The suggestions and descriptions in this chapter are quite brief. For more details, we recommend turning to the building blocks noted above each paragraph.

It is important to note that we pose all these suggestions as potential sources of inspiration, not a checklist of all the things that necessarily should be included. After all, there is a practical limit to what can be taught within a single course. Furthermore, as also discussed in *Foundation 6: The Didactics of Economics Education* and *Tool 7: Learning Objectives*, courses can benefit from making more use of active learning activities. Even if this limits the amount of content that can be 'covered', it will likely increase the amount of content that students will 'master' (Hansen, 2011).

For the most up to date version of suggestions for all fourteen standard economics courses, including a wider selection and more up-to-date range of teaching materials, see our website. We welcome comments and contributions, and offer a platform for discussion with colleagues worldwide.
economy.st/adapt

1 Microeconomics

First, we set out the typical contents of current microeconomics courses. Second, we provide our suggested additions and changes.

Typical contents of current courses

Most introductory courses on microeconomics start from the neoclassical idea of the perfect market. This market is generally described as 'perfect' in the sense that it is, normatively speaking, optimal, and that it has exactly the following characteristics: rational self-interested behaviour, complete markets, perfect information, perfect factor mobility, no market power, no transaction costs, and no externalities. Later in the course and more advanced microeconomics courses, much attention is devoted to how such perfect markets interact with each other (general equilibrium theory). As well as what happens if one of the assumptions does not apply and the market is imperfect. For example: market power is central in industrial organisation, externalities in environmental economics, transaction costs in the theory of the firm, and information asymmetries in information economics. And finally, welfare economics focuses on whether such market imperfections justify government intervention in the market.

Frequently used textbooks:
- *Principles of Microeconomics* by Gregory Mankiw
- *Microeconomic Theory: Basic Principles and Extensions* by Walter Nicholson and Christopher M. Snyder
- *Microeconomics and Behaviour* by Robert Frank and Edward Cartwright
- *Microeconomics* by Anthony Partrick O'Brien and Glenn Hubbard
- *Microeconomics* by Austan Goolsbee and Steven Levitt
- *Microeconomics* by Daniel L. Rubinfeld and Robert Pindyck
- *Microeconomics* by Paul Krugman and Robin Wells
- *Microeconomics: Principles, Problems, and Policies* By Campbell McConnell, Stanley Brue and Sean Flynn
- *Microeconomics: Theory and Applications with Calculus* by Jeffrey M. Perloff
- *Intermediate Microeconomics* by Patrick M. Emerson
- *Intermediate Microeconomics: A Modern Approach* by Hal R. Varian
- *Intermediate Microeconomics: A Tool-Building Approach* by Samiran Banerjee
- *Advanced Microeconomic Theory: An Intuitive Approach with Examples* by Felix Munoz-Garcia

Suggested additions and changes

Practical skills and real-world knowledge

When teaching students how markets work, it can be particularly useful to let them explore and analyse real markets and sectors. Here we advise going beyond the typical example boxes in textbooks. While these are useful didactical tools to bring theory across, they do not give students substantial concrete knowledge about the actual economies. Instead, we recommend also treating real markets and sectors as topics in their own right, using theory as a tool rather than as the sole aim of the course.

This could be done by spending a lecture on a sector, its structure, its different actors, its dominant business models or other ways of functioning, and its relationship to the rest of the economy. Subsequently, students could be given assignments to conduct further analyses of the sector, through case studies and/or quantitative research. Here it can also be especially enriching for students to go and talk to people in the sector. Guest lectures are one form for this, but these contacts could also double as research methods training: interviews or field visits.

For more detail, see *Building Block 2: Know Your Own Economy* and *Building Block 9: Problems & Proposals*.

A range of analytical tools and approaches

When teaching students microeconomics it is helpful and important to make students realise that what they are learning are theories, not direct descriptions of reality. This might seem like an obvious point for any economist or scientist, but it is often not for students, including ourselves when we started studying economics. Before going into the various theories and ideas, courses could, for example, pay attention to philosophy of science and what it means to scientifically study the (economic) world and develop theories about it.

For more detail, see *Building Block 7: Research Methods & Philosophy of Science*.

It can be very useful to teach students other theories too, besides neoclassical microeconomic theory. The concept of competition is central to microeconomics and therefore it would help students to explain both the classical and neoclassical conceptions of competition.

Besides markets, households play a key role in microeconomics. Students could benefit from learning about neoclassical ideas to do with rational utility maximisation within the household as well as feminist economics on the unequal division of unpaid labour.

Relatedly, it is important for students to learn that power relations and institutions have an enormous impact on markets and on economic processes more broadly. In this case we advise going beyond the mainstream notions of market power and transaction costs, and also include insights from Marxian and feminist economics to better understand how class, gender and politics play crucial roles in the economy.

Finally, it is relevant to discuss the meaning of consumption with students, as this has a uniquely central role in microeconomics courses. Besides neoclassical ideas, institutional and ecological economics are of particular importance as these focus on how preferences are socially constructed and how material consumption relates to human wellbeing.

Pragmatic Pluralism offers more detail on the above topics, especially in the sections *Markets, Households, Inequality* and *Consumption*.
economy.st/pragmatic

Teaching Materials

- *Economics After The Crisis* by Irene van Staveren, from 2015, chapters 1, 2, 3, 4, and 5. This textbook discusses the topics of households, consumption, firms and markets from the neoclassical, institutional, social and post-Keynesian perspectives.
- *Economics: The User's Guide* by Ha-Joon Chang, from 2014, chapter 6, 7 and 9. This book provides a pluralist and accessible introduction into, among others, different economic approaches, the world of production, happiness and inequality.
- *Introducing a New Economics* by Jack Reardon, Maria A. Madi, and Molly S. Cato, from 2017, chapters 4, 9, 10, and 13. This textbook introduces the topics of economic value, markets, firms, consumption, and power from the post-Keynesian, Austrian, Marxian, and neoclassical perspectives.
- *The Economy* by The CORE Team, from 2017, chapters 3, 4, 5, 6, 7, 8, 11, 12, and 19. This textbook discusses many microeconomic topics, such as supply and demand, the firm, social interactions, power and inequality, while including recent mainstream insights and empirical findings.
- *The Microeconomics of Complex Economies: Evolutionary, Institutional, Neoclassical and Complexity Perspectives* by Wolfram Elsner, Torsten Heinrich, and Henning Schwardt, from 2014, chapter 17. This innovative textbook makes readers familiar with new insights coming from frontier mainstream economic research, with particular attention to

game theory, agent-based modelling, system dynamics, and empirical realities.

- *Rethinking Economics: An Introduction to Pluralist Economics* by Liliann Fischer, Joe Hasell, J. Christopher Proctor, David Uwakwe, Zach Ward Perkins, Catriona Watson, from 2017. This collection of essays provides an accessible introduction into post-Keynesian, Marxian, Austrian, institutional, feminist, behavioural, complexity and ecological economics.
- *Real World Micro*, by Dollars & Sense, most recent edition from 2020. This collection of essays explores the empirical reality of many microeconomic topics, such as the minimum wage, trade policy, and stock markets.
- *Towards a political theory of the firm*, by Luigi Zingales, from 2017. In this paper Zingales argues for paying more attention to the role of power in firms as well as providing a brief history of different theories of the firm.
- *Firms as political entities* by Isabelle Ferreras, from 2017. A provocative book on the economic history and theories of the firm, arguing for a reappreciation of the role of power in the firm.
- *An Evolutionary Alternative to Mainstream Microeconomics* by Joseph E. Pluta, from 2015. A critical book proposing a more dynamic approach to the microeconomics of firms and markets building on behavioural, institutional as well as evolutionary insights as the title suggests.
- *Classical vs. Neoclassical Conceptions of Competition* by Lefteris Tsoulfidis, 2011. This paper juxtaposes the static and dynamic views of competition, respectively held by neoclassical economists on the one hand, and classical, Marxian, Austrian economists and business scholars on the other hand.
- *Rethinking Microeconomics: A Proposed Reconstruction* by Anwar Shaikh, from 2012. Shaikh argues microeconomics education could be more robust, rigorous and empirically grounded, building on old and new insights, in particular concerning emergent properties and shaping structures. Interestingly, he also builds on the insight of Becker (1962, "Irrational Behavior and Economic Theory." Journal of Political Economy) that the key empirical consumption patterns, such as downward sloping demand curves, Engel's Law, and Keynesian type consumption functions, can be derived without assuming rational utility maximisation and only requires two assumptions: that there is a budget constraint and a minimum level of consumption for necessary goods. His book *Capitalism* can also be useful for teaching.

Institutions and different ways of organising the economy

Microeconomic courses are generally centred on studying markets. The market is, however, only one of the coordination and allocation mechanisms through which economies are organised. Commons and hierarchies (both private and public) are other widespread mechanisms, and crucial concepts for understanding how economies function. Microeconomic courses could thus be enriched by adding other coordination and allocation mechanisms, such as hierarchies and commons. Besides discussing mechanisms, it could also be fruitful to discuss the different forms of economic organisation with students, ranging from multinational corporations, state institutions, and households to democratic cooperatives, family firms and civic organisations.

For more detail, see *Building Block 5: Economic Organisations & Mechanisms*.

Teaching Materials
- *Introducing a New Economics* by Jack Reardon, Molly S. Cato, Maria A. C. Madi, from 2018, chapters 10, 11 & 12. Three accessible and brief chapters, with accompanying classroom activities and questions, introducing students to what public goods, commons and firms are and how they can be governed, for example as a corporation owned by shareholders or as a cooperative owned by its workers or consumers.
- *Economics: The User's Guide* by Ha-Joon Chang, from 2014, chapter 5. A short well-written chapter on different economic actors and organisational forms, from multinational corporations, cooperatives, and labour unions, to governments and a variety of international organisations.
- *Organisations: A Very Short Introduction* by Mary Jo Hatch, from 2011. A brief, accessible and yet highly informative book full with scientific theories and ideas on what organisations are, how they can be structured, how they change, and their internal dynamics and interaction with markets and society.
- *Governing the Commons: The Evolution of Institutions for Collective Action* by Elinor Ostrom, most recent edition from 2015, chapters 1, 2 & 3. A sharp and rigorous discussion of commons, how they are different from markets and hierarchies, how we should theorize them and real-world examples that help us better understand how they can be successful.
- *Contemporary Capitalism: The Embeddedness of Institutions* by J. Rogers Hollingsworth and Robert Boyer, most recent edition from 2012, chapter 1. An instructive analytical introduction and overview of different coordination and allocation mechanisms, such as markets, public and private hierarchies, networks, communities and associations.

Societal relevance and normative aspects
Like economics 101 courses, microeconomics courses could benefit from helping students understand what it means to be studying the economy,

what it is and why it is relevant. Microeconomic courses can further be enriched by explicitly discussing the variety of normative principles that guide decision making. Here, it is particularly enriching to discuss both utilitarian welfare criteria and other normative principles such as fairness, legitimacy, and stability. The main goal would be to help students understand normative trade-offs and be able to clearly communicate them to non-economists.

In addition, when discussing markets and other coordination and allocation mechanisms, one could make students familiar with normative debates about what their roles in the economy should be. A particularly relevant debate seems to be whether the entirety of human life and society should be marketized and commodified, or whether there should be 'moral limits of markets' and if so where should those limits be.

Finally, students could be introduced to the normative aspects of theoretical approaches. Showing students that analytical tools have values embedded in them can be an eye-opener that will help them in their future careers to be able to identify and distinguish normative and positive aspects. For instance, show a few examples of values embedded in analytical tools, such as the normative assumptions made in cost-benefit analyses or those underlying theoretical approaches like neoclassical, Marxian and ecological economics, as discussed in chapter *Foundation 4: Values*.

For more details, see *Building Block 1: Introducing the Economy* and *Building Block 10: Economics for a Better World*.

Teaching Materials

- *Economic Analysis, Moral Philosophy, and Public Policy* by Daniel Hausman, Michael McPherson, and Debra Satz, most recent edition from 2016. A great introduction into normative economics, covering its many areas and topics from welfare economics and utility theory to liberty, equality and justice.
- *A Guide to Ethics and Public Policy: Finding Our Way* by D. Don Welch, from 2014. A brief but insightful book providing a broad framework for evaluating policy proposals and outcomes, organised around five moral principles: benefit, effectiveness, fairness, fidelity, and legitimacy.
- *Political Ideologies: An Introduction* by Andrew Heywood, most recent edition from 2021. A useful and accessible introduction into a wide variety of political ideologies, from liberalism, socialism, and conservatism to feminism, nationalism, and green ideology, that shape much of our normative thinking on the economy.
- *Moral Views on Market Society* by Marion Fourcade and Kieran Healy, from 2007. An insightful overview paper on the key different normative

perspectives on capitalism, enabling readers to better understand and place ideas and arguments prevalent in many debates about the economy.

- *What Money Can't Buy: The Moral Limits of Markets* by Michael J. Sandel, most recent edition from 2012. A highly influential and well-written book reflecting on the moral place of markets in society and asking the key question whether everything should be up for sale. The Institute for New Economic Thinking has also launched a video series on the book and topic.

History

When introducing students to (micro)economic concepts, it can be very informative for them to understand when and how these were developed. There is no need to set out how the details of the models evolved over time, but it can be helpful to know of a few important breakthroughs in their development, the context in which they occurred and the contributions they made to the debates within the discipline. Besides this history of economic thought, economic history can also enrich microeconomic courses as it can help students get a better understanding of the roles that markets can play in economies. By discussing the history of markets, key insights and facts can be conveyed to students in a different way from explaining models and theories. Key questions could be: how did markets emerge and evolve over time; which different institutional frameworks concerning markets have existed and how did they perform; are there important differences between different kinds of markets, such as product markets in goods and services, and factor markets in land, labour and capital?

For more detail, see *Building Block 3: Economic History* and *Building Block 4: History of Economic Thought & Methods*.

Teaching Materials

- *The Worldly Philosophers: The Lives, Times and Ideas of the Great Economic Thinkers* by Robert Heilbroner, most recent edition from 1999. While first published in 1953, it remains perhaps the best introduction into the history of economic thought to this day. In a remarkably well-written and accessible manner it discusses the ideas of key economists and puts them into historical context.
- *Grand Pursuit: The Story of Economic Genius* by Sylvia Naser, from 2012. Another very accessible but more recent book introducing the history of economic thought through captivating narratives.
- *A Companion to the History of Economic Thought* by Warren J. Samuels, Jeff E. Biddle, and John B. Davis, from 2003, chapter 24 & 25. An extensive and detailed collection of contributions covering many

periods and developments in the history of economic thought, with two chapters specifically devoted to the history of post-war neoclassical microeconomics and formalist revolution in economics.

■ *The Great Transformation: The Political and Economic Origins of Our Time* by Karl Polanyi, most recent edition from 2001. This classic explores the economic history of the rise and fall of the market economy and how this transformed society.

What to take out

To create space for the above suggested additions, we advise focussing more on the key ideas and intuitions behind the taught models and devote less teaching time to their technicalities and mathematics. As teaching students to reproduce and work through mathematical models often takes up a large part of the teaching time, this would give the teachers the opportunity to devote more time to practical knowledge, the relevance, institutions, and history. Furthermore, a more even balance between neoclassical economics and other economic approaches could be achieved by decreasing the number of neoclassical ideas and models that are taught.

For the most up to date version of these course adaptation suggestions, including a wider selection and more up-to-date range of teaching materials, see our website. We welcome comments and contributions. We also offer a platform for discussion and exchange of teaching materials with colleagues worldwide.

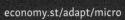
economy.st/adapt/micro

2 Macroeconomics

First, we set out the typical contents of current macroeconomics courses. Second, we provide our suggested additions and changes.

Typical contents of current courses

Current macroeconomics courses typically focus mainly on ideas and models of the neoclassical-Keynesian synthesis, sometimes also called neo-Keynesian macroeconomics, frequently complemented with monetarist critiques and alternative models. Key models to which a lot of teaching time is devoted are the aggregate demand-aggregate supply model, IS-LM model, and the Phillips curve. Sometimes the topic of economic growth, in particular the Solow and Ramsey growth models, are also included. In more advanced macroeconomics courses, dynamic stochastic general equilibrium (DSGE) models, with both their new classical and new Keynesian variants, are often central. In this way, topics, such as unemployment, inflation, growth, monetary and fiscal policy, are analysed using concepts such as adaptive and rational expectations.

Frequently used textbooks:
- *Principles of Macroeconomics* by Gregory Mankiw
- *Macroeconomics* by Andrew B. Abel, Ben Bernanke, and Dean Croushore
- *Macroeconomics* by Campbell R. McConnell, Stanley L. Brue and Sean Masaki Flynn
- *Macroeconomics* by Glenn Hubbard, Anthony Patrick O'Brien and Matthew P. Rafferty
- *Macroeconomics* by Olivier Blanchard
- *Macroeconomics* by Paul Krugman and Robin Wells
- *Macroeconomics* by Robert J. Gordon
- *Macroeconomics* by Stephen Williamson
- *Macroeconomics* by William Boyes, Michael Melvin
- *Macroeconomics: Policy and Practice* by Frederic Mishkin
- *Macroeconomics: Principles and Policy* by Alan Blinder en William Baumol
- *Macroeconomics: Theories and Policies* by Richard T. Froyen
- *Intermediate Macroeconomics* by Dennis W. Jansen, Charles D. Delorme and Robert B. Ekelund
- *Intermediate Macroeconomics* by Robert Barro
- *Advanced Macroeconomics* by David Romer

Suggested additions and changes

Practical skills and real-world knowledge

Macroeconomics courses are often strongly focused on theoretical models. While theory is crucial, it is also important to make students familiar with the real-world economy around them. In particular, it can be useful to teach students about the main institutions that shape the national economy in which the course is given, such as its regulatory or social security system, its economic ministries and central bank, labour unions and employers associations. Besides this, it can be helpful to show students how various indicators, such as unemployment, inflation, life-satisfaction, income and wealth inequality, carbon footprint, and household, corporate, and public debt levels, have developed. These indicators are often variables in models, so this real-world knowledge will enable them to also better understand and put in context the theories they are learning.

For more detail, see *Building Block 2: Know Your Own Economy* and *Building Block 9: Problems & Proposals*.

A range of analytical tools and approaches

Macroeconomic theory is a relatively contested field. Nevertheless, there are many important insights that students could learn. Besides the key ideas and models of the neoclassical-Keynesian synthesis, it could be interesting and relevant to introduce students to Austrian and post-Keynesian ideas about how macroeconomies function and how malinvestment and effective demand are crucial. Since government policy has a central role in macroeconomics, it could also be useful to introduce students to the different economic perspectives on governments with ideas such as discretion, rule-bound policy, the entrepreneurial state and nudging.

The topics *Business Cycles* and *Governments* in the online resource *Pragmatic Pluralism* provide more details.
economy.st/cycles

economy.st/governments

Furthermore, it is important to discuss, and let students debate, how these various theories and models can and should be used and applied in practice. How should one choose a model or theoretical approach when trying to tackle a real-world problem? How should one use the theories, what can they tell you about the world and what are their limitations? These matters can be discussed systematically by teaching philosophy of science to students.

For more detail, see *Building Block 7: Research Methods & Philosophy of Science, Building Block 8: Economic Theories*.

Teaching Materials

- *Macroeconomics in Context* by Neva Goodwin, Jonathan M. Harris, Julie A. Nelson, Pratistha Joshi Rajkarnikar, Brian Roach, and Mariano Torras, most recent edition from 2019. A useful textbook that treats much of the traditional content, but pays considerably more attention to questions related to financial crises, social inequality and environmental sustainability.
- *Economics After The Crisis* by Irene van Staveren, from 2015, chapters 6, 7, 10, and 12. This textbook discusses the topics of the state, public goods, macroeconomic flows, and economic growth from the neoclassical, institutional, social and post-Keynesian perspectives.
- *Economics: The User's Guide* by Ha-Joon Chang, from 2014, chapter 6, 10 and 11. This book provides a pluralist and accessible introduction into, among others, different economic approaches, the world of output, unemployment and the state.
- *Introducing a New Economics* by Jack Reardon, Maria A. Madi, and Molly S. Cato, from 2017, chapters 7, 12, 13 and 14. This textbook introduces the topics of unemployment, investment, financial crises, and fiscal and monetary policy, from the post-Keynesian, Austrian, Marxian, and neoclassical perspectives.
- *Real World Macro*, by Dollars & Sense, most recent edition from 2020. This collection of essays explores the empirical reality of many macroeconomic topics, such as unemployment, inequality, inflation, monetary and fiscal policy.
- *Macroeconomics* by William Mitchell, L. Randall Wray, Martin Watts, from 2019, chapters 20, 21, 22 and 23. This ground-breaking and much-discussed textbook written by three leaders of Modern Monetary Theory (MMT), describes in detail the history of economic thinking about the state and macroeconomy as well as recent theoretical and policy debates.
- *Money and Government: The Past and Future of Economics* by Robert Skidelsky, from 2018. This well-written and insightful book introduces readers to historical and current debates about the macro economy,

with particular attention to neoclassical and Keynesian ideas.

- *The Undercover Economist Strikes Back: How to Run or Ruin an Economy* by Tim Harford, from 2013. An accessible and well-written introduction into macroeconomics, discussing various topics from dealing with recessions, unemployment and inflation, striving for (GNP) growth, happiness, sustainability and more equality.

Institutions and different ways of organising the economy

When teaching students macroeconomics, it can be very enriching and informative to discuss the basics of macroeconomic systems with them. So before going into the various theories about how capitalist economies and their markets function, one could discuss what capitalism is, what varieties it has and what other political-economic systems are. Basic knowledge about these matters enables students to put the taught theories better in perspective and context, allowing students to understand the more fundamental implications of the theories. It also helps students to engage in a more knowledgeable way in political discussions about the economy and reforming it.

For more detail, see *Building Block 6: Political-Economic Systems*.

Teaching Materials:

- *Capitalism* by Geoffrey Ingham, from 2008. A highly insightful introduction into capitalism with chapters on key ideas from Smith, Marx, Weber, Schumpeter and Keynes, and core institutions, such as market exchange, the enterprise, money, capital, financial markets and the state.
- *Capitalism: A Very Short Introduction* by James Fulcher, most recent edition from 2015. A brief and yet useful book on capitalism's definition, historical evolution, varieties, global networks, and recurring crises.
- *Comparative economics in a transforming world economy* by J. Barkley Rosser, Jr. and Marina V. Rosser, most recent edition from 2018. A highly useful and broad book describing many varieties of advanced market capitalism, varieties of transition among socialist economies, and alternative paths among developing economies, with chapters on many countries, such as the United States, Russia, Sweden, China, India, Iran, South Africa, Mexico, and Brazil. It is particularly useful for students to learn about their own country. If their country is not included in the book, as is the case for us as Dutch citizens, it can be useful to supplement the book with teaching material on the national political-economic system.

Societal relevance and normative aspects

When teaching students about the core economic indicators, such as GDP, it can also be helpful to discuss different ideas about how important the various indicators are. Many, if not all, of these indicators are developed because people thought they were important in themselves, or through their impact on other outcomes. Here it can be particularly useful to discuss the most prominent indicator today, GDP, and what its normative relevance is. Furthermore, alternatives to GDP, such as the OECD Better Life Index, Genuine Progress Indicators, and the World Happiness Report, are important. As with indicators, when discussing political-economic systems, it can be useful to also discuss normative views on them. Moral ideas about how the economy should look are at the core of public and political debates. As Robert Heilbroner (1953, p. 14) put it : *"A man who thinks that economics is only a matter for professors forgets that this is the science that has sent men to the barricades"*. As future economists, students would do well to learn about these normative ideas on economic systems.

For more detail, see *Building Block 1: Introducing the Economy* and *Building Block 10: Economics for a Better World*.

Teaching Materials

- *Moral Views on Market Society* by Marion Fourcade and Kieran Healy, from 2007. An insightful overview paper on the key different normative perspectives on capitalism, enabling readers to better understand and place ideas and arguments prevalent in many debates about the economy.
- *Macroeconomics in Context* by Neva Goodwin, Jonathan M. Harris, Julie A. Nelson, Pratistha Joshi Rajkarnikar, Brian Roach, and Mariano Torras, most recent edition from 2019, chapters 0, 1, 5, and 6. A useful textbook that treats much of the traditional content, but pays particular attention to questions related to the goals of the economy and the measurement of them.
- *Introducing a New Economics* by Jack Reardon, Molly S. Cato, Maria A. C. Madi, from 2018, chapters 1, 3, 4, & 5. An accessible textbook which introduces students to what economics is, how it is embedded in society and the environment, and major societal challenges, such as climate change, poverty, financial instability, and inequality.
- *Economics: The User's Guide* by Ha-Joon Chang, from 2014, chapters 1 & 2. Perhaps the most accessible and yet insightful introduction book into economics, with particular attention to why it is relevant to learn economics and what economics is in the first place.
- To help students get an idea of the main societal challenges of today, it can be useful to have them take a look at reports, such as the *Sustainable Development Goals Reports*, *World Development Reports*, and *World*

Happiness Reports. It can also be useful to use more engaging types of materials, such as documentaries and coverage of political protests and debates. Furthermore, it can be interesting and useful for students to also be exposed to material on the key issues in the domestic, rather than global, economy.

- *The Value of Everything: Making and Taking in the Global Economy* by Mariana Mazzucato, from 2017. This well-written and influential book takes readers through the history of thinking about economic value up to the present day.

History

Economic history is a particularly useful tool when teaching macroeconomics. It helps make the content lively and concrete, giving students more feeling for the matters that are discussed. Here the history of capitalism and business cycles seems specifically relevant as these are at the core of macroeconomic courses. Besides economic history, the history of macroeconomic thought can also be interesting and useful to teach to students, as it can help them better understand ideas, how they were developed and relate to other ideas.

For more detail, see *Building Block 3: Economic History* and *Building Block 4: History of Economic Thought & Methods*.

Teaching Materials

- *A Companion to the History of Economic Thought* by Warren J. Samuels, Jeff E. Biddle, and John B. Davis, from 2003, chapter 26. An extensive and detailed collection of contributions covering many periods and developments in the history of economic thought, as well as covering historiography and different ways of approaching that history.
- *Macroeconomics* by William Mitchell, L. Randall Wray, Martin Watts, from 2019, chapters 3, 27, 28, 29 and 30. This ground-breaking and much-discussed textbook written by three key leaders of Modern Monetary Theory (MMT), describes in detail the history of economic thinking about the state and macroeconomy as well as recent theoretical and policy debates.
- *Money and Government: The Past and Future of Economics* by Robert Skidelsky, from 2018. This well-written and insightful book introduces readers to historical and current debates about the state, with particular attention to neoclassical and Keynesian ideas.
- *Capitalism* by Geoffrey Ingham, from 2008, chapters 1 and 2. A highly insightful introduction into capitalism with chapters on key ideas from Smith, Marx, Weber, Schumpeter and Keynes, and core institutions, such as market exchange, the enterprise, money, capital, financial markets and the state.

- *Capitalism: A Short History* by Jürgen Kocka, from 2016. A concise and yet broad-ranging account of how capitalism developed from early merchants, colonialism and slavery to the recent wave of globalisation and financialisation, accompanied by discussions of capitalism's key thinkers, such as Smith, Marx, Weber, and Schumpeter.
- *Economics: The User's Guide* by Ha-Joon Chang, from 2014, chapters 2 & 3. Two short and well written chapters on how the economy has changed over the last centuries and how capitalism evolved.
- *Global Economic History: A Very Short Introduction* by Robert C. Allen, from 2011. A brief but insightful introduction into the economic history of the world with chapters on industrialisation, the rise of the West, great empires, the Americas and Africa.

What to take out

To create space for the above suggested additions, we advise to focus more on the key ideas and intuitions behind the taught models and devote less teaching time to their technicalities and mathematics. As teaching students to reproduce and work through mathematical models often takes up a large part of the teaching time, this would give the teachers the opportunity to devote more time to practical knowledge, the relevance, institutions, and history. Furthermore, a more even balance between neoclassical economics and other economic approaches could be achieved by decreasing the number of neoclassical ideas and models that are taught.

For the most up to date version of these course adaptation suggestions, including a wider selection and more up-to-date range of teaching materials, see our website. We welcome comments and contributions. We also offer a platform for discussion and exchange of teaching materials with colleagues worldwide.
economy.st/adapt/macro

3   Public Economics

First, we set out the typical contents of current public economics courses. Second, we provide our suggested additions and changes.

Typical contents of current courses

Courses on public economics today generally focus on neoclassical (partial or general) equilibrium models with the aim of establishing what would be the 'optimal' course of government (in)action. Government intervention is justified on the basis of market imperfections, such as externalities, public goods, imperfect competition and asymmetrical information. But students are also taught to be wary of market distortions and government failures arising from self-interested rational behaviour of politicians, voters, and civil servants. In this way, students often learn to think in terms of trade-offs between equity and efficiency. Recently, behavioural insights on policy design are increasingly incorporated in public economics courses. These theoretical ideas and models are used to treat a broad range of topics from taxation and redistribution to pensions, social policy and public finance.

Frequently used textbooks:
- *Economics of the Public Sector* by Joseph Stiglitz
- *Fundamentals of Public Economics* by Jean-Jacques Laffont
- *Public Economics* by Gareth D. Myles
- *Public Economics: The Macroeconomic Perspective* by Burkhard Heer
- *Public Finance and Public Policy* by Jonathan Gruber
- *Public Finance* by Harvey S. Rosen and Ted Gayer
- *The Economics of Taxation* by Bernard Salanié
- *The Economics of the Welfare State* by Nicholas Barr
- *Intermediate Public Economics* by Gareth D. Myles and Jean Hindriks

Suggested additions and changes

Practical skills and real-world knowledge
When teaching students about the economics of the state, it can be informative and motivating to discuss not only economic theories, but also the real world. Rather than just talking about government organisations and policies in the abstract, one could make use of (recent and local) cases and spell out questions and dilemmas that arise from these. Besides learning about the real world through case studies, students can benefit from learning about the specific institutions and government structures that shape the (national) economy.

Students can also benefit from learning about practical policy tools. A key part of the work of professional economists is analysing specific cases and possible policy interventions. To prepare students for this, it is useful to devote time to teach them about practical policy tools. The most famous of these is the traditional cost-benefit analysis, based on neoclassical economics. Recently new policy tools, such as risk-opportunity analysis based on complexity economics and participatory evaluation inspired by the cultural approach, have been developed and these are increasingly applied in practice. To ensure students acquire up to date knowledge and skills we suggest also teaching these younger approaches and exposing students to recent developments in the field.

For more detail, see *Building Block 2: Know Your Own Economy* and *Building Block 9: Problems & Proposals.*

Teaching Materials

- To introduce the policy tools, reading materials can be of use, but they will probably have the most lasting impact when combined with practical exercises in which students have to apply the tools themselves. For cost-benefit analysis, a useful book is: *Cost-Benefit Analysis: Concepts and Practice* by Anthony E. Boardman, David H. Greenberg, Aidan R. Vining, David L. Weimer, most recent edition from 2018. For participatory evaluation, the following book can be of help: *Participatory Evaluation Up Close: An Integration of Research Based Knowledge* by J. Bradley Cousins and Jill A. Chouinard, from 2012. Risk-opportunity analysis is newer and has yet to be explained in a textbook, but an useful working paper explaining the tool and providing examples of applications is: *Risk-opportunity analysis for transformative policy design and appraisal* by Jean-Francois Mercure, Simon Sharpe, Jorge Vinuales, Matthew Ives, Michael Grubb, Hector Pollitt, Florian Knobloch and Femke Nijsse, from 2020.
- *The Oxford Handbook of Public Policy* by Robert E. Goodin, Michael Moran, and Martin Rein, from 2008. An extensive book, which provides a useful overview of different aspects of public policy, such as the role of economic policy tools, engagement of stakeholders, and producing and evaluating policy.
- *Handbook of Policy Formulation* by Michael Howlett and Ishani Mukherjee, from 2017. Another extensive book, which focuses on how policy is made with its different aspects, such as choosing policy goals and instruments, policy appraisal techniques, and the politics of defining and resolving policy problems.

A range of analytical tools and approaches

There are many different economic perspectives on the state, but in a course one cannot practically treat all these in detail. Current courses focus mainly on neoclassical ideas, increasingly accompanied by some attention on behavioural ideas. We propose to present students with a broader and more balanced overview of economic debates about the state. Neoclassical and (post-) Keynesian ideas are generally most prominent and students should become familiar with their conflicting ideas about the roles of the state. Recently, new ideas on the state coming from evolutionary economics, such as the concepts of the entrepreneurial state and mission economy, are increasingly influential and therefore relevant for students to learn about. If there is more teaching time (made) available, students could also be made familiar, in more and less detail, with the other perspectives on the state, such as the Marxian, behavioural, Austrian, historical, complexity and classical perspectives.

For more detail, see *Building Block 7: Research Methods & Philosophy of Science*, *Building Block 8: Economic Theories*.

The topic *Governments* in the online resource *Pragmatic Pluralism* also provides more details.
economy.st/governments

Teaching Materials

- *Economics: The User's Guide* by Ha-Joon Chang, from 2014, chapter 11. This brief and accessible pluralist book contains a useful introductory chapter on the role of the state.
- *Economics After The Crisis* by Irene van Staveren, from 2015, chapter 6. This well-written textbook sets out the neoclassical, post-Keynesian, social economic and institutional perspectives on the state.
- *The Economy* by The CORE Team, from 2017, chapters 14, 15 and 22. This successful textbook provides an introduction into mainstream ideas and empirical findings on fiscal, monetary and public policy.
- *Principles of Economics in Context* by Jonathan Harris, Julie A. Nelson and Neva Goodwin, most recent edition from 2020, chapter 12 and 25. This useful textbook, which pays particular attention to social and environmental challenges, devotes two chapters to tax and fiscal policy in specific.
- *The Entrepreneurial State: Debunking Public vs. Private Sector Myths* by Mariana Mazzucato, from 2013. An influential and well-written book, inspired chiefly by evolutionary economics, on the role of the state in innovation.

- *Alternative Theories of the State* by S. Pressman, from 2006. A useful and informative collection of essays which introduces readers to the institutional, Marxist, post-Keynesian, feminist and behavioural perspectives on the state.
- *Money and Government: The Past and Future of Economics* by Robert Skidelsky, from 2018. This well-written and insightful book introduces readers to historical and current debates about the state, with particular attention to neoclassical and Keynesian ideas.
- *Political Economy: The Contest of Economic Ideas* by Frank Stilwell, most recent edition from 2011. A well-written textbook, with parts devoted to classical, Marxist, neoclassical, institutional, and Keynesian economics and particular attention to ideas surrounding the state, reform, policy and economic systems.

Institutions and different ways of organising the economy

States come in many shapes and forms. Students should become at least somewhat familiar with the wide varieties in (welfare) state arrangements, and more generally political-economic systems. Knowledge of these varieties will help students in their careers to situate and contextualise the problems and cases they have to deal with, in the broader systems that they are part of.

For more detail, see *Building Block 6: Political-Economic Systems*.

Teaching Materials

- *The Three Worlds of Welfare Capitalism* by Gøsta Esping-Andersen, from 1990. This classic describes three types of welfare states, the liberal, conservative and social democratic regimes, by exploring their social policies, pension systems, power relations, and labour markets.
- *Varieties of Capitalism: The Institutional Foundations of Comparative Advantage* by Peter A. Hall and David Soskice, from 2001. Another highly influential classic on differences in economic systems, here with a central distinction between liberal and coordinated market economies with respect to industrial relations, social and monetary policy, corporate governance, vocational training and education, and inter-firm relations.
- *Debating Varieties of Capitalism: A Reader* by Bob Hancké, from 2009. An insightful collection of essays provides a good overview of the debates surrounding theoretical and empirical controversies that followed the publication of Hall and Soskice's classic. Besides this reader there are many useful studies and papers on the varieties of capitalism, including of Latin American and Asian varieties. This can be of help as it can be particularly useful for students to read material on the variety of capitalism of their own country.

- *Comparative economics in a transforming world economy* by J. Barkley Rosser, Jr. and Marina V. Rosser, most recent edition from 2018. A highly useful and broad book describing many varieties of advanced market capitalism, varieties of transition among socialist economies, and alternative paths among developing economies, with chapters on many countries, such as the United States, Russia, Sweden, China, India, Iran, South Africa, Mexico, and Brazil. It is particularly useful for students to learn about their own country. If that country is not included, as is the case for us as Dutch citizens, it can be useful to supplement the book with teaching material on the national political-economic system.
- *Understanding and Managing Public Organizations* by Hal G. Rainey, most recent edition from 2014. A useful textbook discussing how to understand the dynamic context in which government organisations operate and strategies and dimensions relevant for managing them.

Societal relevance and normative aspects

Government (in)action is the central matter of debate in politics. For any economists working on the matter, it thus is critical to be familiar with the various normative perspectives on public policy. These concern both normative principles for decision-making and normative visions for the economy as discussed in *Building Block 10: Economics for a Better World*. Courses often already discuss utilitarian principles and assumptions, but could be further enriched by also discussing other normative principles and approaches.

Besides learning about these more general principles and visions, it can be useful to discuss recent debates about key policy issues. This can be done by juxtaposing the different problem analyses and proposed solutions related to the issue at hand. This can help make normative differences more concrete as well as bringing together normative, analytical and practical aspects.

For more detail, see *Building Block 10: Economics for a Better World*.

Teaching Materials

- *Economic Analysis, Moral Philosophy, and Public Policy* by Daniel Hausman, Michael McPherson, and Debra Satz, most recent edition from 2016. A great introduction into normative economics, covering its many areas and topics from welfare economics and utility theory to liberty, equality and justice.
- *A Guide to Ethics and Public Policy: Finding Our Way* by D. Don Welch, from 2014. A brief but insightful book providing a broad framework for evaluating policy proposals and outcomes, organised around five moral principles: benefit, effectiveness, fairness, fidelity, and legitimacy.

- *The Routledge Handbook of Ethics and Public Policy* by Annabelle Lever and Andrei Poama, from 2019. This useful collection of essays treats many different aspects of the ethics of public policy, from monetary, tax and trade policies to the minimum wage, anti-discrimination and social policies.
- *The Oxford Handbook of Professional Economic Ethics* by George F. DeMartino and Deirdre McCloskey, from 2016, chapters 25-33. This insightful collection of essays explores the different aspects of ethics in economics, with one part devoted to ethical issues related to economic policy advice and analysis.

History

The history of the state, from an economic point of view, is a fascinating topic that could enrich public economics courses. The role of the state in the economy has drastically changed over time, so learning about these historical developments can help students imagine a broader range of possibilities as well as understand the current situation and its unique characteristics better. The state has also played a central role in economic thinking, particularly in macroeconomics. Besides teaching about the history of the state itself, it could thus also be useful to treat the history of ideas about the government.

For more detail, see *Building Block 3: Economic History* and *Building Block 4: History of Economic Thought & Methods*.

Teaching Materials

- *A Companion to the History of Economic Thought* by Warren J. Samuels, Jeff E. Biddle, and John B. Davis, from 2003, chapter 27. An extensive and detailed collection of contributions covering many periods and developments in the history of economic thought, with a chapter specifically devoted to the history of economic thought about governments.
- *Money and Government: The Past and Future of Economics* by Robert Skidelsky, from 2018. This well-written and insightful book introduces readers to historical and current debates about the state and macroeconomy, with particular attention to neoclassical and Keynesian ideas.
- *Austerity: The History of a Dangerous Idea* by Mark Blyth, from 2013. This influential and well-written book traces the intellectual history of the ideas of austerity and expansionary fiscal contraction, connecting it to wider developments in economic thinking and reality.
- *States versus Markets: The emergence of a global economy* by Herman Schwartz, most recent edition from 2010. This book explores the history of the global economy, with particular attention to the role of markets and the state.

What to take out

To create space for the above suggested additions, we advise focussing more on the key ideas and intuitions behind the taught models and devote less teaching time to their technicalities and mathematics. As teaching students to reproduce and work through mathematical models often takes up a large part of the teaching time, this would give the teachers the opportunity to devote more time to practical knowledge, the relevance, institutions, and history. Furthermore, a more even balance between neoclassical economics and other economic approaches could be achieved by decreasing the number of neoclassical ideas and models that are taught.

For the most up to date version of these course adaptation suggestions, including a wider selection and more up-to-date range of teaching materials, see our website. We welcome comments and contributions. We also offer a platform for discussion and exchange of teaching materials with colleagues worldwide.

economy.st/adapt/public

4 Finance

First, we set out the typical contents of current finance courses. Second, we provide our suggested additions and changes.

Typical contents of current courses

Over the last decades, financial markets have grown exponentially and their complexity has also increased drastically. Finance courses try to help students make sense of this imposing world by explaining different kinds of financial products and markets. Moreover, courses teach neoclassical theories of how the financial world can be understood as being in efficient equilibria brought about by rational optimising behaviour. Typically, courses start from a highly simplified world in which everything is certain, markets are 'perfect' and all available information is incorporated in prices. Then (calculable) risk and market imperfections are introduced to account for the complex reality of our world. Building on these ideas, a number of neoclassical models such as the capital asset pricing model (CAPM), arbitrage pricing theory, the Black-Scholes model, and intertemporal equilibrium models, are taught. And with the help of these models, financial products such as derivatives, fixed-income securities, and options, are discussed. Recently some courses are also integrating insights from behavioural and complexity economics, which focus on irrational and unpredictable behaviour.

Frequently used textbooks:
- *Asset Pricing* by John H. Cochrane
- *Financial Economics* by Frank Fabozzi, Ted Neave and Gaofu Zhou
- *Money and Banking* by Robert E. Wright and Vincenzo Quadrini
- *Money, Banking and Financial Markets* by Stephen Cecchetti and Kermit Schoenholtz
- *Money, Banking, and the Financial System* by Glenn Hubbard and Anthony Patrick O'Brien
- *Principles of Financial Economics* by Stephen F. LeRoy, Jan Werner and Stephen A. Ross
- *Quantitative Financial Economics: Stocks, Bonds and Foreign Exchange* by Keith Cuthbertson and Dirk Nitzsche
- *The Econometrics of Financial Markets* by John Y. Campbell
- *The Economics of Financial Markets* by Hendrik S. Houthakker and Peter J. Williamson
- *The Economics of Financial Markets* by Roy Bailey
- *The Economics of Money, Banking & Financial Markets* by Glenn Hubbard and Anthony P. O'Brien

Suggested additions and changes

Practical skills and real-world knowledge

It is important that students get to know the actual financial world, not only theoretical ones, for four reasons. First, it motivates students because it makes the often abstract material come alive. By visiting a financial institution, or market, it is no longer just numbers and equations, but also actual people of flesh and blood. Second, it can help students better understand the theory. This is often how the real world is currently incorporated in courses. With the help of examples, the theory is demonstrated to help students grasp what is meant by abstract statements. Third, exposing students to the real world helps them better understand it. This sounds almost tautological, but it is important to note as understanding the real world is too often underappreciated as a goal in itself. By giving students assignments, case studies and lectures that focus on explaining the complex and messy real world, rather than a theory about it, they will learn how theories can help them but also what their limitations are. Finally, making students familiar with the workings and details of actual financial institutions and markets is crucial as it helps them acquire practical skills and knowledge that they will need in their future work. Many of these skills and knowledge will be of little theoretical significance, but nevertheless vital for students' later functioning in an organisation.

For more detail, see *Building Block 2: Know Your Own Economy* and *Building Block 9: Problems & Proposals*.

A range of analytical tools and approaches

Current finance courses could be enriched by incorporating post-Keynesian insights into fundamental, or Knightian, uncertainty, credit dynamics, and animal spirits. We applaud the recent incorporation of behavioural and complexity insights, often related to systematic irrationality and systemic risk, in some finance courses, and encourage teachers to do so even more. To broaden the scope further, cultural insights, among other things into how analytical constructs, such as economic models, can shape real world markets, can be incorporated.

For more detail, see *Building Block 7: Research Methods & Philosophy of Science*, *Building Block 8: Economic Theories*.

The topic *Finance* in the online resource *Pragmatic Pluralism* also provides more details.
economy.st/finance

Teaching Materials

- *Economics After The Crisis* by Irene van Staveren, from 2015, chapter 9. This useful and pluralist textbook discusses financial markets from the neoclassical, institutional, social and post-Keynesian perspectives.
- *Economics: The User's Guide* by Ha-Joon Chang, from 2014, chapter 8. This book provides a pluralist and accessible introduction, with one chapter specifically devoted to finance.
- *Introducing a New Economics* by Jack Reardon, Maria A. Madi, and Molly S. Cato, from 2017, chapters 13, 14 and 17. This textbook introduces the topic of finance in a pluralist and real-world manner.
- *The Economy* by The CORE Team, from 2017, chapters 10 and 17. This textbook introduces students to money, banks and financial crises by explaining recent mainstream insights and empirical findings.
- *Principles of Economics in Context* by Jonathan Harris, Julie A. Nelson and Neva Goodwin, most recent edition from 2020, chapter 26. This textbook, which pays particular attention to social and environmental challenges, devotes one chapter specifically to money and finance.
- *Macroeconomics* by William Mitchell, L. Randall Wray, Martin Watts, from 2019, chapter 10. This textbook written by three leaders of Modern Monetary Theory (MMT) has one chapter specifically devoted to money and banking.
- *The Handbook of Economic Sociology* by Neil J. Smelser and Richard Swedberg, from 2005, chapters 22, 23 and 24. This extensive and yet accessible book for non-sociologists, provides an impressive and useful overview of the field of economic sociology, including a chapter on finance.
- *The anthropology of money* by Bill Maurer, from 2006. An insightful review article discussing money and finance from a cultural, social and performative perspective.
- *"No one saw this coming": Understanding Financial Crisis Through Accounting Models* by Dirk Bezemer, from 2009. A useful article discussing how equilibrium models were not able to anticipate the credit crisis, while accounting models were.
- *An Engine, Not a Camera: How Financial Models Shape Markets* by Donald MacKenzie, from 2006. A book on the performative perspective on finance, looking at how economists' analytical tools can influence how financial markets work.
- *Behavioral Finance: Psychology, Decision-Making, and Markets* by Lucy Ackert and Richard Deaves, from 2010. A book on the behavioural perspective on finance, looking at how cognitive limitations and irrationalities shape how financial markets work.
- *The Routledge International Handbook of Financialization* by Philip Mader, Daniel Mertens, and Natascha van der Zwan, from 2020. A useful and extensive collection of essays on different aspects and perspectives on financialisation, a key development of the last decades.

Institutions and different ways of organising the economy

Financial systems are complex human constructions that know many varieties. To function well in this environment in their later careers, students need to become familiar with the various ways in which financial systems can be organised. This ranges from different micro-level practices and rules inside banks and specific markets, to macro-level structures that determine what characteristics and dynamics shape the system as a whole. Given the limited teaching time, it can be useful to focus on giving a brief overview of the wide variety of possibilities that have existed around the world throughout history, or have been proposed, and then going in more detail into the current domestic institutional framework.

For more detail, see *Building Block 5: Economic Organisations & Mechanisms* and *Building Block 6: Political-Economic Systems.*

The topics *Finance* and *Money* in the online resource *Pragmatic Pluralism* provide more details.
economy.st/finance

economy.st/money

Teaching Materials

- *Modern Financial Systems: Theory and Applications* by Edwin H. Neave, from 2011. This textbook explores how financial systems can be structured, with market and non-market governance forms, different kinds of market activities and relations, intermediation by banks and regulation.
- *Comparing Financial Systems* by Franklin Allen, Douglas Gale, and Julius Silver, from 2001. This textbook compares the financial systems of different countries and discusses the different options in terms of corporate governance and banking structure.
- *The Financial System, Financial Regulation and Central Bank Policy* by Thomas F. Cargill, from 2017. A book on how the financial system is structured and has emerged, discussing historical and current ideas and real-world developments.
- *Principles of Sustainable Finance* by Dirk Schoenmaker and Willem Schramade, from 2018. An accessible and well-structured textbook explaining to students how finance can become sustainable, paying attention to integrated reporting, long-term value creation, internalizing externalities, and approaching equity, bonds, banking and

insurance differently.

- *Between Debt and the Devil: Money, Credit, and Fixing Global Finance* by Adair Turner, from 2015. A book on the current financial problems and innovative ideas to solve them coming from an influential 'insider'.
- *The End of Alchemy: Money, Banking and the Future of the Global Economy* by Mervyn King, from 2016. Another book by an 'insider' which connects personal insights with an accessible description of how our thinking has developed over time, and how the financial system does and should work.

Societal relevance and normative aspects

A finance course without attention to ethics is incomplete. However, we should not stick to a narrow conception of ethics in finance, discussing illegal trading practices or other obvious forms of deceit. Ethical questions concern the core of finance itself and how financial systems are organised. What is the goal of finance, or what should it be? This is a key normative question for students to discuss. Why does finance exist, in the first place? And how is the financial system connected to the rest of the economy and our broader society?

Current courses are often (implicitly) based on the idea that the main goal in finance is to make the highest financial returns possible, and therefore focus mainly on teaching how to put an 'optimal' portfolio together. This normative premise should be discussed and this is a good opportunity to let students themselves debate, in written or oral form. What are the implications of this focus on maximising profits for other societal concerns?

What would need to change if these other normative goals were given more priority? Environmental, Social, and (corporate) Governance (ESG) is increasingly important in actual financial markets, so to provide future-proof education it is important that students become familiar with these and how to deal with them. Rather than only asking how one can earn the highest returns, one can ask how financial professionals can best serve society and provide students with the tools to do so.

For more detail, see *Building Block 1: Introducing the Economy* and *Building Block 10: Economics for a Better World*.

Teaching Materials

- *Ethics and Finance* by John Hendry, from 2013. A useful introduction into the many (a)moral aspects of finance, such as the ethics of lending and borrowing, trading, speculation, financial products, and regulation.
- *The Oxford Handbook of Ethics and Economics* by Mark D. White, from

2019, chapter 17. This highly useful and extensive collection of essays explores the many moral dimensions of economics, with one chapter devoted to the ethics of finance and money.

- *The Oxford Handbook of Professional Economic Ethics* by George F. DeMartino and Deirdre McCloskey, from 2016, chapters 14 & 15. This insightful collection of essays explores the different aspects of ethics in economics, with two chapters devoted to economists' (non)ethical behaviour in the build-up to the global financial crisis of 2007-2008 and the lessons we can learn from it.

History

Good history lessons are a uniquely strong tool to present the complex reality through captivating stories. Historical knowledge of finance also allows students to place current events in context and better grasp their significance and origins. This does not have to be the deep past: the history of recent financial developments can be just as informative and useful.

Besides the history of financial markets themselves, the history of ideas about finance is also fascinating. The intellectual history of finance is largely characterised by two main long-standing strands of thinking. The first strand, deductive in nature, is often referred to as equilibrium models. It originates from the physiocrats in the 18th century and is a central part of modern-day neoclassical economics. The second, more inductive approach, is known as accounting or stock-flow consistent models. This strand of thought was born in the ideas of Jean-Baptiste Say and can today be found in modern-day post-Keynesian economists. This history can help students better understand the different theoretical ideas and models about how finance works.

For more detail, see *Building Block 3: Economic History* and *Building Block 4: History of Economic Thought & Methods*.

Teaching Materials

- *A Concise History of International Finance: From Babylon to Bernanke* by Larry Neal, from 2015. A detailed history of how finance has evolved over time, with particular attention to financial innovations, crises, government regulation, and international dynamics.
- *Money and Government: The Past and Future of Economics* by Robert Skidelsky, from 2018. This well-written and insightful book introduces readers to historical and current debates about money, with particular attention to neoclassical and Keynesian ideas.
- *The Oxford Handbook of Banking and Financial History* by Youssef Cassis, Catherine R. Schenk, and Richard S. Grossman, from 2016. An impressive collection of essays on the history of finance, with its many

different aspects, from banking types and varieties of financial markets, to financial crises and the role of the state.

- *The Ascent of Money: A Financial History of the World* by Niall Ferguson, from 2008. A well-written and accessible book on the fascinating history of money and finance. There is also an accompanying documentary by the same name, as there are many other informative documentaries and movies on finance and the global financial crisis of 2007-2008 in specific, such as Inside Job, The Warning, Boom Bust Boom, Margin Call, The Big Short, and Money, Power and Wall Street.
- *Crashed: How a decade of financial crises changed the world* by Adam Tooze, from 2018. A detailed and well-written account of the global financial crisis of 2007-2008 and the decade that followed it, with accessible explanations of the technical workings of finance and theories about it as well as sharp descriptions of the role of politics and close up personal accounts of individuals making decisions.
- *Manias, Panics, and Crashes: A History of Financial Crises* by Charles P. Kindleberger, most recent edition from 2015. A classic in the genre, describing in a highly accessible and even entertaining way the complex history of financial crises.
- *Boom and Bust: A Global History of Financial Bubbles*, by William Quinn and John D. Turner. A more recent book devoted to the fascinating history of financial crises, with specific chapters devoted to questions related to predicting bubbles and more recent developments in China and Japan.

What to take out

To create space for the above suggested additions, we advise focussing more on the key ideas and intuitions behind the taught models and devote less teaching time to their technicalities and mathematics. As teaching students to reproduce and work through mathematical models often takes up a large part of the teaching time, this would give the teachers the opportunity to devote more time to practical knowledge, the relevance, institutions, and history. Furthermore, a more even balance between neoclassical economics and other economic approaches could be achieved by decreasing the number of neoclassical ideas and models that are taught.

For the most up to date version of these course adaptation suggestions, including a wider selection and more up-to-date range of teaching materials, see our website. We welcome comments and contributions. We also offer a platform for discussion and exchange of teaching materials with colleagues worldwide.
economy.st/adapt/finance

Tool 3
Curriculum Review

A tool to scan existing programmes and identify major gaps, using the Economy Studies building blocks.

Step 1
Overview by
Building Block

Step 2
Overview Within
Building Blocks

Curriculum Review

Step 3
Formulating
Recommendations

Since most of us do not have the luxury of designing programmes from scratch, this chapter lays out how existing curricula can be reviewed and improved using the building blocks developed in this book. Such a curriculum review helps indicate what is missing in the current programme and what might be ways to improve it.

Using the resulting overview, staff and students can make personal and collective judgments as to which things they find most important to improve and where to focus their activities on. This can help both students and faculty to work with the existing curricula and improve them.

This chapter sets out the steps of the curriculum review tool, and applies them to the Harvard undergraduate program in economics as a demonstration of the method. The first step is a rough overview: scan per building block whether any courses cover parts of it. The second step is more detailed, and looks within the building blocks, to see which of their various sections have been covered. The third and final step sets out how to go from this curriculum overview to more concrete recommendations for improving the programme.

The methodology for analysing curricula described in this chapter differs markedly from existing methodologies (Proctor, 2019), mainly in that this methodology is less time-consuming. Rather than reviewing what is *included*, it focuses on what is *absent* in existing programmes.

The steps outlined below provide a simple guide to reviewing existing curricula, using the Harvard undergraduate economics programme of 2018-2019 as an example.

Step 1: Overview by Building Block

The first step is to make a column for every one of the 10 building blocks. Assign every course of the programme in question to one or several of the columns. This step gives an overview of what types of skills and knowledge the current programme emphasises, and which building blocks are not covered in the programme. It thus allows you to see where most headway could be made.

BB1: Introducing the Economy	BB2: Know Your Own Economy	BB3: Economic History	BB4: History of Economic Thought & Methods	BB5: Economic Organisations & Mechanisms
		Economic history		

Figure 11a: An overview of the undergraduate economics curriculum at Harvard University 2018-2019 by building block (building blocks 1-5).

BB6: Political-Economic Systems	BB7: Research Methods & Philosophy of Science	BB8: Economic Theories	BB9: Problems & Proposals	BB10: Economics for a Better World
	Mathematics	Principles of Economics: Microeconomics		
	Statistics	Principles of Economics: Macroeconomics		
	Econometrics	Sophomore Tutorial		
		Intermediate Microeconomics		
		Intermediate Macroeconomics		
		Development		
		Environmental Economics		
		Finance		
		Game theory / Decision theory		
		Health economics		
		Industrial organisation		
		International economics		
		Labor economics		
		Microeconomic theory		
		Macroeconomics – Monetary and Fiscal Policy		
		Behavioural economics		
		Public economics		

Figure 11b: An overview of the undergraduate economics curriculum at Harvard University 2018-2019 by building block (building blocks 6-10).

As the above overview shows, the undergraduate economics curriculum at Harvard University 2018-2019 has a strong focus on *Building Block 8: Economic Theories*. *Building Block 7: Research Methods & Philosophy of Science* also gets serious attention with three mandatory courses. And besides these analytical tools, there is one elective course on *Building Block 3: Economic History*.

The overview also makes clear that various building blocks are still missing, which serves to identify low-hanging fruit for improvement of the programme. Building blocks 1, 2, 4, 5, 6, 9 and 10 are currently not covered. In order to improve the curriculum, one or more of these building blocks could be incorporated. For instance, to provide students with a more solid grounding in the normative aspects of economic questions, one could advocate for including a course on *Building Block 10: Economics for a Better World*.

Whilst Harvard University has been chosen here as an example, its curriculum and the elements missing are hardly unique. Therefore, the overview here should not be seen as a critique of Harvard University, but rather as an analysis of what most economics programmes currently and often leave out. Colander and McGoldrick (2010, pp. 29-30) summarise the currently most prevalent curriculum structure:

"At most schools, the undergraduate economics major almost always includes one or two introductory courses (usually called principles of microeconomics and macroeconomics), intermediate theory courses in both microeconomics and macroeconomics, one or two quantitative methods courses covering basic statistics, regression models and estimation techniques, a few elective upper-level "field" courses and ideally a senior seminar or capstone course that includes an extensive research and writing component. Often, there is a calculus requirement, but that requirement is often designed more as an analytic filter for who can major in economics than as an actual needed requirement. The introductory and intermediate microeconomics courses concentrate on presenting a constrained optimization model in either a geometric or calculus format. The introductory and intermediate macroeconomics courses concentrate on presenting geometric AD/AS and IS/LM models."

Step 2: Overview Within Building Blocks

The rough overview described above is useful for identifying the main elements which are currently missing in a curriculum. However, a more detailed overview might be necessary, which delves into the building blocks, asking which of their core features are included and which parts have been left out. This fine-grained analysis helps students and faculty to see the focal points or strengths of the programme and its individual courses more clearly, as well as pinpointing where there is room for improvement.

To create a more detailed overview, compare the courses in every building block column (from step 1) with the main elements of that building block, as shown on the first page of that building block's chapter in this book. For instance, for the building block column *Research Methods & Philosophy of Science*, analyse whether the following elements are included: (a) Quantitative data gathering (b) Quantitative data analysis (c) Qualitative data gathering (d) Qualitative data analysis (e) Philosophy of Science.

Philosophy of Science	Quantitative data gathering	Quantitative data analysis	Qualitative data gathering	Qualitative data analysis
		Mathematics		
		Statistics		
		Econometrics		

Figure 12: A detailed breakdown of the main elements of Building Block 7: Research Methods & Philosophy of Science.

As step 1 of this analysis showed, the Harvard programme does teach material from *Building Block 7: Research Methods & Philosophy of Science*. However, the more detailed breakdown, allows us to see more precisely which elements of this field are taught. Table 2, above, shows that all emphasis is on quantitative data analysis. The other main elements of *Research Methods and Philosophy of Science*, quantitative data gathering, qualitative data gathering, qualitative data analysis, and philosophy of science, are not included in the programme.

Based on these findings, one could argue for the creation of a course in qualitative research, philosophy of science or in quantitative data gathering. Alternatively, if there were no room for an entire new course, such elements could be incorporated into existing courses. The existing Methods courses at Harvard could, for example, incorporate discussions about philosophy of science and/or quantitative data collection.

Thus, the detailed overview (step 2) helps to identify gaps within the building blocks which do not become visible through the rough overview (step 1). One could also go into more detail than given here by, for example, looking at what specific quantitative data analysis methods are included in the programme and what methods are left out. Such analysis might show that descriptive statistics and regression analysis are included, while network analysis is not. Students and staff can then determine for themselves which level of detail is useful for them to pursue when reviewing a curriculum.

A particular note on *Building Block 8: Economic Theories* is necessary, as this building block is substantially larger than the others, as well as being the building block where most currently taught courses fit in. In essence this building block consists of two elements: (a) the topics, and (b) the theoretical perspectives. First, one checks which topics are taught and which are not. This gives an idea about which economic topics that are not covered in the programme. Then, for the topics that are taught, one can analyse whether this is done in a pluralist or monist way. Or in other words, whether it does include multiple perspectives or not.

With the help of the table provided in *Tool 1: Pragmatic Pluralism*, one can transform courses to be taught in a more pluralist fashion. Again, a more detailed analysis is also possible. Instead of simply looking at whether the teaching is done in a pluralist way, one could analyse which specific perspectives are included and excluded. Such an analysis gives deeper insight into the specific ideas that are taught, and which are missing.

Firms	Households	International trade	Labour	Other Economic Topics
Industrial organisation: Monistic		International economics: Monist	Labour economics: Monist	
Microeconomic theory: Monist				

Figure 13: A detailed breakdown of the main elements of Building Block 8: Economic Theories (abbreviated breakdown, showing only 4 economic topics).

As can be seen in table 3, the Harvard programme does include courses on firms, international trade, and labour. However, it does not teach students about households. Furthermore, whilst it teaches students about firms, international trade, and labour, it does so in a monistic way, meaning it only includes one perspective. Other faculties or programmes will often have at least one or more courses which are pluralist in their treatment of economic theories.

Step 3: Formulating Recommendations

By using the quick scan methodology described in this chapter, it is possible to identify areas of serious improvement to an existing programme with only a few hours of work. For the Harvard programme, our recommendations would include the following:

- Incorporate new material on building blocks 1, 2, 4, 5, 6, 9, 10. In particular, discuss values and aspects of the real world, rather than limiting the programme to theories and methods only.
- Incorporate additional theoretical approaches in the theory courses (see *Tool 1: Pragmatic Pluralism*).
- Incorporate additional work on research methods, including qualitative research methods, quantitative data gathering and philosophy of science.

Do you want to use this method to create a quick scan of your own programme? Our website provides a useful spreadsheet.

economy.st/reviewtool

Tool 4

Example Courses

A number of example courses, made using the Economy Studies building blocks and the principles: pluralism, real-world and values.

1
Example Course:
The Challenges
of Our Time

2
Example Course:
Argentina and the IMF

3
Example Course:
The Economics of Oil

4
Example Course:
A Historical Perspective
on Economic Success

5
Do It Yourself:
Design Your Own
Curriculum, Step by Step

Online:
Seven Additional
Example Courses

In this chapter, we demonstrate how to create actual courses using the *Economy Studies* design toolkit, showing four example courses. Each of these courses flows from our central philosophy: teach students how to study the economy, rather than teaching them one form of economic thinking in the abstract. In terms of our principles, they vary: some of these example courses focus more on pluralism, others on real-world economics, others yet on thinking about values. As for the building blocks, each of the example courses uses at least one of the ten building blocks, while most use more than one.

These courses are described rather briefly in this chapter, as full syllabi, slides or exam questions would take up too much space in a physical book. More extensive course descriptions, syllabi and teaching material can be found in the online database of our partner organisation *Exploring Economics*.

The courses shown here are highly diverse, and mainly intended to inspire and to show the range of possibilities. Depending on the knowledge available within a department, the courses designed there could be vastly different from the examples shown here.

The chapter starts with four very different example courses: *The Challenges of Our Time*, *Argentina and the IMF*, *The Economics of Oil* and *A Historical Perspective on Economic Success*. We also provide a step-by-step method to design your own ideal course. On our website we provide a number of extra example courses.

To reiterate, the *Economy Studies* design method is built up in steps, from abstract to concrete. The philosophy and three principles are considerations and points of departure, but by themselves remain abstract. The following section, the building blocks, are descriptions of content, coupled with suggestions for teaching materials. But they are intended as flexible design tools, not ready-made courses: one building block could be spread out over several courses, or several building blocks could be combined into a single course. This chapter takes it to the next step, showing how the *Economy Studies* design method and materials can be used to create actual courses.

These courses are described rather briefly in this chapter, as full syllabi, slides or exam questions would take up too much space in a physical book. More extensive course descriptions, syllabi and teaching material can be found in the online database of our partner organisation *Exploring Economics*. Course descriptions in this database generally contain full descriptions of reading assignments, week-by-week lecture and workshop plans and suggestions for exam questions.
economy.st/exploring

The first two example courses were written by the main two authors of this book. The other two were designed by students at international *Rethinking Economics* gatherings, and participants of an online course design competition within the network. This is noted on the page of those courses. In the overview below, we have noted the main building blocks used in each example course.

Book: Four very different example courses
- The Challenges of Our Time (Main BB1, Additional BB2, BB3, BB8, BB9, BB10)
- Argentina and the IMF (Main BB9, Additional BB2, BB3, BB6, BB8, BB10)
- The Economics of Oil (Main BB8, Additional BB3, BB6)
- A Historical Perspective on Economic Success (Main BB4, Additional BB1, BB6)

Online: A larger database to explore
- The Digital Economy of South Korea (Main BB2, Additional BB3, BB5, BB6)
- Agent-Based Modelling (Main BB7, Additional BB4, BB9)
- The World of Production (Main BB8, Additional BB2, BB3, BB4, BB5)

- The Political-Economic System of India (Main BB6, Additional BB2, BB3, BB10)
- Economics for a Better World (Main BB10, Additional BB1, BB2)
- Coordination and Allocation Mechanisms in Norwegian Agriculture (Main BB5, Additional BB2, BB3)
- The Economics of Financial Crises (Main BB8, Additional BB3, BB4, BB6)

Do you know of a unique economics course, or do you have a good idea for a topic and course design? Send it in through our website.
economy.st/excourses

1 Example Course: The Challenges of Our Time

Delving into the real-world knowledge, theoretical ideas, empirical studies, and normative visions surrounding today's main challenges.

Course outline

The course starts out with a sweeping overview of the key human challenges throughout history, such as poverty, hunger, war and violence. The focus here is mainly on a factual overview and getting an understanding of how today's world relates to earlier periods. Then the focus shifts to current challenges. Before delving into the specifics about the various challenges, we discuss which issues dominate the political agenda, contrasted with the public opinion on what the main issues are as these two often differ.

After this broad introduction into previous and today's challenges, each week is devoted to one specific challenge. Every week consists of three sessions: a guest lecture by an expert on the issue to ensure a good basic understanding of the matter; a normal lecture on the economics and policy debates concerning the issue; and finally an interactive seminar in which students debate with each other over how they understand the issue, its causes and potential solutions. The first week is devoted to climate change, with a climate scientist giving the guest lecture. The second week is about financial instability, with a banker as guest lecturer. The third week focuses on pandemics with a medical specialist. The fourth week on digitisation with a software engineer. And the fifth and last challenge is inequality with a guest lecture by a sociologist.

For the final assignment students choose one of these five challenges and work in groups to write a short policy report on the issue. In this report, they need to discuss recent developments, analyse the problem making use of available theoretical and empirical literature, and propose and argue for solutions that would tackle the issue.

Required knowledge

None, this is an introductory course.

Nominal workload

7,5 ECTS (225 hrs)

This course uses the following building blocks:

Main:

Introducing the Economy (BB1).

Additional:

Problems & Proposals (BB9),
Economics for a Better World (BB10),
History of the Economy (BB3),
Know Your Own Economy (BB2),
Economic Theories (BB8)

2 Example Course: Argentina and the IMF

Training in problem analysis and solution design through a case study in international and macroeconomics.

Course outline

This master's course in a fictitious Argentinian university is organised around one real world issue: what policies should the IMF pursue concerning Argentina? For this reason, the course is made in collaboration with the IMF and Argentinian government, as they are able to provide guest lectures, information, relevant assignments, useful contacts and potentially also internship places.

The first half of the course is about teaching students the relevant theoretical, empirical and real-world knowledge so that they can properly fulfil the case study. This consists of three parts: learning about the Argentinian economy, the IMF, and about international and macroeconomics in general. Regarding the Argentinian economy, it is important that students become familiar with its history, as well as its current structure and institutions. Regarding the IMF, students need to learn how it functions and how this has changed over time, with internal structure and external power pressures, dominant ideas and models, key practices and methods, and the relation it has had with and the impact its policies has had on various countries, in particular Argentina. Finally but crucially, students need to become familiar with the different approaches and recent developments in international and macroeconomics. This part of the course is concluded with an exam testing the students' knowledge of the Argentinian economy, the IMF, and international and macroeconomics.

The second half of the course focuses on the current situation and problems in Argentina and how the IMF should respond to these. It starts out with a few (guest) lectures to introduce students to the current situation and different ideas about the causes of the problems and solutions to them. The main part of the second half of the course, however, consists of project group work. In small groups students are asked to write a policy report to either the IMF or the Argentinian advising them on what they should do regarding the agreements between the IMF and Argentina.

As such, the report has an explicit goal and audience, and students are assessed based on how well they are able to make their case accordingly. Students have to convince the reader of their understanding of the problem, and that the theoretical ideas and empirical studies they build upon are most relevant. Furthermore, they need to make the case for their policy proposals with both analytical and normative arguments. The assessment is done together by the academic teacher and policymakers at the IMF and Argentinian government in order to focus on both the analytical and real-world aspects.

Required knowledge

Master's course, requiring advanced knowledge of Economic Theories (BB8), Economic History (BB3), Know Your Own Economy (BB2), Political-Economic Systems (BB6).

Nominal workload

12 ECTS (360 hrs)

This course uses the following building blocks:

Main:

Problems & Proposals (BB9).

Additional:

Economic Theories (BB8),
Economic History (BB3),
Know Your Own Economy (BB2),
Political-Economic Systems (BB6),
Economics for a Better World (BB10).

3 Example Course:
The Economics of Oil

An exploration of the economic issues surrounding oil and, in particular, the economic fortunes of oil-rich countries.

By: Andrew Graham (Queen's University Belfast)

Course outline

As oil is a commodity familiar to all of us, it is an ideal lens through which fundamental economic concepts such as supply, demand, elasticity, externalities, power relations, and property rights can be intuitively examined. It can also provide a lens on macroeconomic and geopolitical issues such as inflation, international trade, exchange rates, national and global power struggles. These topics will be investigated through studying specific cases, such as the oil crises of the 1970s.

This course will also include an analysis of the causes and consequences of the economic divergence of oil-rich nations. Countries such as Venezuela and Iraq haven't been able to sustainably develop their economies, while countries such as Norway and Qatar have amassed great wealth. In addressing this divergence, the economic impact of factors such as government policy and conflict will be discussed. Furthermore, the future direction of these countries will be debated as they face environmental and economic pressures to diversify their economies. Important elements here are the history of climate change and the lobbying power of oil companies.

Required knowledge
Introducing the Economy (BB1)

Nominal workload
7,5 ECTS (225 hrs)

This course uses the following Building Blocks:
Main:
Economic Theories (BB8).

Additional:
Economic History (BB3),
Politica-Economic Systems (BB6).

4 Example Course: A Historical Perspective on Economic Success

Examining how thinking about the objectives of the economy has evolved in different societies across time and place.

By Jamie Barker, Rita Guimarães, Ben Pringle and Cecilie Christensen (Rethinking Economics UK, Portugal, and Denmark)

Course outline

Week 1: Clarifying what we mean by the 'aims' or 'objectives' of an economy. Covering the main actors within the economy, looking at who does the 'aiming' when we ask what our economy is aiming for. For example, what objectives do governments, businesses, trade unions and civil society groups have in their economic activity?

Week 2: Discussion between students about what 'economic success' means to them, and what it could potentially mean for others. Review of the different goals that different societies have around the world now (Gross National Happiness, Gross Domestic Product, full employment, sustainability, etc.).

The rest: Progressing chronologically through different historical societies around the world, probably starting with the Ancient Greeks. For each society we investigate the historical context it was situated in, what they considered to be economic success, the power dynamics and values which influenced this view, and the policies and institutional structures that were created as a result. Students would also discuss their own views on the objective(s) of that economy and consider what people from that society would think of our economy now.

The final week: Proposals for objectives that have not yet been widely adopted such as the Genuine Progress Indicator, or Kate Raworth's Doughnut.

Assessment: Group presentations on each society to start each week, as well as a take-home exam at the end of term.

Required knowledge

None, this is an introductory course.

Nominal workload

7,5 ECTS (225 hrs)

This course uses the following building blocks:

Main:

History of Economic Thought (BB4).

Additional:

Introducing the Economy (BB1),
Political-Economic Systems (BB6).

5 Do It Yourself: Design Your Own Course, Step by Step

An interesting exploratory exercise is to design an economics curriculum like those above from scratch, with a small group of faculty, students, or ideally both. This can be a great way to start thinking outside the box. It can be done with students or with teaching staff, or ideally with a mixture. Here is a basic roadmap for conducting such a workshop.

Step 1: Choose the central theme

Brainstorm about the central theme of the course. Will it be centred on the values at play in economics? Focused on the real-world economy, perhaps a specific country? Built around a certain sector? The building blocks can be useful here. Choose one, two or three of them and make them the anchoring points for the course.

Step 2: Sketch the broad strokes

What kind of theories would students need for this purpose, if any? Would the course include any kind of methods training? What kind of practical assignments might be part of the course? Which other disciplines or practitioners could provide an interesting guest lecture?

Step 3: Design the core lessons

It is easiest to start the design process with a few of the key lectures. This helps organise your thinking, and can form an initial framework around which to design the other parts of the course. The examples in this chapter may also provide inspiration for workshop participants.

Step 4: Create a structure

What would be the best order in which to take students through the key lessons? Here one can consider which lessons are particularly motivating for students, providing a good introduction into the field and triggering the interests of students.

Step 5: Get it on paper

Make sure that all ideas are written down: use post-its in the brainstorm phase and a worksheet to bring it all together into a structure. Think of a good slogan or tagline for the course. This helps to attract students but it also helps to keep the raison-d'être of the course front and centre.

Step 6: Present the course designs

It also works well to do this exercise with a few groups of 3-5 people each. Afterwards, each group presents their course in a 1-minute pitch to the group. Maybe there is even a prize for the best course design, by group vote?

→ *You have designed your own course!*

On our website, we provide additional practical resources for this workshop. In addition, within the Rethinking Economics network there is a group of trained *Economy Studies* workshop facilitators who could conduct this workshop at your faculty. Alternatively, we can provide you with the worksheets, PowerPoint slides and other materials.
economy.st/workshops

Tool 5

Example Curricula

A number of example bachelor and master programmes, made using the Economy Studies building blocks and the principles: real-world, pluralism and values.

1
**Bachelor in
Economics with a
Theoretical Focus**

2
**Bachelor in Economics
with a Real-World Focus**

3
**Major Economics in
a Liberal Arts and
Sciences Programme**

4
**Master in
Public Economics**

5
**Design Your
Own Curriculum,
Step by Step**

Online: **6**
**Master in Financial
Economics**

Online: **7**
**Master in Economics
of Climate Crises**

Example Curricula

Online: **8**
**Research Master
in Industrial
Economics**

This chapter provides examples of how economics programmes could look and be structured. Such proposals help make the debate concrete and bring out potential trade-offs. This is important because critics of current programmes often simply ask to teach more and more, without considering practical limits on time and content. Curriculum proposals help us to flesh out not only what could be added to a programme, but also what could be left out. In addition, these examples show how the building blocks of *Economy Studies* can be combined to form coherent programmes.

We present four examples in this book and three more on our website, all created through the Economy Studies design approach: two bachelor programmes, an economics major in a Liberal Arts & Sciences programme and four master programmes. These example curricula demonstrate how our building blocks can either be used independently or combined together into ready-to-teach courses.

This chapter is also intended to make clear once again: *Economy Studies* is not a blueprint of a single, 'ideal' curriculum. It is possible to design a wide variety of programmes with these building blocks, and it is our hope that they will be used for this. We firmly believe that the world is best served with a wide variety of economists. One size does not fit all.

Before going into our own example curricula, we want to shortly discuss a few prominent curriculum proposals that have inspired us. In 2010, INET published a curriculum proposal for UK undergraduate economics education. The first year of the bachelor programme would focus on width, with courses on the *Economics of the Real World*, philosophy of science, basic theoretical concepts and methodological tools in economics, economic history, the history of economic thought, and current debates in economics. The second year focuses on further developing students' conceptual and technical competencies, with adjusted versions of the standard micro- and macro-economics and econometrics courses, and a course on the different languages and approaches used in economics. These "adjusted" courses would include ideas from other theoretical approaches, such as post-Keynesian, Austrian and behavioural economics, and pay more attention to the limitations of the dominant neoclassical theories. The purpose of the third and final year is to go into greater depth and apply economic concepts and tools to real-world problems. They propose to do this through the bachelor thesis, specialised elective courses and practically oriented case studies.

In 2014, the French economics student group PEPS made the case for pluralism by analysing existing French programmes as well as proposing an alternative curriculum. This 3-year undergraduate programme consists of courses on contemporary economic and social issues, key economic topics, normative economic questions, institutions, history of economic thought, economic history, and quantitative and qualitative research methods.

The same year, Jack Reardon presented a curriculum proposal in the final chapter of a volume he edited with Maria Alejandra Madi – *The Economics Curriculum: Towards a Radical Reformulation* (2014). The 4-year undergraduate programme starts out by delving into a diverse range of topics from the history of capitalist systems to philosophy, the history of intellectual thought, world literature, and quantum physics. The second year introduces the discipline of economics, different schools of thought, modelling, communicating, as well as the topics of finance, credit and money. The third year focuses on the topic of poverty and related issues, such as international trade and power relations, governments, firms and industry structures. The fourth and last year is organised around the issue of sustainability with attention to matters such as resource use, economic growth and climate policy.

In this chapter we build on the above work, by setting out how the *Economy Studies* foundations and building blocks could be used to shape economics curricula. Our suggestions differ from the above, in the sense that we do not propose one 'ideal' curriculum. Instead, we provide a number of example curricula that each makes use of the logic and ingredients discussed in this book, but at the same time are different from each other. We do not think there could exist such a thing as an 'optimal' curriculum that should be taught everywhere. Diversity of programmes is something to encourage, and we try to show the flexibility of the *Economy Studies* framework in this chapter. The variety between these curricula speaks to the great diversity of economists our society needs.

Beyond these "demand" factors, there might also be "supply" reasons for varying programmes, as universities have different specialisations in their research expertise. As Colander and McGoldrick (2010, p. 21) put it: *"A program heavily endowed with historians of economic thought might want to offer a rather different program than one with primarily game theorists and econometricians. There is room for much positive variation within the economics major; there is no one size fits all"*.

We present four examples here in the book, and several more on the website, all created through the *Economy Studies* approach. The first two are 3-year undergraduate programmes, one more theoretical and the other more real-world focused. The third example curriculum is an economics major within a liberal arts and sciences programme (1,5 years worth of courses). The fourth is a one-year master programme in public economics. Online, we describe three more master programmes: one-year programmes in financial economics and on the climate crisis and a two-year research master in industrial economics.

These example curricula demonstrate how our building blocks can either be used independently or combined together into ready-to-teach courses. Building on the framework described in *Tool 1: Pragmatic Pluralism*, they show the idea of a 'thematic course', which teaches a pluralist range of theory around a single economic theme. The second curriculum also introduces the 'sectoral course', which starts from a specific economic sector and introduces a variety of theoretical insights and real-world knowledge on that basis. In addition, that curriculum demonstrates how other disciplines could contribute to a broader economics education.

The thesis is perhaps the element that is least fleshed out in these examples, so a word on that is in order here. We suggest that it could in many cases be less of a stripped-down academic research paper, and more of a concrete case study. The thesis would still be a piece of independent research, using the theories and methods learned during the preceding programme. The result, however, would be less suitable for a peer-reviewed journal, and instead more suitable as an input to a discussion between professionals, a decision-making body in a private or public organisation, or to feed public debate.

While these seven curricula are quite diverse, each of them is built with the same philosophy and three basic principles in mind, and makes use of the same ten building blocks. We deliberately made them fairly diverse, to demonstrate that the framework of Economy Studies enables a broad array of possible programmes. These are far from the only possible curricula that could be built from these principles and building blocks, they are simply examples. Nonetheless, we hope that they will help to inspire you in your own educational efforts.

1 Bachelor in Economics with a Theoretical Focus

Programme slogan: A diverse toolkit for understanding the economy.

This programme is a general economics bachelor programme, preparing students for a master's in economics and for work in government agencies or the private or non-profit sector. At the end of the degree, students will have gained a thorough overview and understanding of the main body of economic theory and the economic system in which they live and will work. They will have gained some experience in applying this theory to solve concrete problems, will be able to conduct independent research using a range of methods, and will have a brief specialisation in either inequality or competition.

This programme stacks the ten building blocks of *Economy Studies* in a relatively simple and straightforward way. The first year of the programme includes real-world economics (BB2, BB3, BB9), its normative relevance (BB1, BB10), and introductory courses in methodological and theoretical tools and concepts (BB4, BB7, BB8). In these courses, students explore their chosen topic of study, 'the economy'. They become knowledgeable about the main societal challenges of our time and the economics underpinning them. They learn more about the vital sectors and institutions of the economy around them, and learn to see in what ways this complex system is intermingled with areas such as our personal lives, the environment and international political relations. In addition, they are introduced to the basic toolkits of the academic world: theories and methods.

The second year is focused on specialised methods courses (BB7) and deep-dives into theory (BB8). Besides these theory and method courses, students are also taught conceptual and real-world knowledge about the different ways in which economic processes can be organised, both at the micro and meso level (BB5) as well as at the macro level (BB6). The second semester of the second year also picks up on the real-world economics (BB2) and normative aspects (BB10) discussed in the first year. The theory electives are organised using the Pragmatic Pluralism approach, teaching subject-based theory courses on issues like economic development, nature, and consumption. In each theory course, the subject is approached from 2-4 theoretical angles. This serves to highlight different aspects of the economic subject in question. It also teaches students the vital academic skill of selecting and combining the most relevant perspectives. The methods courses allow students to specialise in specific sets of methods that fit their personal talents and ambitions.

In the third year of this example curriculum, students have the choice between two majors: Competition, or Inequality. We assume, for the sake of the example, that the department teaching this particular programme has strong expertise there, but such choices would always depend on the locally available knowledge. Both of these majors have the same basic structure. They start with side-by-side courses on the history of the economic phenomenon in question (competition or inequality) and the different ways of thinking about that phenomenon.

In the case of the inequality major, these two courses are followed up by a practically oriented policy course on how to address inequality and a specialised methodological course on how to best capture and understand inequality by making use of qualitative or quantitative research tools. Students choosing the competition major continue with a theoretical course on the varying institutional structures which markets can have, coupled with a practically oriented policy course devoted to better understanding current developments in competition, the nuts and bolts of managing these, and its future directions.

In the last semester of the programme there is the 15-ECTS bachelor thesis project, in which students tackle a concrete economic question themselves. There are also two final courses. One is an additional theories course. The other is a 'sectoral elective', a deeper dive into a specific sector, tying together much of the theoretical material taught earlier by applying it to a real economic sector.

This example curriculum, in short, provides a straightforward use of the *Economy Studies* building blocks and principles, as well as the theme-centred theory teaching described in *Tool 1: Pragmatic Pluralism*.

Programme overview

	First quarter	Second quarter	Third quarter	Fourth Quarter
Year 1	**Introducing the Economy** (BB1) Getting a feeling for economic matters. What is the economy, why is it important, how is it embedded in the larger social and natural world? What role do its experts, economists, play?	**Challenges of Our Time** (BB1/BB9/BB10) Starting from factual knowledge about the big challenges of our time, such as climate change, inequality, financial instability, and pandemics. With this knowledge of the current developments, students have to choose one specific issue concerning a challenge and work on a project basis to figure out how this specific issue could be addressed.	**History of the Economy** (BB3) Knowledge of how economies developed over time and what kinds of economies there have been throughout history.	**History of Economic Thought** (BB4) History of economic thought that includes mainstream and heterodox economics, as well as other disciplines studying the economy.
	Introducing Economic Perspectives (BB8/BB10) Introduction into the basic assumptions and core elements of the different economic perspectives (including their normative aspects).	**Methods 1: Philosophy of Science** (BB7) What is research for? How can valuable analyses be done? What are the fundamental assumptions on which analyses are based? A good grounding in the different ideas on why science is helpful and how science should be done.	**Methods 2: Quantitative** (BB7) Acquiring knowledge and skills in survey research, descriptive statistics, and regression analysis (including learning to use software).	**Methods 3: Qualitative** (BB7) Acquiring knowledge and skills in interviews, non-participatory observation, case studies, and qualitative data analysis (including learning to use software).
	Ribbon course: **Know Your Own Economy (1)** (BB2) The basic structure of the national economy, its economic class composition, and its basic statistics.		**Internship** (1 day per week)	
Year 2	**Economic Organisations & Mechanisms** (BB5) The different economic logics and organisational forms – how market, bureaucratic, associational, familial, cooperative, and communal mechanisms together make up the economy.	**Political-Economic Systems** (BB6) The macro-structures of economies – how economies are organised, which institutions they have, and how their power relations look.	**Know Your Own Economy (2)** (BB2/BB9) A deeper look at the national economy and its most important institutions and sectors. With this knowledge, students have to choose one specific sector and study its structure, institutions and current developments in detail.	**Economics for a Better World** (BB10) What normative principles and visions can guide action to make the world a better place and address the major challenges of our times?
	Theory Elective (1) (BB8) The Economics of Economic Development OR The Economics of Nature OR The Economics of Money	**Methods Elective #1** (BB7) Big Data and Network Analysis OR Experiments OR Interviews and Focus Groups	**Theory Elective (2)** (BB8) The Economics of Business Cycles OR The Economics of Households OR The Economics of International Trade	**Methods Elective #2** (BB7) Econometrics OR Qualitative Data Analysis OR Agent-based Modelling

Part III

Year 3 (OPTION 1: major in Inequality)	Perspectives on Inequality (BB8) A pluralist exploration of the Marxian, neoclassical, cultural, feminist, and social network perspectives on inequality.	Addressing Inequality (BB9) What policies have been used to address inequality and what have been their consequences? What new insights and policy ideas are currently being debated and what are their merits?	Thesis project	
	History of Inequality (BB3/BB6) How different political-economic systems throughout history created different levels and forms of inequality.	Methods Elective (BB7) Quantitative: Measuring Inequality OR Qualitative: Experiencing Inequality	Theory Elective (3) (BB8) The Economics of Finance OR The Economics of the State OR The Economics of Consumption	Sector Elective (BB2/BB8) The Economics of Energy OR The Economics of Entertainment and Information OR The Economics of Textile
Year 3 (OPTION 1: major in Competition)	Perspectives on Competition (BB8) Introducing students to the two main views on competition: as a harmonious outcome versus a ruthless process. Then moving into the theoretical insights into markets and firms from the evolutionary, cultural, behavioural, social network, institutional, and field perspective.	The structures of markets (BB5) Delving into the different forms and ways markets can be constructed and shaped. Exploring how relationships between different actors can look.	Thesis project	
	History of Competition (BB3/BB4) The history of how competition has evolved and changed over time. From the mercantilist forms of competition to the current digital forms.	Recent Developments in Competition (BB8) The rise of new forms of competition, because of globalisation, digitalisation, and automation. Ideas on how to shape and deal with these developments, from the perspective of companies, governments, and individuals.	Theory Elective (3) (BB8) The Economics of Finance OR The Economics of the State OR The Economics of Consumption	Sector Elective (BB2/BB8) The Economics of Energy OR The Economics of Entertainment and Information OR The Economics of Textile

2 Bachelor in Economics with a Real-World Focus

Programme slogan: Economic thinking starts from the real world.

This programme puts real-world knowledge first. The majority of the theory courses start from economic history or sectoral analysis, only introducing the theoretical concepts later in the course. This is most visible in the first year, where the economic sectors of housing, retail and healthcare are all covered using this approach. The programme prepares students to work as an economist in government or in larger companies or non-profits. At the end of the degree, students will have gained a wide range of real-world knowledge of the economy, and be able to approach concrete economic questions in a practical and problem-solving oriented manner.

These sectoral courses include valuable knowledge on the real economy, but are also used to introduce a number of theoretical insights – which will be remembered all the better because they are taught on the basis of something concrete, rather than only as an abstract mathematical model. The first sectoral course (on housing) teaches students something about the role of law in the economy, the various levels of government that shape the sector, and the degree to which finance is interwoven with households in our daily economy. The second sectoral course (on retail) introduces theories about market mechanisms, market power, global value chains and digitisation. The third sectoral course (on healthcare) introduces a sector where public and private economic mechanisms are tightly interwoven, many products and services are primarily state-provided, professional associations hold a powerful position and ethical discussions on issues like the value of human life come front and centre in economic considerations.

The first year also has a double course on economic history. This course starts with the history of the economy, from which the history of economic thought then emerges. Students are provided with a basic overview of the various economic schools of thought, including their foundations and origins. This knowledge is not only taught for its own sake, but also to provide a firm basis for the thematic courses in Year 2.

These are taught on a more theoretical basis than the sectoral courses, but still start with, and continue to present, a large amount of real-world economic knowledge. Besides these thematic courses, the second year has three methods courses. As with the sectoral courses in Year 1, these are organised around actual topics of research, with students now creating their own data and working to answer real research questions.

This particular example curriculum has one additional goal: it presents a way to teach an *Economy Studies*-based programme at a faculty with a smaller staff. Besides having fewer economics electives, this shows in the structure of Year 3, which taps into the capacities of other social science faculties. Students choose from three different Interdisciplinary Minor programmes, each of which takes a deeper dive into an economic topic. As well as teaching students about that specific topic, it also provides them with an introduction to the frameworks of several other disciplines (mostly social sciences). This takes students out of the box of economic approaches and will help them in later life to more easily communicate with professionals trained in other disciplines. The final courses look ahead by exploring how the topics that were covered in the second-year thematic courses might look in the future.

In summary, this programme builds from the real world towards theory and methods, rather than the other way around. It also introduces students to other disciplines' approaches to economic questions, lightening the teaching load of the economics department, whilst at the same time broadening students' perspectives.

Programme overview

	First quarter	Second quarter	Third quarter	Fourth Quarter
Year 1	**Welcome to the Economy** (BB1/BB2) Starting from the economy around us and connecting this to concepts that help us think. Discussing big questions (what is the economy, how does it relate to the broader social and ecological world?), while also acquiring factual knowledge (about institutions and sectors).	**The Economics of Housing** (BB2/BB5) Combining concrete knowledge of the housing sector (BB2), with a study of economic coordination and allocation mechanisms (BB5) through a study of the rental housing, mortgage markets, housing cooperatives and various government policies. Course incorporates theory on the state.	**The Economics of Retail** (BB2/BB5) Combining concrete knowledge of the retail sector (BB2), with a study of economic coordination and allocation mechanisms (BB5) through a study of market power and competition, global value chains, corporate social (ir)responsibility, consumption culture, and digitalisation. Course incorporates theory on markets.	**The Economics of Healthcare** (BB2/BB5) Combining concrete knowledge of the health care sector (BB2), with a study of economic coordination and allocation mechanisms (BB5) through a study of the public and private hospitals, professional associations, innovation and intellectual property, public-private partnerships, and population aging. Course incorporates theory on firms.
	History of Economic Reality and Thought – part 1 (BB3/BB4) From the beginning of humankind to the second world war. Focuses mostly on the history of the economy and differing ways in which economies have been organised. But always links these facts to the economic thinking of the time.	**Methods 1: Methodology & Basic Methods** (BB7) Learning research methods and methodology through conducting a study into the housing sector (linked the course above). While applying survey analysis and interviews to concrete cases, it is key that students become familiar with economic methodology.	**History of Economic Reality and Thought – part 2** (BB3/BB4) From the second world war until the present. Focus mostly on the history of thought and the different ways in which recent challenges and developments have been understood. Second half of the course becomes more theory-focused as the various recent schools are introduced.	**Professional and Academic Skills** Teaching students through (inter)active exercises how to find good literature and data, but most importantly how to communicate. This includes both academic writing and presenting economic insights to a broad public in written and spoken form. Professional codes of ethics.
	Why do we care about the economy? (BB1/BB10) Delving into the big issues that shape the world, such as climate change, inequality, pandemics, international (economic) tension, and financial instability. These issues are connected to positive visions for how the future economy could look and the underlying goals and values on which they are based.		**Methods 2: Finding, Reading and Assessing Research** (BB7) Learning how to find good empirical studies and read them quickly but also thoroughly by learning what things to pay attention to. How should one assess empirical evidence for arguments and can different studies be compared to each other? This course should teach students to identify the different chains in arguments and assess the strength of the evidence for each of them.	

Year 2	The Economics of Economic Development (BB3/BB8) Combining theoretical insights into economic development (BB8) with the history of how different countries around the world developed (BB3).	The Economics of Business Cycles (BB2/BB3/BB8) Combining theoretical insights into business cycles (BB8) with the history of booms and busts (BB3), and knowledge of the institutions that have been built to address economic instability (BB2).	The Economics of Households and Consumption (BB1/BB8) Combining theoretical insights into households and consumption (BB8) with discussions about the goals of the economy and the current challenges it faces (BB1).	The Economics of Money and Finance (BB2/BB5/BB8) Combining theoretical insights into money and finance (BB8) with knowledge about current and alternative financial and monetary institutional frameworks (BB2/BB5).
	Methods 3: Quantitative Methods (BB7) Learning descriptive statistics and regression analysis by investigating questions on economic development. While directed towards the real world, students acquire statistical skills.	Comparative Economics (BB2/BB6) How do economies differ around the world? And how does your own economy look in comparison to other economies? Understanding these real world questions with the help of concepts about political-economic systems (BB6).	Methods 4: Elective (BB7) Network analysis OR Assessing data quality OR Advanced econometrics OR Participatory observation	Research project (BB7/BB9) Becoming familiar with the entire research cycle through conducting a full research project into a specific real world problem. This problem has to be located within the housing, retail, or health care sector, so that students can build on and use previously acquired knowledge.
Year 3	Interdisciplinary minor / International exchange / Internship Interdisciplinary minor options:		Thesis project	

Environmental Policy
- The economics of nature and consumption behaviour (pluralist theory course)
- Systems thinking in ecology (biology)
- The Politics of Paris and Kyoto (political science)
- Environmental regulation (law)

Labour
- Labour economics (pluralist theory course)
- History of labour institutions (history)
- The social institution of work (sociology)
- Industrial relations (political science)

A Look Into the Future: Elective
(BB8/BB10)
The Future of Economic Development
OR
The Future of Business Cycles
OR
The Future of Households and Consumption
OR
The Future of Money and Finance

International Economic Relations
- International economics and finance (pluralist theory course)
- Economic geography (human geography)
- The politics of international trade and tax havens (political science)
- Globalisation: its old and recent past (history)

3 Major Economics in a Liberal Arts and Sciences Programme

Programme slogan: An introduction into the economic world.

This undergraduate programme is shorter than the two above, as it describes a major in economics that lasts for one and a half years as part of a three-year long Liberal Arts and Sciences programme. A Liberal Arts education gives students a broad and interdisciplinary education, whilst also allowing them to specialise in the single discipline that they are most interested in. The economics programme here is thus not very interdisciplinary, as the other half of the liberal arts and sciences programme will already be in other fields of study.

The programme shows how each of the ten building blocks can be included in only three semesters. For most building blocks, this is done in a very straightforward way by devoting one course to each building block. The exceptions are that history of economic thought and economic history are merged together in one course, and that there are two methods courses and three theory courses, to provide students with a basis in analytical tools.

Programme overview

	First quarter	Second quarter	Third quarter	Fourth Quarter
Year 1	**Introducing the Economy** (BB1) Getting a feeling for economic matters. What is the economy, why is it important, how is it embedded in the larger social and natural world? What role do its experts, economists, play?	**Know your own economy** (BB2) The basic structure of the national economy, its economic class composition, its main economic sectors and institutions, and its basic statistics.	**Economic Organisations & Mechanisms** (BB5) The different economic logics and organisational forms – how market, bureaucratic, associational, familial, cooperative, and communal mechanisms together make up the economy.	**Political-Economic Systems** (BB6) The macro-structures of economies – how economies are organised, which institutions they have, and how their power relations look.
	History of Economic Reality and Thought (BB3/BB4) Connecting the history of the economy to that of ideas about it. Both are covered in a broad-sweeping course, providing overviews as well as several more in-depth examples.	**Methods #1: Methodology & Basic Data Collection Methods** (BB7) Learning about the basics of economic methodology and qualitative and quantitative research. Students will become familiar with the basics of doing interviews and surveys.	**Theory #1** (BB8) The Economics of Markets and Firms OR The Economics of Money and Finance	**Methods #2: Econometrics** (BB7) Students learn more about how to properly perform regression analysis and also how to assess more advanced econometric analyses when reading other research.
Year 2	**Theory #2** (BB8) The Economics of Households and Labour OR The Economics of Nature and Consumption	**Theory #3** (BB8) The Economics of Business Cycles and the State OR The Economics of Economic Development and International Trade	Rest of the liberal arts and sciences programme.	
	Problems & Proposals (BB9) Practical skills to critically and constructively analyse real world problems, with a focus on the economic aspect, and work on proposals to address them.	**Economics for a better world** (BB10) What normative principles and visions can guide action to make the world a better place and address the major challenges of our times?		

4 Master in Public Economics

Programme slogan: Economics for the common good

This master's programme prepares students for a position in the public or semi-public sector. It focuses not so much on the market-related functions of the state such as regulation, but rather on its core activities. This includes the organisation of public services such as physical infrastructure, education and healthcare, and its activities such as taxation and welfare support.

The programme is somewhat less academic and more practical than most example curricula in this book. It is very much focused on the real world of public policy, rather than abstract theory and academic research methods. The first semester does start, however, with a broader, more theoretical discussion of the state, as seen from various perspectives in economics and neighbouring disciplines. This is coupled with a course on the process of public policy in practice. The following courses bring in discussions about the normative questions involved in government activities, as well as providing hands-on experience with various policy tools.

The second semester introduces a theme elective, diving deeper into several of the aforementioned core functions of the state, as well as a methods elective focused on practically oriented research skills. The programme is concluded with a thesis, written in the form of a practical policy paper on a real-world issue that the government in that country is currently dealing with. This is alongside a course on recent developments in policy-making, which provides an overview of the major challenges defining the current era, as well as several possible and actual state responses to them.

	First quarter	Second quarter	Third quarter	Fourth Quarter
Block Courses	**Perspectives on the State** (BB4/BB8) Short introduction into the sociological and political science perspectives on the state. Then move towards the economic perspectives on the state. Use the history of economic thought as a way to introduce the classical, Marxian, historical, neoclassical, and Keynesian perspectives on the state.	**Moral Dilemmas in Running the State** (BB5/BB6/BB10) An introduction into the different normative perspectives on the state. Coupled with discussions about different political-economic systems and mechanisms, and how the state can take differing forms and shapes depending on these.	**Theme elective** (BB2/BB5/BB8/BB10) Taxation (tax evasion, distribution, incentives) OR Social welfare (unemployment, old age, disability) OR Public services (education, health care, defence) OR Land, housing, and infrastructure	**Thesis**

Block Courses	Public Policy in Practice (BB2/BB3/BB5)	Policy Tools (BB5/BB7/BB9)	Methods Elective (BB7)	Recent Developments and Debates (BB1/BB8)
	What key institutions determine how public policy looks? How do these institutions work internally and interact with each other? How have the roles the state plays in society changed over the last century?	A good understanding of how statistical and modelling work influences policy and public debates and how these numbers come to be. Knowledge about policy evaluation and skills in stakeholder management.	Interviews & focus groups OR Modelling policy and econometrics	Starting with an overview of the most important recent trends, current challenges, and changes in policy. After this, focusing on recent insights in public economics by evolutionary (the entrepreneurial state), behavioural (nudging), modern monetary theory (connecting monetary and fiscal policy), and complexity economists (tool diversity and flexibility).

5   Design Your Own Curriculum, Step by Step

An interesting exploratory exercise is to design an economics curriculum like those above from scratch, with a small group of faculty, students, or ideally both. This can be a fascinating way to start thinking outside the box, even further than would be possible when designing a single course. Here is a basic roadmap for conducting such a workshop.

Step 1: Choose the central theme

Brainstorm about the central theme of the programme. Will it be centred on the values at play in economics? Focused on the real-world economy, perhaps a specific country? Built around a certain sector? Will it prepare students mostly to work for policy agencies, in the financial or commercial world, or in other places yet such as journalism, research or education?

Step 2: Sketch the broad strokes

What kind of theory would students need for this purpose? What kind of methods might be most useful? What kind of practical assignments might form a capstone course? Which other disciplines could contribute knowledge to this programme?

Step 3: Create the key courses

It is easiest to create a few of the key courses early on. This helps organise your thinking, and can form an initial framework to design other courses around. The examples in chapter Tool 4: Example courses may provide inspiration, as well as the course design workshop explained at the end of that chapter.

Step 4: Rethink the standard courses

Every programme will have a few methods courses, some theory 101 work, and so forth. How could those standard courses be redesigned, to better fit the particular purposes of this programme? The chapter *Tool 2: Adapting Existing Courses* can provide inspiration.

Step 5: Create the structure

Create a list of the courses designed in step 3 and 4. What would be the best order in which to put these courses? Here it can help to think of what knowledge courses can build on or require students to have beforehand. But one can also consider which courses are particularly motivating for students, providing a good introduction into the field and triggering the interests of students.

Step 6: Check if something is still missing

Look at the programme structure created in step 5 and check if there is still relevant content missing. Here, one can see whether the three principles are included, or for a more thorough check one can use chapter *Tool 3: Curriculum Review* to see which building blocks (and which sections of these) are still absent. It is important to note here that it is not necessarily a bad thing if a building block is not present in the programme. Every programme is finite, and therefore cannot include everything. The check is thus whether any relevant content is still missing. If so, create a new course to include it, or incorporate it into one or more of the courses already in your plan.

→ *You have designed your own curriculum!*

Tool 6

Courses for Non-Economists

Teaching economics to high school students and to those specialising in other disciplines.

1
Foundations

2
Building Blocks

3
**A High School
Economics Course**

4
**An Economics Course in
a Business Programme**

Courses for Non-Economists

Online:
**An Economics Course in a
Public Administration
& Law Programme**

Online:
**An Academic
Minor in
Economics**

The book so far has mainly focused on how economists should be prepared for their future roles in society. Economists are, however, not the only ones who receive an economics education. In fact, the majority of people who are taught economics will never become an economist or even take a specialisation in the topic. This includes high school programmes, economics minors aimed at students from other disciplines, and economics courses in neighbouring programmes, such as business and public administration.

While these students will never call themselves economists, they do take in economic ideas and will apply these in their later work and personal life. Thus, economics education to non-economists still has a large impact on the world.

This chapter starts with the application of the *Foundations* part of this book to the education of non-economists. We discuss the implications of teaching economics from the perspective of the individual who engages with economic systems in various ways, we go into the application of the principles *real-world*, *pluralism* and *values*, and we argue for the democratisation of economics through the notion of the *citizen economist*. Then, we go through the ten building blocks, separated in three categories: those we consider core, those which are optional, and those we would not recommend focusing on for non-economists. For each of these categories, we suggest teaching materials which seem most suitable for teaching economics to non-economists, such as high school students or those from other disciplines.

Teaching economics briefly, to those who do not specialise in the discipline, is an art in itself. For high school economics education specifically, we also recommend Maier and Nelson's teacher's guide *Introducing Economics: A Critical Guide for Teaching*: a practical handbook for the various dilemmas surrounding the teaching of critical economic thinking to students at a basic level. For the sake of brevity, however, in this chapter we stick to the *Economy Studies* approach, applying the principles and building blocks developed in this book to economics education for non-economists and taking out those elements that seem most important.

1   Foundations

The Philosophy of Economy Studies

The central aim of economics education for non-economists is different from that of the education of economists, on which we focused in the chapter *Foundation 1: The Philosophy of Economy Studies*. Rather than preparing experts on the economy for their future societal roles, economics education for non-economists is about helping non-economists better engage with the economic world in their everyday lives, as everyone participates in the economy in a couple of respects.

First and most obviously, during our working lives we fulfil crucial economic roles and tasks, and have to deal with many economic issues, both through our work and concerning our labour relations. Therefore, it is helpful for non-economists to learn more about the economic world of production and labour in general as well as more specific skills, such as how to get a job, negotiate working conditions, or (help) run a company. Besides these, occupation specific economic knowledge and skills are important. For accountants, the economics of firms seem particularly relevant, while the economics of the state seem more important for students of public administration.

Second, outside of our working hours we engage in various economic activities, such as consuming, householding, and investing our savings. Education related to this is often called financial literacy. It can help people make better informed decisions and prevent them from making unwise financial decisions. A stark example of this is the US student debt crisis and the financial problems people face because of unwise decisions, such as choosing forbearance over income-based repayment.

There is, however, also criticism on financial literacy programmes as they are normally taught, for focusing too narrowly on individual consumer misconduct. While this is important, it leaves out the more critical and collective action aspects of financial literacy. Besides learning what the smartest option is when choosing a loan, it is helpful to have a rough understanding of how the system works, what actors it has and what their interests are. This can help people recognize wrongdoings by companies and organisations as well as dysfunctionalities in an economic system. To put it simply, it is important for students to learn that when they have a problem, it might not be their fault. Besides individual responsibility, good economic structures and regulation are thus key. And for this, public awareness and collective action are important.

To come back to the earlier example, the reason for many unwise decisions related to US student debt is not only a lack of financial literacy. It is also misinformation by student loan services. It should be illegal for institutions to misinform their clients or withhold information from them. Critical financial literacy thus not only helps people make better individual consumer choices, but also helps them better engage in collective action and fight wrongdoings by companies and organisations. An informed person would, for example, note the misinformation and can signal this to regulators.

The content of financial literacy programmes is, however, often made in collaboration with financial institutions, who often have an incentive to prevent the more critical aspects of financial literacy from being taught (Hütten et al., 2018). Therefore, it is important to also engage civil society organisations, regulatory agencies and independent scholars in the creation of the financial literacy content. This allows students to develop a broader, better and more critical understanding of the matters, and can help prevent financial literacy programmes from turning into advertisement (or even propaganda) programmes by special interest groups. And this also creates useful overlap with the third point.

Third, as citizens and members of our local, national and international communities, we engage in many economic processes and decisions. The economics education of non-economists should therefore focus on a broad understanding of economic systems and issues. In public debates about government budgets, for example, there are often misunderstandings, such as the idea that public finances work in the same way as personal household finances. Without any economics education such misunderstandings are very likely as people do have personal experience with personal finances, but have never learned anything about public finances. The goal of economics education for non-economists should thus be to help people better understand the larger economic systems they are part of and also understand counter-intuitive insights. And since most students will not continue to specialise in economics, it is important that economics education for non-economists *"focuses primarily on preparing students for citizenship rather than for intermediate theory courses"* (Nelson, 2009, p. 62).

Overall, economics education for non-economics should thus be about preparing people for their future engagement with the economic world, and in particular in their working, private and public lives.

Principles: Real-World, Pluralism & Values

Each of the three principles set out in this book is also relevant for economics education for non-economists. The only difference is the way in which these principles can be applied and put into practice, with as main difference the more limited amount of teaching time with which to convey them to students.

Firstly, pluralism. It is crucial that non-economists are exposed to different economic ideas and that they realise that these ideas of economists are theories about the world, rather than direct descriptions of how the world works. This may sound rather obvious for any economists, or any academically trained person. But many non-academics tend to think of experts as simply knowing 'the truth', rather than that they have different ideas about how the world *may* work and perform empirical analyses to see what the evidence suggests. To use Alfred Korzybski's words, it is important that students learn that "the map is not the territory" (1931).

We think that this fundamental realisation best sinks in when students are exposed to a couple of contrasting economic debates. It does not require teaching full theoretical frameworks and mathematical models. This can be done by simply juxtaposing ideas about a certain economic issue, such as whether to tackle the problem of unemployment and a shrinking economy through government stimulus or austerity. Useful materials, ordered from light to heavy: the Keynes vs Hayek rap battles *Fear the Boom and Bust* & *Fight of the Century*, London School of Economics debate *Keynes v Hayek* with Selgin, Skidelsky, Weldon and Whyte, the book *Austerity vs Stimulus: The Political Future of Economic Recovery* by Skidelsky and Fraccaroli, or the book *Austerity: When It Works and When It Doesn't* by Alesina, Favero and Giavazzi.

Secondly, real-world. Especially when teaching non-economists, it is crucial to link the concepts that are discussed to the real world and the experiences of the students. If matters are only discussed in the abstract, it is likely that many students will not be able to see how it is relevant for the world around them, which will likely diminish their interest in the topic. Therefore, we advise bringing the real world in as much as possible.

As discussed in the chapter *Foundation 3: Real-World*, this can be done by using case studies, the news and economic history, visiting or having guest lectures by employees of economic institutions and companies, and exposing students to current public debates about economic issues. In doing so, we would encourage teachers to feel free to also do so in a playful manner. One could, for example, let students read an economics cartoon book, such as *Economix: How and Why Our Economy Works (and Doesn't Work) in Words and Pictures* by Goodwin and Bach. This may sound silly and of little educational value, but we would argue the opposite is true. As long as the materials are carefully selected to ensure their content is of good quality, the more playful manner in which these contents are communicated to students simply facilitates, rather than prevents, learning and is likely to leave behind longer lasting impressions on students. While the cartoon book is funny, it is surprisingly informative, helping readers better understand what the economy is about, economic history, the history of economic thought, different ways of organising economies, economic theories, normative aspects of economies and economic policies debates.

Thirdly, values. It is essential that non-economists learn to see and think about values and normative issues in the economy. This is also precisely where the views and ideas of non-economists are most relevant. They have just as much to say about value judgements related to economic issues as economists do (see more about this below in *Democratising Economics*). So students need to learn to identify value judgements in order to be able to properly interpret, value and make use of advice by experts without needing to blindly follow them. Interesting books and video's might be the book and INET video series by Michael Sandel both called *What Money Can't Buy*, Mariana Mazzucato's book *The Value of Everything* and her related TED talk *What is economic value, and who creates it?*, Robert Skidelsky's INET video *Ethics & Economics* and the chapter carrying the same title in his book *What's Wrong with Economics? A Primer for the Perplexed*.

Democratising Economics

Economics education for non-economists currently too often discourages, rather than encourages, people to participate in economic debates. The strong focus on technicalities and mathematics causes economics classes to often feel more like tests or competitions of mathematical talent and economic jargon, than places of learning and questioning. In a democratic society, all citizens should, however, engage in debates about important issues that influence their lives and futures. Therefore, we strongly advise to facilitate, rather than to hinder, this through economics education for non-economists. So instead of focusing on teaching technicalities, we advise to focus on teaching substantive knowledge about the economy in an accessible way. It is also important that students learn how to ask questions and participate in economic debates. Such an open, critical and active learning process can help create *citizen economists* according to Earle et al. (2016, p. 154):

"We propose the idea of the 'Citizen Economist', an individual who has the basic knowledge, confidence and interest to engage critically with economic discourse in politics, the news and their local communities. Citizen Economists are able to see the links between their individual circumstances and the operation of the economy on a systemic level. They are able to engage with economic statements and narratives made by politicians, economists and media commentators about the performance of the economy and evaluate the values and assumptions behind their arguments. A society of Citizen Economists is one in which individuals have more understanding and thus control over their circumstances. It is a society where there are always alternatives and all of society plays an active role in proposing, debating and scrutinising them, ultimately deciding collectively and individually which paths to take."

In a world in which expertise is often despised, this might read as an argument to make people mistrust economists, but it's actually the opposite. We believe blind public trust in economic experts is a recipe for disaster. Not only would this lead to undemocratic debates and decision making related to economic issues, it will lead to mistrust of economists and has arguably already done so. If something goes wrong or is seen as unfair, and citizens have no say in the matter, then the fault must be with the experts who claim the exclusive right to discuss economic issues, or at least this accusation is easily made and difficult to refute when the message is that citizens should not have a say in economic affairs.

What we need is more mutual understanding between economists and citizens. In recent years, economists have often been criticised for being 'out of touch with normal people' and they, for example, often misjudged how citizens would receive their economic expert advice related to the Brexit referendum. And the other side of the coin is the topic of this chapter: economics education for non-economists. This will not make everyone an economic expert, but it will help them better participate in public debates about economic issues. And it will also enable them to better understand economists as well as being better able to critically scrutinize and question their arguments.

2 Building Blocks

While all ten of our building blocks could be applied and used in economics education for non-economists, some are more relevant than others. Here we discuss the building blocks from high to low priority for economics education for non-economists.

Core building blocks

We advise putting the following building blocks at the core of economics education for non-economists:

- Building Block 1: Introducing the Economy
- Building Block 2: Know Your Own Economy
- Building Block 5: Economic Organisations & Mechanisms
- Building Block 6: Political-Economic Systems
- Building Block 8: Economic Theories
- Building Block 9: Problems & Proposals
- Building Block 10: Economics for a Better World

Before we go into the various building blocks, it is important to note that each of the building blocks will have to be treated more lightly than in full economics programmes. So here we suggest using elements of these building blocks, not trying to cover the full scope and depth of each in a course for non-economists. Courses can differ in how much they go into detail into economic theories, real world knowledge, or ways of organising the economy. We advise trying to cover these various topics, even if briefly, but if this is not possible one can choose to leave one or more out.

Building Block 1: Introducing the Economy

The first step in any economics course is to explain to students what the economy is and why it is important to learn about. This can be done in many different ways, from giving students a good academic or cartoon book, watching a documentary or letting them do their own online research, to giving them exercises to go outside of the classroom and observe parts of the economy for themselves and interview people about. Key topics for such exercises can be recent changes in the local economy, the main societal challenges of the day, and what people are concerned about and find most important.

Materials

- *Economics: The User's Guide* by Ha-Joon Chang, from 2014, chapters 1 & 2. Perhaps the most accessible and yet insightful introduction book into economics, with particular attention to why it is relevant to learn economics and what economics is in the first place.
- *Introducing a New Economics* by Jack Reardon, Molly S. Cato, Maria A.

C. Madi, from 2018, chapters 1, 3, 4, & 5. An accessible textbook which introduces students to what economics is, how it is embedded in society and the environment, and major societal challenges, such as climate change, poverty, financial instability, and inequality.

- *Principles of economics in context* by Neva Goodwin, Jonathan M. Harris, Julie A. Nelson, Brian Roach, Mariano Torras, most recent edition from 2019, chapters 0, 1, 20, and 21. This economics textbook covers many of the traditional economic topics, but pays more attention to why studying the economy is relevant and concerns, such as human wellbeing, ecological sustainability, distributional equity, and the quality of employment.
- To help students get an idea of the main societal challenges of today, it can be useful to have them take a look at reports, such as the *Sustainable Development Goals Reports*, *World Development Reports*, and *World Happiness Reports*. It can also be useful to use more engaging types of materials, such as documentaries and coverage of political protests and debates. Furthermore, it can be interesting and useful for students to also be exposed to material on the key issues in the domestic, rather than global, economy.

Building Block 2: Know Your Own Economy and Building Block 9: Problems & Proposals

Building on the suggestions above, it can be very useful for students to acquire basic factual knowledge about the economic world they live in. As described in more detail in *Building Block 2: Know Your Own Economy*, this can be done by looking at and discussing key indicators, institutions and sectors. One can also take the core current problems and let students create factual overviews of them. With this, students do not only acquire factual knowledge but also practical skills to tackle economic problems. Perhaps the most often applied policy tool, which often also plays a central role in the public debate, is cost-benefit analysis. For this reason, it can be worthwhile to make students familiar with the basics of the method and its limitations, enabling them to ask critical questions and properly interpret the results. Furthermore, it is useful to also discuss different approaches to comparing policy options, such as participatory evaluation and risk-opportunity analysis, as this widens students' understanding of how policy options can be assessed.

Materials

- Material on the national economy as described in *Building Block 2: Know Your Own Economy*.
- To introduce the policy tools, reading materials can be of use, but they will probably have the most lasting impact when combined with practical exercises in which students have to apply the tools themselves.

- For cost-benefit analysis, a useful book is: *Cost-Benefit Analysis: Concepts and Practice* by Anthony E. Boardman, David H. Greenberg, Aidan R. Vining, David L. Weimer, most recent edition from 2018.
- For participatory evaluation, the following book can be of help: *Participatory Evaluation Up Close: An Integration of Research Based Knowledge* by J. Bradley Cousins and Jill A. Chouinard, from 2012.
- Risk-opportunity analysis is newer and has yet to be explained in a textbook, but a useful working paper explaining the tool and providing examples of applications is: *Risk-opportunity analysis for transformative policy design and appraisal* by Jean-Francois Mercure, Simon Sharpe, Jorge Vinuales, Matthew Ives, Michael Grubb, Hector Pollitt, Florian Knobloch and Femke Nijsse, from 2020.

Building Block 8: Economic Theories

Theory is normally the meat and bones of economics courses, and for a good reason. It is critical that students learn about different analytical ideas about the economy. So while we advise to pay more attention to other matters than theory, it is still of great importance. Our main suggestion is to focus on making students familiar with different ways of looking at the economy, rather than on teaching them only rudimentary theoretical models. In *Building Block 8: Economic Theories*, we explain in more detail how this could be done by first explaining the basic elements of different economic approaches and then focusing on the main approaches per economic topic. To prepare students for their economic citizenship, different economic ideas about the form and function of government can be particularly useful as these are often central to the public debate. For suggestions, see the section *Government* in chapter *Tool 1: Pragmatic Pluralism*.

Materials

- *Economics: The User's Guide* by Ha-Joon Chang, from 2014. This book provides a brief and accessible pluralist introduction to a broad range of theoretical insights the discipline has to offer. While theoretical, this book is never dry. It is clearly written and has a very succinct style.
- *Rethinking Economics: An Introduction to Pluralist Economics* by Liliann Fischer, Joe Hasell, J. Christopher Proctor, David Uwakwe, Zach Ward Perkins, Catriona Watson, from 2017. This collection of essays provides an accessible introduction into post-Keynesian, Marxian, Austrian, institutional, feminist, behavioural, complexity and ecological economics.
- The website *Exploring Economics:* www.exploring-economics.org/en/. This website provides sharp and helpful introductions into the different economic perspectives and furthermore gives many useful overviews of related teaching materials, video's and existing (online) courses.

- *Principles of Economics in Context* by Jonathan Harris, Julie A. Nelson and Neva Goodwin, most recent edition from 2020. A useful textbook that treats much of the traditional content, but also consistently discusses the social and environmental challenges inherent in economic questions.
- *Economics After The Crisis* by Irene van Staveren, from 2015. This well-written textbook describes twelve central topics in economics at an introductory level from four different perspectives: the neoclassical, institutional, social and post-Keynesian perspectives.
- *The Economy* by The CORE Team, from 2017. This highly successful textbook, freely available online with additional resources, provides a treasure trove of empirical data, context and recent research. The CORE Team has also been working on developing teaching material for high school economics education, see their website for the latest materials: www.core-econ.org
- *Introducing a New Economics* by Jack Reardon, Maria A. Madi, and Molly S. Cato, from 2017. This ground-breaking textbook introduces many of the core issues in economics today and weaves together pluralist theory and real-world knowledge in an eminently readable way.
- *Political Economy: The Contest of Economic Ideas* by Frank Stilwell, most recent edition from 2011. This well-written textbook provides a good introduction to economic ideas from multiple perspectives, with particular attention to classical, Marxist, neoclassical, institutional, Keynesian and more recent insights related to capitalism.

Building Block 5: Economic Organisations & Mechanisms and Building Block 6: Political-Economic Systems

Economic Organisations & Mechanisms and *Political-Economic Systems* are about showing to students that there are multiple ways of organising and thinking about economies. In both cases, the point is not that students need to remember and reproduce specifics. The focus should, however, be on making them realise the economic world can be organised and thought about in multiple ways and giving them a rough idea of the various options and perspectives that exist. This can be done by discussing various economic organisations, mechanisms and theories in an accessible, engaging and non-technical way. This knowledge can help students understand the different options that are discussed (or ignored) in the public debate or in an organisation they are involved in.

Materials
- *Introducing a New Economics* by Jack Reardon, Molly S. Cato, Maria A. C. Madi, from 2018, chapters 10, 11 & 12. Three accessible and brief chapters, with accompanying classroom activities and questions, introducing students to what public goods, commons and firms are

and how they can be governed, for example as a corporation owned by shareholders or as a cooperative owned by its workers or consumers.

- *Economics: The User's Guide* by Ha-Joon Chang, from 2014, chapter 5. A short well-written chapter on different economic actors and organisational forms, from multinational corporations, cooperatives, and labour unions, to governments and a variety of international organisations.
- *Organisations: A Very Short Introduction* by Mary Jo Hatch, from 2011. A brief, accessible and yet highly informative book full with scientific theories and ideas on what organisations are, how they can be structured, how they change, and their internal dynamics and interaction with markets and society.
- *Capitalism* by Geoffrey Ingham, from 2008. A highly insightful introduction into capitalism with chapters on key ideas from Smith, Marx, Weber, Schumpeter and Keynes, and core institutions, such as market exchange, the enterprise, money, capital, financial markets and the state.
- *Capitalism: A Very Short Introduction* by James Fulcher, most recent edition from 2015. A brief and yet useful book on capitalism's definition, historical evolution, varieties, global networks, and recurring crises.
- *Socialism: A Very Short Introduction* by Michael Newman, most recent edition from 2020. A similar brief and yet useful book, but then on capitalism's main rival socialism, with chapters on its varieties around the world, historical traditions and more recent developments.

Building Block 10: Economics for a Better World

The public debate about the economic matters is often normatively loaded and focused. Therefore, it is of great importance that students become familiar with the normative foundations and ideas on which economic debates are built. As discussed in more detail in *Building Block 10: Economics for a Better World*, this can be done by discussing normative principles for decisions and visions for the economy. The point here is not that students should learn political philosophies by heart or make sophisticated normative arguments. It is rather about giving them a basic understanding and feeling for the different ways in which normative issues can be looked at.

Materials

- *A Guide to Ethics and Public Policy: Finding Our Way* by D. Don Welch, from 2014. A brief but insightful book providing a broad framework for evaluating policy proposals and outcomes, organised around five moral principles: benefit, effectiveness, fairness, fidelity, and legitimacy.
- *Political Ideologies: An Introduction* by Andrew Heywood, most recent

edition from 2021. A useful and accessible introduction into a wide variety of political ideologies, from liberalism, socialism, and conservatism to feminism, nationalism, and green ideology, that shape much of our normative thinking on the economy.

■ *Moral Views on Market Society* by Marion Fourcade and Kieran Healy, from 2007. An insightful overview paper on the key different normative perspectives on capitalism, enabling readers to better understand and place ideas and arguments prevalent in many debates about the economy.

■ *What Money Can't Buy: The Moral Limits of Markets* by Michael J. Sandel, most recent edition from 2012. A highly influential and well-written book reflecting on the moral place of markets in society and asking the key question whether everything should be up for sale. The Institute for New Economic Thinking has also launched a video series on the book and topic: https://www.ineteconomics.org/perspectives/videos/what-money-cant-buy

Additional building blocks

If the teacher has a personal affinity with these topics, we recommend including them, but otherwise they do not have priority:

■ Economic History (BB3)
■ History of Economic Thought and Methods (BB4)

While we would argue that the two building blocks devoted to history are not of the highest priority, we think they can be of great value added if it is done well. As such, we would thus advise to include it if history is of particular interest to the teacher and he or she knows how to use it well to engage students more with economic ideas and realities. So rather than putting it at the core of economics education for non-economists, we see it as a didactical option to possibly teach the other contents in a more interesting way. It should be noted that this is not the case for full economics programs, for which a basic understanding of the histories of economic ideas and realities is essential.

Materials

■ *Capitalism: A Short History* by Jürgen Kocka, from 2016. A concise and yet broad-ranging account of how capitalism developed from early merchants, colonialism and slavery to the recent wave of globalisation and financialisation, accompanied by discussions of capitalism's key thinkers, such as Smith, Marx, Weber, and Schumpeter.

■ *Economics: The User's Guide* by Ha-Joon Chang, from 2014, chapters 2 & 3. Two short and well written chapters on how the economy has changed over the last centuries and how capitalism evolved.

■ *Global Economic History: A Very Short Introduction* by Robert C. Allen, from 2011. A brief but insightful introduction into the economic history of the world with chapters on industrialisation, the rise of the West, great empires, the Americas and Africa.

- *The Worldly Philosophers: The Lives, Times and Ideas of the Great Economic Thinkers* by Robert Heilbroner, most recent edition from 1999. While first published in 1953, it remains perhaps the best introduction into the history of economic thought to this day. In a remarkably well-written and accessible manner it discusses the ideas of key economists and puts them into historical context.
- *Grand Pursuit: The Story of Economic Genius* by Sylvia Naser, from 2012. Another very accessible but more recent book introducing the history of economic thought through captivating narratives.

Less relevant building blocks

Finally, we would recommend avoiding the following building block when teaching non-economists:

- Research Methods (BB7)

Research methods are, of course, of great importance, but given the aim of economics education for non-economists we would argue that teaching time can be better spent on the other building blocks. Non-economists are not prepared to do detailed analyses of economic issues, as economics students are. Rather, non-economists need to acquire a rough understanding of economic issues and learn about how to deal with them. Learning the specifics of various research methods will only very indirectly help with this and have therefore least priority. Another important downside of focusing on econometrics and mathematics-heavy material, is that it makes economic ideas and topics inaccessible for those without an affinity for mathematics. The current focus on technique harms students from understanding the economy: *"If a student is not capable of understanding graphs, then subsequent success in one's economics class is less likely. ... It could be that if the intention is to prepare students to use economics to understand policy and everyday life, graphs generate more harm than good."* (Hoyt & McGoldrick, 2012, p. 338). Economics education for non-economists should therefore be understandable for everyone and not require a high level of mathematical expertise.

This also relates to another point: Do not focus on techniques. What matters is that students gain more knowledge about the substance of economic ideas and topics. Whether students are able to work with a model and have technical skills related to statistics, should not matter. Especially when considering that the technical skills they could acquire will be too minimal to be of any significant use in the real world. If an organisation needs someone to construct or work with a mathematical model about an economic topic, this person would need considerably more training to do so properly. In fact, many organisations consider even a full university economics programme not enough and hire trained mathematicians and statisticians to work on the technical aspects. Furthermore, leaving the technical aspects out frees up teaching time to focus on the various things discussed above. In the current dominant way of teaching, the technical and substantive aspects are often supposed to be conveyed to students by teaching them a few simplified models. This demands a lot from teachers to be able to convey both at the same time to all students, especially considering the different levels of talent for the technical and substantive aspects that the students have. Putting the focus (exclusively) on the substantive aspects will make it more doable for teachers to convey economic ideas and real-world knowledge to students.

Example Courses

Whether it is for economics majors or for a smaller side programme such as described in this chapter, the *Economy Studies* framework can be flexibly applied to create a wide variety of courses. To illustrate this in practice, we provide in this section an example economics course for high school students and one for business students, both built on the basis of the *Economy Studies* framework. Online, we provide two more examples: an economics course in a public administration and law programme, and an academic minor in economics.

3   A High School Economics Course

Title:
Preparing 'Citizen Economists' for their future personal economic lives and participation in public life

Required background knowledge:
None

Nominal workload:
1-2 years of economics classes in high school education

Course goals:
This course enables students to better understand the economic world they are part of, to understand political debates about it, to envision their own roles in it and to be practically able to play those roles.

Course outline:
The course is divided into the following three parts:
1   Welcome to the economic world
2   The key problems of our times
3   How should we organize the economy?

Part 1: Welcome to the economic world
The first part of the course focuses on giving students a basic understanding of what the economy is and why it is relevant. This is done through a combination of explanations of relatively abstract concepts and explorations of the real-world economy the students live in. The purpose here is helping students realise that their personal lives and experiences are connected to a larger economic world.

Besides teaching basic conceptual and real-world knowledge about the economy, students learn practical skills needed for their current and future roles in the economy as consumers, citizens, household members, students and (future) workers. Financial literacy is a part of this, but it is broader than that. It also relates to life choices about choosing what to study and what kind of career to pursue, as well as practical skills related to, for example, finding a job or negotiating.

The course focuses not only on instrumental knowledge that can help students themselves, but also enables them to reflect on the broader implications of their economic decisions, for example when it comes to their personal consumption.

For more details, teaching materials and practical advice on teaching these topics, see the following building blocks:

- Building Block 1: Introducing the Economy
- Building Block 2: Know Your Own Economy
- Building Block 9: Problems & Proposals

Part 2: The key problems of our times

The second part of the course focuses on the current big societal challenges, such as climate change, economic instability, aging populations, and growing economic inequality. The first step is always to explain to students what the challenge is and providing them some basic factual knowledge about the current state of the issue. Creating such factsheets could also be an assignment for students.

To help students grasp the relevance of these issues, a couple of things can help. Firstly, to connect the material to the personal lives of students. How are, or will, they and the people around them be influenced by these big societal problems? Secondly, to make use of more engaging material, such as documentaries, music, poems, and news articles, next to the more dry (written or academic) material on the issues.

Once students have acquired a basic understanding of the issue, the focus is on the main different perspectives on the issue, its causes, mechanisms, consequences and potential solutions. The chapter *Tools: Pragmatic Pluralism* can be helpful in determining which perspectives are most relevant for the issue at hand.

Having learned different ways of thinking about the problem, students are given the assignment to write an essay in which they have to advocate a solution of their choosing and present this to the class. Following this, they are matched with another student who advocated a different solution and are given the assignment to reach a compromise together.

For more details, teaching materials and practical advice on teaching these topics, see the following building blocks:

- Building Block 1: Introducing the Economy
- Building Block 8: Economic Theories
- Building Block 9: Problems & Proposals
- Building Block 10: Economics for a Better World

Part 3: How should we organize the economy?
The last part of the course centres on making students familiar with the different ways of organising an economy and arguments for and against them. The focus is first on economic organisations and mechanisms. This is mainly to prepare students for their personal future lives both at work and outside of it, as they will participate in organisations for their career but also through their community and civic life, as well as their hobbies and sports. Besides explaining the different organisational forms and mechanisms as abstract concepts, students will also visit actual organisations and be required to analyse them.

After this the focus shifts towards macro political-economic systems. The goal here is to enable students to more critically and confidently follow and participate in (future) political debates about how the economy should be organised or reformed. To help them do so, the different political-economic systems and their varieties are discussed, giving most attention to the current domestic one (most likely, a particular variety of capitalism) and prominent proposed alternatives to it. As an assignment, students are tasked to analyse and reflect on recent developments and changes in the domestic political-economic system, enabling them to get a better and more nuanced understanding.

For more details, teaching materials and practical advice on teaching these topics, see the following building blocks:
- Building Block 5: Economic Organisations & Mechanisms
- Building Block 6: Political-Economic Systems
- Building Block 8: Economic Theories
- Building Block 10: Economics for a Better World

4 An Economics Course in a Business Programme

Title:
Introducing business students to the world of economic thinking

Required background knowledge:
None

Nominal workload:
Equivalent of 6 ECTS (180 hrs)

Course goals:
This course enables business students to understand how businesses are embedded in the economy at large. It provides them with an overview of the economic system and the various types of organisations in it such as commercial, cooperative and non-profit entities, as well as various forms of government which interact with the private sector. It also provides students with a basic, intuitive understanding of the main theories about firms and markets.

Course outline:
The course is divided into the following three parts:
1 The role of business in society
2 The composition of the business world
3 Economic theories about markets and firms

Part 1: The role of business in society
The first part of the course concerns the role of business in society. It starts with a discussion of the concept 'the economy', including the question where its boundaries lie and how this system is embedded in a broader ecological and social context. Students also learn about the concept of capitalism as a political-economic system. Using several readings, they discuss with each other the advantages of this system and its inherent problems.

The discussion then zooms in on the societal role of business. Various perspectives are discussed, from the shareholder value theory to democratic and stakeholder theories. Possible materials:
■ The series of articles on the shareholder-stakeholder debate *'Milton Friedman 50 Years Later'* edited by Zingales, Kasperkevic, & Schechter, from 2020.

- The book *Change Everything: Creating an Economy for the Common Good* by Christian Felber, from 2015.
- The fierce yet constructive video debate between Zingales and Felber *'The Future of Capitalism #10: Can a Different Market Economy Work in Practice?'*, from 2020.

A case study is presented on the interplay between government and commercial actors in Germany's famous and relatively early turn to green energy production (*Grüne Wende*). This case study is mainly used to demonstrate how the commercial sectors are interwoven with each other, how big firms and small- to medium-sized enterprises together make up an industrial ecosystem. It also demonstrates to students how change can occur in an economy, in this case a deliberately orchestrated transition from polluting forms of energy production to cleaner techniques.

For more details, teaching materials and practical advice on teaching these topics, see the following building blocks:
- Building Block 1: Introducing the Economy
- Building Block 6: Political-Economic Systems
- Building Block 10: Economics for a Better World

Part 2: The composition of the business world

The second part of this course focuses on a real-world overview of the main economic sectors in the country, and their relation with public and civil sectors. For instance, say this course were to be taught in Germany, students might learn about the structure of the automobile industry, the mechanical engineering sector, the chemical industry and the electrical industry.

This second part of the course also introduces to students the wide variety of economic organisations: from commercial firms to cooperatives to non-profits. The concept of cooperatives is illustrated with the German cooperative banking sector, including a brief historical overview, from their local formation by citizen collectives to the subsequent series of mergers between them to form larger organisations.

For more details, teaching materials and practical advice on teaching these topics, see the following building blocks:
- Building Block 2: Know Your Own Economy
- Building Block 5: Economic Organisations & Mechanisms

Part 3: Economic theories about markets and firms

In the third part of the course, the focus becomes more systemic. Students learn of the main government policies regarding the country's commercial sectors, both those designed to stimulate and protect them and those designed to regulate their impacts on the environment and their potential monopoly powers. Students also gain a brief overview of the sectors' relations with civil society, such as labour unions and NGOs, and the main points of contention between these parties.

This part also introduces students to the main economic theories about markets and firms. On firms, there is a short presentation of field theory, which sets out how firms stabilise and shape power relations in an economic system, and of institutional economics, which sees firms as a way to limit the transaction costs, which would be impossibly large if an economy only consisted of individual free agents. On markets, students are presented with the contrasting views of neoclassical economics, which sees competition as a harmonious process with an optimal outcome, and classical economics, which sees competition as a ruthless process more akin to war.

For more details, teaching materials and practical advice on teaching these topics, see the following building blocks:
- Building Block 6: Political-Economic Systems
- Building Block 8: Economic Theories

For two more examples, visit our website.
- An Economics Course in a Public Administration and Law Programme (30 ECTS)
- An Academic Minor in Economics (30 ECTS)
economy.st/nonecon

Part III

Tool 7
Learning Objectives

Designing economics courses not from the question 'what does the teacher know best?' but from 'what do the students need to know, to be prepared for their future societal roles?'.

1
**Traditional
Learning Objectives:
Chalk and Talk**

2
**The Proficiencies
Approach**

Learning Objectives

3
**Example Learning
Objectives Based on
the Building Blocks**

When designing a course, it is key to start with the learning objectives. Based upon these learning objectives content, teaching material, exercises and assessment forms can subsequently be chosen, and not in the reversed order. Teachers should not start from their own knowledge or current research, but from what students need to fulfil their future societal roles. Learning objectives require teachers to think critically about what the ultimate goals are of the course and be concrete and transparent about it to students and other faculty members.

The most frequently used form of learning objective is still connected to the traditional 'chalk and talk' teaching techniques: students need to be able to reproduce their notes from lectures or textbooks, and to demonstrate their mastery of the mathematics behind the theory. We suggest using Hansen's (1986) proficiencies approach instead, coupled with O'Donnell's (2002) additions on critical thinking.

Based on the proficiencies approach, we provide three example learning objectives for each of our ten building blocks.

When designing a course, it is key to start with the learning objectives. Based upon these learning objectives content, teaching material, exercises and assessment forms can subsequently be chosen, and not in the reversed order. Teachers should not start from their own knowledge or current research, but from what students need to fulfil their future societal roles, thereby ensuring curriculum alignment (Anderson, 2002; Biggs, 2003; Squires, 2012). Learning objectives require teachers to think critically about what the ultimate goals are of the course and be concrete and transparent about it to students and other faculty members.

1 Traditional Learning Objectives: Chalk and Talk

The traditional approach to learning objectives focuses on reproducing knowledge in individual and largely isolated courses (Hoyt & McGoldrick, 2012). Learning objectives, in these cases, often describe that students need to be able to describe or reproduce theory X and can use or solve model Y. Students are passively taking notes in lectures in which the teacher explains the material described in the textbook, also known as 'chalk and talk' (Watts & Becker, 2008). At the end of the course, students take a (written) exam which tests how well they are able to reproduce the taught content.

The danger of this approach is that students gain knowledge and develop skills that are of little or no use in their future career and life. For instance, calculating the market equilibrium of a fictitious market using abstract numbers is an interesting mathematical puzzle. But for most students it does not lead to much additional insight or intuition for economic mechanisms. Nor will most students use this skill in their subsequent working lives. Such exercises crowd out other valuable knowledge and skills, such as practically applying and effectively explaining economic concepts and critical independent thinking.

Research among economics graduates and their employers indicates that economists need a broader range of skills and knowledge to properly fulfil their societal and professional roles (O'Donnell, 2009; van Dalen et al., 2015b; Yurko, 2018). Economists not only need to have knowledge of economic theories and technical econometric skills, but also need to be able to effectively communicate them and work together (with non-economists), think critically and independently, reflect on their role and position, and be able to think creatively outside the conventional framework making use of new ideas and different viewpoints. To better prepare economics students for their future careers, different approaches to learning objectives in economics education have therefore been developed.

2 The Proficiencies Approach

Over the last decades, Hansen (1986, 2001, 2011) has developed a proficiencies approach for economics through experimenting, debating with other teachers and interviewing employers of economics graduates in the public, private and non-profit sectors. The emphasis in Hansen's proficiencies approach is on doing economics, rather than only learning to think about. He built on the cognitive domain of the general educational Bloom's taxonomy and applied it to economics education (Bloom, 1956). The updated core of the taxonomy for the cognitive domain is a hierarchy of the following six learning objectives which sequentially increase in level of complexity: (1) Remember, (2) Understand, (3) Apply, (4) Analyse, (5) Evaluate, and (6) Create (Anderson & Krathwohl, 2001).

Hansen added one learning objective on critical reflection and asking questions, thereby coming to the following seven proficiencies for economics education (2011, pp. 188-190):

1 *"Accessing existing knowledge*: Retrieve, assemble, and organize information on particular topics and issues in economics. Locate published research in economics and related fields. Track down economic data and data sources. Find information about the generation, construction and meaning of economic data.
2 *Displaying command of existing knowledge*: Explain key economics theories and concepts, and describe how they can be used. Write a precis or summary of a published journal article. Summarize in a two-minute monologue or a 300-word written statement what is known about the current condition of the economy and the economic outlook. Summarize the principal ideas of an eminent economist; summarize a current controversy in the economics literature; state succinctly the dimensions of a current economic policy issue.
3 *Interpreting existing knowledge*: Explain and evaluate what economic concepts and principles are used in economic analyses published in articles from daily newspapers, weekly news magazines and academic journals. Describe how these concepts aid in understanding the analysis. Do the same for nontechnical analyses written by economists for general purpose publications.
4 *Interpreting and manipulating economic data*: Explain how to understand and interpret data found in published articles, such as the annual Economic Report of the President. Be able to identify patterns and trends in published data such as those found in the Statistical

Abstract of the United States. Construct tables from already available data to illustrate an economic issue. Describe the relationships among several different measures (e.g. unemployment, prices, and gross domestic product).

5 **_Applying existing knowledge_**: Prepare an organised, clearly written three-page analysis of a current economic problem. Assess in a four-page paper the costs and benefits of an economic policy proposal. Prepare a two-page decision memorandum for your employers that recommends some action on an economic decision faced by the organisation. Write a 600-word op-ed essay on some local economic issue.

6 **_Creating new knowledge_**: Identify and formulate a question or series of questions about some economic issue that will facilitate its investigation using the tools of economics. Synthesize the literature on a topic to determine gaps in our existing knowledge and how those gaps might best be filled. Prepare a five-page proposal describing a potentially useful research project and how that project might be undertaken. Complete a research study whose results are presented in a carefully edited twenty-page paper or in an undergraduate thesis. Engage in a group research project that prepares a detailed research proposal and/or a finished research paper.

7 **_Questing for knowledge and understanding_**: Demonstrate an understanding of questions that stimulate productive discussion (factual, interpretative, and evaluative) and help keep discussions centered on the economic issues under discussion. Develop a line of questions that probe the meaning or seek to interpret the meaning of a reading selection written by a well-known economist. Show how a questioning approach can get to the heart of substantive issues by focusing, for example, on the equity and efficiency implications of alternative arrangements, policies, and programmes (e.g.: What are the benefits? What are the costs? How do the benefits and costs compare? Who pays? Who gains?)."

Hansen (2011) proposes focusing on the first three proficiencies in introductory courses, three to five in intermediate courses, four to six in advanced field courses, and seven on all levels. Using this approach to economics education, according to Hansen, might mean 'covering' less content in class, but will likely increase the amount of content students will 'master'. Furthermore, it is important that students acquire skills to connect conceptual knowledge to real problems and contexts (Kneppers et al., 2012).

The approach has a lot of implications for economics education, in particular for the didactics. It requires moving away from passive learning activities towards more active, constructive and interactive learning activities (Chi, 2009). To achieve the proficiencies students need to actively engage and practise with close reading, writing, speaking, discussing, reasoning, thinking and creating, rather than simply listening and remembering.

In terms of assessment, Hansen argues for making more use of oral exams, writing assignments, summarising and discussing non-textbook reading assignments, capstone courses, thesis seminars, research projects, and practical policy- and problem-focused projects (for an extensive discussion of assessing the proficiencies see Myers et al., 2009). He also proposes making a table which lists the 7 proficiencies above in the columns, and the different exercises and assessments of the course in the rows. This allows teachers to create a good overview of how often and when certain proficiencies receive attention, helping them to ensure enough variety and good timing.

O'Donnell (2002) proposed to amend and improve upon the seven proficiencies of Hansen. While Hansen, rightfully according to O'Donnell, emphasizes the importance of practical skills, more attention should be devoted to the broader intellectual development of students. These skills relate to awareness and dealing with different ideas, economics approaches, and disciplines, as well as critically reflecting on one's role and being aware of weaknesses and limitations of economics. Students need to learn to make their own informed decisions amidst controversies and debates. As such, economics education should have both more vocational aspects, focusing on practical skills, and more liberal arts aspects, focusing on broader intellectual skills.

O'Donnell (2002, pp. 52-53), therefore, proposes to add the following three learning objectives to the Hansen's proficiencies:

8 *"Display Awareness of the Nature of Economics*: Write a paper on: definitions of economics; the nature of economic reasoning(s) in either theoretical or policy matters; whether economics is a science or not; if a science, whether it belongs to the social sciences or natural sciences; the capacities and limitations of economics in analysing social and individual phenomena; whether assumptions constrain the applicability of theories; whether the gap between theory and reality matters and how to deal with it if it does; whether institutions are central or peripheral to economic analysis; the methods available for testing the implications of economic theories and whether such tests

are ever conclusive; the relations between micro and macro.

9 *Display Awareness of Controversy in Economics*: Write a paper on: a controversy in economics concerning content or methodology, or micro or macro; whether controversies are ever resolved in economics and, if so, how; whether there is only one true conceptual framework for economics or whether economics is essentially pluralist with multiple conceptual frameworks; whether faith, dogmatism and ideology are significant factors in economic controversies.

10 *Display Awareness of Links Between Economics and Other Disciplines*: Write a paper on: the links between economics and at least one other related discipline such as psychology, history, sociology, politics, anthropology or philosophy; what economics can learn from other disciplines; whether, in discourse with other disciplines, economics has preferred the role of teacher to that of learner."

Before we go on, it is important to note that there is often a gap between the intentions of the teacher and the experience of the student. While many teachers agree with most of the proficiencies above and believe they have already incorporated them (fully) in their teaching, evidence coming from surveys among students and employers of economists suggest otherwise (Earle et al., 2016; Proctor, 2019; Yurko, 2018). We do not doubt that teachers want their students to gain a deeper understanding of material and the ability to apply it in practice. The widespread use of *'chalk and talk'* teaching style, however, prevents students from developing the different proficiencies. When students are largely passive in class, learn only one perspective, are not encouraged to question and challenge presented ideas, lectures are conducted in front of hundreds of students, small group classes are used to solve equations and assessment is primarily through exams that request the regurgitation of material, then it is not very likely that students will develop the various proficiencies. We recognise that some of these features are often outside of the control of individual lectures and ask deans and programme directors to enable teachers to address them. But fortunately, many of these aspects can be changed fairly easily by teachers and we encourage teachers to take their role and tackle these barriers when setting out learning objectives for courses.

3 Example Learning Objectives Based on the Building Blocks

So, what could learning objectives look like when making use of the *Economy Studies* framework? We recommend keeping an eye on covering the proficiencies discussed above as well as the building blocks of the *Economy Studies* framework. In principle, nearly every proficiency could be combined with every building block, but in actual courses sharp choices have to be made.

We provide a number of examples of possible learning objectives for every building block making use of the different proficiencies. For brevity, we number the proficiencies in the same way as we did above, as follows:

The ten learning proficiencies of Hansen (2011) and O'Donnell (2002)

1   Accessing existing knowledge
2   Displaying command of existing knowledge
3   Interpreting existing knowledge
4   Interpreting and manipulating economic data
5   Applying existing knowledge
6   Creating new knowledge
7   Questing for knowledge and understanding
8   Display awareness of the nature of economics
9   Display awareness of controversy in economics
10 Display awareness of links between economics and other disciplines

Building Block 1: Introducing the Economy
- Students can define and explain what the economy is and how it relates to the larger social and ecological world. Proficiencies: 2, 3, 8, 10.
- Students are able to ask stimulating questions about the relevance and importance of economic topics and issues. Proficiencies: 3, 7.
- Students display awareness of and can critically reflect on the roles economists have in society. Proficiencies: 7, 8, 9, 10.

Building Block 2: Know Your Own Economy
- Students can describe the basic structure, main institutions, and dominant sectors of the national economy. Proficiencies: 2, 3.
- Students are able to assemble, organize, interpret and present data and basic facts on the domestic economy. Proficiencies: 1, 3, 4.
- Students are able to connect abstract economic concepts to their personal experiences and the real-world economy around them. Proficiencies: 3, 5.

Building Block 3: Economic History

- Students can summarize how economies worldwide have evolved over time. Proficiencies: 2, 3.
- Students are able to put recent events into historical context. Proficiencies: 5, 6.
- Students command knowledge about how the domestic economy developed into its current state. Proficiencies: 2, 3.

Building Block 4: History of Economic Thought & Methods

- Students can describe main strands of economic thinking and research in history and how they developed. Proficiencies: 2, 3, 9.
- Students are able to connect developments in economic thinking to developments in the real-world economy. Proficiencies: 5, 6.
- Students command knowledge about how the discipline of economics and its relations with other disciplines evolved over time. Proficiencies: 2, 3, 9, 10.

Building Block 5: Economic Organisations & Mechanisms

- Students command knowledge about different organisational forms and economic mechanisms. Proficiencies: 2, 3.
- Students are able to find information and ask questions that help understand how organisations function and are structured. Proficiencies: 1, 5, 7.
- Students can recognize economic mechanisms in their daily lives and connect these personal experiences to abstract theories. Proficiencies: 2, 3, 5.

Building Block 6: Political-Economic Systems

- Students can describe the main political-economic systems and their key varieties. Proficiencies: 2, 3.
- Students can analyse actual political-economic systems making use of analytical concepts, academic literature and empirical data. Proficiencies: 1, 4, 5, 6.
- Students can reflect on how societal problems and reform ideas are related to political-economic systems. Proficiencies: 5, 6, 7.

Building Block 7: Research Methods & Philosophy of Science

- Students are able to collect and analyse quantitative data, draw substantive and theoretical implications from it, and effectively communicate the findings. Proficiencies: 1, 4, 5, 6.
- Students are able to collect and analyse qualitative data, draw substantive and theoretical implications from it, and effectively communicate the findings. Proficiencies: 1, 4, 5, 6.
- Students are able to assess which research methods can help better understand a topic and reflect upon the implication of methodological choices. Proficiencies: 4, 5, 7, 8.

Building Block 8: Economic Theories

- Students can understand and distinguish economic approaches and different ways of looking at the economy. Proficiencies: 2, 3, 8, 9.
- Students are able to recognize and connect insights from other disciplines on the economy to economic theory. Proficiencies: 2, 3, 10.
- Students can explain the key theories and insights on topic X. Proficiencies: 2, 3, 9.

Building Block 9: Problems & Proposals

- Students are able to perform a sector or topic scan and create a useful overview of the findings. Proficiencies: 1, 4, 5, 6.
- Students can perform practical problem analyses and identify relevant factual, normative and theoretical aspects. Proficiencies: 1, 4, 5, 6.
- Students can write and evaluate proposals to tackle real-world issues. Proficiencies: 5, 6, 7.

Building Block 10: Economics for a Better World

- Students have the ability to argue morally as well as analytically, and to clearly distinguish the two. Proficiencies: 7, 8.
- Students can describe and apply different normative principles for decisions and visions for the economy. Proficiencies: 2, 3, 5.
- Students are able to collect, assemble and reflect on information on citizens' normative preferences related to an economic issue and possible solutions. Proficiencies: 1, 4, 6, 7.

Conclusion

In this concluding chapter, we briefly review what this book has offered and then look forward, offering practical suggestions and ideas for economics teachers and professors, programme directors and students.

1 A New Vision for Economics Education

Our rapidly changing world is faced with many economic challenges, such as increasing debt levels, staggering inequalities and serious forms of ecological breakdown. These challenges are complex and cross multiple dimensions of our social and natural systems. To face them, it is not nearly enough for economists to hold knowledge in formal, theoretical abstractions. Whilst these may be sophisticated, they only reflect a fraction of what is actually going on in the real world. We need broadly trained economists with an understanding of the real-world economy. We need economists who know for example how the main industries work, who can grasp the interfaces between state and corporate systems and who can see how economies are embedded in society and nature at large.

This requires open minds that can examine issues from a variety of perspectives. Given the multifaceted nature of economic systems, no single theoretical framework or methodology can answer all questions, or capture all of its dimensions and mechanisms. Instead, economists need the ability to think critically and evaluate the appropriateness of a range of fundamentally different approaches. In doing so, they also need to be able to clearly distinguish and explicitly discuss the moral dilemmas and normative trade-offs involved in economic decisions.

This book sets out a concrete path towards building such a pluralist and real-world based economics curriculum. While we envision a large diversity of possible economics programmes, we suggest that all programmes would be improved by following these three principles: a *pluralist* toolkit of theories and methods, sufficient *real-world* economic knowledge and practical skills, and active training in the consideration of *values* and moral and social questions. To flesh out these principles, we propose ten concrete building blocks: practical material for the creation of courses. These building blocks include introductory material, history of economic thought and reality, forms of economic organisation, research methods, theoretical approaches, normative ideas, practical skills and knowledge of the real economy.

The entire book carries a CC-BY Creative Commons licence, meaning that any part can be freely used, redistributed, or built upon without restrictions. We encourage people to make use of this and apply, edit and adapt the material for their own purposes.

What kind of graduates would a programme based on these ideas and materials produce? It is important to acknowledge that they would not have all the skills that current-day graduates have. They would have less mathematical sophistication, less expertise in econometric analysis, and less knowledge of neoclassical theory. Instead, students would gain a deeper understanding and more concrete knowledge of the economy they live and will work in. This includes:

- An understanding of the linkages between the economy, the environment and society.
- The ability to analyse different types of economic topics and problems, by using a variety of theoretical and methodological approaches.
- An integral understanding of how various smaller mechanisms make up larger economic systems.
- Practical skills for investigating and resolving questions of economic policy: both understanding the context and choosing the right tool.
- The ability to argue morally as well as analytically, and to clearly distinguish the two.

In short, such programmes would produce academically trained professional economists: broad thinkers and practical scholars, rather than students who are trained to write academic research papers.

2 Change Is Necessary and Possible

It will not be easy to build such programmes. We fully realise that these changes cannot be introduced overnight. Surprisingly rare is the academic economist who can teach even a basic introductory course on their national economic sectors and institutions. The structure of the discipline – highly internationalised, methods-centred and organised around a single pyramid structure of journals – does not facilitate the creation of such knowledge. The same applies to pluralism in economic theory: the decades-long marginalisation of valuable schools of thought has left us with a dearth of suitably trained academics.

In addition, academic programmes tend to have a strong path-dependency. Most are only updated infrequently and changed piecemeal. Long-running courses have to be adjusted, the order in which courses build upon each other has to be reconsidered, new courses have to be developed and new expertise has to develop in the economics departments. In many countries, national or international frameworks regulate academic programme content. In short, this is a long road, but one that we believe is both necessary and possible.

The changes we propose are necessary. The devastating impact of our economy on the life-sustaining ecological systems of this planet is increasingly visible, making the realistic study of that economy all the more urgent. The unprecedented centrality of the economy in our society and the big role of economic ideas in political decision-making make it all the more vital for economists to be firmly rooted in the real world, to have a pluralist perspective and to be trained in distinguishing the moral tangles inherent to economic questions. We need to prepare a new generation of economists, and we should start this work now.

The changes we propose are possible. Indeed, they are happening, thanks to the energy of a growing worldwide network of students and academics. More and more pluralist and real-world textbooks, course formats, readers, best practices and other materials are becoming available (see the online *Teaching Materials* resource chapter at economy.st/materials for many examples). Increasingly, faculties are teaching economics primarily as a subject-based pluralist discipline, rather than a method-centred monist approach. Economic faculties are hiring academics from other theoretical schools and other disciplines, thus reversing the narrowing of the past decades and enriching both students and colleagues with fresh insights. Various universities are starting to experiment with teaching-based career tracks, enabling staff to focus on developing better teaching materials rather than focusing almost exclusively on publishing in mainstream academic journals. Pluralist programmes are springing up inside and outside of traditional economics departments, throughout the academic world. Perhaps most importantly, more and more faculties are opening up to the idea of widening their student's view beyond the traditional theories and methods.

3 Calls to Action

While there are hopeful signs of change, this is only the start. We need more students, teachers, programme directors and deans to make a difference and help ensure that the economists of the future are prepared for their roles in society. So what can each of us do to bring economics education to a higher plane?

Students, be critical of what you are learning. Do not just ask: *"Is this part of the exam?"*. Instead, ask: *"Does this reflect the real world?"*, *"In what other way could one also look at this issue?"*, and *"What are the moral dilemmas surrounding this case?"*. Look up the course you are following in chapter *Tool 2: Adapting Existing Courses* and discuss the suggested additions and changes with your teacher. Design your own ideal course with the tool of chapter *Tool 4: Example Courses* and campaign to make your dream into a reality. Talk to your lecturers and find out who is interested in your ideas. Build public support by publishing an open letter or petition that advocates for the creation of this new course.

Get in touch with the programme committee and apply *Tool 3: Curriculum Review* to your programme to see what could be improved. Build, or join, a local team of critical students. Organise a reading group or an event. If you want, you can become affiliated with the international *Rethinking Economics* network and benefit from the experience, contacts and resources of a large worldwide network of student groups. Doing it together will not only help you last longer and achieve more impact, it will also be more fun.

Teachers, think about what you are preparing your students for. Less than 3% of them will become academic economists, the rest will work inside government agencies, policy institutes and think-tanks, (central) banks and other financial corporations, private sector and not-for-profit companies, NGOs and campaign groups, and journalistic entities. As such, they will work on tackling practical and real-world problems, rather than publishing academic articles. So, confront your students with the messy and complex real world, let them practise tackling actual cases, start lectures with today's newspaper, ask guest speakers from the relevant field, and let students go out of the classroom and experience the economy with their own eyes.

Stimulate open discussions and active participation from students, bring in literature from other disciplines, actively expose the weaknesses of the theories you are teaching. Make normative assumptions explicit and let students struggle with the resulting moral dilemmas. Make sure that you are not just pushing through a textbook; be proud of your role as a teacher and *use* it. Make use of the suggestions provided throughout this book, and in particular in *Tool 2: Adapting Existing Courses*. Kick-start discussions, and play the devil's advocate. Trigger students to start thinking, critically and independently.

Most academics reach many more people through their teaching than through their academic papers. Yet today, teaching is underappreciated and under-rewarded. Often, the time allocated for teaching is not nearly enough. Please speak out about this. Challenge that status quo, with the students as your allies.

Deans and programme directors, support and facilitate good teaching. Make sure that your faculty have enough resources and time available for teaching. Enable them to constantly improve their teaching and update the taught material. Give students a voice and role in designing and adapting the courses. Ask yourself: how is our programme built? Was it created through a departmental power struggle about which professors' specialisation is more important and deserves most space in the programme? Or is it carefully designed based on a clear idea of the societal roles students are being prepared for? How is it updated based on changes in society and academic thinking?

Do not be afraid to deviate from the standard programme at other universities. Variety in programmes makes economics education stronger, not weaker. It also makes your university stand out. Take a look at the chapter *Tool 5: Example Curricula* and draw inspiration from other innovative programmes. Try your hand at *Tool 3: Curriculum Review*, to see where in your programme there might be gaps in terms of relevant knowledge or skills. You could also ask teachers or students to run this analysis, and set up a series of meetings to discuss the outcomes. Or you could ask members of the international *Rethinking Economics* movement to organise a workshop or conference to further explore how the programme could be improved. Attention and open discussion about how to better economics education can only be positive, contributing to better prepared future economists.

Governments, create the right conditions for good economics education. Look at how resources for teaching and research are distributed. Does this encourage relevant, open-minded and interdisciplinary research and teaching, or does it encourage scoring on the intellectual square millimetre through a competitive 'publish or perish' system? Are universities stimulated to offer their faculty career options focused on education and reward good teaching? Governments could also follow the French example (French Government, 2014) and initiate an independent and in-depth investigation of the state of the economics education in the country.

Climate change, inequality, economic instability, ageing, power concentration, pandemics, biodiversity loss, social polarisation, resource depletion, migration, poverty; these are core challenges for the world of today and tomorrow. Economists have a central role in society and need to tackle these challenges head-on. Reforming and modernising economics education is therefore of great importance not only to the students and teachers directly involved in it, but also to society as a whole. Let's build better courses and programmes, together.

References

Advani, A., Ash, E., Cai, D., & Rasul, I. (2021). Race-related research in economics and other social sciences. *Working Paper of the Econometric Society World Congress.*

Akerlof, G. A. (1978). The market for "lemons": Quality uncertainty and the market mechanism. In *Uncertainty in economics* (pp. 235-251). Elsevier.

Akerlof, G. A. (2020). Sins of Omission and the Practice of Economics. *Journal of Economic Literature, 58*(2), 405-418.

Aldred, J. (2019). *Licence to be bad: How economics corrupted us.* Penguin UK.

Allan, B. B., & Meckling, J. O. (2021). Creative Learning and Policy Ideas: The Global Rise of Green Growth. *Perspectives on Politics,* 1-19.

Allgood, S., Badgett, L., Bayer, A., Bertrand, M., Black, S. E., Bloom, N., & Cook, L. D. (2019). *AEA Professional Climate Survey: Final Report* https://www.aeaweb.org/resources/member-docs/final-climate-survey-results-sept-2019

Almond, G. A. (1991). Capitalism and democracy. *PS: Political Science and Politics, 24*(3), 467-474.

Anderson, L. W. (2002). Curricular alignment: A re-examination. *Theory into practice, 41*(4), 255-260.

Anderson, L. W., & Krathwohl, D. R. (2001). *A taxonomy for learning, teaching, and assessing: A revision of Bloom's taxonomy of educational objectives. .* Longman.

Andre, P., & Falk, M. (2021). *What's worth knowing? Economists' opinions about economics.* Working Paper.

Antecol, H., Bedard, K., & Stearns, J. (2018). Equal but inequitable: Who benefits from gender-neutral tenure clock stopping policies? *American Economic Review, 108*(9), 2420-2441.

Babcock, L., Recalde, M. P., Vesterlund, L., & Weingart, L. (2017). Gender differences in accepting and receiving requests for tasks with low promotability. *American Economic Review, 107*(3), 714-747.

Backhouse, R. E. (1994). *Economists and the economy: the evolution of economic ideas.* Transaction Publishers.

Backhouse, R. E., & Medema, S. G. (2009a). Defining economics: the long road to acceptance of the Robbins definition. *Economica, 76,* 805-820.

Backhouse, R. E., & Medema, S. G. (2009b). Retrospectives: On the definition of economics. *Journal of economic perspectives, 23*(1), 221-233.

Bartels, L. M. (2016). *Unequal democracy.* Princeton University Press.

Basole, A., & Jayadev, A. (2018). A Better Economics for the Indian Context. *Economic & Political Weekly, 53*(24).

Bauman, Y., & Rose, E. (2011). Selection or indoctrination: Why do economics students donate less than the rest? *Journal of Economic Behavior & Organization, 79*(3), 318-327.

Bayer, A. (2018). The Economics Profession's Unique Problem With Diversity. *The Minority Report*(10), 17.

Bayer, A., Bhanot, S. P., Bronchetti, E. T., & O'Connell, S. A. (2020). *Diagnosing the learning environment for diverse students in introductory economics: An analysis of relevance, belonging, and growth mindsets* (Vol. 110).

Bayer, A., & Rouse, C. E. (2016). Diversity in the economics profession: A new attack on an old problem. *Journal of economic perspectives, 30*(4), 221-242.

Becker, G. S. (1973). A theory of marriage: Part I. *Journal of Political economy, 81*(4), 813-846.

Becker, G. S. (1976). *The economic approach to human behavior* (Vol. 803). University of Chicago press.

Becker, G. S. (2010). *The economics of discrimination.* University of Chicago press.

Beinhocker, E. D. (2006). *The Origin of Wealth: The Radical Remaking of Economics and What it Means for Business and Society.* Harvard University Press.

Berggren, N., Jordahl, H., & Stern, C. (2009). The Political Opinions of Swedish Social Scientists. *Finnish economic papers, 22*(2), 75-88.

Bertrand, M., & Mullainathan, S. (2004). Are Emily and Greg more employable than Lakisha and Jamal? A field experiment on labor market discrimination. *American Economic Review, 94*(4), 991-1013.

Bewley, T. F. (1999). *Why wages don't fall during a recession.* Harvard University Press.

Biggs, J. (2003). Aligning teaching for constructing learning. *Higher Education Academy, 1*(4).

Blaug, M. (2001). No history of ideas, please, we're economists. *Journal of economic perspectives, 15*(1), 145-164.

Bloom, B. S. (1956). *Taxonomy of educational objectives.* McKay.

Boardman, A. E., Greenberg, D. H., Vining, A. R., & Weimer, D. L. (2017). *Cost-benefit analysis: concepts and practice.* Cambridge University Press.

Boring, A., & Zignago, S. (2018). *Economics: where are the women?* Banque de France. https://blocnotesdeleco.banque-france.fr/en/blog-entry/economics-where-are-women

Boumans, M., & Davis, J. B. (2015). *Economic methodology: Understanding economics as a science.* Macmillan International Higher Education.

Bowles, S., & Carlin, W. (2020). What students learn in economics 101: Time for a change. *Journal of Economic Literature, 58*(1), 176-214.

Bowles, S., & Gintis, H. (2012). *Democracy and capitalism: Property, community, and the contradictions of modern social thought.* Routledge.

Brillant, L. (2018). Ursula Hicks' and Vera Lutz's contributions to development finance 1. In K. Madden & R. W. Dimand (Eds.), *The Routledge Handbook of the History of Women's Economic Thought* (pp. 341-357). Routledge.

Butler-Sloss, S., & Beckmann, M. (2021). *Economics journals' engagement in the planetary emergency: a misallocation of resources?* Economists for Future. https://econ4future.org/wp-content/uploads/2021/04/economics-journals-engagement-in-the-planetary-emergency-v3.pdf

Butler, A. (2009). The illusion of objectivity: implications for teaching economics. In R. F. Garnett Jr, E. Olsen, & M. Starr (Eds.), *Economic pluralism* (pp. 258-271). Routledge.

Butler, G., Jones, E., & Stilwell, F. J. (2009). *Political economy now!: The struggle for alternative economics at the University of Sydney.* Darlington Press.

Butterfield, H. (1931). *The Whig interpretation of history.* WW Norton & Company.

Carlin, B. A., Gelb, B. D., Belinne, J. K., & Ramchand, L. (2018). Bridging the gender gap in confidence. *Business Horizons, 61*(5), 765-774.

Carlin, W. (2021). *Personal Communication.*

Carruthers, B. G., & Ariovich, L. (2010). *Money and credit: A sociological approach* (Vol. 6). Polity.

Casselman, B., & Tankersley, J. (2020). Economics, Dominated by White Men, Is Roiled by Black Lives Matter. *The New York Times.* https://www.nytimes.com/2020/06/10/business/economy/white-economists-black-lives-matter.html

Ceballos, G., Ehrlich, P. R., & Dirzo, R. (2017). Biological annihilation via the ongoing sixth mass extinction signaled by vertebrate population losses and declines. *Proceedings of the national academy of sciences, 114*(30), E6089-E6096.

Ceci, S. J., Ginther, D. K., Kahn, S., & Williams, W. M. (2014). Women in academic science: A changing landscape. *Psychological science in the public interest, 15*(3), 75-141.

Cedrini, M., & Fontana, M. (2018). Just another niche in the wall? How specialization is changing the face of mainstream economics. *Cambridge journal of economics, 42*(2), 427-451.

Cedrini, M. A., & Fontana, M. (2015). Mainstreaming. Reflections on the origins and fate of mainstream pluralism. *CESMEP Working Paper Series.*

Chang, H.-J. (2012). When Brian Eno met Ha-Joon Chang. *The Guardian*. https://www.theguardian.com/music/2012/nov/11/brian-eno-ha-joon-chang

Chang, H.-J. (2014). *Economics: the user's guide* (Vol. 1). Bloomsbury Publishing USA.

Chase-Dunn, C., & Hall, T. D. (1997). *Rise and demise: Comparing world-systems*. Routledge.

Chelwa, G. (2016). Decolonizing the teaching of economics. *Africa Is a Country*. https://africasacountry.com/2016/04/decolonizing-the-teaching-of-economics

Cherrier, B. (2016). Is there really an empirical turn in economics. *Institute for New Economic Thinking blog 29th September*. https://www.ineteconomics.org/perspectives/blog/is-there-really-an-empirical-turn-in-economics

Chi, M. T. (2009). Active-constructive-interactive: A conceptual framework for differentiating learning activities. *Topics in cognitive science, 1*(1), 73-105.

Clower, R. W. (1995). Axiomatics in economics. *Southern Economic Journal, 62*(2), 307-319.

Coase, R. H. (1960). The problem of social cost. In C. Gopalakrishnan (Ed.), *Classic papers in natural resource economics* (pp. 87-137). Springer.

Coase, R. H. (1978). Economics and contiguous disciplines. *The Journal of Legal Studies, 7*(2).

Coase, R. H. (1999). Opening Address. The Annual Conference of the International Society of New Institutional Economics, Washington, DC, USA.

Coase, R. H. (2012). *The firm, the market, and the law*. University of Chicago press.

Coates, D. (2005). *Varieties of capitalism, varieties of approaches*. Springer.

Cohen, A. J., & Harcourt, G. C. (2003). Retrospectives: whatever happened to the Cambridge capital theory controversies? *Journal of economic perspectives, 17*(1), 199-214.

Colander, D. (1992). Retrospectives: The lost art of economics. *Journal of economic perspectives, 6*(3), 191-198.

Colander, D. (2000). The death of neoclassical economics. *Journal of the History of Economic Thought, 22*(2), 127-143.

Colander, D. (2001). *The lost art of economics: Essays on economics and the economics profession*. Edward Elgar Cheltenham.

Colander, D. (2003). Caveat lector: Living with the 15% rule. In *The stories economists tell: Essays on the art of teaching economics* (pp. 33-43). McGraw-Hill.

Colander, D. (2008). *The making of an economist, redux*. Princeton University Press.

Colander, D., & Klamer, A. (1987). The making of an economist. *Journal of economic perspectives, 1*(2), 95-111.

Colander, D., & Landreth, H. (1998). Political Influence on the Textbook Keynesian Revolution. In *Keynesianism and the Keynesian Revolution in America* (pp. 59-72). Edward Elgar.

Colander, D., & McGoldrick, K. (2009). The Teagle Foundation Report: the economics major as part of a liberal education. In *Educating economists: The Teagle discussion on re-evaluating the undergraduate economics major*. Edward Elgar.

Colander, D. C., & McGoldrick, K. (2010). *Educating economists: The Teagle discussion on re-evaluating the undergraduate economics major*. Edward Elgar.

Comaroff, J., & Comaroff, J. (2012). Theory from the South: or How Euro-America is evolving towards Africa. *Boulder/London: Paradigm*.

Conti-Brown, P. (2009). A proposed fat-tail risk metric: disclosures, derivatives, and the measurement of financial risk. *Washington University Law Review, 87*, 1461.

CORE-Team. (2017). *The Economy: Economics for a Changing World*. Oxford University Press.

Courvisanos, J., Doughney, J., & Millmow, A. (2016). *Reclaiming Pluralism in Economics*. Routledge.

Cousins, J. B., & Chouinard, J. A. (2012). *Participatory evaluation up close: An integration of research-based knowledge*. Information Age Publishing.

Coyle, D. (2012). *What's the Use of Economics? Teaching the Dismal Science After the Crisis*. London Publishing Partnership.

Crawford, C., Davies, N. M., & Smith, S. (2018). *Why do so few women study economics? Evidence from England*. Institute for Fiscal Studies. https://www.res.org.uk/uploads/assets/uploaded/6c3fd338-88d6-47ea-bf2f302dfee7f37e.pdf

Da Costa, P. N. (2017). The 'sobering' gender and racial gap among economists is hurting everyone. *Business Insider* https://www.businessinsider.nl/gender-and-racial-gaps-in-economics-are-hurting-everyone-2017-9?international=true&r=US

Daly, H. E., & Farley, J. (2011). *Ecological economics: principles and applications*. Island press.

Das, J., Do, Q.-T., Shaines, K., & Srikant, S. (2013). US and them: The geography of academic research. *Journal of Development Economics, 105*, 112-130.

Davies, H. T., & Nutley, S. M. (2000). *What works?: Evidence-based policy and practice in public services*. Policy Press.

Davis, J. B. (2002). Review: The Lost Art of Economics, Essays on Economics and the Economics Profession. *History of Economic Ideas, 10*(2).

Davis, J. B. (2006). The turn in economics: neoclassical dominance to mainstream pluralism? *Journal of institutional economics, 2*(1), 1-20.

De Benedictis, L., & Di Maio, M. (2011). Economists' views about the economy: Evidence from a survey of Italian economists. *Rivista italiana degli economisti, 16*(1), 37-84.

de Goede, M., Belder, R., & De Jonge, J. (2014). *Promoveren in Nederland: Motivatie en loopbaanverwachtingen van promovendi.* Rathenau Instituut.

de Langhe, R. (2009). Why should I adopt pluralism? In R. F. Garnett Jr, E. Olsen, & M. Starr (Eds.), *Economic pluralism* (pp. 109-120). Routledge.

Decker, S., Elsner, W., & Flechtner, S. (2018). *Advancing pluralism in teaching economics: International perspectives on a textbook science.* Routledge.

Decker, S., Elsner, W., & Flechtner, S. (2019). *Principles and Pluralist Approaches in Teaching Economics: Towards a Transformative Science* (Vol. 41). Routledge.

DeMartino, G. F., & McCloskey, D. N. (2016). *The Oxford handbook of professional economic ethics.* Oxford University Press.

Denis, A. (2009). Pluralism in economics education. *International Review of Economics Education, 8*(2), 6-22.

Dequech, D. (2017). Some institutions (social norms and conventions) of contemporary mainstream economics, macroeconomics and financial economics. *Cambridge journal of economics, 41*(6), 1627-1652.

Dolar, V. (2021). The gender gap in economics is huge – it's even worse than tech. *The Conversation.* https://theconversation.com/the-gender-gap-in-economics-is-huge-its-even-worse-than-tech-156275

Dow, S. (2009). History of Thought, Methodology and Pluralism. *The Handbook of Pluralist Economics Education, London, Routledge,* 43-53.

Dutch Government. (2020). *Beantwoording Kamervragen private equity in de kinderopvang.* https://www.rijksoverheid.nl/documenten/kamerstukken/2020/09/14/beantwoording-kamervragen-private-equity-in-de-kinderopvang

Dutch Parliament. (2019). *Rondetafelgesprek: Private equity in de kinderopvang.* https://www.tweedekamer.nl/debat_en_vergadering/commissievergaderingen/details?id=2019A01311

Earle, J., Moran, C., & Ward-Perkins, Z. (2016). *The econocracy: the perils of leaving economics to the experts.* Manchester University Press.

Eliassen, R. L. (2016). *On the liberty of thought and discussion in economics.* Anglia Ruskin University.

Ely, R. T. (1898). Fraternalism vs. Paternalism in Government. *The Century Magazine.*

Ely, R. T. (1906). *Studies in the Evolution of Industrial Society.* The MacMillan Company.

European-Commission. (2021). *Sustainable finance*. https://ec.europa. eu/info/business-economy-euro/banking-and-finance/ sustainable-finance_en

FEE. (2017). *The Case against Pluralism in Economics*. https://fee.org/articles/ the-case-against-pluralism-in-economics/

FEE. (2021). *Mission*. https://fee.org/about/

Fine, B., & Milonakis, D. (2009). *From economics imperialism to freakonomics: The shifting boundaries between economics and other social sciences*. Routledge.

Fourcade, M. (2009). *Economists and societies*. Princeton.

Fourcade, M., & Healy, K. (2007). Moral views of market society. *Annual review of Sociology, 33*.

Fourcade, M., Ollion, E., & Algan, Y. (2015). The superiority of economists. *Journal of economic perspectives, 29*(1), 89-114.

Francis, D., & Opoku-Agyeman, A. G. (2020). Economists' Silence on Racism Is 100 Years in the Making. *Newsweek*. https://www.newsweek.com/ economists-silence-racism-100-years-making-opinion-1509790

Frank, R. H. (2011). Less is more: The perils of trying to cover too much in microeconomic principles. In G. M. Hoyt & K. McGoldrick (Eds.), *International handbook on teaching and learning economics*. Edward Elgar Publishing.

Freeman, A., Chick, V., & Kayatekin, S. (2014). Samuelson's ghosts: Whig history and the reinterpretation of economic theory. *Cambridge journal of economics, 38*(3), 519-529.

Freeman, S., Eddy, S. L., McDonough, M., Smith, M. K., Okoroafor, N., Jordt, H., & Wenderoth, M. P. (2014). Active learning increases student performance in science, engineering, and mathematics. *Proceedings of the national academy of sciences, 111*(23), 8410-8415.

French-Government. (2014). *L'avenir des sciences économiques à l'Université en France*. https://cache.media.enseignementsup-recherche.gouv.fr/file/ Formations_et_diplomes/05/1/Rapport_Hautcoeur2014_328051.pdf

Friedman, M. (1962). *Capitalism and Freedom*. University of Chicago Press

Fullbrook, E. (2003). *The Crisis in Economics: the post-autistic economics movement: the first 600 days* (Vol. 22). Psychology Press.

Fullbrook, E. (2007). *Real world economics: a post-autistic economics reader* (Vol. 1). Anthem Press.

Fullbrook, E. (2008). *Pluralist economics*. Zed Books.

Galbraith, J. K. (1981). *A life in our times*. Plunkett Lake Press.

Gans, J. S., & Shepherd, G. B. (1994). How are the mighty fallen: Rejected classic articles by leading economists. *Journal of economic perspectives, 8*(1), 165-179.

Garnett Jr, R. F., Olsen, E., & Starr, M. (2009). *Economic pluralism* (Vol. 122). Routledge.

Gilens, M. (2012). *Affluence and influence: Economic inequality and political power in America*. Princeton University Press.

Gilens, M., & Page, B. I. (2014). Testing theories of American politics: Elites, interest groups, and average citizens. *Perspectives on Politics, 12*(3), 564-581.

Ginther, D. K., & Kahn, S. (2004). Women in economics: moving up or falling off the academic career ladder? *Journal of economic perspectives, 18*(3), 193-214.

Girardi, D., Mamunuru, S. M., Halliday, S. D., & Bowles, S. (2021). Does economics make you selfish? *UMass Amherst Economics Department Working Paper Series*.

Goodwin, N., Harris, J. M., Nelson, J. A., Roach, B., & Torras, M. (2019). *Principles of economics in context*. Routledge.

Gräbner, C., & Strunk, B. (2020). Pluralism in economics: its critiques and their lessons. *Journal of Economic Methodology, 27*(4), 311-329.

Graeber, D. (2005). Value: anthropological theories of value. In J. Carrier (Ed.), *A handbook of economic anthropology*. Edward Elgar Publishing.

Granovetter, M. (1985). Economic action and social structure: The problem of embeddedness. *American Journal of Sociology, 91*, 22-45.

Greenwald, A. G., & Banaji, M. R. (1995). Implicit social cognition: attitudes, self-esteem, and stereotypes. *Psychological review, 102*(1), 4.

Greenwald, A. G., & Krieger, L. H. (2006). Implicit bias: Scientific foundations. *California law review, 94*(4), 945-967.

Groenewegen, J. (2007). *Teaching pluralism in economics*. Edward Elgar Publishing.

Grossbard, S. (1993). *On the Economics of Marriage-A Theory of Marriage, Labor and Divorce*. Westview Press.

Guba, E. G., & Lincoln, Y. S. (1989). *Fourth generation evaluation*. Sage.

Haberl, H., Wiedenhofer, D., Virág, D., Kalt, G., Plank, B., Brockway, P., Fishman, T., Hausknost, D., Krausmann, F., & Leon-Gruchalski, B. (2020). A systematic review of the evidence on decoupling of GDP, resource use and GHG emissions, part II: synthesizing the insights. *Environmental Research Letters, 15*(6), 065003.

Halpern, D. F., Benbow, C. P., Geary, D. C., Gur, R. C., Hyde, J. S., & Gernsbacher, M. A. (2007). The science of sex differences in science and mathematics. *Psychological science in the public interest, 8*(1), 1-51.

Hansen, W. L. (1986). What knowledge is most worth knowing--for economics majors? *The American Economic Review, 76*(2), 149-152.

Hansen, W. L. (2001). Expected proficiencies for undergraduate economics majors. *The Journal of Economic Education, 32*(3), 231-242.

Hansen, W. L. (2011). An expected proficiencies approach to the economics major. In G. M. Hoyt & K. McGoldrick (Eds.), *International handbook on teaching and learning economics*. Edward Elgar Publishing.

Hardoon, D., Fuentes-Nieva, R., & Ayele, S. (2016). *An Economy for the 1%: How privilege and power in the economy drive extreme inequality and how this can be stopped.* Oxfam International. https://www-cdn.oxfam. org/s3fs-public/file_attachments/bp210-economy-one-percent-tax-havens-180116-en_0.pdf

Hart, K. (2005). Money: one anthropologist's view. In J. Carrier (Ed.), *A handbook of economic anthropology.* Edward Elgar Publishing.

Harvey, J. T. (2019). Do Women Avoid Economics...Or Does Economics Avoid Women? *Forbes.* https://www.forbes.com/sites/ johntharvey/2019/01/11/do-women-avoid-economics-or-does-economics-avoid-women/?sh=2220d1422f32

Hayek, F. (1974). The Nobel Banquet Speech.

Heilbroner, R. L. (1953). *The worldly philosophers: The lives, times and ideas of the great economic thinkers.* Simon and Schuster.

Heilbroner, R. L. (1960). *The future as history.* Harper & Row.

Hengel, E. (2017). Publishing while female are women held to higher standards? Evidence from peer review. https://www.aeaweb.org/ conference/2018/preliminary/paper/FZ9iRYss

Hickel, J. (2020). *Less is more: How degrowth will save the world.* Random House.

Hickel, J., & Kallis, G. (2020). Is green growth possible? *New political economy, 25*(4), 469-486.

Hirschman, A. O. (1982). Rival interpretations of market society: Civilizing, destructive, or feeble? *Journal of Economic Literature, 20*(4), 1463-1484.

Ho, K. (2009). *Liquidated: an ethnography of Wall Street.* Duke University Press.

Hodgson, G. M., Mäki, U., & McCloskey, D. N. (1992). Plea for a pluralistic and rigorous economics. *American Economic Review, 82*(2), 25.

Howard, M., & King, J. E. (2001). 'State capitalism'in the Soviet Union. *History of Economics Review, 34*(1), 110-126.

Hoyt, G. M., & McGoldrick, K. (2012). *International handbook on teaching and learning economics.* Edward Elgar Publishing.

Hurston, Z. N. (1942). *Dust tracks on a road: an autobiography.* Hutchinson & Co.

Hütten, M., Maman, D., Rosenhek, Z., & Thiemann, M. (2018). Critical financial literacy: an agenda. *International Journal of Pluralism and Economics Education, 9*(3), 274-291.

IDEAS. (2021). *Female representation in Economics, as of April 2021.* https:// ideas.repec.org/top/female.html

Ihlanfeldt, K., & Mayock, T. (2009). Price discrimination in the housing market. *Journal of Urban Economics, 66*(2), 125-140.

INET. (2011). *Three-Year Economics Undergraduate Curriculum.*

Ingham, G. (2013). *Capitalism: With a new postscript on the financial crisis and its aftermath.* John Wiley & Sons.

Jackson, W. A. (2018). Strategic pluralism and monism in heterodox economics. *Review of Radical Political Economics, 50*(2), 237-251.

Javdani, M. (2019). The way to fix bias in economics is to recruit more women. *Financial Times.* https://www.ft.com/content/5b9b47d2-2e12-11e9-80d2-7b637a9e1ba1

Javdani, M., & Chang, H.-J. (2019). Who said or what said? Estimating ideological bias in views among economists. *Discussion Paper Series of the Institute of Labor Economics, 12738.*

Jo, T.-H. (2016). The Social Provisioning Process and Heterodox Economics. *MPRA Working Paper Series.*

Kelton, S. (2018). *Stephanie Kelton on MMT and debunking budget deficit myths.*

Keynes, J. M. (1924). Alfred Marshall. *The Economic Journal, 34*(135), 311-372.

Keynes, J. M. (1930). Economic possibilities for our grandchildren [2010 Edition]. In *Essays in persuasion* (pp. 321-332). Springer.

Keynes, J. M. (1936). *The general theory of employment, interest, and money.* Springer.

Keynes, J. M. (1938). Letter to Sir Roy Harrod [2012 edition]. In E. Johnson & D. Moggridge (Eds.), *The Collected Writings of John Maynard Keynes.* Cambridge University Press.

Keynes, J. N. (1891). *The scope and method of political economy.* Routledge.

Khaldun, I. (1377). *The Muqaddimah: An Introduction to History [2015 Abridged Edition].* Princeton University Press.

Kimenyi, M. S., & Shughart, W. F. (1986). Economics of suicide: Rational or irrational choice. *Atlantic Economic Journal, 14*(1), 120-121.

Klein, D. B., & Stern, C. (2006). Economists' policy views and voting. *Public Choice, 126*(3), 331-342.

Kneppers, L., Van Boxtel, C., & van Hout-Wolters, B. (2012). The road to transfer: concept and context approaches to the subject of economics in secondary school. *International Review of Economics Education, 11*(1), 36-56.

Knight, F. H. (1933). *The economic organization.* Transaction Publishers.

Korzybski, A. (1931). A non-Aristotelian system and its necessity for rigour in mathematics and physics. In *Science and Sanity.* Institute of General Semantics.

Krugman, P. (2009). How did economists get it so wrong? *The New York Times, 2*(9), 2009. https://www.nytimes.com/2009/09/06/magazine/06Economic-t.html

Krugman, P., & Wells, R. (2012). *Economics.* Worth Publishers.

Kuhn, T., Nicoli, F., & Vandenbroucke, F. (2020). Preferences for European unemployment insurance: a question of economic ideology or EU support? *Journal of European Public Policy*, 27(2), 208-226.

Kvangraven, I. H., Styve, M. D., Kufakurinani, U., & Santanta, F. (2017). *Dialogues on Development Volume 1: Dependency*. Institute for New Economic Thinking.

Lawson, T. (2012). *Reorienting economics*. Routledge.

Lee, F. (2009). *A history of heterodox economics: challenging the mainstream in the twentieth century*. Routledge.

Lewis, S. L., & Maslin, M. A. (2015). Defining the anthropocene. *Nature*, 519(7542), 171-180.

Lewis, W. A. (1955). *Theory of economic growth*. Routledge.

Lindblom, C. E. (1982). The market as prison. *The Journal of Politics*, 44(2), 324-336.

Lopez, I. F. H. (2000). Institutional racism: Judicial conduct and a new theory of racial discrimination. *Yale Law Journal*, 1717-1884.

Lundberg, S., & Stearns, J. (2019). Women in economics: Stalled progress. *Journal of economic perspectives*, 33(1), 3-22.

Maas, H. (2014). *Economic methodology: A historical introduction*. Routledge.

MacKenzie, D. (2008). *An engine, not a camera: How financial models shape markets*. MIT Press.

MacKenzie, D., & Millo, Y. (2003). Constructing a market, performing theory: The historical sociology of a financial derivatives exchange. *American Journal of Sociology*, 109(1), 107-145.

MacKenzie, D., Muniesa, F., & Siu, L. (2007). *Do Economists Make Markets? On the Performativity of Economics*. Princeton University Press.

Martyn, R. (2017). What even is economic pluralism? *Rethinking Economics*. https://www.rethinkeconomics.org/journal/what-even-is-economic-pluralism/

Marx, K. (1867). *Das Kapital. Kritik der politischen Ökonomie*. Verlag von Otto Meisner.

Marx, K., & Engels, F. (1848). *The Communist Manifesto*. https://www.marxists.org/archive/marx/works/download/pdf/Manifesto.pdf

May, A. M., McGarvey, M. G., & Whaples, R. (2014). Are disagreements among male and female economists marginal at best?: A survey of AEA members and their views on economics and economic policy. *Contemporary Economic Policy*, 32(1), 111-132.

Mazzucato, M. (2018). *The value of everything: Making and taking in the global economy*. Hachette UK.

Mearman, A., Wakeley, T., Shoib, G., & Webber, D. (2011). Does pluralism in economics education make better educated, happier students? A qualitative analysis. *International Review of Economics Education, 10*(2), 50-62.

Meckling, J., & Allan, B. B. (2020). The evolution of ideas in global climate policy. *Nature Climate Change, 10*(5), 434-438.

Mengel, F., Sauermann, J., & Zölitz, U. (2019). Gender bias in teaching evaluations. *Journal of the European Economic Association, 17*(2), 535-566.

Mercure, J.-F., Sharpe, S., Vinuales, J., Ives, M., Grubb, M., Pollitt, H., Knobloch, F., & Nijsse, F. (2020). Deciding how to decide: Risk-opportunity analysis for transformative policy design and appraisal. *UCL IIPP Working Paper Series*. https://www.ucl.ac.uk/bartlett/public-purpose/sites/public-purpose/files/final_iipp_2021-03_roa_simon_sharpe_et_al_21_jan.pdf

Morgan, J. (2015). *What is neoclassical economics?: debating the origins, meaning and significance*. Routledge.

Morgan, M. S. (2012). *The world in the model: How economists work and think*. Cambridge University Press.

Morgan, M. S., & Rutherford, M. (1998). From interwar pluralism to postwar neoclassicism. *History of Political Economy, 30*.

Mounk, Y. (2018). *The people vs. democracy: Why our freedom is in danger and how to save it*. Harvard University Press.

Myers, S. C., Nelson, M. A., & Stratton, R. W. (2009). Assessing an economics programme: Hansen proficiencies, ePortfolio, and undergraduate research. *International Review of Economics Education, 8*(1), 87-105.

Naritomi, J., Sequeira, S., Weigel, J., & Weinhold, D. (2020). RCTs as an opportunity to promote interdisciplinary, inclusive, and diverse quantitative development research. *World Development, 127*, 104832.

Nelson, E. (2019). Economics needs to do more than attract women to solve its gender problem. *Quartz*. https://qz.com/1637906/diversity-in-economics-depends-on-more-than-just-attracting-women/

Nelson, J. A. (2009). The principles course. *The handbook of pluralist economics education, 9*, 57.

Nelson, J. A. (2018). Gender and Failures of Rationality in Economic Analysis. *Gender in the Economics Profession II by the American Economic Association*.

Nicoli, F., Kuhn, T., & Burgoon, B. (2020). Collective identities, European solidarity: identification patterns and preferences for European social insurance. *JCMS: Journal of Common Market Studies, 58*(1), 76-95.

Nolan, P., & Lenski, G. (2003). *Human societies*. Oxford University Press.

North, D. C. (1990). *Institutions, institutional change and economic performance*. Cambridge university press.

O'Donnell, R. (2002). What kind of economics graduates do we want? *Australasian Journal of Economics Education, 1*(1), 41-60.

O'Doherty, R., Street, D., Webber, C., & Lane, C. (2007). The skills and knowledge of the graduate economist. *University of the West of England, Bristol*.

O'Donnell, R. (2009). Economic pluralism and skill formation. In R. F. Garnett Jr, E. Olsen, & M. Starr (Eds.), *Economic pluralism*.

OECD. (2018). Including unpaid household activities: An estimate of its impact on macro-economic indicators in the G7 economies and the way forward. https://www.oecd.org/officialdocuments/publicdisplayd ocumentpdf/?cote=SDD/DOC(2018)4&docLanguage=En

OECD. (2021). *Green growth and sustainable development*. https://www.oecd. org/greengrowth/

Ostrom, E. (1990). *Governing the commons: The evolution of institutions for collective action*. Cambridge University Press.

Oswald, A., & Stern, N. (2019). Why are economists letting down the world on climate change. *VoxEU*. https://voxeu.org/article/ why-are-economists-letting-down-world-climate-change

Parvin, M. (1992). Is Teaching Neoclassical Economics as the Science of Economics Moral? *The Journal of Economic Education, 23*(1), 65-78.

Pawson, R. (2002). *Evidence-Based policy: The Promise of Realist Synthesis, Centre for Evidence Based Policy & Practice Working Paper 4*.

Pawson, R., & Tilley, N. (2001). Realistic evaluation bloodlines. *American Journal of Evaluation, 22*(3), 317-324.

PEPS. (2014). The case for pluralism: what French undergraduate economics teaching is all about and how it can be improved. *International Journal of Pluralism and Economics Education, 5*(4), 385-400.

Perez, C. C. (2019). *Invisible women: Exposing data bias in a world designed for men*. Random House.

Perry, K. (2020). Rethink economics to help marginalized people. *Nature, 582*(7812), 341-341.

Polanyi, K. (1944). *The Great Transformation*. Farrar & Rinehart.

Pomorina, I. (2012). Economics graduates' skills and employability. *Economics Network*. https://www.economicsnetwork.ac.uk/sites/ default/files/Ashley/EN%20Employers%20Survey%202012%20-%20 Full%20Report(2).pdf

Proctor, J. C. (2019). *Mapping Pluralist Research: An overview of research within the student movement for pluralism in economics*. oikos International. https://cdn.oikos-international.org/intl/old/2019/03/Mapping-Pluralist-Research-0319.pdf?fbclid=IwAR32UXbUMbF6YHAbv1WiO6iRgEv7ABCyEsR3VwSUr4CLj3r5PVAZZt9WIlE

Purdie-Vaughns, V., Steele, C. M., Davies, P. G., Ditlmann, R., & Crosby, J. R. (2008). Social identity contingencies: how diversity cues signal threat or safety for African Americans in mainstream institutions. *Journal of personality and social psychology*, 94(4), 615.

Raveaud, G. (2009). A pluralist teaching of economics: why and how. In R. F. Garnett Jr, E. Olsen, & M. Starr (Eds.), *Economic pluralism* (Vol. 122). Routledge.

Reardon, J. (2009). *The handbook of pluralist economics education*. Routledge.

Reardon, J., & Madi, M. A. (2014). *The economics curriculum: towards a radical reformulation*. College Publications.

Rethinking Economics, & Ecnmy. (2018). *Doing Economics Differently*. https://www.ecnmy.org/wp-content/uploads/2018/10/RE-Economy-Doing-Economics-Differently-Report-September-2018-DIGITAL.pdf

Robbins, L. (1932). *An essay on the nature and significance of economic science*. Ludwig von Mises Institute.

Robinson, J. A., & Acemoglu, D. (2012). *Why nations fail: The origins of power, prosperity and poverty*. Profile London.

Rodrik, D. (2011). *The globalization paradox: why global markets, states, and democracy can't coexist*. Oxford University Press.

Rodrik, D. (2015). *Economics rules: The rights and wrongs of the dismal science*. WW Norton & Company.

Roncaglia, A. (2017). The economist as an expert: a prince, a servant or a citizen. *Institute for New Economic Thinking blog*. https://www.ineteconomics.org/perspectives/blog/the-economist-as-an-expert-a-prince-a-servant-or-a-citizen

Roosenboom, P. (2020). Vijf jaar private equity: Hogere prijzen, meer schuld en grotere deals. *M&A Magazine*. https://repub.eur.nl/pub/129152

Salanti, A., & Screpanti, E. (1997). *Pluralism in economics: new perspectives in history and methodology*. Edward Elgar Publishing.

Samuels, W. J., Biddle, J. E., & Davis, J. B. (2008). *A companion to the history of economic thought*. John Wiley & Sons.

Samuelson, P. A. (1987). Out of the closet: a program for the whig history of economic science. *Journal of the History of Economic Thought*, 9(1), 51-60.

Samuelson, P. A. (1990). Foreword. In P. Saunders & W. B. Walstad (Eds.), *The Principles of Economics Course*. McGraw-Hill.

Sandberg, S. (2013). *Lean in: Women, work, and the will to lead.* Random House.

Sarsons, H., Gërxhani, K., Reuben, E., & Schram, A. (2021). Gender differences in recognition for group work. *Journal of Political economy, 129*(1), 000-000.

Say, J.-B. (1803). *A treatise on political economy: or the production, distribution, and consumption of wealth.* Grigg & Elliot.

Schakel, W., Burgoon, B., & Hakhverdian, A. (2020). Real but unequal representation in welfare state reform. *Politics & Society, 48*(1), 131-163.

Schulak, E.-M., & Unterköfler, H. (2011). *The Austrian school of economics: A history of its ideas, ambassadors, and institutions.* Ludwig von Mises Institute.

Schumpeter, J. A. (1911). *The theory of economic development: An inquiry into profits, capital, credit, interest, and the business cycle [translated in 1934]* (Vol. 1). New Brunswick

Schumpeter, J. A. (1942). *Capitalism, Socialism and Democracy.* Columbia University Press.

Schumpeter, J. A. (1954). *History of economic analysis.* Routledge.

Sen, A. (1987). *On Ethics and Economics.* Blackwell Publishing.

Sen, A. (2005). *Sen, McCloskey, and the Future of Heterodox Economics* [Interview]. Post-Autistic Economics Review. http://www.paecon. net/PAEReview/issue35/Garnett35.htm

Sent, E.-M. (2006). Pluralisms in economics. In S. H. Kellert, H. E. Longino, & C. K. Waters (Eds.), *Scientific Pluralism* (pp. 80-101).

Shaikh, A. (2016). *Capitalism: Competition, conflict, crises.* Oxford University Press.

Siegfried, J. J., Bartlett, R. L., Hansen, W. L., Kelley, A. C., McCloskey, D. N., & Tietenberg, T. H. (1991). The status and prospects of the economics major. *The Journal of Economic Education, 22*(3), 197-224.

Siegfried, J. J., & Walstad, W. B. (2014). Undergraduate coursework in economics: A survey perspective. *The Journal of Economic Education, 45*(2), 147-158.

Smelser, N. J., & Swedberg, R. (2010). *The handbook of economic sociology.* Princeton University Press.

Smith, A. (1776). *An Inquiry into the Nature and Causes of the Wealth of Nations* (Vol. 1). Librito Mondi.

Soll, J. B., Milkman, K. L., & Payne, J. W. (2014). A user's guide to debiasing. In G. Keren & G. Wu (Eds.), *Wiley-Blackwell Handbook of Judgment and Decision Making.*

Solow, R. M. (1983). Teaching Economics in the 1980s. *The Journal of Economic Education, 14*(2), 65-68.

Solow, R. M. (1994). Science and ideology in economics. In D. M. Hausman (Ed.), *The Philosophy of Economics: An Anthology* (pp. 239-251).

Spiegler, P. M., & Milberg, W. (2013). Methodenstreit 2013? Historical perspective on the contemporary debate over how to reform economics. *Forum for Social Economics*, 42(4), 311-345.

Squires, D. (2012). Curriculum alignment research suggests that alignment can improve student achievement. *The Clearing House: A Journal of Educational Strategies, Issues and Ideas*, 85(4), 129-135.

Stame, N. (2004). Theory-based evaluation and types of complexity. *Evaluation*, 10(1), 58-76.

Stevenson, B., & Zlotnik, H. (2018). *Representations of men and women in introductory economics textbooks* (Vol. 108). American Economic Association.

Stigler, G. J. (1962). The Problem of the Negro. *The New Guard*, 11-12.

Strassmann, D., & Starr, M. (2009). Raising dissonant voices: Pluralism and economic heterodoxy. In R. F. Garnett Jr, E. Olsen, & M. Starr (Eds.), *Economic pluralism* (pp. 83-95). Routledge.

Su, H.-C. (2012). Beyond the positive-normative dichotomy: some remarks on Colander's Lost Art of Economics. *Journal of Economic Methodology*, 19(4), 375-390.

Tetlow, G. (2018). Where are all the female economists? *Financial Times*. https://www.ft.com/content/0e5d27ba-2b61-11e8-9b4b-bc4b9f08f381

The Economics Network. (2015). *'Employers' Survey 2014-2015*. https://www.economicsnetwork.ac.uk/projects/surveys/employers14-15

Theobald, E. J., Hill, M. J., Tran, E., Agrawal, S., Arroyo, E. N., Behling, S., Chambwe, N., Cintrón, D. L., Cooper, J. D., & Dunster, G. (2020). Active learning narrows achievement gaps for underrepresented students in undergraduate science, technology, engineering, and math. *Proceedings of the national academy of sciences*, 117(12), 6476-6483.

Thornton, T. B. (2016). *From Economics to Political Economy: The problems, promises and solutions of pluralist economics*. Routledge.

Tieleman, J., De Muijnck, S., Kavelaars, M., & Ostermeijer, F. (2017). *Thinking like an Economist: A quantitative analysis of economics bachelor curricula in the Netherlands*. Rethinking Economics NL. https://www.economicseducation.org/s/Thinking-like-an-economist.pdf

Turner, A. (2010). Market Efficiency and Rationality: Why Financial Markets are Different. Lionel Robbins Memorial Lectures, London School of Economics.

United Nations. Economic Commission for Africa (2015). *Illicit financial flows: report of the High Level Panel on illicit financial flows from Africa*. United Nations, Addis Ababa.

Van Bavel, B. (2016). *The invisible hand?: how market economies have emerged and declined since AD 500*. Oxford University Press.

Van Bussel, M. (2020). Commerciële kinderopvang is niet slecht. *Management Kinderopvang, 26*(2), 28-30.

Van Dalen, H., & Klamer, A. (1996). *Telgen van Tinbergen: het verhaal van de Nederlandse economen*. Balans.

Van Dalen, H., Klamer, A., & Koedijk, C. (2015a). Het gekantelde wereldbeeld van economen. *Me Judice*. https://www.mejudice.nl/artikelen/detail/het-gekantelde-wereldbeeld-van-economen

Van Dalen, H., Klamer, A., & Koedijk, K. (2015b). De ideale econoom staat onder druk. *Me Judice*. https://www.mejudice.nl/artikelen/detail/de-ideale-econoom-staat-onder-druk

Van de Weijenberg, A. (2018). Private equity in kinderopvang: lust of last? *Management Kinderopvang, 24*(6), 10-13.

Van den Bergh, J. C. (2011). Environment versus growth – A criticism of "degrowth" and a plea for "a-growth". *Ecological economics, 70*(5), 881-890.

Van den Bergh, J. C., & Kallis, G. (2012). Growth, a-growth or degrowth to stay within planetary boundaries? *Journal of Economic Issues, 46*(4), 909-920.

Varathan, P. (2017). A Princeton economist has a theory for why there are so few women in economics. *Quartz*. https://qz.com/1165891/why-there-are-so-few-women-economists-according-to-princeton-economist-anne-case/

Velthuis, O. (1999). The Changing Relationship Between Economic Sociology and Institutional Economics. *American journal of economics and sociology, 58*(4), 629-649.

Wallerstein, I., Alatas, S., Brumann, C., Calhoun, C., Hall, J., Madan, T., & Wallerstein, I. (2003). Anthropology, sociology, and other dubious disciplines. *Current Anthropology, 44*(4), 453-465.

Wamsley, L. (2020). World's Largest Asset Manager Puts Climate At The Center Of Its Investment Strategy. *NPR*. https://www.npr.org/2020/01/14/796252481/worlds-largest-asset-manager-puts-climate-at-the-center-of-its-investment-strate

Wang, L., Malhotra, D., & Murnighan, J. K. (2011). Economics education and greed. *Academy of Management Learning & Education, 10*(4), 643-660.

Watts, M., & Becker, W. E. (2008). A little more than chalk and talk: Results from a third national survey of teaching methods in undergraduate economics courses. *The Journal of Economic Education, 39*(3), 273-286.

Watts, M., & Schaur, G. (2011). Teaching and assessment methods in undergraduate economics: A fourth national quinquennial survey. *The Journal of Economic Education, 42*(3), 294-309.

Weber, M. (2009). *From Max Weber: essays in sociology*. Routledge.

Weintraub, E. R. (2002). *How economics became a mathematical science*. Duke University Press.

Wight, J. B. (2017). The ethics behind efficiency. *The Journal of Economic Education, 48*(1), 15-26.

Wilber, C. K. (2004). Teaching economics as if ethics mattered. In E. Fullbrook (Ed.), *A Guide to What's Wrong with Economics* (pp. 147-157).

Wolf, E. R. (1982). *Europe and the People without History*. University of California Press.

Wolf, M. (2021). Humanity is a cuckoo in the planetary nest. *Financial Times*. https://www.ft.com/content/a3285adf-6c5f-4ce4-b055-e85f39ff2988

Wolff, R. D. (2012). *Democracy at work: A cure for capitalism*. Haymarket books.

Wu, A. H. (2017). Gender stereotyping in academia: Evidence from economics job market rumors forum. *Working Paper UC Berkeley*.

Wu, S. (2005). Where do Faculty Receive their PhDs? A Comparison Across Six Disciplines. *Academe, 91*(4), 53-54.

Yurko, A. (2018). *Employers Report*. Rethinking Economics. https://issuu.com/rethinkeconomics/docs/uk_employers_report_2018

Zandt, D. (2013). Dear Sheryl Sandberg: 'Leaning In' Doesn't Fix What's Actually Broken for Working Women. *Forbes*. https://www.forbes.com/sites/deannazandt/2013/02/25/dear-sheryl-sandberg-leaning-in-doesnt-fix-whats-broken-for-working-women/?sh=1861fdd13638

Ziliak, S., & McCloskey, D. N. (2008). *The cult of statistical significance: How the standard error costs us jobs, justice, and lives*. University of Michigan Press.